Global Criminal and Sovereign Free Economies and the Demise of the Western Democracies

Much has been written about the many economic benefits of globalization and the triumph and spread of democratic liberalism with the end of the Cold War, following the demise of the Soviet Union.

This work takes issue with such "wine and roses" perspectives about the future of the Western democracies and their faith-based views on the moral purity of a globalized marketplace. It also questions many of the assumptions found in the status quo reinforcing discipline of international political economy (IPE)—a discipline that focuses on the formal and legitimate economies and the façade they present that international relations and commerce is still dominated and dictated solely by the old Westphalian state centric system.

Having highlighted these concerns, this book looks at two major themes. The first theme focuses on the theoretical perception that a "Dark Renaissance" is taking place globally—one in which the Western liberal democracies and its citizens are ill prepared to respond because it exists at the trans-civilization level, bridging the modern to the post-modern world. The second theme focuses on the actual process of state deconstruction that is taking place. This process is leading to what may become the very undoing of the democracies.

Drawing together experts from a variety of backgrounds, this work explores the increasing shift away from formal based capitalism and evaluates through case studies how different states are responding to the challenges they face. This work will be of great interest to students and scholars of international political economy.

Robert J. Bunker is a Distinguished Visiting Professor and Minerva Chair at the Strategic Studies Institute, US Army War College, USA.

Pamela Ligouri Bunker is a past senior officer of the Counter-OPFOR Corporation and has professional experience in research and program coordination in University, Non-Government Organization (NGO), and City Government settings.

Routledge advances in international political economy

Global Criminal and Sovereign Free Economies and the Demise of the Western Democracies

Dark Renaissance

Edited by Robert J. Bunker and Pamela Ligouri Bunker

 Routledge
Taylor & Francis Group

LONDON AND NEW YORK

First published 2015
by Routledge
2 Park Square, Milton Park, Abingdon, Oxon OX14 4RN

and by Routledge
711 Third Avenue, New York, NY 10017

Routledge is an imprint of the Taylor & Francis Group, an informa business

British Library Cataloguing in Publication Data
A catalogue record for this book is available from the British Library

Library of Congress Cataloging-in-Publication Data
Global criminal and sovereign free economies and the demise of the
Western democracies / edited by Robert J. Bunker and Pamela Ligouri
Bunker.
    pages cm. – (Routledge advances in international political economy; 23)
    Includes bibliographical references and index.
    1. Political corruption–Economic aspects. 2. Executive power–Moral
    and ethical aspects. 3. Heads of state. 4. Democracy. 5. Political
    science–Economic aspects. I. Bunker, Robert J. II. Bunker, Pamela
    Ligouri.
    JF1081.G565 2014
    364.4'04561–dc23   2014011181

ISBN: 978-1-138-80243-8 (hbk)
ISBN: 978-1-315-75426-0 (ebk)

Typeset in Times New Roman
by Wearset Ltd, Boldon, Tyne and Wear

Printed and bound in the United States of America by Publishers Graphics,
LLC on sustainably sourced paper.

Contents

Figures[1]

Note

1 Figures 5.3–5.8 can be accessed online, available at: http://scholarship.claremont.edu/cgu_facbooks/27/

Tables

Contributors

Editors

Robert J. Bunker is a Distinguished Visiting Professor and Minerva Chair at the Strategic Studies Institute, US Army War College, USA. He is also Adjunct Faculty, Division of Politics and Economics, Claremont Graduate University. Past positions include Futurist in Residence, Training and Development Division, Behavioral Science Unit, Federal Bureau of Investigation Academy; Director of Research (Contract) Counter-OPFOR Program, National Law Enforcement and Corrections Technology Center-West; and Fellow, Institute of Land Warfare, Association of the US Army. He holds a Doctorate in Political Science from Claremont Graduate University, degrees in Government, Behavioral Science, Social Science, Anthropology-Geography and History, and has undertaken hundreds of hours of counter-terrorism and counter-cartel training. Dr. Bunker has hundreds of publications including the edited works *Criminal Insurgencies in Mexico and the Americas* (Routledge, 2012); *Narcos Over the Border* (Routledge, 2011); *Criminal-States and Criminal-Soldiers* (Routledge, 2008); *Networks, Terrorism and Global Insurgency* (Routledge, 2005); and *Non-State Threats and Future Wars* (Routledge, 2002).

Pamela Ligouri Bunker is a past senior officer of the Counter-OPFOR Corporation and has professional experience in research and program coordination in University, Non-Government Organization (NGO) and City Government settings. She graduated from California State Polytechnic University Pomona with a BS in Anthropology/Geography and a BS in Social Science, and from The Claremont Graduate University with an MA in Public Policy, with additional post-graduate work completed in comparative politics and government. Her writings have been published in academic and professional journals and in book chapter form, and range from topics related to criminal states and urban terrorism through illicit organizations and dark spirituality. She is presently in the graduate program at the Handa Centre for the Study of Terrorism and Political Violence at University of Saint Andrews, Scotland.

Contributing authors

Tanya Buhler Corbin is an Assistant Professor at Radford University and previously was a Visiting Assistant Professor of Political Science, University of Alaska Fairbanks. She holds a Master's in Public Policy and a Doctorate in Political Science from Claremont Graduate University and a Bachelors in Sociology from University of New Orleans. Dr. Corbin has taught numerous courses in Political Economy, Public Policy and American Politics, and published co-authored articles in the *California Journal of Politics and Policy* and *Women and Politics*. Her primary area of research focuses on the politics and policy changes that are proposed and adopted after crises and disasters and their interrelationship to traditionally marginalized groups. In recent research, she has studied policy entrepreneurship and congressional agenda setting, and disaster recovery after Hurricane Katrina. She is currently engaged in a research project comparing local communities' policy responses after the Exxon-Valdez and BP oil spills.

Mark Galeotti is Professor of Global Affairs at New York University's SCPS Center for Global Affairs. Previously, he was head of the History department at Keele University in the United Kingdom, Visiting Professor of Public Security at Rutgers-Newark, and an advisor to the British Foreign and Commonwealth Office, He is a consultant for a range of organizations, from the US State Department and FBI, to Interpol, Europol and national police forces. He read History at Cambridge University then took his Doctorate in Government at the London School of Economics. Dr. Galeotti has written 13 books on Russian crime, politics and security, most recently *Russian Security and Paramilitary Forces since 1991* (Osprey, 2013) and *The Politics of Security in Modern Russia* (Ashgate, 2010) and is currently working on a study of Russian organized crime.

Luis Jorge Garay Salamanca is a Visiting Scholar at the universities of Oxford and Cambridge (United Kingdom), Visiting Scholar and Consultant at the Inter-American Development Bank, the United Nations, the National Planning Department and Ministries of Finance, Foreign Trade and Foreign Affairs in Colombia, and Director of the National Process of Verification of Human, Social and Economic Rights of the forced displaced population in Colombia. Dr. Garay is an Industrial Engineer and Magister in Economics, Universidad de los Andes, Bogotá, Colombia, and a PhD in Economics, Massachusetts Institute of Technology, Cambridge, United States. He has authored more than 40 books, numerous essays and scientific articles, in topics including international migration and remittances, international trade and economic integration, foreign debt management, industrial development and international competitiveness, globalization, corruption and capture of state, and social exclusion.

Nils Gilman is Associate Chancellor at the University of California, Berkeley. Dr. Gilman is the author of *Mandarins of the Future: Modernization Theory* *in Cold War America* (John Hopkins University Press, 2007) and the co-editor of *Deviant Globalization: Black Market Economy in the 21st Century* (Continuum, 2011); *Staging Growth: Modernization, Development, and the Global Cold War* (University of Massachusetts Press, 2003); and the journal *Humanity: An International Journal of Human Rights, Humanitarianism, and Development.* He holds a BA, MA and PhD in History from the University of California, Berkeley.

T.X. Hammes is a Distinguished Research Fellow at the Institute for National Strategic Studies, National Defense University and an Adjunct Professor at Georgetown University. In his 30 years in the Marine Corps, he served at all levels in the operating forces to include command of a rifle company, a weapons company, an intelligence battalion, an infantry battalion and the Chemical Biological Incident Response Force. He participated in stabilization operations in Somalia and Iraq as well as training insurgents in a number of locales. He holds a Master's and a Doctorate in Modern History from Oxford University. Dr. Hammes is the author of *Forgotten Warriors: The 1st Provisional Marine Brigade, the Corps Ethos, and the Korean War* (University Press of Kansas, 2012) and *The Sling and the Stone: On War in the Twenty-First Century* (Zenith Press, 2006), chapters in 13 books and over 100 articles and opinion pieces. He has lectured widely at US and International Staff and War Colleges.

Nicole Hendrix is an Associate Professor in the Department of Criminal Justice at Radford University. She earned her Doctoral degree from the University at Albany. Her research has bridged the academic and professional realms within the field of criminal justice and included a number of projects involving agencies and institutions within criminal justice across Virginia and in other states. These projects have included a study of the use of force by Roanoke City Police Officers, an examination of nuisance offenses in the City of Radford, an investigation of patterns of sexual assault in Charlotte-Mecklenburg, NC, and a study of the state level firearms sales data available from the Virginia State Police. Dr. Hendrix has completed an introduction to criminal justice textbook that incorporates technology and innovative pedagogy into the building of foundational knowledge. At present, she is collaborating with a colleague on another textbook project that examines the role of media in modern criminal justice issues.

T.L. Moore is Adjunct Professor in the Center for Peace and Security Studies Program at The Edmund A. Walsh School of Foreign Service, Georgetown University. Past positions include Program Director at the Claremont Graduate University, Assistant Professorships at the Naval War College, the National Defense University, the United States Marine Corps Command and Staff College, the United States Military Academy (West Point) and the University of Miami. He holds a Master's degree in Government and a Doctorate in International Relations from the Claremont Graduate School and a law degree from the University of Miami. Dr. Moore has spoken to various governmental, professional and academic audiences including at the Association of the United States Army national meeting and the American Bar Association. Publications include book chapters, reports, papers and encyclopedia essays. He was the principal writer and analyst contributing to the *Comprehensive Report of the Special Advisor to the President on Iraq's WMD* (Washington: USGPO, 2005).

Eduardo Salcedo-Albarán is the Founder and Director of Scientific Vortex, a transnational research group that provides inputs for policymaking under integrative science principles. He holds Master's in Political Science, Universidad de los Andes, Bogota, Colombia. Eduardo has researched in the areas of organized crime, kidnapping, corruption, drug-trafficking and state capture. He is part of EDGE Foundation, with thinkers "who are at the center of today's intellectual, technological, and scientific landscape." He has collaborated for different books and magazines, as a researcher and also as an activist on science and empirical knowledge. He has taught in the areas of Introduction to Scientific Thought, Evolution, Genetics and Artificial Intelligence for Social Scientists and Philosophers. As Fellow Researcher, partner and consultant, he currently researches on Transnational Criminal Networks with institutes and Universities in North, Central and South America, Europe and Africa. His visual work on illicit networks was presented at the Serpentine Gallery, London, UK.

John P. Sullivan is a career police officer. He currently serves as a lieutenant with the Los Angeles County Sheriff's Department. He is also an Adjunct Researcher at the Vortex Foundation in Bogotá, Colombia; a Senior Research Fellow at the Center for Advanced Studies on Terrorism (CAST); and a Senior Fellow at *Small Wars Journal—El Centro*. He is co-editor of *Countering Terrorism and WMD: Creating a Global Counter-Terrorism Network* (Routledge, 2006) and *Global Biosecurity: Threats and Responses* (Routledge, 2010) and co-author of *Mexico's Criminal Insurgency: A Small Wars Journal—El Centro Anthology* (iUniverse, 2011) and *Studies in Gangs and Cartels* (Routledge, 2013). He completed the CREATE Executive Program in Counter-Terrorism at the University of Southern California and holds a BA in Government from the College of William and Mary, an MA in Urban Affairs and Policy Analysis from the New School for Social Research, and a PhD in Information and Knowledge Society, from the Internet Interdisciplinary Institute (IN3) at the Open University of Catalonia.

Yelena A. Tuzova is an Assistant Professor at Claremont Graduate University. She has more than ten years of experience in academia (University of Colorado at Denver, University of Minnesota and Wesleyan College), industry (Renault, Inc.) and the consulting sector (NEXT, LLC and Crowns Consulting, LLC). She received her PhD in Economics at the University of Minnesota-Twin Cities in addition to having a BA in Linguistics and Music.

Dr. Tuzova specializes in macroeconomic policy analysis and quantitative modeling. Her primary interests include optimal taxation, the role of government and corruption. She is presently conducting research under a *BLAIS Research Grant* ($25,000.00 award). Dr. Tuzova has a large spectrum of computational skills (MatLab, STATA, RATS and SPSS) and expertise in macroeconomics and time-series analysis. Over the last two years, she has been actively engaged in forecasting projects in collaboration with Claremont McKenna College and the UCLA Anderson Forecast. She is a native Russian speaker and is fluent in English and French.

Abbreviations

AiS	Agents inside of the state
AoS	Agents outside of the state
APC	Armored personnel carrier
AStC	Advanced stage state capture
AUC	Autodefensas Unidas de Colombia
AUMF	Authorization for Use of Military Force
BDU	Battle dress uniform
CEE	Central and Eastern European countries
CHN	Crédito Hipotecario Nacional
COW	Correlates of War Database
CStR	Co-opted state reconfiguration
DAS	Departamento Administrativo de Seguridad
DHS	Department of Homeland Security
ECHR	European Court of Human Rights
ECSC	European Coal and Steel Community
EEC	European Economic Community
EPI	Economic Policy Institute
EU	European Union
FARC	Fuerzas Armadas Revolucionarias de Colombia
FATA	Federally Administered Tribal Areas
FSU	Former Soviet Union
GAC	Governance and Anticorruption
GCR	General currency-ratio approach
GDP	Gross domestic product
GLS	Generalized least squares
HMRC	Her Majesty's Revenue and Customs
IBC	International business companies
IMF	International Monetary Fund
IRGC	Iranian Revolution Guard Corps
IRS	Internal Revenue Service
MAD	Mutually assured destruction
MEND	Movement for the Emancipation of the Niger Delta
MIMIC	Multiple indicators multiple causes

MS-13	Mara Salvatrucha
NDAA	National Defense Authorization Act
nEM	Nano explosive material
NIPA	National Income and Product Accounts
NRP	National Research Program
OECD	Organisation for Economic Co-operation and Development
OOTW	Operations other than war
PMC	Private military company
PTC	Propensity to corrupt
RMA	Revolution in military affairs
RPMA	Revolution in political and military affairs
SGP	Stability and Growth Pact
SNA	Social network analysis
SNAP	Supplemental Nutrition Assistance Program
StC	State capture
SWAT	Special weapons and tactics
TCMP	Taxpayer Compliance Measurement Program
TINS	Taxpayer ID numbers
UHNWI	Ultra-high-net-worth individual
VAT	Value Added Tax
VDTO	Violent Drug Trafficking Organization
VNSA	Violent non-state actor
WEF	World Economic Forum

Editors' note

This book has its origins in late 2011 as a theoretical linking component to earlier work done on Epochal Change—initially developed during the mid-to-late 1980s at the Claremont Graduate University by T. Lindsay Moore and Robert Bunker—and the criminal insurgencies construct later articulated by John Sullivan, Los Angeles County Sheriff's Department, in 2008. The work also draws heavily upon the insights provided in the early 2011 work *Deviant Globalization* by Nils Gilman and his fellow authors.

The intent of this project is to bring in a supra-national (top down) component as a complement to the sub-national (bottom up) component expressed by criminal insurgency derived from the illicit economy. This supra-national component was to be known as plutocratic insurgency and derived from the sovereign free economy. Together these two insurgency forms, and the concurrent economies upon which they are drawn, are viewed as compressing the Westphalian state, the formal economy upon which it rests, and the middle class based social structure it exhibits. After consultation with Routledge representatives it was decided by mid-2012 to undertake this project as an international political economy (IPE) focused work—albeit a non-formal based one—focusing on illicit, off the books and deviant forms, what can be considered "Dark IPE." In support of this research effort a pilot course, *Underground Economies and Shadow Governments*, was taught in the fall of 2012 at the Claremont Graduate University by a team of three professors. This transdisciplinary course explored quite a number of themes that would later appear in this work and also helped to serve as a sounding board via ongoing discussions with the graduate students taking the course.

Editing this work and contributing to it has been both the proverbial blessing and a bane for us. Like many works of this nature—especially when new theoretical ground is being broken—the workload is far more than first expected, however, editors are always delighted when a project ultimately completes the process from the initial vision to the finished polished product. Writing on the subject matter, however, has been difficult for two reasons. The first is that one of the original contributors—Desmonette Hazly, a bright new PhD—was forced to leave the project due to health reasons. She co-taught the earlier mentioned CGU course with one of the editors and another professor and was fully engaged in supporting this research effort. As a result this work is dedicated to her, with the additional hope for her speedy recover. The second difficulty with working on this project concerns the perspectives gained. The old saying "Ignorance is bliss" has great relevance in this regard. Living within a time of transition is always difficult, but seeing the changes for what they are and being able to place in context the economic erosion of fellow middle class individuals and families—in fact family, friends and associates—is very disheartening. Hopefully the theories presented, constructs developed and words written in the many pages of this project will do some good in that regard. If this material could somehow find its way into the hands of a congressional or MP (or Lord) led committee and influence the public policy process that would be a very good thing indeed.

In facilitation of this project we would like to thank Paul Rich and Thomas Durrell-Young for their initial sage advice, and the early help and support of Steve Thompson, Heidi Bagtazo, Alexander Quayle, Andrew Taylor, Charlotte Endersby and the Routledge IPE editorial board in helping to transition the project into a special volume. We must also thank Jean Schroedel for being part of that CGU pilot course and introducing us to some of faculty members in her research network who have joined in on the project. Also the support of the Minerva Chairs program in promoting this and other "Dark Globalization" research to inject expertise from the social sciences at the strategic level to promote new Department of Defense insights into the human dimension of its understanding is noted. Finally, we wish to thank Tanya Buhler Corbin, Mark Galeotti, Nils Gilman, T.X. Hammes, Nicole Hendrix, T. Lindsay Moore, Luis Jorge Garay Salamanca, Eduardo Salcedo-Albarán, John P. Sullivan and Yelena A. Tuzova for their contributions to this important project and the many suggestions they have provided in order to improve it. Without their time, dedication and professionalism provided to us over the course of a number of years, this special volume of the Routledge Advances in International Political Economy series would have not come to fruition.

Of course all mistakes and errors contained in this work are those of the editors. Further, the views expressed in this work are those of the authors and do not necessarily reflect the official policy or position of the Department of the Army, the Department of Defense or the US government.

Robert J. Bunker
Pamela Ligouri Bunker
Claremont, CA
February 2014

Foreword

The twin insurgency—facing plutocrats and criminals

Nils Gilman

> Everywhere the ceremony of innocence is drowned.
>
> William Butler Yeats, 1919

States within the global political economy today face a twin insurgency: one from below, another from above. On the one hand, there are a series of interconnected *criminal insurgencies*, in which the global disenfranchised resist, coopt and route around states as they seek ways to empower and enrich themselves in the shadows of the global economy. Drug cartels, human traffickers, computer hackers, counterfeiters, arms dealers and others exploit the loopholes, exceptions and failures of governance institutions to build global commercial empires that, in turn, provide them the resources to corrupt, coopt or challenge incumbent political actors. On the other hand, there exists a *plutocratic insurgency*, in which globalized elites seek to disengage from traditional national obligations and responsibilities. From libertarian activists, to tax haven lawyers, to currency speculators, to mineral-extraction magnates, the new global super-rich and their hired help are waging a broad-based campaign that aims either to limit the reach and capacity of government tax collectors and regulators or to manipulate these functions as a tool in their own cut-throat business competition. Unlike classic twentieth-century insurgents, who sought control over the state apparatus in order to implement social reforms, criminal and plutocratic insurgents do not seek to take over the state. Nor do they wish to destroy the state, since they rely, like parasites, on the state to provide the legacy goods of social welfare: health, education, infrastructure and so on. Rather, their aim is simpler: to carve out de facto zones of autonomy for themselves by crippling the state's ability to constrain their freedom of (economic) action.

The failures of social modernism

Understanding how we arrived at these twin insurgencies requires a brief return to the anterior period. During the social modernist era (1945–1971), virtually all states—whether capitalist or communist, industrialized or developmental, great power or postcolonial—aimed to legitimate themselves by serving the interests of a middle class whose size they sought to expand (Woodiwiss, 1993; Gilman, 2003). Both capitalist and communist accumulation strategies were based on the nurturing of industrial laborers, who were expected to work for a living and who, in turn, were told that the state not only would steadily improve their standard of living, but also would cushion them from outrageous misfortune via various forms of social security (Westad, 2006). These states were "welfare states" in the sense that they sought to provide for the *general welfare*, rather than to protect or lift up the poor or defend the prerogatives of the rich. In the non-communist world, the wealthy were taxed not out of class hostility but in order to finance *public goods* for society as a whole (Lambert, 1993). Health care, pensions, schools and so on were represented less as individual "entitlements" than as collectively enjoyed public goods. While a diversity of social contracts existed during this period (Evans *et al.*, 1985; Esping-Andersen, 1990), in virtually every country elites felt a duty to play a "muscular and essential role in steering the economy and underwriting the well-being of the middle class" (Mizruchi, 2013), and inequality of income steadily decreased. For Western elites in particular, the fact that the Cold War order made thinkable radical alternatives to capitalism no doubt helped concentrate a certain commitment to larger moral, social and political purposes.[1]

By the 1970s, however, it was becoming undeniable that social modernist states across each of the "three worlds of development" were failing to deliver on their promises (Pletsch, 1981; Slater, 2008). In the West, the stagflation of the 1970s undermined the technical foundations of the Bretton Woods financial order, as well as the technocratic consensus in favor of Keynesian demand management and the political consensus in favor of sharing productivity gains between labor and capital. In the East, centrally planned economies were revealing themselves as not only politically repressive but also economically inefficient and environmentally catastrophic. In the Global South, while the commodity boom of the 1970s led to a golden age for primary producers, Import Substitution Industrialization failed to deliver sustained growth and transition to high per capita incomes,[2] and the commodity price crash of the early 1980s precipitated a debt crisis that put to rest any dreams of global redistribution (Reinhart and Reinhart, 2008). From the late 1970s through the early twenty-first century, a period of reaction to state-centric models of development set in (Harvey, 2007; Caryl, 2013; Sargent, forthcoming). Levels of economic inequality began to grow again, eventually reaching heights not seen since the 1920s, and prompting some financial analysts to describe the new economy as a "plutonomy" (Kapur *et al.*, 2005). At the same time, states stopped trying to create a more egalitarian society or to provide for the general welfare; instead they increasingly sought legitimacy by claiming to maximize the opportunities of individuals (Bobbitt, 2002). From this perspective, the creation of plutocrats counted not as a defeat, but as a success for the new model of governance.

When Communism collapsed in 1989, what died was not just the particular collectivist economic system and authoritarian politics of the Soviet Union and its satellites. Cremated along with the corpse of Communism was the civic-minded conception of development as the central responsibility of the state and allied elites—a conception shared by communists and liberals alike during the Cold War. It wasn't just that the state "retreated" (Strange, 1996) from the "commanding heights" (Yergin, 1998) of the economy, but also that the very ambitions of the state found itself in eclipse. The best face that the World Bank could put on the new order was to say that, henceforth, the role of the state would be to "steer" rather than to "row" (World Bank, 1997). By the turn of the millennium, even the left had come to doubt whether states could be relied on to effectively and disinterestedly promote the public interest (Scott, 1998).

The nature of the new order was made most explicit in two texts published the year that the Berlin Wall fell, Francis Fukuyama's "The End of History?" (1989) and John Williamson's "The Washington Consensus" (1990). Fukuyama proposed that big-H History (in the Hegelian sense of ideological contestation over the proper relationship between state and civil society) had come to an end with a universal agreement that liberal, democratic capitalism was not just the best but in fact the only reasonable form of socio-political-economic organization. Williamson's text was more pragmatic than metaphysical, filling in the details of this "post-historical" policy consensus with specific imperatives around fiscal discipline, the redirection of public spending away from subsidies, the rollback of progressive tax codes, the floating of currencies, the liberalization of trade and cross-border investment, the privatization of state enterprises and deregulation of private ones, and above all the sacrosanctification of private property rights. Taken together, these texts involved not just a dethroning of the state, but a wholesale challenge to the idea that technocratic leadership was the primary way to ensure collective social well-being. Pioneered as domestic policy in Margaret Thatcher's Great Britain and Ronald Reagan's United States, the programs associated with the Washington Consensus—above all, the privatization of national industrial assets (especially of state owned firms and utilities) and deregulation (especially of financial firms)—soon became a model that London and Washington sought to export to the Global South and the post-Communist world under the rubric of "structural adjustment" and "shock therapy" (Fourcade-Gourinchas and Babb, 2002; Rajan and Zingales, 2003). As Dani Rodrik concluded: " 'Stabilize, privatize, and liberalize' became the mantra of a generation of technocrats who cut their teeth in the developing world and of the political leaders they counseled" (Rodrik, 2006).

This transformation of the role of the state in the wake of the Cold War has led to a very different sort of landscape of political contestation. With the social modernist state in ideological crisis, the middle classes whose interests it was designed to promote find themselves in an increasingly precarious position. From above, they are threatened by a global financial elite in league with ultra-wealthy compradors, who seek to cut the social services that are paid for by taxes that these elites depict as a form of illegitimate expropriation. From below, they find themselves exposed to various forms of criminals, who have reacted to the collapse of hope for inclusion in the middle class by taking their futures into their own hands. Let us consider each of these phenomena in turn.

Plutocratic insurgency: the revolt of mainstream globalization's winners

This ideological retreat of the social modernist state represents the central event that has enabled plutocratic insurgency. During the 1990s, a new class of globe-trotting economic elites emerged, enriched by the opportunities created by globalizing industrial firms, deregulated financial services and new technology platforms. This new class is an order of magnitude richer in absolute terms than previous generations of the ultra-wealthy.[3] The rise of the new plutocrats reflects an historic shift in the structure of capital accumulation (Irvin, 2007). The accumulation regime that predominated during the heyday of social modernism was predicated on creating a new class of workers who could afford the goods that they were producing (Harvey, 2001). The great fortunes of the late nineteenth and early twentieth century were built on the backs of masses of worker-consumers in primarily inward-looking national contexts. By contrast, today's plutocrats make their fortunes selling their goods and services globally—in real terms, therefore, their ongoing success is less connected to the fortunes of their fellow national citizens than was that of previous generations. Moreover, the two signature types of massive wealth accumulation in the early twenty-first century have been high technology and financial services—both industries that do not rely on masses of laborers, and whose productivity is therefore detached from the health of any particular national middle class. The result has been a dramatic rise in inequality within countries, even as wealth inequality transnationally has narrowed.

The rise in a new class of plutocrats has been marked by the emergence of new ideological self-conceptions (Freeland, 2013). Many of these contemporary plutocrats see themselves as "the deserving winners of a tough worldwide competition" (Freeland, 2011) and regard efforts to make them to pay for public goods as little more than organized theft. Whereas the threat of Communism during the Cold War acted as a check on the maximalist ambitions of the ultra-rich, the political and ideological collapse of the Soviet Union removed that constraint, enabling an ideological shift in how a significant segment of the new wealthy conceive their relationship with their societies. While some among the wealthy continue to see themselves as owing a debt of obligation to the societies in which they have enriched themselves, there exists a significant subset—particularly among financial elites (Huffschmid, 2008)—who do not see their personal achievements as tied to the success of the national societies in which they reside (Taylor and Harrison, 2008). Instead of seeing themselves as the ultimate winners of the systems in which they work (Domhoff, 2009), they characterize themselves as rebels, outsiders who have made it on their own despite the restraints presented by incumbents, loafers and parasites in government and society (Frank, 2007). The popularity of the pseudo-philosophical novels of Ayn Rand—whose ideas George Monbiot (2012) refers to as "the Marxism of the new right"—represents the most visible manifestation of this ideology that poses the rich as "makers" as opposed to the mass of shiftless "takers" (Burns, 2009;

Weiss, 2012). From Washington to London, plutocrat-funded think tanks are devoted to creating a body of usable ideas and policy proposals geared at dismantling social modernism (James, 1993; Medvetz, 2012). This ideological shift heralds the arrival of plutocratic insurgency.[4]

The defining feature of plutocratic insurgency is the effort on the part of holders of this ideology to *defund or de-provision public goods*, in order to defang a state that they see as a threat to their prerogatives (Pack, 1987).[5] Practically speaking, plutocratic insurgency takes the form of efforts to *lower taxes*, which necessitates the cutting of spending on public goods; to *reduce regulations* that restrict corporate action or that protect workers; and to *defund or privatize public institutions*, such as schools, health care, infrastructure and social space. The political strategy associated with plutocratic insurgency is to use austerity in the face of economic shocks to *rewrite social contracts on the basis of a much narrower set of mutual social obligations* (Klein, 2007), with the ultimate effect of de-collectivizing social risks (Beck, 2008). As a palliative for the loss of public goods and state-backed programs to improve public welfare, plutocratic insurgents typically promote the idea of philanthropy—directed toward ends defined not democratically but, naturally, by themselves (Barkan, 2013). "There's no such thing as society," Margaret Thatcher famously declared, issuing the *cri de cœur* of insurgent plutocrats everywhere—since, if there's no such thing as society, then the very category of social services collapses, along with any responsibility on the part of the rich to contribute to them. From this perspective, plutocratic insurgency signifies the re-importation back into the industrial core of the aforementioned policies of structural adjustment that were applied across the Global South during the 1980s and 1990s.

For plutocratic insurgents, this strategy is dictated at bottom by a raw cost–benefit analysis: the price the social modernist state asks them to pay in taxes and the regulatory burdens it imposes on them outweighs the benefit they believe they personally receive from living in such a state. Plutocratic insurgents believe they can afford (and therefore everyone should be required) to buy for themselves the sorts of goods that before required a state to provide. They live in gated communities, travel via personal jets and private bus fleets, and send their children to exclusive schools (Freeland, 2012). While each of these decisions may at first be motivated by lifestyle choices or a desire for social differentiation, the result is a progressive moral disinvestment and civic disengagement from the quality of these traditionally public services (Bickford, 2000; Sengupta, 2008; Blakely, 2012), especially as the habit of opting out of public services trickles down from the oligarchs to the upper middle classes (Caldeira, 2000). Leaving aside the matter of the undemocratic nature of such private services, or the adverse selection problems that arise from partial privatizations, what marks the arrival of plutocratic insurgency is when the rich begin to revolt against paying taxes for public services they never plan to use. The result is a reinforcing cycle, whereby plutocratic insurgents increasingly see no reason to contribute anything to their host societies, and indeed actively make war on the idea that citizenship imbues them with economic or social responsibilities.

Criminal insurgency: the revolt of deviant globalization's winners

Many of the same processes that are driving plutocratic insurgency also underpin the process of criminal insurgency: the globalization of economic flows, growing wealth inequality and a collapse of state provisioning of public goods and services. From Latin America to Africa to the former Eastern bloc, the 1980s and 1990s structural adjustment and shock therapy programs led to the "hollowing out" of the state: the physical buildings and institutions of "adjusted" states remained in place, but their ambitions and capacities shriveled (Milward and Provan, 2000). The states in these countries dramatically decreased their spending on social services—ranging from subsidies for food and fuel to broader social services like public health and pensions. State-owned industries were either shut down or privatized, with wages and employment slashed. The state, in other words, further decreased its capacity to deliver a decent life to its citizens, leading to a collapse in the popular expectation that the state should serve as a guarantor of progress (Duffield, 1998; Ferguson, 1999; Parenti, 2011). At the same time, however, the economies of these countries opened rapidly to cross-border financial and trade flows. This combination of the failure of the public goods-providing state and a dramatic increase in the openness of national economies created both the opportunity for enterprising individuals to make money in new ways and an imperative to do so, as a matter of survival. These effects were in fact the explicit intention of the structural adjustment and shock therapy programs: rolling back the dirigiste state and opening up the economy was meant to unleash a flood of pent-up entrepreneurial energy and, indeed, it did.

Alas, the structural-adjustment- and shock-therapy-driven globalization of the formerly closed economies of the Eastern Bloc and the Global South turned out to have an unfortunate bug (Los, 2003; Glenny, 2008). While the mainstream globalization celebrated by the likes of Thomas Friedman (2005) grabbed the headlines, what most distinguished the post-Cold War global economy from the earlier era was the parallel development of a shadowy "deviant" globalization in industries like narcotics, immigration, wildlife harvesting and antiquities. Though the weakness of the post-Communist and post-developmental state represented a dire problem for mainstream businesses and for imploding middle classes in these countries, it offered certain comparative advantages for illicit commerce. Deviant entrepreneurs realized that arbitraging the moral and regulatory differences that existed in different jurisdictions worldwide presented fantastic business opportunities. While big multinational corporations were able to sew up the licit opportunities afforded by the integration of the global economy, they were unable to play in arenas of goods and services banned for moral reasons (Gilman *et al.*, 2011). The great unsung globalizers of the 1990s and 2000s, therefore, were the criminals who rapidly scaled up their local mom-and-pop criminal organizations to become globe-spanning deviant commercial empires (Saviano, 2006; Keefe, 2012).

These avatars of deviant globalization are also the leaders of the second of our twin insurgencies—the criminal sort. What distinguishes criminal insurgents from classic social revolutionaries is that rather than seeking to build or capture institutionalized state power, they seek merely to protect their rents in various (usually deviant) markets that they control. Organizations such as the First Command of the Capital in Brazil, the 'Ndrangheta in Italy, or the Zetas in Mexico have no interest in taking over the states in which they operate. Instead, like plutocratic insurgents, what criminal insurgents seek is to cripple the state, that is, to establish a zone of economic autonomy while continuing to rely on the state to supply vestigial social services.[6] These actors thrive in (and indeed prefer and try to foster) weak-state environments, and their activities reinforce the conditions of this weakness. As deviant globalization takes root in a particular locale, however, it soon begins to generate a positive feedback loop, in much the same way that many successful animal and plant species, as they invade a natural ecosystem, reshape their ecosystem in ways that improve their ability to exclude competitors (Sullivan and Bunker, 2002; Manwaring, 2005; Arias, 2006). The state weakness that at first was merely a permissive enabling condition for their business becomes something that the now empowered criminal insurgents seek to perpetuate and even exacerbate. They siphon off money, loyalty and sometimes territory; they increase corruption; and they undermine the rule of law. They also force well-functioning states in the global system to spend an inordinate amount of time, energy and attention trying to control what comes in and out of their borders.

In building their business empires, deviant globalizers inevitably come into conflict with host states in three distinct ways that render them de facto political actors. First, they control huge, growing swathes of the global economy, operating most prominently in places where the state is hollowed or hollowing out. Corruption fueled by drug money on both sides of the US–Mexico border exemplifies this point (Miller, 2009). Second, many deviant entrepreneurs control and deploy a significant quota of violence—an occupational hazard for people working in extralegal industries, who cannot count on the state to adjudicate their contractual disputes. This use of violence brings deviant entrepreneurs into primal conflict with one of the state's central sources of legitimacy, namely its monopoly (in principle) over the socially sanctioned use of force, transforming them from merely deviant businessmen into criminal insurgents. Third, these criminal insurgents in some cases begin to emerge as private providers of justice, health care and infrastructure —that is, precisely the kind of goods that functional states are supposed to provide to their citizens. (However, since they are provided privately, to the deviant entrepreneurs' personal constituents, they are not "public goods" in the sense of goods equally accessible to all citizens.) Criminal syndicates in Brazil (Langewiesche, 2007), the MEND in Nigeria (Junger, 2007), narco-traffickers like the Sinaloa Cartel in Mexico (Keefe, 2012)—all are criminal insurgents who not only have demonstrated that they can shut down areas of their host states' basic functional capacity, thereby upsetting global markets half a world away, but who are also providing social services to local constituencies (Robb, 2007).

Criminal insurgency is thus the form that deviant globalization takes as it scales and reaches political self-consciousness. On the one hand, the more deviant industries grow, the more damage they do to the political legitimacy of the states within which the criminal insurgents operate, thus undermining the capacity of the state to provide the infrastructure and services that the criminal insurgents want to free ride on. On the other hand, the people living in the semi-autonomous zones controlled by criminal insurgents increasingly recognize the insurgents rather than the hollowed out state as the real source of local power and authority (Finnegan, 2010). Of course, just because these deviant providers of alternative governance functions end up seeming "legitimate" in the eyes of local stakeholders, this type of governance is usually poorly institutionalized and untransparent about both ends and means. Nonetheless, as these groups take over functions that would have been expected of the state, their stakeholders increasingly lose interest in the hollowed-out formal state institutions (Davis, 2010). Thus, even though criminal insurgents have no desire to kill their host state, they may end up precipitating a process whereby the state implodes catastrophically.

The enclavization of microsovereignties and the end of the middle class

During the 1990s, it became fashionable to declare that in the new post-Cold War era, the state was destined to wither away. In fact, something more subtle was taking place: the double collapse of social modernist state's capacity and legitimacy was giving birth not to the post-historical utopia of universal consensus in favor of liberal democratic capitalism, but rather to a conjoined monster in the form of plutocratic secession and deviant globalization. Instead of projects of collective emancipation, what both plutocratic and criminal insurgents desire is for the social modernist state to remain intact *except insofar as it impinges on them personally*. Neither criminal nor plutocratic insurgents are revolutionaries in the classic modernist sense of political actors who seek to take over the state.[7] As the social modernist state failed to realize its promise, the very notion of a revolution that aspires to a project of national-scale collective social reform (Skocpol, 1979) has come to seem quaint. Neither category of insurgent is interested in taking control over the state to enact a process of national (or international) social reform. Nor do they seek a political revolution in the Arendtian or Burkean sense of a contest for direct operational and ideological control over the organs of the state (Arendt, 1963; Burke, 1983). Instead of being in revolt against a particular political regime, with the goal of building better government, they aim instead to cripple their host states in order to gain de facto zones of private autonomy that can enable individual, tribal, or interest-group enrichment.[8] They are thus parasitic in a very specific sense: they wish to free ride on the institutional legacy of social modernism so as to avoid costs to their businesses.

Seen from a spatial perspective, what both insurgencies represent is the replacement of the liberal ideal of uniform authority and rights within national spaces by *a kaleidoscopic array of de facto and de jure microsovereignties.* Rather than a single national space in which power is exercised and rights are enjoyed in a consistent and homogeneous way by all residents, the cartography of the dual insurgency represents diverse enclaves of political authority and of social service provisioning arrangements (Ong, 2000; Sidaway, 2007). As these unique arrangements emerge, national and local authorities proliferate a variety of increasingly one-off exceptions to the general rules, incrementally traducing the liberal notion of equality before the law. Just as the 1930s saw a multiplication of conditions poised between war and peace, so our present conjuncture witnesses the multiplication of various forms of authority between the full-blown modern state and outright anarchy, symbolized by the blurring lines between police, military and private security contractors, in terms of both kinetic capabilities and legal authorities (Singer, 2001; Lambert, 2013; Shank and Beavers, 2013). The process itself is, of course, self-reinforcing: the proliferation of exceptional and unique microsovereignties only increases the scope for the insurgents to engage in jurisdictional arbitrage, and further demands by other insurgents for their own personalized sovereign exceptions. In the space of the dual insurgency, citizenship no longer signifies the liberal ideal of an identical package of rights for all, but instead means very different things depending on where individuals are in physical and social space (Krijnen and Fawaz, 2010).

Within plutocratic enclaves, the source of authority and loyalty is, at bottom, money. From a geographic perspective, plutocratic insurgents seek to create zones of private authority and legal autonomy where they can privately command goods once considered public, including not just security (Caldeira, 2000; Hope, 2000; Abrahamsen and Williams, 2011) but also increasingly schooling, transportation, health care, shopping, legal enforcement and so on (Dezelay and Garth, 1998; Rodenbeck, 2013). The paradigmatic case for plutocratic spatial segregation and secession are so-called gated communities, which rightly have become the subject of a minor academic subfield (Lister *et al.*, 2003). These spaces are much more than simple residential enclaves, but increasingly offer full-service operations that contain virtually everything their denizens need, so that residents only need to leave in order to travel to other such enclaves (Connell, 1999; Webster, 2001; Sengupta, 2008; Breitung, 2012). Rights within such spaces, it goes without saying, accrue to dollars rather than to citizenship. The vision of the future here is of a global archipelago of "privatopias" (McKenzie, 1996), linked by air and Internet to other such spaces, protected by high ramparts from the roiling dystopian ocean of the hoi polloi (Graham and Marvin, 2001; Davis, 2005). Moreover, in addition to these zones of physical separation, plutocratic insurgents also seek out (or seek to create) virtual zones of legal exception, in the form of offshore tax havens (which allow them to avoid income taxes—Baldacchino, 2010; Shaxson, 2011) and special economic zones (which allow them to avoid tariffs as well as laws designed to protect labor or the environment—Bach, 2011). Plutocratic insurgents are adept at playing off one jurisdiction against another, threatening to take their capital elsewhere if the local authorities do not grant them the exceptions that they seek.

The enclaves of the criminal insurgents are more precarious, as one would expect. Unlike the visible separation that the plutocratic insurgents enjoy in the form of high walls and armed guards, the autonomous zones of the underclass are more temporary and, naturally, less secure for their masters. From the favelas of Sao Paolo (Langewiesche, 2007), the slums of Karachi (Kaker, 2014), the waterfront of Kingston (Kilcullen, 2013), and the suburbs of Beirut (Fawaz *et al.*, 2012) or Naples (Saviano, 2006) to the remotest corners of Afghanistan (Hetherington, 2011), Honduras (Schwartz, 2014) or Sudan (Omeje, 2010), such autonomous spaces take the form of feral "no-go zones" (no-go, that is, to the rich) in which some notionally social modernist state may claim authority, but in which true power is wielded by warlords, gangsters, or other kinds of organized criminals, who take de facto control over local security and whatever meager social service provisioning may be on offer (Norton, 2003; Bunker and Sullivan, 2011; Marten, 2012). In these zones, sources of authority and loyalty and the application of raw power tends toward what might be called "neo-tribalism"— "neo" in the sense that primal loyalties adhere not just to those who share (perceived) bonds of ancient kinship, but rather in accordance to all manner of intense and ritualized personal connections among young male specialists in the use of violence (Ronfeldt, 2006; Robb, 2007). In short, while globalization is indeed undermining national political institutions and thus national identities and loyalties, what appears to be replacing the national is not a "global" political identity—as "cosmopolitical" dreamers have long aspired to (Cheah and Robbins, 1998)—but rather a return to localized identities rooted in clan, sect, ethnicity, corporation and gang. Understanding the nature of social relations in such spaces of social fracture may best be approached by a literary rather than a strictly social scientific sensibility (DiMaggio, 2011).

The central difficulty that both plutocratic and criminal insurgents face is that it is unclear whether the political objective they seek can produce stable equilibria of governance. There are least two separate reasons to question the ability of these arrangements to produce stability. First, the fracturing of sovereign homogeneity increases transaction costs for people traversing them—it requires a constant expenditure of time and effort to determine exactly what zone of governance one is in and who, therefore, is due respect and obeisance. This is equally true whether one considers the spaces of the plutocratic or the criminal insurgency: in the former case, the price is paid to lawyers, in the second to gangsters. Second, the kaleidoscope proliferates opportunities for arbitrage and defection of customers and foot soldiers to other governance spaces (Hirschman, 1970). The ultimate losers in all of this, of course, are the middle classes—the sorts of people who try to "play by the rules" by going to school and getting traditional middle class jobs whose chief virtue is stability. These sorts of people— who lack the ruthlessness to act as criminal insurgents and the resources to act as plutocratic insurgents—can only watch with a certain passivity as the institutions that were built over the course of the twentieth century to ensure a high quality of life for a broad majority of citizens are progressively eroded. As the social bases of solidaristic collective action crumble, individuals within the middle classes increasingly face the choice of accepting a progressive loss of social security and de facto social degradation, or attempting to join one of the two insurgencies.[9]

Notes

1 The ideal of the modernist welfare state may have been mainly honored in the breach but the point is that it was in fact honored despite contestation of the liberal-welfarist model by various actors, whether by leftists who sought a more explicit policy of class leveling, or by rightists who sought to uphold or enforce various forms of racial, national, or class-based exclusions. The liberal welfare state remained firmly ensconced as the hegemonic model during this period—that is, as the baseline against which other political discourses and proposed political-economic models had to define themselves. With that said, the relations between labor and management in the West (and particularly in the United States) were conflictual even during the postwar heyday of social modernism. Plutocratic pushback against both organized labor and the regulatory and tax reach of the liberal state was present from the beginning of the New Deal and became a formal political strategy by mid-1940s (Phillips-Fein, 2006, 2009; Burgin, 2012). As Nelson Lichtenstein has observed, "There was no 'labor-management accord,' although labor's strength did generate a kind of armed truce in key oligopolistic sectors of the economy" (Lichtenstein, 2000: 261). Despite this pre-history of the plutocratic insurgency, however, it is clear that the end of the Cold War represented a watershed. One cannot help but contrast Tony Judt's (2005) descriptions of Europe's public-minded postwar statesmen to the shameless way that ex-presidents (G.H.W. Bush, Clinton), chancellors (Schroeder) and prime ministers (Blair) are happy to receive $100m+ payouts from hedge funds and foreign governments upon leaving office.
2 Key texts in the normative shift away from ISI were Baer, 1972 and Balassa, 1978.
3 Just a few statistics give a sense of the scale. When *Forbes* magazine first started tracking the ultra-rich in 1982, there were 12 billionaires in the United States; by 2012, there were 425 (Kroll, 2012). In 1982, there were fewer than 200,000 millionaires in the United States; by 2012, there were over 3.7m (CapGemini, 2013). In 2013, there were also 98,700 "ultra-high net worth individuals" (with assets >$50m), of which 45 percent were American (Credit Suisse, 2013). To speak of the habits, ideological or otherwise, of the very rich is thus largely to speak of Americans.
4 The locus of the plutocratic insurgency today lies in the West—in particular, the world headquarters for the global plutocratic insurgency is London, the world's largest "off-shore" financial center that is home to (or at any rate has the homes of) more plutocrats than any other city (Vellacott, 2012; Shaxson, 2013). Elsewhere, the evidence is less clear: Russia experienced a huge plutocratic insurgency in the 1990s, but the arrival of Putin and the defenestration of the first-generation oligarchs represented the reassertion of the prerogatives of the state—that is, a successful *plutocratic counterinsurgency*. In China, the rise of the super-rich has happened mainly through state-sponsored (though not state-owned) enterprises, which means that plutocrats there remain dependent on the state and the Communist Party and, as such, are relatively insecure politically. There, and elsewhere in East Asia, rent-seeking rather than insurgent remains the norm among plutocrats.
5 Conceptually, plutocratic insurgencies differ from kleptocracies—the latter involve the use the institutions of state to loot the population, whereas the former wish to neutralize those institutions in order to facilitate private sector looting. In practice, these may overlap or co-mingle.
6 Liberal enthusiasts of globalization (most prominently: Barnett, 2005 and Friedman, 2005) assert poverty, insecurity and state fragility are the result of "disconnectedness"

from the world economy. This is false: even paradigmatically "failed" states—Congo, Somalia, Afghanistan—are deeply connected to the global economy. While it is true that they remain weakly connected to the *formal* and *legal* parts of the global economy, such places are *deviantly* connected—via the illicit trade in minerals, via piracy, or via the global drug trade, and so on. The crucial issue, in other words, is not connectedness or disconnectedness, but rather *what kind* of connectedness.

7 Rebels who seek to take over or direct the state toward projects of social reform do continue to exist of course—from Marx-inspired movements like the Zapatistas in Mexico or the Naxalites in India, to Allah-inspired movements like Al-Shabaab in Somalia or the Moro insurgency in the Philippines. These sorts of movements, as well as the so-called "color revolutions" that have befallen various post-Soviet states represent a different phenomenon than either described in this essay.

8 The ideological collapse of the labor-centric, social welfare-providing nationalist state helps to explain why the post-2007 crisis has failed to produce organized opposition movements geared at reining in the secessionist impulses of plutocrats or at addressing the abjections that drive deviant globalization (Fraser, 2013).

9 The popularity of the American television series "Breaking Bad" stems in no small part from its dramatization of this precise moral dilemma.

References

Abrahamsen, R. and Williams, M. (2011) *Security beyond the State: Private Security in International Politics*. Cambridge: Cambridge University Press.

Arendt, H. (1963) *On Revolution*. New York: Penguin.

Arias, E. (2006) "The Dynamics of Criminal Governance: Networks and Social Order in Rio de Janeiro." *Journal of Latin American Studies*. Vol. 38. No. 2: 293–325.

Bach, J. (2011) "Modernity and the Urban Imagination in Economic Zones." *Theory, Culture and Society*. Vol. 28. No. 5: 98–122.

Baer, W. (1972) "Import Substitution and Industrialization in Latin America: Experiences and Interpretations." *Latin American Research Review*. Vol. 7. No. 1: 301–328.

Balassa, B. (1978) "Exports and Economic Growth: Further Evidence." *Journal of Development Economics*. Vol. 5. No. 2: 181–189.

Baldacchino, G. (2010) *Island Enclaves: Offshoring Strategies, Creative Governance, and Subnational Island Jurisdictions*. Montreal: McGill-Queen's Press.

Barkan, J. (2013) "Plutocrats at Work: How Big Philanthropy Undermines Democracy." *Dissent*. Fall. Online, available at: www.dissentmagazine.org/article/plutocrats-at-work-how-big-philanthropy-undermines-democracy.

Barnett, T. (2005) *The Pentagon's New Map: War and Peace in the Twenty-First Century*. New York: Putnam.

Beck, U. (2008) *World at Risk*. New York: Polity, 2008.

Bickford, S. (2000) "Constructing Inequality: City Spaces and the Architecture of Citizenship." *Political Theory*. Vol. 28. No. 3: 355–376.

Blakely, E. (2012) "In Gated Communities, a Dangerous Mind-Set." *Washington Post*. April 6. Online, available at: www.washingtonpost.com/opinions/in-gated-communities-such-as-where-trayvon-martin-died-a-dangerous-mind-set/2012/04/06/gIQAwWG8zS_story.html.

Bobbitt, P. (2002) *The Shield of Achilles: War, Peace, and the Course of History*. New York: Knopf.

Breitung, W. (2012) "Enclave Urbanism in China: Attitudes towards Gated Communities in Guangzhou." *Urban Geography*. Vol. 33. No. 2: 278–294.

Bunker, R. and Sullivan, J. (2011) "Integrating Feral Cities and Third Phase Cartels/Third Generation Gangs Research: The Rise of Criminal (Narco) City Networks and Black-For." *Small Wars and Insurgencies*. Vol. 22. No. 5: 764–786.

Burgin, A. (2012) *The Great Persuasion: Reinventing Free Markets since the Depression*. Cambridge: Harvard University Press.

Burke, E. (1983 [1790]) *Reflections on the Revolution in France*. New York: Penguin.

Burns, J. (2009) *Goddess of the Market: Ayn Rand and the American Right*. New York: Oxford University Press.

Caldeira, T. (2000) *City of Walls: Crime, Segregation, and Citizenship in São Paulo*. Berkeley: University of California Press.

CapGemini (2013) "World Wealth Report 2013." Online, available at: www.capgemini.com/resource-file access/resource/pdf/wwr_2013_0.pdf.

Caryl, C. (2013) *Strange Rebels: 1979 and the Birth of the 21st Century*. New York: Basic Books.

Cheah, P. and Robbins, P. eds. (1998) *Cosmopolitics: Thinking and Feeling beyond the Nation*. Minneapolis: University of Minnesota Press.

Connell, J. (1999) "Beyond Manila: Walls, Malls, and Private Spaces." *Environment and Planning A*. Vol. 31. No. 3: 417–439.

Credit Suisse (2013) "Global Wealth Report 2013" Online, available at: https://publications.credit-suisse.com/tasks/render/file/?fileID=BCDB1364-A105–0560–1332EC9100FF5C83.

Davis, D. (2010) "Irregular Armed Forces, Shifting Patterns of Commitment, and Fragmented Sovereignty in the Developing World." *Theory and Society*. Vol. 39. No. 3–4: 397–413.

Davis, M. (2005) *Evil Paradises: Dreamworlds of Neoliberalism*. New York: The New Press.

Dezelay, Y. and Garth, B. (1998) *Dealing in Virtue: International Commercial Arbitration and the Construction of a Transnational Legal Order*. Chicago: University of Chicago Press.

DiMaggio, K. (2011) "Seceding from the Narrative: How the Criminal Underworlds in William Burroughs' Naked Lunch Map out a Non-Linear Narrative through the Creation of 'Temporary Autonomous Zones.'" *International Journal of the Book*. Vol. 8. No. 1: 11–18.

Domhoff, G. (2009) *Who Rules America? The Triumph of the Corporate Rich*, 7th edition New York: McGraw-Hill.

Duffield, M. (1998) "Post-modern Conflict: Warlords, Post-adjustment States and Private Protection." *Civil Wars*. Vol. 1. No. 1: 65–102.

Esping-Andersen, G. (1990) *The Three Worlds of Welfare Capitalism*. Cambridge: Polity Press.

Evans, P., Rueschemeyer, D. and Skocpol, T. eds. (1985) *Bringing the State Back In*. Cambridge: Cambridge University Press.

Fawaz, M., Harb, M. and Gharbieh, A. (2012) "Living Beirut's Security Zones: An Investigation of the Modalities and Practice of Urban Security." *City and Society*. Vol. 24. No. 2: 173–195.

Ferguson, J. (1999) *Expectations of Modernity: Myths and Meanings of Urban Life on the Zambian Copperbelt*. Berkeley: University of California.

Finnegan, W. (2010) "Silver or Lead." *New Yorker*. May 31. Online, available at: www.newyorker.com/reporting/2010/05/31/100531fa_fact_finnegan.

Fourcade-Gourinchas, M. and Babb, S. (2002) "The Rebirth of the Liberal Creed: Paths to Neoliberalism in Four Countries." *American Journal of Sociology*. Vol. 108. No. 3: 533–579.

Fraser, N. (2013) "A Triple Movement?" *New Left Review*. Vol. 81. May–June. Online, available at: http://newleftreview.org/II/81/nancy-fraser-a-triple-movement.

Frank, R. (2007) *Richistan: A Journey through the 21st Century Wealth Boom and the Lives of the New Rich*. New York: Piatkus.

Freeland, C. (2011) "The Rise of the New Global Elite." *Atlantic*. Vol. 307. No. 1: 44–55.

Freeland, C. (2012) *Plutocrats: The Rise of the New Global Super-Rich and the Fall of Everyone Else*. New York: Penguin.

Freeland, C. (2013) "An Elite Deserving of the Name." *Democracy: A Journal of Ideas*. No. 29. Summer. Online, available at: www.democracyjournal.org/29/an-elite-deserving-of-the-name.php?page=all.

Friedman, T. (2005) *The World is Flat: A Brief History of the Twenty-first Century*. New York: Macmillan.

Fukuyama, F. (1989) "The End of History?" *National Interest*. Vol. 16. No. 3: 3–18.

Gilman, N. (2003) *Mandarins of the Future: Modernization Theory in Cold War America*. Baltimore: Johns Hopkins University Press.

Gilman, N., Goldhammer, J. and Weber, S. eds. (2011) *Deviant Globalization: Black Market Economy in the 21st Century*. New York: Continuum.

Glenny, M. (2008) *McMafia: A Journey through the Global Criminal Underworld*. New York: Knopf.

Graham, S. and Marvin, S. (2001) *Splintering Urbanism: Networked Infrastructures, Technological Mobilities and the Urban Condition*. New York: Routledge.

Harvey, D. (2001) *Spaces of Capital: Toward a Critical Geography*. New York: Routledge.

Harvey, D. (2007) *A Brief History of Neoliberalism*. New York: Oxford University Press.

Hetherington, T. (2011) "Into the Korengal." *World Policy Journal*. Vol. 28. No. 1: 60–70.

Hirschman, A. (1970) *Exit, Voice, and Loyalty*. Cambridge: Harvard University Press.

Hope, T. (2000) "Inequality and the Clubbing of Private." Hope, T. and Sparks, R. eds. *Crime, Risk, and Insecurity: Law and Order in Everyday Life and Political Discourse*. New York: Routledge: 83–106.

Huffschmid, J. (2008) "Finance as a Driver of Privatization." *Transfer: European Review of Labour and Research*. Vol. 14. No. 2: 209–236.

Irvin, G. (2007) "Growing Inequality in the Neo-liberal Heartland." *Post-Autistic Economics Review*. Vol. 43: 1–23.

James, S. (1993) "The Idea Brokers: The Impact of Think Tanks on British Government." *Public Administration*. Vol. 71. No. 4: 491–506.

Judt, T. (2005) *Postwar: A History of Europe since 1945*. New York: Penguin.

Junger, S. (2007) "Blood Oil." *Vanity Fair*. February. Online, available at: www.vanity-fair.com/politics/features/2007/02/junger200702.

Kaker, S. (2014) "Enclaves, Insecurity and Violence in Karachi." *South Asian History and Culture*. Vol. 5. No. 1: 1–15.

Kapur, A., Macleod, N. and Singh, N. (2005) "Plutonomy: Buying Luxury, Explaining Global Imbalances." Citigroup Research. October 16. Online, available at: http://cryptome.org/0005/rich-pander.pdf (Mirrored).

Keefe, P. (2012) "How a Drug Cartel Makes its Billions." *New York Times*. June 15. Online, available at: www.nytimes.com/2012/06/17/magazine/how-a-mexican-drug-cartel-makes-its-billions.html?_r=0.

Kilcullen, D. (2013) *Out of the Mountains: The Coming Age of the Urban Guerrilla*. New York: Oxford University Press.

Klein, N. (2007) *The Shock Doctrine: The Rise of Disaster Capitalism*. New York: Knopf.

Krijnen, M. and Fawaz, M. (2010) "Exception as the Rule: High-end Developments in Neoliberal Beirut." *Built Environment*. Vol. 36. No. 2: 245–259.

Kroll, L. (2012) "Forbes World's Billionaires 2012." *Forbes*. July 3. Online, available at: www.forbes.com/sites/luisakroll/2012/03/07/forbes-worlds-billionaires-2012/.

Lambert, L. (2013) *Weaponized Architecture: The Impossibility of Innocence*. Barcelona: DPR-Barcelona.

Lambert, P. (1993) *The Distribution and Redistribution of Income*. Manchester: Manchester University Press.

Langewiesche, W. (2007) "City of Fear." *Vanity Fair*. April 1. Online, available at: www.vanityfair.com/politics/features/2007/04/langewiesche200704.

Lichtenstein, N. (2000) "Class Politics and the State during World War Two." *International Labor and Working-Class History*. No. 58: 261–274.

Lister, D., Atkinson, R. and Flint, J. (2003) *Gated Communities: A Systematic Review of the Research Evidence*. Bristol: ESRC Centre for Neighbourhood Research.

Los, M. (2003) "Crime in Transition: The Post-Communist State, Markets, and Crime." *Crime, Law and Social Change*. Vol. 40. No. 2–3: 145–169.

McKenzie, E. (1996) *Privatopia: Homeowner Associations and the Rise of Residential Private Government*. New Haven: Yale University Press.

Manwaring, M. (2005) *Street Gangs: The New Urban Insurgency*. Carlisle: Strategic Studies Institute, US Army War College. March 1. Online, available at: www.strategicstudiesinstitute.army.mil/pubs/display.cfm?pubID=597.

Marten, K. (2012) *Warlords: Strong-Armed Brokers in Weak States*. Ithaca: Cornell University Press.

Medvetz, T. (2012) *Think Tanks in America*. Chicago: University of Chicago Press.

Miller, J. (2009) "The Mexicanization of American Law Enforcement." *City Journal*. Vol. 19. No. 4. Autumn. Online, available at: www.city-journal.org/2009/19_4_corruption.html.

Milward, H. and Provan, K. (2000) "Governing the Hollow State." *Journal of Public Administration Research and Theory*. Vol. 10. No. 2: 359–380.

Mizruchi, M. (2013) *The Fracturing of the American Corporate Elite*. Cambridge: Harvard University Press.

Monbiot, G. (2012) "A Manifesto for Psychopaths." *Guardian*. March 6. Online, available at: www.monbiot.com/2012/03/05/a-manifesto-for-psychopaths/ (Mirrored).

Norton, R. (2003) "Feral Cities: The New Strategic Environment." *Naval War College Review*. Vol. 56. No. 4: 97–106.

Omeje, K. (2010) "Markets or Oligopolies of Violence? The Case of Sudan." *African Security*. Vol. 3. No. 3: 168–189.

Ong, A. (2000) "Graduated Sovereignty in South-East Asia." *Theory, Culture and Society*. Vol. 17. No. 4: 55–75.

Pack, J. (1987) "Privatization of Public Sector Services in Theory and Practice." *Journal of Policy Analysis and Management*. Vol. 6. No. 4: 523–540.

Parenti, C. (2011) *Tropic of Chaos: Climate Change and the Geography of Violence*. New York: Nation Books.

Phillips-Fein, K. (2006) "American Counterrevolutionary: Lemuel Ricketts Boulware and General Electric, 1950–1960." Lichtenstein, N., ed., *American Capitalism: Social*

Thought and Political Economy in the Twentieth Century. Philadelphia: University of Pennsylvania Press: 249–270.

Phillips-Fein, K. (2009) "Business Conservatives and the Mont Pèlerin Society." Mirowski, P. and Plehwe, D. eds. *The Road from Mont Pèlerin: The Making of the Neoliberal Thought Collective*. Cambridge: Harvard University Press: 280–301.

Pletsch, C. (1981) "The Three Worlds, or the Division of Social Scientific Labor, circa 1950–1975." *Comparative Studies in Society and History*. Vol. 23. No. 4: 565–590.

Rajan, R. and Zingales, L. (2003) "The Great Reversals: The Politics of Financial Development in the Twentieth Century." *Journal of Financial Economics*. Vol. 69. No. 1: 5–50.

Reinhart, C. and Reinhart, V. (2008) *Capital Flow Bonanzas: An Encompassing View of the Past and Present*. No. w14321. National Bureau of Economic Research. September. Online, available at: www.nber.org/papers/w14321.

Robb, J. (2007) *Brave New War*. New York: Wiley.

Rodenbeck, E. (2013) "Mapping Silicon Valley's Gentrification Problem through Corporate Shuttle Routes." *Wired*. June 9. Online, available at: www.wired.com/opinion/2013/09/mapping-silicon-valleys-corporate-shuttle-problem/.

Rodrik, D. (2006) "Goodbye Washington Consensus, Hello Washington Confusion? A Review of the World Bank's Economic Growth in the 1990s: Learning from a Decade of Reform." *Journal of Economic Literature*. Vol. 44. No. 4: 973–987.

Ronfeldt, D. (2006) *Tribes: The Once and Forever Form*. WR-433-RPC. Santa Monica: RAND Corporation. December. Online, available at: www.rand.org/content/dam/rand/pubs/working_papers/2007/RAND_WR433.pdf.

Sargent, D. (forthcoming) *A Superpower Transformed: History, Strategy, and American Foreign Policy in the 1970s*. New York: Oxford University Press.

Saviano, R. (2006) *Gomorrah: A Personal Journey into the Violent International Empire of Naples' Organized Crime System*. Milan: Mondadori.

Schwartz, M. (2014) "A Mission Gone Wrong: Why Are We Still Fighting the Drug War?" *New Yorker*. January 6. Online, available at: www.newyorker.com/reporting/2014/01/06/140106fa_fact_schwartz.

Scott, J. (1998) *Seeing Like a State: How Some Schemes to Improve the Human Condition Have Failed*. New Haven: Yale University Press.

Sengupta, S. (2008) "Inside Gate, India's Good Life; Outside, the Servants' Slums." *New York Times*. June 9. Online, available at: www.nytimes.com/2008/06/09/world/asia/09gated.html.

Shank, M. and Beavers, E. (2013) "America's Police Are Looking More and More Like the Military." *Guardian*. October 7. Online, available at: www.theguardian.com/commentisfree/2013/oct/07/militarization-local-police-america.

Shaxson, N. (2011) *Treasure Islands: Tax Havens and the Men Who Stole the World*. London: Bodley Head.

Shaxson, N. (2013) "A Tale of Two Londons." *Vanity Fair*. April 1. Online, available at: www.vanityfair.com/society/2013/04/mysterious-residents-one-hyde-park-london.

Sidaway, J. (2007) "Enclave Space: A New Metageography of Development?" *Area*. Vol. 39. No. 3: 331–339.

Singer, P. (2001) *Corporate Warriors: The Rise of the Privatized Military Industry*. Ithaca: Cornell University Press.

Skocpol, T. (1979) *States and Social Revolution: A Comparative Analysis of France, Russia and China*. Cambridge: Cambridge University Press.

Slater, D. (2008) *Geopolitics and the Post-Colonial: Rethinking North-South Relations*. Malden: Blackwell.

Strange, S. (1996) *The Retreat of the State: The Diffusion of Power in the World Economy*. Cambridge: Cambridge University Press.

Sullivan, J. and Bunker, R. (2002) "Drug Cartels, Street Gangs, and Warlords." *Small Wars and Insurgencies*. Vol. 13. No. 2: 40–53.

Taylor, J. and Harrison, D. (2008) *The New Elite: Inside the Minds of the Truly Wealthy*. New York: Amacom.

Vellacott, C. (2012) "London Impoverished by Rise of the Plutocrats." *Reuters*. March 20. Online, available at: http://uk.reuters.com/article/2012/03/20/uk-london-incomedisparity-idUKLNE82J02420120320.

Webster, C. (2001) "Gated cities of tomorrow." *Town Planning Review*. Vol. 72. No. 2: 149–170.

Weiss, G. (2012) *Ayn Rand Nation: The Hidden Struggle for America's Soul*. New York: St. Martin's Press.

Westad, O. (2006) *The Global Cold War: Third World Interventions and the Making of Our Times*. Cambridge: Cambridge University Press.

Williamson, J. (1990) "What Washington Means by Policy Reform." Williamson, J., ed., *Latin American Adjustment: How Much Has Changed*. Washington: Institute for International Economics: 7–40.

Woodiwiss, A. (1993) *Postmodernity USA: The Crisis of Social Modernism in Postwar America*. Thousand Oaks: Sage Publications.

World Bank Staff (1997) *World Development Report 1997: The State in a Changing World*. New York: Oxford University Press.

Yergin, D. (1998) *The Commanding Heights: The Battle between Government and the Marketplace that is Remaking the Modern World*. New York: The Free Press.

Overview

Dark Renaissance—crime, corruption, and global class warfare

Robert J. Bunker and Pamela Ligouri Bunker

> Ciudad Juarez is all our futures. This is the inevitable war of capitalism gone mad.
>
> Ed Vulliamy, 2011

Much has been written about the many economic benefits of globalization and the triumph and spread of democratic liberalism with the end of the Cold War, following the demise of the Soviet Union. The scholar Francis Fukuyama went so far as to proclaim "The End of History." The final form of human governance was said to be achieved—a form of government derived from a universalization of Western liberal democracy (Fukuyama, 1989, 1992). Implicit in such a position is that those very democracies do not become dysfunctional and that the economic paradigm they are founded on, in this instance laissez-faire capitalism, remains infallible—especially when operating at the supra-national level as a result of globalization.

This work takes issue with such "wine and roses" perspectives about the future of the Western democracies and their faith-based views on the moral purity of a globalized marketplace. It also, in fact, questions many of the assumptions found in the status quo reinforcing discipline of IPE—a discipline that focuses on the formal and legitimate economies and the façade they present that international relations and commerce are still dominated and dictated solely by the old Westphalian state centric system.[1] For such a young and interdisciplinary field of study such as IPE to be so heavily influenced, some could even say captured, by the "dead hand of the past" is an intellectual tragedy. Further, from an applied perspective, it is increasingly diminishing the relevance of its contribution to future discourse and debate about global human political and economic relations. It's focus on the ideal world of the past, is increasingly separated from the real—a more nasty and brutish world that is to be found not only in regions of the developing world but also in what were once considered the "safe havens" in the West anchored by a productive and burgeoning middle class.

Having highlighted these concerns, this overview will next delve into two of the major themes of the work prior to providing a short summary of the contents of the book itself. The first theme focuses on the theoretical perception that a

"Dark Renaissance" is taking place globally—one in which the Western liberal democracies and its citizens are ill prepared to respond because it exists at the trans-civilization level, bridging the modern to the post-modern world. The second theme focuses on the actual process of state deconstruction that is taking place. This process is leading to what may become the very undoing of the democracies and their peoples as they now attempt to sail a dangerous course, reminiscent of the Homeric passage through the Strait of Messina, with criminal and plutocratic forces representing Scylla and Charybdis, respectively.

Dark Renaissance

The political science literature is abundantly blessed with theories, constructs, and insights about the adverse and potentially calamitous changes that have been taking, and are continuing to take, place in the state based international system and to states themselves in the face of the rising power of both violent non-state actors (VNSAs), essentially armed criminal entities, and multinational corporations and sovereign wealth funds, operated by extremely rich and privileged family dynasties. While the views of one scholar may be discounted as the proverbial "lone voice in the wilderness," the choral nature of an increasingly vocal scholarly symphony cannot be so easily discounted. For an early example, concerning the privileged position of the state as the dominant human social and political form, Martin van Creveld has written on both the loss of the state's monopoly on war making and the gradual demise of the Westphalian state form itself (1991, 1999). Phillip Bobbitt, in turn, has gone on to project the rise of the market state and its variants (e.g. entrepreneurial, mercantile, and managerial) as a successor to the modern state form (2002). A few years earlier, Rosecrance projected the rise of a virtual state that is world market, rather than territorially, based (1999: 4).

With the rise of new state forms, a very different state system is projected to develop. Perspectives on the new international environment now emerging have likened it to a new medievalism as states recede (Bull, 1977; Rapley, 2006) and even offer the potential for a new dark age (Williams, 2008). These are reminiscent of Robert Kaplan's earlier "coming anarchy" concerns (1994) and are complementary to the works on the exponential growth of global slums (Davis, 2006; Neuwirth, 2006), now containing an estimated 860 million inhabitants (UN, 2012). Such ungovernable slums create "vacuums of governance" that can be exploited. This results in questions arising about alternatives to state authority in ungoverned spaces (Clunan and Trinkunas, 2010) and how governance will develop without a state (Risse, 2011).

One answer may come from scholars focusing on transnational crime and armed non-state actors. In 1985, a body of work focusing on "war making and state making as organized crime" first emerged. In that initial work, Charles Tilly described four mutually supporting state agent activities: war making (eliminating/neutralizing external rivals), state making (eliminating/neutralizing internal rivals), protection (eliminating/neutralizing the enemies of their clients—e.g. consumers with whom they have a relationship), and extraction (acquiring the means to carry out the first three activities) that lead to European state creation (Tilly, 1985).[2] This work was greatly expanded by Tilly (1992 [1990]) and has more recently been revisited by Leander (2004) and Felbab-Brown (2010). Leander's contrarian views are significant due to the fact that her "un-state making" insights about contemporary state decentralization and privatization, the dismantling and criminalizing of administrations, and the loss of domestic clientele (i.e. the loss of the loyalty of the citizens) show how the Tillian process is now being reversed by violent non-state actors. This dovetails nicely with Felbab-Brown's focus on how the gangs and cartels in parts of Latin America are now engaging in their own process of proto-state creation amongst their constituents in the territories that they control. Further, such armed non-state groups are rapidly evolving through various gang generations and cartel phases (Bunker and Sullivan, 2013) and are converging together into ever more deadly and adaptive polyglot combinations which are blurring the lines of terrorists, criminals, insurgents and other VNSAs (Hesterman, 2013; Miklaucic and Brewer, 2013). Further, Robert Mandel, breaking with commonly held views, is now calling for accommodation and power sharing arrangements with armed non-state actors in some fragile states in order to facilitate stable governance (2013).

With regard to threats posed by multinational corporations and dynastic elites, we have come a long way from the old 1950s adage "What's good for GM [General Motors] is good for America" (Patterson, 2013).[3] Jessica Matthews in a celebrated article discussed how:

> National governments are not simply losing autonomy in a globalized economy. They are sharing powers—including political, social, and security roles at the core of sovereignty—with businesses, with international organizations, and with a multitude of citizens groups, known as nongovernmental organizations (NGOs). The steady concentration of power in the hands of states that had begun in 1648 with the Peace of Westphalia is over, at least for a while.
>
> (Matthews, 1997: 50)

In the 1960s, multinational corporations were essentially all American but the fear four to five decades later is that increasingly stateless multinationals "are disconnecting from their home countries' national interests, moving jobs, evading taxes, and eroding sovereignty in the process" (Matthews, 1997: 56).

This thinking ties back to the market state projections of Bobbitt and Rosecrance—especially that of Rosecrance who observes that "The newly pruned [downsized] corporation has facilitated the emergence of the virtual state" (Rosecrance, 1999: 9). Stateless and streamlined multinationals, in essence, have reconfigured themselves for the hyper-competitive requirements of a globalized economy. The pursuit of maintaining and increasing profit margins has been a coup for private shareholders and dynastic wealth funds. The losers have been labor and Westphalian states, especially middle class workers in the Western democracies and those states themselves, who are being played off against each other by the multinationals who seek special operating and tax privileges to bolster their bottom lines. A growing literature focusing on how global corporations and the very rich are benefiting from this process exists. See, for instance, Noreena Hertz (2001), Charles Lewis and Bill Allison (2001), David Rothkopf (2008, 2012), Janine Wedel (2009), Chrystia Freeland (2012), and Jeff Faux (2012).

Where the corporate (licit economy) and criminal (illicit economy) intersect is also of significance to the Dark Renaissance now unfolding before our eyes. The core arguments drawn from the work *Deviant Globalization* (Gilman *et al.*, 2011: 2–5) are as follows:

- ...*deviant globalization is inextricably linked to and bound up with mainstream globalization.*
- ...*it would be a grave mistake to view deviant globalization as a mere sideshow* to what "really matters" in the global political economy.
- ...*we have to abandon the assumption that deviant globalization is a removable cancer* in an otherwise healthy global economy.

Hence, with globalization—the *cross-border integration of value-added economic activity*—promoting the formal economy, comes a deviant "illicit" doppelganger shadowing virtually every mainstream industry (Gilman *et al.*, 2011: 6, 13). As a result, stateless multinationals now exist in both licit and illicit forms with a surprising amount of permeability existing between them in the informal (gray) economic region and in international money laundering schemes. Moreover, licit and illicit elites in authoritarian states readily work together for mutual economic benefit in places such as Russia, Pakistan, and China or even merge as has taken place in North Korea (Kan *et al.*, 2010).

A great example of such criminal and corporate forces simultaneously imperiling the sovereignty of a state can be seen recently in Honduras. That state of about eight million citizens has a gang population of about 35,000 members belonging to MS-13, Barrio-18, and various homegrown *Maras*. It has also been penetrated by the Sinaloa, Gulf, Zetas, Loco Barrera and Rastrojos cartels, who have fielded armed paramilitary units. The threat to the state—which serves as a transit point for South American cocaine coming north, a safe haven for cartel operations, and as a possible synthetic drug production hub—by these groups is extremely high, with the potentials for a de facto narco-state emerging (Dudley, 2013). During the same time as these criminal groups were seizing control of both urban and rural regions and turning Honduras into the homicide capital of the world, a major development project was proposed by the Honduran government. The project sought to allow the creation of "charter cities." These proposed cities, essentially quasi-independent city-states built and managed by multinational corporations and defended by private security firms, would become free-market islands of economic production and global trade to spur investment and growth in the beleaguered local economy (*The Economist*, 2011; Fernandez, 2012). As can be seen, neither the criminal insurgent activities of the gangs and cartels nor the neo-colonial corporatist response of the government, installed after a 2009 coup, bode well for democratic rule or social class mobility in that state.

The many scholarly works highlighted, and no doubt numerous others not drawn upon, both complement and reinforce the Epochal Studies/RPMA literature first developed in 1987 by T. Lindsay Moore (2003 [1987 unpublished]) and Robert J. Bunker (1994, 1997).[4] Over the last 25 years, numerous publications related to this literature have been published.[5] Components of this body of work have focused on various attributes of the epochal change taking place with the ongoing global transition from the modern to post-modern eras. Attributes of this change include advances in human civilizational energy sources, economies, state organization, technology (weaponry), battlespace dimensionality, and military force structures. The blurring of crime and war, the returning of mercenaries to the battlefield, and the increasing failure of the Westphalian state model have also been identified. Major social class reorganization, as an additional component of this change, has been long projected (Bunker, 1999) with this book providing a significant, regarding the near term, foray into such analysis.

Figure O.1 is representative of one conceptual model used to view epochal change (shifts) in Western civilization. T. Lindsay Moore will provide a detailed description and analysis of this process, along with a more granulated figure portraying the historical epochs, later in this book. Suffice to say that, since 1500 CE, Western civilization has spread throughout the globe and that, during this epochal shift, not only will that civilization transition into a post-modern form of human social and political organization but so too will the rest of the world's civilizations. Quite likely this will occur at uneven rates and with unimaginable levels of disruption and strife, as is only beginning to take place within a number of Islamic states, as part of the process. Further, at least for the West, the historical clashes "*in* civilization" have been characterized as the dark ages and a renaissance, respectively. While those epochal shifts spanned centuries, this

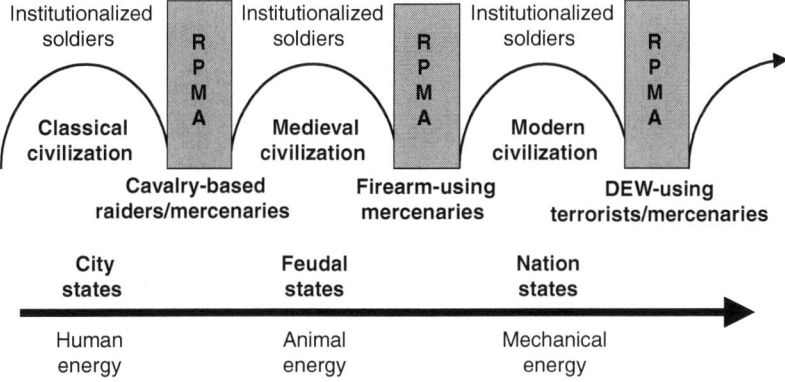

Figure O.1 Epochal change (shifts) in Western civilization.

epochal shift, due to historical compression beginning in the ~1820 period will likely see Westphalian state deconstruction and the state successor process measured in possibly a century or less. Because elements of both a dark age and a renaissance are readily apparent in this shift into the post-modern (fourth) epoch of human civilization, akin to globalization plagued by a deviant "illicit" doppelganger shadow (Gilman *et al.*, 2011), the term being used to describe it is that of a Dark Renaissance.

In defining a Dark Renaissance, it can be said that a transition is taking place from one historical era (epoch) to another derived from the qualitative advancement of civilizational knowledge, rather than a relearning of such knowledge. The negative—or dark—attributes of this transition are defined from the perspective of the "existential threat" this represents to the integrity of the Western democracies with whom the scholars writing this book have allegiance as citizens, legal residents, and fiduciary agents. While civilizational progress is typically viewed as a positive element of human mastery over the environment with technology use and development a process of this advancement, the actual transitional phase sees the fall of one temporal civilization (e.g. classical, medieval, modern) and the rise of a new one.

Crime, corruption, and global class warfare

The "existential threat" highlighted above can be viewed in Figure O.2: Demise of the Western democracies. What we are witnessing is the compression of the middle zone—our modern Westphalian based world—by the forces of post-modernity. The supra- and sub-state actors ushering in this change are taking us down the path of crime, corruption, and, very likely, global class warfare. The last potentiality is of great significance. Still, it should be remembered that great levels of inequality have existed between the "West and the rest"; developed countries and underdeveloped states, as well as between the elites (haves) and the masses (have-nots) in authoritarian states around the globe for centuries. According to Ignacio Ramonet of *Le Monde diplomatique*:

> On a worldwide level, poverty continues to be the rule and welfare the exception. The different forms of inequality have become a structural feature of our times. They continue to worsen, creating an ever widening gulf between rich and poor. The 225 greatest fortunes in the world represent a total of over a trillion euros, or the equivalent of the earnings of the poorest 47 percent of the world's population (2.5 billion human beings!). Today there are individuals richer than many states: the sum total of the wealth of the 15 richest people in the world is greater than the GNP of all the sub-Saharan African countries.
>
> (Ramonet, 2004: 6)

However, dramatically rising levels of inequality are now becoming apparent within the Western states as well, with concerns being openly voiced by scholars including Lawrence Jacobs and Theda Skocpol (2005), Thom Hartmann (2006), Jeff Faux (2006, 2012), Benjamin Page and Lawrence Jacobs (2009), and James Galbraith (2009). These scholars, and others like them, are not from the "historical materialism" tradition of Karl Marx (1859) and Frederick Engels (1892). With the demise of the Soviet Union—based on a centrally planned economy—in 1991 and the acceptance of a market economy by the Chinese Communist Party in the 1990s, those political-economic views, which had brought about the twentieth-century "Cold War" between communism and capitalism, have been fully discredited. Rather, these are scholars allied with capitalism. They are recognizing that the present globalized strain of capitalism has now gone greatly amiss—much of it is predatory, facilitated by corrupt officials, and even criminally linked. It is creating an emerging world in which not only do "haves and have-nots" exist in the less developed and under resourced Global South but one in which this condition is increasingly apparent in the more developed and resource rich Global North exemplified by the Western democracies.

It is as if the hands of the labor movement clock are now being slowly turned back in time towards the lives of immigrant workers in the meat packing plants of turn of the century Chicago (Sinclair, 1906) and to the even earlier industrial deprivations of Victorian London. Where the spreading condition of the "haves and have-nots" now comes full circle is, indeed, back to seemingly Marxist views of class conflict. The Western middle classes had enjoyed for many generations relatively high wages as laborers (e.g. the proletariat) that allowed them many of the benefits of owners of capital (e.g. the bourgeoisie). Beginning in the 1970s, the fortunes of the middle class, specifically in America, began to take a turn for the worse (Pizzigati, 2012). They have been backsliding ever since with the advent of the supply-side (trickle-down) Reaganomics of the 1980s. Similar trends also began to take place in Britain under Margaret Thatcher by the 1980s, with the reduction in power of the trade unions, and have since spread throughout Western Europe. Rising levels of inequality in the West with the loss of industrial age jobs has over time bifurcated the ranks of the middle class. This has served to create a far larger demographic group composed of families relying on part-time and low paying service jobs, devoid of benefits, upon which to live as versus the smaller pool of highly paid knowledge workers which has emerged (Rifkin, 1995; Wilson, 1996). The big winners, however, have been the CEOs of the major corporations who 30 years ago were already being paid on average 42 times what the average worker earned. Those same CEOs in 2012, on average, made $12.3 million which is now 354 times the rank-and-file salary (Lazarus, 2013: B4).

Perhaps this is why in 2006 Warren Buffett, consistently listed as one of the richest persons in the world and not a Marxist by any stretch of the imagination, acknowledged "There's class warfare, all right, … but it's my class, the rich class, that's making war, and we're winning" (Stein, 2006). This recognition spurred Buffet to donate the bulk of his fortune to the Bill and Melinda Gates Foundation, the founders of which, like himself, are making a noble gesture that is simply too little and too late to influence the broader currents of rising

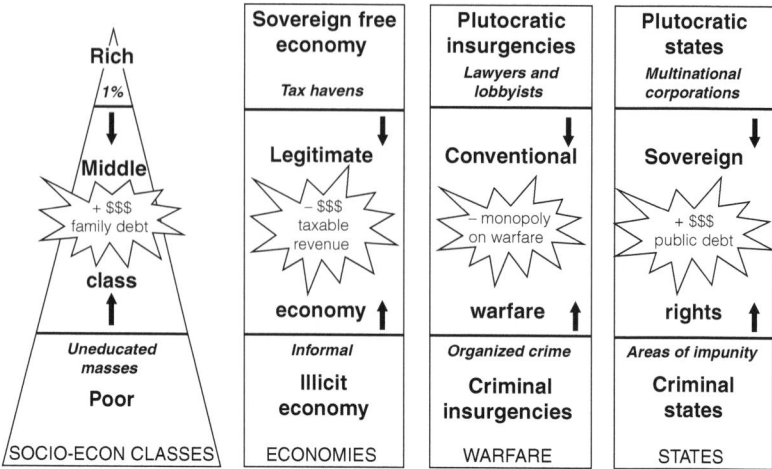

Figure O.2 Demise of the Western democracies.

inequality.[6] In contrast, however, the typical plutocratic response is more akin to the utter disdain shown by the "great princess" of Rousseau's pen, whose callous remark about the starving French peasants with no bread was simply, "Let them eat cake" (Rousseau, 1782–1789).

The premise of this book is thus that this marked rise in inequality in the Western democracies along with other deleterious trends in effect are an outcome of the historical transition—the process of epochal change—taking place across multiple components of modern civilization. For the purposes of this book project, meant to advance our understanding of this process vis-à-vis IPE, the focus will be on the changes taking place to socio-economic classes, economies, warfare and states. A general description of these changes to each civizational component follows:

Socio-economic classes

The modern era, within the Western states, is characterized by a socio-economic structure derived from the benefits of industrialization beginning in the mid-to-late nineteenth century. A growing middle class emerged, which, by the mid-twentieth century, prospered from governmental policies that protected the various trade and worker unions that had developed. These Global North states have since seen a reversal of middle class fortunes and the thinning out of the middle strata of society, with changes in the economy and tax code shifts that have benefited primarily the wealthy. This polarization between the 1 percent and 99 percent was evident in the Occupy and 15-M protests—"We are the 99 percent"—in many American and European cities during the 2011–2012 period of the financial meltdown. Sites related to these protests are still active (e.g. occupywallst.org), though the protests themselves have subsided and are being more actively broken up (UPI, 2013). One of the mechanisms being utilized by middle class families to retain their standards of living and to educate their college age children is to incur increasing private debt loads. In the United States, the average individual debt load, which includes higher credit card interest rate debt, is presently at about $47,000. The average student loan debt is now about $23,000. This is in contrast to the average US salary of roughly $42,000 in 2010 (McCluskey, 2012). To be fair, however, the loss for the Western middle class has been a boon for rising social strata in Chinese, Indian and other industrializing states, who are now seeing their own middle classes emerge at an accelerated rate. As a result, in a fully globalized and post-modern economy, we may someday witness the emergence of a global class structure resulting in some form of equilibrium, wherein a greatly thinned out Western middle class is mirrored by a relatively small and only partially developed middle class in the more recently industrialized countries of the Global South.

Economies

The Western states draw the vast bulk of their revenues from the formal (licit) economy. While some benefits do accrue from the informal, and can even be traced back to the criminal economy (Andreas, 2013)—for example, much of the Miami skyline was originally built on 1980s cocaine money—our increasingly convoluted and bureaucratic tax code is legal economy focused. Four basic issues now exist between Western states and the formal economy. The first one is that the legitimate economy is shrinking relative to the two other economies that exist. This means that the potential revenue pool, a segment of which is provided by the middle class, is steady state if not diminishing in size. Loss of higher paying union jobs and their substitution with "Walmart" and other such part time employment translates into much lower taxable incomes for tax filers. This trend has also spread to upper class medical professionals with general practice MDs seeing a marked decrease in their incomes relative to the insurance companies, which have done a good job of squeezing out the profits between medical practitioners and their clients. The second issue is that the illicit economy appears to be growing in size while remaining highly profitable. The Western states are expending large sums of revenues to nominally combat violent non-state actors, such as the cartels and gangs, who benefit from the illicit economy—whereas, in actuality, they are attempting to fight an economy itself which can be a daunting challenge. The third issue is that a sovereign free economy has emerged that is increasingly being utilized by multinational corporations and the global 1 percent. Legitimate revenues earned in the Western democracies thus become sheltered by business entities residing in tax havens and which have seen legislation enacted that benefits their profit margins. These plutocratic-derived strategies are ensuring that the revenue streams of the Western states are being further truncated. Finally, the fourth issue, revolves around Chinese and Indian businesses, and many of the more pragmatic multinational corporations, which willingly embrace any profits that they can extract from the informal and, more importantly, criminal economies. These four issues result in the Western democracies becoming revenue starved while non-state actors, multinationals, and other less "legalistic" entities remain profitable in the more globalized and largely amoral economy that exists.

Warfare

Changes to modern warfare ultimately stem from the loss of the monopoly on political violence—a privilege granted to states since the Treaty of Westphalia in 1648—and have resulted in a diminution in state-on-state conventional war. While one cause of this condition is attributed to the development of nuclear weapons and their proliferation in a number of greater and lesser powers, which makes conventional warfare simply too dangerous for states to engage in (van Creveld, 2008), much of this loss stems from the actions of both non-state and supra-state actors.[7] Unconventional, asymmetric, and hybrid forms of warfare have been gaining in importance for decades now. One of the newer terms for one form of violent non-state actor derived warfare is that of "criminal insurgency" (Sullivan and Bunker, 2012) which has its basis in the older "commercial insurgency" literature (Metz, 1993). Even more recently, a newer form of warfare being waged by multinational corporations and the superrich has been postulated; "plutocratic insurgency" (Bunker and Gilman, 2012). It is principally co-optive—lawyer and lobbyist—based in nature, and represents an insider threat to the international state system. Themes relating to both of these new forms of warfare will be evident throughout the book.

States

Westphalian states are not only having their sovereign rights challenged but are also buckling under the strain of materially and ideologically providing for the needs of their citizens. Both international free-trade agreements, such as NAFTA (North American Free Trade Agreement) and the European Single Market, and the increasing growth and importance of the global World Wide Web are posing challenges to state sovereignty. An addition concern for a number of European states is that extreme secularization to the detriment of ideology and extremely low indigenous birth rates have combined to make the concept of nationalism passé—if not outright unacceptable—particularly given the association of ultra-nationalism with groups on the extreme right. Heavy migration and higher fecundity within migrant groups has resulted more often in a form of tribalization rather than a process of integration, causing additional levels of societal stress. Further, for many Western states, the ravages of internal corruption, decay and other organizational maladies are resulting in internal dysfunction becoming evident—simply look at the budgetary and deficit issues and general loss of consensus plaguing the US Congress. The rising public debt levels in the United States and many of the Western European states—simply to keep governments running and providing basic services to their citizens—are indicative of these trends. Furthermore, armed non-state actors are threatening the integrity of weaker states, which can result in the criminalization of their institutions. If such institutions are fully compromised, the emergence of actual criminal-states becomes a viable concern (Bunker and Bunker, 2006; Miklaucic and Naim, 2013). Weak states are also as subject to capture by multinational corporations and other plutocratic interests as much as they are to collusion between criminal (bottom up) and elite (top down) interests (Casas-Zamora, 2013).

The work

The book is divided into three main parts along with front and back sections. The initial section of the work contains an editors' note, foreword, introduction, and this overview. The foreword by Nils Gilman focuses on the dichotomy and interrelationship of the plutocratic and criminal insurgencies discussed in quite a few of the special volume chapters. It is divided into an overview of the failures of social modernism, a discussion concerning plutocratic insurgency (a revolt of mainstream globalization's winners) and criminal insurgency (a revolt of deviant globalization's winners), and the resulting enclavization of microsovereignties and the end of the middle class. Gilman's composition is the first of its kind, conceptually linking the twin insurgency threat—one from above (supranational) and one from below (subnational)—now challenging the Westphalian state, its institutions, the political economy upon which it rests, and its social class structure. Following the eloquent foreword is a penetrating introduction to the work written by Mark Galeotti. It highlights the relationships of kleptocracies, warlords, and mafias in uniform to predation, coercion and legitimacy and the fact that these result from inadequate controls by civil society. When such controls are inadequate—or even worse non-existent—economic coercion and plundering take place. Consequently, some sort of moderating force, principally a democratic state via its policing and judicial system, is required to keep the excesses of such organized criminals in check. This has very real implications for the rest of this work, which views both the illicit and sovereign free economies, and the entities that function within them, as falling outside the moderating influence of the Westphalian state.

Part I of the work provides context and allows us to better understand the changing twenty-first-century global environment. Specifically, these chapters focus on the attributes of energy, economics and war, their interrelationship to globalization, and what impact this may have vis-à-vis the future of the Western democracies. The chapter by T. Lindsay Moore focuses on the contemporary clash *in* Western civilization. The thesis presented is that the emergence of a new system of energy results in civilizational shifts. These shifts promote the introduction of innovative technologies for waging war and designing, fabricating and assembling new products. Novel transportation and communications systems also develop. Taken together, the many changes transform politics and economics and even the social class structures of Western civilization. The next chapter, by Yelena A. Tuzova, focuses on the illicit and sovereign free IPEs. It provides an overview of the underground economy, an explanation of why individuals and firms would seek to embrace it, methods of its measurement, estimates of its size around the globe, its positive and detrimental effects, and concluding thoughts. This discussion of the theoretical and empirical literature advances our understanding of dark IPE, outlines the debates and disagreements inherent in analyzing it, and attempts to explain why the illicit economy appears to continue to expand and grow so fast. The final chapter, by T.X. Hammes, concerns criminal enterprises, private military companies (PMCs), smart robots and their implications for both the international order and state sovereignty. His conclusions are mixed and range from the not-so-good, even often times grim, through the more optimistic. He also brings a futuristic flare to his chapter concerning his analysis of the marriage of robotics with computer power—a union that he views as having more impact, at least initially, on economic production and the replacement of human workers than on warfare. This will likely help to create more instability in the developing world. Further, many of the trends highlighted are also viewed to increase both a state's security capabilities along with the disruptive capability of terrorists and insurgents. Totalitarian, democratic, private military corporations and criminal leaders will all benefit from these technologies. By extension, this also means that plutocratic enclaves and cities will also be readily able to defend themselves with their own mercenary and armed robotic forces from the aggressions of both states and criminal organizations if required to do so in the future.

Part II of this special volume focuses on criminal and sovereign free change and conflict. The initial chapter, by Luis Jorge Garay Salamanca and Eduardo Salcedo-Albarán, explores the reconfiguring of institutions by illicit networks in Colombia, Guatemala and Mexico. The chapter goes beyond basic concepts of coercion and corruption and explains how drug traffickers and other unlawful organizations are reconfiguring states in the western hemisphere. It builds upon the state capture (StC) literature by utilizing a process known as co-opted state reconfiguration (CStR). Social network analysis (SNA) is then utilized in the chapter to graph the CStR taking place in the three case study states. Node/agent concentrations provide a convincing argument that state institutional capture and reconfiguration is taking place. This research provides an excellent glimpse into the process by which gangs, cartels and other entities waging a criminal insurgency—utilizing the technique of *¿Plata O Plomo?* (Silver or Lead)—are able to eat away at the institutions of the state and co-opt them for their illicit economic benefit. The companion chapter, by Robert J. Bunker, provides an analysis of public looting for private gain. It does so by explaining the rise of predatory capitalism, exploring its facilitators—multinational corporations and the global elites that control them—and then analyzes the plutocratic insurgency construct in comparison to the better known criminal insurgency one. The chapter then goes on to highlight some of the instances of how the United States and United Kingdom—and their middle classes—have suffered at the hands of the plutocratic insurgency that is taking place. It concludes with a short discussion of how a capitalist "civil war" has essentially broken out, pitting the supra-bourgeoisie, representative of globalized capitalism, directly against the petty-bourgeoisie, representative of moderated state capitalism.

Part III of the book highlights the demise of the Western democracies. The first chapter, by Tanya Buhler Corbin and Nicole Hendrix, is concerned with the demise of the American middle class and the rise of the police state. The authors explore the precarious position of the middle class and the increased, and often unchecked, use of militaristic law enforcement strategies as a response to both criminal and terrorist activity. They conclude with some reflections and the need for reform concerning the convergence of these two negative trends since they point toward a potential Orwellian societal shift. This potential shift is one in which many individual liberties are lost in a nation squarely divided between the masses of the poor and a much smaller group of power elites. The second chapter of this part of the book, by Pamela Ligouri Bunker, focuses on the crisis in Europe. It provides an overview of the relationship of established Westphalian states to the European Union and then focuses on the crises of sovereignty and the legitimacy that are taking place within those states. As a result of these twin processes, forces acting from both within and without are deconstructing the modern welfare state that has arisen in Europe, resulting ultimately in the demise of the middle class.

The concluding section of the special issue contains an afterword by Robert J. Bunker, Pamela Ligouri Bunker and John P. Sullivan, which addresses the twenty-first-century IPE with regard to the Westphalian state and the near and far future of the middle class. It also provides a short commentary about IPE themes developed in the book and the effects of the plutocratic and criminal insurgency forms—as they relate to states and epochal change—on the work's case studies focusing on Colombia, Guatemala and Mexico; the United States; and the states of the European Union.

Notes

1 IPE courses on transnational organized crime and the illicit economy are very much the exception. IPE programs do not normally provide illicit economy tracks or concentrations of study. One of the authors was involved in a team-taught pilot course on underground economies and shadow governments at the Claremont Graduate University in the fall of 2012. The three professors teaching the course were forced to list it under transdisciplinary studies, rather than politics and economics, because it was considered too non-traditional for the IPE program.

2 See also the work of the late economic historian Frederic C. Lane on sixteenth-century Europe, and Venice in particular.

3 This is a continually misquoted 1953 line attributed to Charles Wilson, then CEO of GM, who became secretary of defense under President Eisenhower. Still, it portrayed the then close relationship between corporate America and the country itself.

4 The strategic level acronym RPMA (revolution in political and military affairs), dating from the 1990s, was meant to encompass both the RMA (revolution in military affairs) and OOTW (operations other than war) operational level analysis then being undertaken by the US military.

5 These include many Routledge, and other, works edited by Robert J. Bunker in collaboration with dozens of scholars.
6 As Nils Gilman has pointed out, this is payback to society on the plutocrat's terms rather than letting the voters decide what is in their best interest.
7 Two other major attributes of this change, though not directly addressed in this work, are derived from battlespace dimensionality (e.g. fifth-dimensional space–time dynamics) and qualitatively advanced weaponry utilizing directed energy to create barriers/shielding and scalable effects on targets. These attributes will become more pronounced over the coming decades.

References

Andreas, P. (2013) *Smuggler Nation: How Illicit Trade Made America.* Oxford: Oxford University Press.

Bobbitt, P. (2002) *The Shield of Achilles: War, Peace, and the Course of History.* New York: Anchor Books.

Bull, H. (1977) *The Anarchical Society: A Study in Order in World Politics.* New York: Columbia University Press.

Bunker, R. (1994) "The Transition to Fourth Epoch War." *Marine Corps Gazette.* September, Vol. 78. No. 9: 20–32.

Bunker, R. (1997) "Epochal Change: War over Social and Political Organization." *Parameters.* Summer, Vol. 27. No. 2: 15–25.

Bunker, R. (1999) "Enhanced and Unenhanced Humans: The Social Classes of a Dark Renaissance." *Crime and Justice International Online.* September. Online, available at: http://oicj.acsp.uic.edu/spearmint/public/pubs/cjfarrago/cjf_enhanced.cfm (link is terminated).

Bunker, R. and Bunker, P. (2006) "Defining Criminal-states." *Small Wars and Insurgencies.* Vol. 7. No. 3: 365–378.

Bunker, R. and Gilman, N. (2012) "Plutocratic Insurgency." *Small Precautions.* September 5. Online, available at: http://smallprecautions.blogspot.com/2012/09/plutocratic-insurgency.html.

Bunker, R. and Sullivan, J. (2013) *Studies in Gangs and Cartels.* London: Routledge.

Casas-Zamora, K., ed. (2013) *Dangerous Liaisons: Organized Crime and Political Finance in Latin America and Beyond.* Washington, DC: Brookings Institution Press.

Clunan, A. and Trinkunas, H. eds. (2010) *Ungoverned Spaces: Alternatives to State Authority in an Era of Softened Sovereignty.* Stanford: Stanford Security Studies.

Creveld, M. van (1991) *The Transformation of War.* New York: Free Press.

Creveld, M. van (1999) *The Rise and Decline of the State.* Cambridge: Cambridge University Press.

Creveld, M. van (2008) "HJS Event: On Counterinsurgency: How to Triumph in the Age of Asymmetric Warfare." The Henry Jackson Society. February 26. Online, available at: http://henryjacksonsociety.org/2008/02/26/hjs-event-on-counterinsurgency-how-to-triumph-in-the-age-of-asymmetric-warfare/.

Davis, M. (2006) *Planet of Slums.* London: Verso.

Dudley, S. (2013) "Central America Besieged: Cartel and Maras Country Threat Analysis." Bunker, R., ed., *Criminal Insurgencies in Mexico and the Americas: The Gangs and Cartels Wage War.* Routledge: London: 177–200.

Engels, F. (1892 [1970]) "General Introduction and the History of Materialism." *Socialism: Utopian and Scientific.* 1892 English translation from 1880 French work. Moscow:

Progress Publishers. Online, available at: www.Marxists.org/archive/marx/works/1880/soc-utop/int-mat.htm.

Faux, J. (2006) *The Global Class War*. Hoboken: John Wiley & Sons, Inc.

Faux, J. (2012) *The Servant Economy: Where America's Elite is Sending the Middle Class*. Hoboken: John Wiley & Sons, Inc.

Felbab-Brown, V. (2010) "Conceptualizing Crime as Competition in State-making and Designing an Effective Response." Brookings Institute. May 21. Online, available at: www.brookings.edu/research/.../21-illegal-economies-felbabbrown.

Fernandez, B. (2012) "Partitioning Honduras: The Advent of Charter Cities." *Aljazeera*, July 14. Online, available at: www.aljazeera.com/indepth/opinion/2012/07/2012711121224.

Freeland, C. (2012) *Plutocrats: The Rise of the New Global Super-Rich and the Fall of Everyone Else*. New York: The Penguin Press.

Fukuyama, F. (1989) "The End of History." *National Interest*. Summer, Vol. 16. No. 3: 3–18.

Fukuyama, F. (1992) *The End of History and the Last Man*. New York: Free Press.

Galbraith, J. (2009) *The Predator State*. New York: Free Press.

Gilman, N., Goldhammer, J. and Weber, S. (2011) *Deviant Globalization: Black Market Economy in the 21st Century*. New York: Continuum.

Hartmann, T. (2006) *Screwed: The Undeclared War against the Middle Class*. San Francisco: Berrett-Koehler Publishers, Inc.

Hertz, N. (2001) *The Silent Takeover: Global Capitalism and the Death of Democracy*. New York: The Free Press.

Hesterman, J. (2013) *The Terrorist-Criminal Nexus: An Alliance of International Drug Cartels, Organized Crime, and Terror Groups*. Boca Raton: CRC Press.

Jacobs, L. and Skocpol, T. eds. (2005) *Inequality and American Democracy*. New York: Russell Sage Foundation.

Kan, P., Bechtol, Jr., B. and Collins, R. (2010) *Criminal Sovereignty: Understanding North Korea's Illicit International Activities*. Letort Paper. Carlisle: Strategic Studies Institute, US Army War College.

Lazarus, D. (2013) "Wealth Gap only Getting Worse." *Los Angeles Times*. October 11: B1, B4.

Leander, A. (2004) "Wars and the Un-making of States: Taking Tilly Seriously in the Contemporary World." Guzzini, S. and Jung, D. eds. *Copenhagen Peace Research: Conceptual Innovations and Contemporary Security Analysis*. London: Routledge.

Lewis, C. and Allison, B. (2001) *The Cheating of America*. New York: William Morrow.

McCluskey, M. (2012) "Do You Have More Debt Than the Average American." *Daily Finance*. July 2. Online, available at: www.dailyfinance.com/2012/07/02/do-you-have-more-debt-than-the-average-american/.

Mandel, R. (2013) *Global Security Upheaval: Armed Nonstate Groups Usurping State Stability Functions*. Stanford: Stanford University Press.

Marx, K. (1859 [1977]) "Preface." *A Contribution to the Critique of Political Economy*. Moscow: Progress Publishers. Online, available at: www.Marxists.org/archive/marx/works/1859/critique-pol-economy/preface.htm.

Matthews, J. (1997) "Power Shift." *Foreign Affairs*. January–February, Vol. 76. No. 1: 50–66.

Metz, S. (1993) *The Future of Insurgency*. Carlisle: Strategic Studies Institute, US Army War College.

Miklaucic, M. and Brewer, J. eds. (2013) *Convergence: Illicit Networks and National Security in the Age of Globalization*. Washington, DC: National University Press.

Miklaucic, M. and Naim, M. (2013) "Chapter 9: The Criminal State." Miklaucic, M. and Brewer, J. eds. *Convergence: Illicit Networks and National Security in the Age of Globalization*. Washington, DC: National University Press: 149–170.

Moore, T.L. (2003 [1987 unpublished]) "The Structure of War: Early Fourth Epoch War Research." Bunker, R., ed., *Non-State Threats and Future Wars*. London: Routledge: 159–170.

Neuwirth, R. (2006) *Shadow Cities: A Billion Squatters, a New Urban World*. London: Routledge.

Page, B. and Jacobs, L. (2009) *Class War? What Americans Really Think about Economic Inequality*. Chicago: University Of Chicago Press.

Patterson, R. (2013) "What's Good for America..." *National Review Online*. July 1. Online, available at: www.nationalreview.com/article/352429/whats-good-america-robert-w-patterson.

Pizzigati, S. (2012) *The Rich Don't Always Win*. New York: Seven Stories Press.

Ramonet, I. (2004) *Wars of the 21st Century: New Threats, New Fears*. Melbourne: Ocean Press.

Rapley, J. (2006) "The New Middle Ages." *Foreign Affairs*. Vol. 85. No. 3: 95–103.

Rifkin, J. (1995) *The End of Work*. New York: G.P. Putnam's Sons.

Risse, T., ed. (2011) *Governance without a State?* New York: Columbia University Press.

Rosecrance, R. (1999) *The Rise of the Virtual State: Wealth and Power in the Coming Century*. New York: Basic Books.

Rothkopf, D. (2008) *Superclass: The Global Power Elite and the World They Are Making*. New York: Farrar, Straus and Giroux.

Rothkopf, D. (2012) *Power, Inc.: The Epic Rivalry between Big Business and Government—and the Reckoning That Lies Ahead*. New York: Farrar, Straus and Giroux.

Rousseau, J. (1782–1789 [2000]) *Confessions*. Scholar, A., trans. New York: Oxford University Press.

Sinclair, U. (1906) *The Jungle*. New York: Doubleday, Jabber & Company.

Stein, B. (2006) "In Class Warfare, Guess Which Class is Winning." *New York Times*. November 26. Online, available at: www.nytimes.com/2006/11/26/business/your money/26every.html?_r=2&.

Sullivan, J. and Bunker, R. (2012) *Mexico's Criminal Insurgency: A Small Wars Journal—El Centro Anthology*. Bloomington: iUniverse.

The Economist (2011) "Hong Kong in Honduras." December, 10. Online, available at: www.economist.com/node/21541392.

Tilly, C. (1985) "War Making and State Making as Organized Crime." P. Evans, D. Rueschemeyer and T. Skocpol, eds. *Bringing the State Back In*. Cambridge: Cambridge University Press.

Tilly, C. (1992) *Coercion, Capital and European States: AD 990–1992*. Revised edition. Malden: Blackwell Publishers, Inc.

United Nations (2012) "Housing and Slum Upgrading are a Key Area of the UN-Habitat's Mandate." UN Habitat. September 5. Online, available at: www.unhabitat.org/content. asp?cid=11441&catid=5&typeid=6&subMenuId=0.

United Press International (2013) "Protesters Gather on Wall Street for Occupy Second Anniversary." September 17. Online, available at: www.upi.com/Top_News/US/2013/ 09/17/Protesters-gather-on-Wall-Street-for-Occupy-second-anniversary/UPI-9570137 9437664/.

Vulliamy, E. (2011) "Ciudad Juarez is All of our Futures. This is the Inevitable War of Capitalism Gone Mad." *Guardian*. June 20. Online, available at: www.theguardian.com/commentisfree/2011/jun/20/war-capitalism-mexico-drug-cartels.

Wedel, J. (2009) *Shadow Elite: How the World's New Power Brokers Undermine Democracy, Government, and the Free Market*. New York: Basic Books.

Williams, P. (2008) *From the New Middle Ages to a New Dark Age: The Decline of the State*. Carlisle: Strategic Studies Institute, US Army War College.

Wilson, W. (1996) *When Work Disappears: The World of the New Urban Poor*. New York: Vintage Books.

1 Introduction

Kleptocracies, warlords and mafias in uniform

Mark Galeotti

The term "kleptocracy" is surprisingly new. According to the Oxford English Dictionary, its first use was in 1819, but then this term for a "government by thieves" languished until 1968, when it seems to have been revived for discussion of Mobutu Sese Seko's Zaire (Congo). Of course, Mobutu deserves particular opprobrium given the extravagant scale of his plunder of his own country, but can it be true that kleptocracy as a phenomenon has only really been around for the past half-century?

The answer, of course, is no. Instead, the emergence of the term kleptocracy essentially reflects changing norms, different expectations in the relationship between rulers and ruled, governors and the governed. This has been a long-term process, from the end of patrimonialism and the development of a sense that there was some distinction between the assets of the state and those of the monarch, through to a modern concept of equality before the law and a clear sense of a division between legitimate and illegitimate ways of enriching oneself through one's position. In other words, what once was—to a greater or lesser extent—the norm, has become the sinful exception.

But just how exceptional an exception? Terms such as kleptocrat (and warlord, and Mafioso...) are widely and loosely used, for everything from Wall Street executives to well-paid civil servants. Beneath this rather banal point is what may prove to be a growing dissatisfaction, especially since the 2008 financial crisis, with a global system seemingly underpinned by the self-interest of relatively small, wealthy and powerful elites, eager to maintain governance regimes that work to their advantage. True kleptocrats, though, are rulers and national elites who plunder countries and territories under their control for their personal gain. In the process, they distort or ignore institutions and cultural norms intended to protect the commonweal, typically resorting to coercion when necessary to maintain and retain their ability to steal. Kleptocracy and coercion are thus inextricably linked, but what distinguishes the kleptocrat from the bandit is the third element: at least partial legitimacy, the result of occupying a position within a government or pseudo-governmental structure. Ruling kleptocrats, local warlords and criminal organizations within military and security apparatuses are thus three main expressions of this combination of predation, coercion and legitimacy.

Kleptocracy

Kleptocracy takes many forms, from dictatorships to pseudo-democracies. Indeed, it should not be considered a form of governance in its own right so much as a particular pathology especially prone to afflict regimes with weaker cultures and institutions of accountability and transparency. Susan Rose-Ackerman (1997) has conceptualized four kinds of corrupt states, based on the number of bribe-givers and bribe-takers:

In her typology, a kleptocracy is a state in which a single ruler or a small circle exploit resources for their personal gain, exploiting the many. Classic examples would be Mobutu, Haiti's "Papa Doc" Duvalier or Indonesia's Suharto. This is different from a Competitive-Bribery State, where numerous corrupt officials prey on large numbers of ordinary citizens, such as in modern China, Russia or Nigeria. Conversely, a Bilateral Monopoly State is shaped by the relationship of a single corrupt ruler and a single major briber, such as Guatemala under Colonel Castillo Armas (1954–1957), who was closely aligned with the United Fruit Company. At the other extreme, a Mafia-Dominated State is characterized by a weak and disorganized state in which many officials seek to access a relatively small number of major bribe-givers, typically organized crime syndicates.

In practice, though, a kleptocracy is not—cannot be—purely for the benefit of one individual, or even one small ruling family. Power needs to be maintained, enemies spied on or eliminated, rebellions put down, money moved and managed. In the process, access to plundered resources must be spread around. The true mark of kleptocracy is thus the systematic and widespread extra-legal (or borderline extra-legal, perhaps observing the letter of the law but certainly breaking its spirit) exploitation of a country for financial gain by a ruling elite.

The kleptocrats may still be a relatively small circle, a dominant or uncontrolled segment of society, or a government elite as a whole. In Equatorial Guinea, for example, the ruling Obiang family has maintained a tight control over the potential profits of power. In 2011, the US government launched a campaign to seize $70.8 million in property owned by Teodoro Nguema Obiang Mangue, son of president Teodoro Nguema Obiang Mbasogo and at the time his agriculture and forestry minister. According to the case, unresolved as of writing, on an official salary of less than $100,000 per year, he accumulated a personal fortune of more than $100 million (USDOJ, 2011). What can one do with such a sum? The answer appears to

Table 1.1 Rose-Ackerman's typology of corrupt states

	Multiple bribers	*Few bribers*
Few recipients, concentrated at upper levels of government	Kleptocracy	Bilateral monopoly state
Multiple recipients at lower levels of government	Competitive bribery state	Mafia-dominated state

Source: Rose-Ackerman, S. (1998) "Corruption and Development." Pleskoric, B. and Stiglitz, J., eds., *Annual World Bank Conference on Development Economics*.

have been to buy more than $1.8 million worth of Michael Jackson memorabilia, a $30 million Malibu mansion, a Ferrari and a Gulfstream personal jet. These centralized kleptocracies are often tightly-controlled autocracies. In Central Asia, for example, Turkmenistan's dictatorial Saparmurat Niyazov set the bar: Global Witness (2006) estimated that he embezzled some $3 billion from his impoverished country's gas exports. He was, however, a rank amateur compared with Suharto, whom *The Economist* (2007) dubbed "king of the kleptocrats." His 31-year rule (1967–1998) was marked not only by the zealous plunder of the country—Transparency International (2004) estimated that he and his family embezzled some $35 billion, just under 4 percent of the country's GDP—but also for most of this time by a tightly-controlled militaristic government.

In other cases, the true beneficiaries of kleptocracy are segments, sub-sets of the elite, or the elite as a whole (albeit with some clearly doing better for themselves than others). This shades into what Rose-Ackerman would call the Competitive Bribery State: although the usual assumption is that kleptocracy is very much directed from above, it can simply be that the ruler(s) are willing to sanction illicit exploitation by the elite in return for continued service. In this respect, corruption and kleptocracy, corrosive to the state in the long-term, become tools of governance by the regime in the short-term. In Azerbaijan, for instance, where power became in effect hereditary as president Heidar Aliyev handed his office to his son Ilham, control of the country's oil wealth proved crucial to this succession and the subsequent maintenance of Ilham's power, as he "distributes rents from oil exports through a patronage network in order to ensure the support of allies and various clientelist groups" (Guliyev, 2009: 2).

Whoever they may be, broadly speaking, the kleptocrats illegally enrich themselves in four ways:

Plundering state assets

This is often the easiest for kleptocrats who have managed to establish their control at a national or local level, using their control of, or influence over, government apparatuses simply to divert revenues or assets into private hands, creating a rentier state. This could be directly into their own, or it could take the form of transferring assets to a third party, which, in turn, pays off the kleptocrats. In 1990s Russia, whole swathes of former state assets, especially oil, gas and metals, ended up controlled by a handful of oligarchs thanks to their connections. Conversely, under president Jose Eduardo dos Santos, Angola's extensive oil reserves have been exploited by Western corporations, with his personal oil account allegedly receiving a contribution for every barrel sold (Malaquias, 2001: 528).

Plundering private assets

Those able to deploy the power of the state can also use it to expropriate private assets. This could be as crude a process as Idi Amin's seizure of the businesses of expelled Ugandan Asians through to the modern Russian practice of *reiderstvo*, "raiding"—taking control of companies through the use of the courts and banks, often by presenting spurious but officially-validated "proof" of their sale (Firestone, 2008).

Rent-seeking

Corruption often rests upon charging "rent" to those wanting license to carry out activities, from building houses to sending their children to university. In this respect, the power to approve (or deny) can be monetized. This also extends to criminal operations, as officials may be in a position to turn a blind eye to under-world activities or, conversely, to use the power of the state against them. This need not be incompatible with economic growth—China is a classic case—but more usually it is associated with stagnation, sometimes masked by favorable export opportunities, such as in Nigeria (Anugwom, 2011; Ihonvbere, 2011).

Criminalizing state assets

Finally, kleptocrats may be in a position to divert state assets to specifically criminal purposes, either directly running underworld enterprises or selling or leasing them to the gangsters. Panamanian dictator Manuel Noriega allowed the Medellin cartel to use his country as a cocaine staging post, for example (Dudley, 2011) while the appointment of Henry Rangel Silva—a man designated by the US government as a "drug kingpin" in 2008—as Venezuela's defense minister marked a similar opening of the door to narcotics traffickers (Naim, 2012). As will be discussed later, those pseudo-state violent entrepreneurs we call warlords likewise often "rent" out territory under their control to criminal organizations. In Tajikistan, Gaffor Mirzoev went from being a field commander in the civil wars of the 1990s—in other words, a warlord—to commander of the Presidential Guard and then head of the State Antidrugs Agency, even while being a known drug kingpin himself (Marat, 2006: 106–108).

As Acemoglu *et al.* (2004) have noted, kleptocracies tend to rise in weakly-institutionalized states where rulers can tap into substantial resources and deploy tactics of divide-and-rule. The resources permit kleptocrats to maintain just enough state spending while still enriching themselves and their main allies, as well as providing a dowry, making themselves appealing allies and clients for foreign governments and corporations. Meanwhile,

> Members of society need to cooperate in order to depose a kleptocrat, yet such cooperation may be defused by imposing punitive rates of taxation on any citizen who proposes such a move, and redistributing the benefits to those who need to agree to it.
>
> (Acemoglu *et al.*, 2004: 162)

In short, kleptocrats can often flourish—so long as there is enough for them to steal, to maintain and buy off what de Mesquita and Smith (2011) would call the "winning coalition." In short, so long as the money lasts.

Warlords

Some of the most infamous kleptocrats are often warlords, local strongmen who are able to exploit conditions of state weakness to establish themselves as the rulers of states-within-states. For what it may be worth, the term "warlord" has a relatively recent pedigree, too, having emerged in Ralph Waldo Emerson's 1856 essay on the rise of central power in England, as he noted how "the war-lord [gave way] to the law-lord" (Emerson, 1902: 142). However, conceptually there is again an understanding that they have a rather longer history. Indeed, Emerson's use evokes a traditional view, that warlords should be considered potential state-builders, following parallels perceived especially by Charles Tilly (1985) in the emergence of medieval states from the protean chaos of post-Roman Europe. Of course, the "dark ages" were never really so dark and brutish and the difference is usually that in the modern world warlords are often empowered by external forces who are less interested in state-building than asserting their own influence. Kimberly Marten's work (2012) has perceptively drawn attention to the way that warlords are typically not the legitimate, culturally-consecrated leaders of their communities so much as upstarts, opportunists who have been imposed or imposed themselves. This is a distinction that Boege *et al.* (2009) are also eager to make, that there are culturally-embedded "non-state authorities—like chiefs, religious figures, customary kings, big men, and healers—who are often engaged in confrontation and competition with state institutions" (p. 19) and yet who are not warlords and do not need to maintain their power through coercive patronage.

As a result, these are coercive leaders who depend neither on institutionalized, bureaucratic power, nor on cultural authority. Instead, they need to maintain coalitions through patronage, which typically requires the distribution of money or other assets or else privileged access to channels to acquire them. Today's Afghan warlords, for example, are often heavily involved in the production and sale of opiates to traffickers, raising money that they then disburse to their followers. Conversely, Ramzan Kadyrov, the warlord-president of Russian-controlled Chechnya, not only operates by direct disbursement of funds, he also grants allies positions such as ministerial posts or the mayoralty of Grozny that provide opportunities for direct enrichment. Even the more entrenched, well-armed and politically-connected (or tolerated) Latin American street gangs begin to assume potential warlord status—becoming what Lopes de Souza (2009) calls "micro-level warlords"—thanks to this ability to convert violence and predation into economic, but also political, power.

After all, this requires not just the ability to wield and threaten violence—any street thug can do that—but also wider connections and, usually, the active or tacit blessing of higher-order power structures. After all, by Ahram and King's definition, "warlords are armed agents who wield some degree of civil power and claim some kind of local sovereignty over a defined region while paying allegiance to one or more stronger powers" (Ahram and King, 2011: 172). The Afghan warlords survive largely because they have found ways of coexisting with the Karzai regime in Kabul, while Kadyrov is almost entirely an agent of Moscow's, albeit one who has leveraged his position to assume increasing autonomy. Likewise, perhaps the most feared warlords of the post-Yugoslav Balkans was Željko Ražnatović, known as "Arkan," who seamlessly blended paramilitary operations in the Serb cause and criminal entrepreneurialism, the former excusing or permitting the latter (Glaurdić, 2009; Mladenovic, 2012).

Warlords who are not wholly bankrolled and managed by external backers (which really makes them simply hirelings, mercenaries) will thus near enough by definition also be kleptocrats, both for their personal enrichment but also to feed the voracious appetites of their clients and henchmen. This does not mean, as Jackson (2003) suggests, that the new warlords are necessarily new-generation, post-Cold War state-builders, a point vigorously made by Marten (2012). But it does mean that while they may benefit from a degree of uncertainty and local weakness of metropolitan power, they depend actually on a certain stability of the institutions in which they are embedded. Whether a steady trade with the underworld wholesalers of the global narcotics trade, or the ability to receive, bank and spend money from corporate or government backers, or even just the opportunity to "tax" criminal commerce through their jurisdictions, all these are based on external relationships. For example, Turkish strongmen in the Kurdish region—both pro- and anti-government—for a long time relied on either direct involvement with heroin trafficking or else simply providing safe routes towards Europe (Galeotti, 1998). Likewise, Marten (2012) successfully demonstrates that the power-brokers of Pakistan's Federally Administered Tribal Areas (FATA) are not traditional elders but the product of external interference, originally by the British colonial overlords and then Islamabad, elevating a new breed of opportunistic strongman who both depends on, but also flouts central control.

In this respect, warlordism represents an interesting case of the collusion of upperworld and underworld, the forces of the prevailing global order and those characterized as outsiders, predators and agents of chaos. Warlords may be rooted in local political, social and economic conditions, but they depend on external contacts and backers. However, if warlords represent a case of the outsourcing—sometimes by design, sometimes by default—of coercion and control to kleptocratic local actors, then the rise of organized criminal operations within national militaries (and other security agencies) reflects instead a loss of control over coercive agencies.

Military mafias

Where a state is a kleptocracy, then it may well be fair to assume that its military elite will be no less venal than their peers. Sometimes—although more often in popular legend than reality—the barracks may be a bastion of patriotism and honor, but generally rot spreads throughout the elite. Thus, just as the Russian military has fallen prone to the same levels of corruption evident throughout the ruling class (Bukkvoll, 2008), so too the mid-twentieth-century Brazilian army, which justified its political interventions by citing the malpractices of the political elite, was no less rotten (Smallman, 1997). In Nigeria, Ebbe (2012) depicts the military as involved in the same corruption and criminality as the rest of the elite. Likewise, in Guatemala, the 36-year conflict that led to the 1996 peace process had facilitated the rise of

> political–criminal networks loosely organized around former senior military officials linked to military intelligence and the counter-insurgency structures established during the war. These groups had forged ties with elements of the business elite, corrupt police officers, judiciary and customs officials, and political actors to participate in the highly lucrative international drugs trans-shipment business and an array of other illicit activities.
>
> (Gavigan, 2009: 62)

However, there will also be situations in which the military are *distinctively* criminalized rather than just being exemplars of a kleptocrat elite who happen to wear uniforms. Such "military mafias" tend to take three main forms:

Institutional

Military structures themselves operate illegal businesses, generally with the knowledge or at least acquiescence of the state, and so the criminal hierarchies essentially mirror the military ones. The Iranian Revolution Guard Corps (IRGC), is heavily involved in a range of smuggling operations, for example, from sanctions-busting smuggling of Iraqi oil during the Saddam Hussein embargo (Wahab, 2006) through to drug trafficking. To some extent this could be considered a state measure to raise operational funds for domestic and external operations—much as North Korea uses activities such as methamphetamine trafficking and counterfeiting to supplement its foreign incomes (Perl, 2004)—but this shades into the more overtly criminal as it becomes clear that some IRGC commanders have grown personally rich from these extracurricular activities.

Endemic

There are cases in which corruption and criminality are not state-sanctioned, but they are both pervasive and yet largely insular. In other words, while there may be many criminal organizations within the armed forces, they do not recruit outside their own ranks. As a result, they often will to a degree reflect military hierarchies—more senior officers in charge—but need not do so. In Russia, for example, numerous examples of organized criminal conspiracies have been identified, from smuggling rings within the Border Troops to so-called "werewolves in uniform," gangs within the police (Galeotti, 2006). Likewise, in the 1990s and 2000s, some Chinese naval personnel appear to have been involved in piracy (Dillon, 2000), an activity that would have required the involvement of whole ships' crews and probably port authorities, as well. On a larger scale, Vlassen-root *et al.* (2012) have demonstrated how the Ugandan interventions into neigh-boring Congo were increasingly dominated by the interests of corrupt and exploitative "military entrepreneurs," essentially senior officers working the chain of command to their own advantage.

Recruits

Most often, though, elements of the security forces are instead recruited, singly or en masse, into external or hybrid criminal groups. The notorious Zetas of Mexico, for example, were originally members of Mexico's elite Groupo Aero-movil de Fuerzas Especiales, recruited by Gulf cartel leader Osiel Cardenas Guillen, and later became a gang in their own right (Campbell, 2010).

The same applies to security and police forces and even legitimate private security agencies, which in some cases have become armed gangs, generally when wider conflict or state collapse has opened up new opportunities, removed old constraints and deprived them of former markets. A security force estab-lished to protect oil wells in Serbia in 1992, for example, drawn largely from local traffickers and racketeers, became in due course the Scorpions, a local militia involved in ethnic cleansing and widespread criminality alike (Tanner and Mulone, 2012).

Quite why the security agencies might be tempted into criminality is no great mystery. They have not only the will, training and capacity to deploy violence, they often have control over border areas suitable for smuggling and facilities that can be used for storage or production. In Venezuela, for example, not only did the Chavez regime reach understandings with FARC and other drug traffick-ing organizations, but individual traffickers also struck deals with senior officers able to expedite transfers. Cocaine trafficker Walid Makled, for example, report-edly boasted that "All my business associates are generals. The highest ... I am telling you, we dispatched 300,000 kilos of coke. I couldn't have done it without the top of the government" (Farah, 2012: 42). Military and security personnel also frequently enjoy a privileged legal status that helps organized criminal activity. In Russia, for example, workshops producing counterfeit goods and cig-arettes have been established on army bases, where they cannot be investigated by the civilian police without the base commander's approval, and military transport vessels sailing between St Petersburg and the exclave of Kaliningrad used to move stolen cars and other goods, again because they are not subject to customs controls (Galeotti, 2006).

Under these circumstances, in many ways the question is rather why there are not more military mafias? The main reasons would seem to be discipline and *esprit de corps*—which can sometimes make these criminals especially formid-able, but does seem to reduce criminalization—as well as measures introduced by the government to control them. These range from maintaining oversight and counter-balancing agencies, such as maintaining distinct gendarmeries or pene-tration by separate security agencies, through to efforts to coopt the military elite into the wider civilian one. Sometimes, political elites explicitly try to exclude the military from the opportunities of corruption in order to ensure that they do not develop independent economic power bases but remain dependent on the state. This can, however, backfire. In Egypt, Mubarak's kleptocratic regime sought to accommodate and pacify the military by granting it the right to build and run "a lucrative military-industrial-business complex" (Hashim, 2011: 109). However, as the scale of elite corruption grew and officers found themselves nudged out of key patronage networks—especially by Mubarak's son, Gamal—then this became a bone of contention. The military's eventual decision not to back Mubarak's regime in 2011 reflects in part dissatisfaction with the status quo, and in part the very way that, having been excluded from the grand corruption around Mubarak and his family, they had less to fear from the inevitable corruption investigations that would follow the regime's fall (Pion-Berlin *et al.*, 2012).

Conclusions

Nature may abhor a vacuum, but crime appears to embrace it. Weak or broken states provide great opportunities for "violent entrepreneurs" willing to turn the ability to use force into capital (Volkov, 2002). Phil Williams (2009) has, for example, detailed the interconnection of insurgents, local warlords, government forces and crime gangs in post-invasion Iraq. However, this is not solely the preserve of the failed state, nor of the warlord and thug. Kleptocracies also rest on the ability of those with political and economic power to convert that into coercive capacity to preserve their rule, the complementary form of violent entrepreneurship. Sometimes, this is challenged by criminality and corruption within the security forces, but more often the two are intimately interconnected. As Majeed and Macdonald (2010) have demonstrated, there is a close correlation between the direct and indirect involvement of soldiers in governance and overall levels of corruption.

Often, these exploitative regimes are short-lived. Sometimes, fittingly, it is the very greed of these regimes that brings them down. The brazen theft of emergency relief by the Somoza government in Nicaragua after the 1972 Managua earthquake undoubtedly proved a self-destructive blunder, not least as it alienated the Catholic Church enough that it could later find common cause with the FSLN Sandinistas. At other times, political coalitions built on the distribution of plundered resources collapse when the resources are devalued or begin to run out, as Idi Amin was beginning to discover even before Tanzania invaded in 1979. Sometimes, external intervention will break kleptocracies, which after all frequently lack deep reservoirs of legitimacy and public support, as was visible when Mobutu was overthrown in 1997 and Mubarak in 2011.

However, it would be naïve to assume that kleptocracy, warlordism and the criminalization of security structures are merely transient byproducts of state dysfunction. Instead, they represent three sides of the same problem: inadequate controls by civil society—whether represented by democracy, courts and the press or the organic consensus and social contracts of less institutionalized societies—on those able to exercise coercion, whether through crude force or control of governmental structures and funding streams. After the Arab Spring, and in the context of a modern international system increasingly intolerant of the grand corruption and open plunder of previous years, the kleptocrats and war-lords will instead have to get smarter. Just as an increasing proportion of auto-crats now hide behind the façade of democracy, creating "hybrid regimes" such as modern Russia and Venezuela (Diamond, 2002; Bogaards, 2009; Levitsky and Way, 2010), so too the institutionalized plunder of countries must adapt. However, it hardly seems likely that the temptations of extortion, embezzlement and maintaining the opportunities to do so will disappear anytime soon.

References

Acemoglu, D., Verdier, T. and Robinson, J. (2004) "Kleptocracy and Divide-and-Rule: a Model of Personal Rule." *Journal of the European Economic Association.* Vol. 2. Nos. 2–3: 162–192.

Ahram, A. and King, C. (2012) "The Warlord as Arbitrageur." *Theory and Society.* Vol. 41. No. 2: 169–186.

Anugwom, E. (2011) "From Babangida to Obasanjo: the State, Rent-seeking Behaviour and the Realities of Privatization in Nigeria." *International Journal of Sociology and Anthropology.* Vol. 3. No. 7: 204–216.

Boege, V., Brown, M. and Clements, K. (2009) "Hybrid Political Orders, not Fragile States." *Peace Review.* Vol. 21. No. 1: 13–21.

Bogaards, M. (2009) "How to Classify Hybrid Regimes? Defective Democracy and Elect-oral Authoritarianism." *Democratization.* Vol. 16. No. 2: 399–423.

Brown, B. (2003) "Governance in Central Asia: The Case of Turkmenistan." *Helsinki Monitor.* Vol. 14: 206.

Bukkvoll, T. (2008) "Their Hands in the Till: Scale and Causes of Russian Military Cor-ruption." *Armed Forces and Society.* Vol. 34. No. 2: 259–275.

Bunker, R. and Sullivan, J. (2010) "Cartel Evolution Revisited: Third Phase Cartel Poten-tials and Alternative Futures in Mexico." *Small Wars and Insurgencies,* Vol. 21. No. 1: 30–54.

Campbell, L. (2010) "Los Zetas: Operational Assessment." *Small Wars and Insurgencies,* Vol. 21. No. 1: 55–80.

Chen, C., Li, Z., Su, X. and Sun, Z. (2011) "Rent-seeking Incentives, Corporate Political Connections, and the Control Structure of Private Firms: Chinese evidence." *Journal of Corporate Finance.* Vol. 17. No. 2: 229–243.

Coolidge, J. and Rose-Ackerman, S. (1997) *High-level Rent-seeking and Corruption in African Regimes: Theory and Cases.* No. 1780. The World Bank.

Diamond, L. (2002) "Thinking about Hybrid Regimes." *Journal of Democracy.* Vol. 13. No. 2: 21–35.

Dillon, D. (2000) Piracy in Asia: a Growing Barrier to Maritime Trade. *Heritage Founda-tion Backgrounder.* 1379: 1–5.

Dudley, S. (2011) "Drug Trafficking Organizations in Central America: Transportistas, Mexican Cartels and Maras." Olson, E., Shirk, D. and Selee, A. *Shared Responsibility: US–Mexico Policy Options for Confronting Organized Crime.* Washington, DC: Woodrow Wilson International Center for Scholars: 63–93.

Ebbe, O. (2012) "Organized Crime in Nigeria." Siegel, D. and van de Bunt, H. *Traditional Organized Crime in the Modern World*. Springer: 169–188.

Emerson, R. (1902 [1856]) *English Traits*. London: George Routledge and Sons.

Farah, D. (2012) *Transnational Organized Crime, Terrorism, and Criminalized States in Latin America: An Emerging Tier-One National Security Priority*. Carlisle: US Army War College, Strategic Studies Institute.

Firestone, T. (2008) "Criminal Corporate Raiding in Russia." *International Law*. Vol. 42. No. 4: 1207–1230.

Galeotti, M. (1998) "Turkish Organized Crime: Where State, Crime, and Rebellion Conspire." *Transnational Organized Crime*. Vol. 4. No. 1: 25–41.

Galeotti, M. (2004) "The Transdnistrian Connection: Big Problems from a Small Pseudo-State." *Global Crime*. Vol. 6. No. 3–4: 398–405.

Galeotti, M. (2006) "The Criminalisation of Russian State Security." *Global Crime*. Vol. 7. No. 3–4: 471–486.

Gavigan, P. (2009) "Organized Crime, Illicit Power Structures and Guatemala's Threatened Peace Process." *International Peacekeeping*. Vol. 16. No. 1: 62–76.

Glaurdić, J. (2009) "Inside the Serbian War Machine: The Milošević Telephone Intercepts, 1991–1992." *East European Politics and Societies*. Vol. 23. No. 1: 86–104.

Global Witness (2006) *It's a Gas. Funny Business in the in the Turkmen-Ukraine Gas Trade*. London: Global Witness Publishing, Inc.

Guliyev, F. (2009) "Oil Wealth, Patrimonialism, and the Failure of Democracy in Azerbaijan." *Caucasus Analytical Digest*. February: 2–5.

Hashim, A. (2011) "The Egyptian Military, Part Two: From Mubarak Onward." *Middle East Policy*. Vol. 18. No. 4: 106–128.

Hristov, J. (2010) "Self-Defense Forces, Warlords, or Criminal Gangs? Towards a New Conceptualization of Paramilitarism in Colombia." *TRAVAIL, capital et société*. Vol. 43. No. 2: 14–56.

Ihonvbere, J. (2011) "Economic Crisis, Structural Adjustment and Social Crisis in Nigeria." *World Development*. Vol. 21. No. 1: 141–153.

Jackson, P. (2003) "Warlords as Alternative Forms of Governance." *Small Wars and Insurgencies*. Vol. 14. No. 2: 131–150.

James, M. (2012) "The Other Civil Society: Organised Crime in Fragile and Failing States." *Defence Studies*. Vol. 12. No. 2: 218–256.

Klay Kieh, G. (2011) "Warlords, Politicians and the Post-First Civil War Election in Liberia." *African and Asian Studies*. Vol. 10. No. 2–3: 2–3.

Levitsky, S. and Way, L. (2010) *Competitive Authoritarianism: Hybrid Regimes after the Cold War*. Cambridge: Cambridge University Press.

Lopes de Souza, M. (2009) "Social Movements in the Face of Criminal Power: the Sociopolitical Fragmentation of Space and 'Micro-level Warlords' as Challenges for Emancipative Urban Struggles." *City*. Vol. 13. No. 1: 26–52.

Majeed, M. and Macdonald, R. (2010) *Corruption and the Military in Politics: Theory and Evidence from around the World*. University of Glasgow, Department of Economics Discussion Paper.

Malaquias, A. (2001) "Making War and Lots of Money: the Political Economy of Protracted Conflict in Angola." *Review of African Political Economy*. Vol. 28. No. 90: 521–536.

Marat, E. (2006) "Impact of Drug Trade and Organized Crime on State Functioning in Kyrgyzstan and Tajikistan." *China and Eurasia Forum Quarterly*. Vol. 4. No. 1: 93–111.

Marten, K. (2012) *Warlords: Strong-arm Brokers in Weak States*. Ithaca: Cornell University Press.

Mesquita, B. de, and Smith, A. (2011) *The Dictator's Handbook: Why Bad Behavior is almost always Good Politics*. New York: Public Affairs.

Mladenovic, N. (2012) "The Failed Divorce of Serbia's Government and Organized Crime." *Journal of International Affairs*. Vol. 66. No. 1. Online, available at: http://jia.sipa.columbia.edu/failed-divorce-serbia's-government-and-organized-crime.

Naim, M. (2012) "Mafia States: Organized Crime Takes Office." *Foreign Affairs*. Vol. 91: 100–111.

Perl, R. (2004) "State Crime: The North Korean Drug Trade." *Global Crime*. Vol. 6. No. 1: 117–128.

Pion-Berlin, D., Esparza, D. and Grisham, K. (2012) "Staying Quartered: Civilian Uprisings and Military Disobedience in the Twenty-first Century." *Comparative Political Studies*. Online, available at: http://cps.sagepub.com/content/early/2012/08/02/0010414012450566.

Reno, W. (2009) "Illicit Markets, Violence, Warlords, and Governance: West African Cases." *Crime, Law and Social Change*. Vol. 52. No. 3: 313–322.

Rose-Ackerman, S. (1998) "Corruption and Development." B. Pleskoric and J. Stiglitz, eds. *Annual World Bank Conference on Development Economics: 1998*. World Bank: 149–171.

Smallman, S. (1997) "Shady Business: Corruption in the Brazilian Army before 1954." *Latin American Research Review*. Vol. 32. No. 3: 39–62.

Tanner, S. and Mulone, M. (2013) "Private Security and Armed Conflict A Case Study of the Scorpions during the Mass Killings in Former Yugoslavia." *British Journal of Criminology*. Vol. 53. No. 1: 41–58.

The Economist (2007) "King of the Kleptocrats." June 11. Online, available at: www.economist.com/node/9465434.

Tilly, C. (1985) "War Making and State Making as Organized Crime." Evans, P., Rueschemeyer, D. and Skocpol, T. eds. *Bringing the State Back In*. Cambridge: Cambridge University Press: 169–191.

Transparency International (2004) *Global Corruption Report 2004*. Online, available at: www.transparency.org/research/gcr/gcr_political_corruption.

USDOJ (US Department of Justice) (2011) "Department of Justice Seeks to Recover More Than $70.8 Million in Proceeds of Corruption from Government Minister of Equatorial Guinea." October 25. Online, available at: www.justice.gov/opa/pr/2011/October/11-crm-1405.html.

Vlassenroot, K., Perrot, S. and Cuvelier, J. (2012) "Doing Business out of War: an Analysis of the UPDF's Presence in the Democratic Republic of Congo." *Journal of Eastern African Studies*. Vol. 6. No. 1: 2–21.

Volkov, V. (2002) *Violent Entrepreneurs*. Ithaca: Cornell University Press.

Wahab, B. (2006) "How Iraqi Oil Smuggling Greases Violence." *Middle East Quarterly*. Vol. 8. No. 4: 53–59.

Williams, P. (2009) *Criminals, Militias, and Insurgents: Organized Crime in Iraq*. Carlisle: US Army War College, Strategic Studies Institute.

Part I
Energy, economics and war

2 The contemporary clash *in* civilization

T.L Moore

Destiny is not a matter of chance—it is a matter of choice. It is not a thing to wait for—it is a thing to be achieved.

William Jennings Bryan

Western civilization is in for the time of its life. There prevails throughout the West a restlessness driven by exciting new scientific knowledge and innovative technological possibilities, entwined with fears of collapsing expectations, pervasive terrorist violence, extensive environmental degradation, and a rising antagonism between cultural identities. A growing apprehension that existing institutions may be inadequate to reap this harvest of prospects and cope with its attendant adversities haunts Western thought. The temper of our time is charged by an ever increasing uneasiness.

The times are not unique. What is transpiring today has occurred twice before in the history of Western civilization. The first took place when the classical world collapsed under the onslaught of the barbarians: Mount Olympus gave way to Valhalla and, eventually, Heaven. The second arose when the Christian empire of the medieval world was swept aside in the explosions of the Machiavellian ambitions of princes. On that occasion, Heaven and Earth changed places. Each time, Western civilization launched itself onto a turbulent sea and life became, in Hobbes' pungent phrase, "solitary, poor, nasty, brutish, and short" and remained so until Western civilization created itself anew.

Propelling those two shattering times was the *emergence of a new system of energy.* That new energy system made possible innovative technologies for waging war, for designing, fabricating and assembling new products, together with novel transportation and communication systems. It offered the vision of a future narrative of Western life, a new cultural identity irreconcilable with then existing patterns of living. The result was a *clash in civilization.* In each instance the outcome of the clash was an extraordinary transformation in the West's understanding of the possibilities for living, working, fighting and playing.

Today, a new system of energy, electricity, and its technological offspring (computers, robots, and their "apps"), is altering in profound ways our understanding of the knowledge provided by science, the waging of war, the production of well-being, the relationship of human life to the planet, and the meaning of a civilized life from which the West derives its cultural identity. Electricity generated a research program and a technology that transformed the foundations of knowledge from the classical science of Newton's $F = ma$ into the relativity of Einstein's $E = mc^2$, the quantum physics of Dirac, Heisenberg and Hawking, and the biochemistry of life unraveled by Franklin, Watson and Crick. Nuclear weapons and the shift from conventional to asymmetrical war infused with electronic weaponry are profoundly affecting the relations of nations. Manual labor and skilled craftsmanship in production are being replaced by robotic and other production technologies, previously unimagined except in science fiction. Electronically based communication transmits information around the globe virtually instantaneously. New information is spreading rapidly, stimulating new ideas and creating possibilities for new cultural identities. Electronic life is reaching into regions of the world heretofore denied access to what the West regards as a modern, civilized existence.[1] New visions are on the horizon.[2] The disquiet now experienced by the West signals the onset of a third clash in Western civilization.

There is much to be learned by consulting those earlier clashes in Western civilization. Caution is advised, however, for history is as light refracted through a prism, historical analogy a seductive Lorelei.

Continuity and discontinuity in Western civilization

The history of Western civilization is an epic narrative[3] unfolding in three epochs: classical, medieval, and modern. Although precise dates separating these epochs may be arbitrary, the divisions themselves are not. They reflect the historian's belief that life in the fifteenth century differed from life in the fourteenth century in far more fundamental and profound ways than life in the fourteenth century differed from that of the tenth. This is so even though the first two are separated by a mere century, while the latter are separated by half a millennium. Although much divergence-in-detail is readily apparent, it is the agreement-in-principle that is of interest.

All communities provide security for its membership. These are the structures ensuring the physical safety, productive well-being, and cultural identity and continuity of its membership. Even the most cursory examination of the history of Western civilization is sufficient to reveal that, taken together, these structures displayed a shared pattern of coherent practices within the narratives that constituted each of the three epochs. Whether Greek or Roman, the city-states of classical Western civilization shared a family resemblance. So, too, did the baronial fiefdoms of the Holy Roman Empire, whether French, English, Spanish or German. The structures underlying the contemporary nation state are shared throughout the West—if not the world. Although there are differences between communities within an epoch, they are differences in stylistic development not substantive genre.

This same cursory examination also discloses significant differences in the complexities of communal life from one epoch to another. In one epoch physical safety meant waging battle on foot, in another on horseback, and in a third inside a metal container driven by an internal combustion engine. Productive well-being was once undertaken by artisan-slaves in the countryside or urban shop with rudimentary technologies, later by craftsmen-serfs on a feudal estate or in a rural village, and still later by wage-earners on a factory assembly line driven by steam powered machines. Once upon a time, the West believed the human condition the result of arbitrary, capricious and whimsical gods at play; then the blueprint of a single Judeo-Christian deity; today many believe it is the chance result of a huge cosmic explosion. These discontinuities in the historical record of Western civilization suggest that, rather than proceeding in an unbroken line of cumulative intellectual awakenings, material progress and moral insight, Western civilization erupts from time to time in cataclysmic upheavals. That cataclysm is a clash in civilization.

Today the West is experiencing a third clash in civilization. Beginning with the equations of James Clerk Maxwell uniting electricity and magnetism (1866) and the Mickelson-Morely experiments establishing the constancy of the speed of light (1886) and spanning the cusp of the nineteenth and twentieth centuries— a new form of energy, electricity, replaced the steam-machine nexus. The development of the scientific and technological progeny of electrical power is altering everyday living in ways heretofore found only in science fiction. An increasingly electronic life is overwhelming settled ways of what it means to be alive and human, the waging of war and peace, the structure of wealth and its distribution, the ideas of faith and reason, and the working practices of governance. *Those who look to contemporary scientific research and see the cutting edge of modern civilization are looking to the past; those who see in the contemporary explorations of science bubblings in a primordial soup have their sights fixed keenly and firmly upon the future.*

Energy transformation and a clash of civilization

How might this parade of continuity and discontinuity be explained? Whenever physical action—moving, lifting, pushing, pulling—is taken, whether in the framework of farming, building, making, crafting, sculpting, playing, loving, or fighting, energy is expended and, if action is to continue, must be constantly renewed. Constant renewal is the function of an energy system. An energy system consists of three structures: the *source* of energy (biomass, fossil fuel, minerals), the processes of *converting* that source into power (metabolism, combustion, nuclear fission), and the *form power takes as work* (human, animal, machine). Continuity through an epoch is sustained and driven by an image residing in a distant horizon suggested and constrained by the possibilities inherent in a system of energy. A change in one or more of the energy structures is a change in an energy system.

Development of an energy system *within* an epoch traces a familiar path. The first phase is *experimental* or *entrepreneurial* in character. At some point an exceptionally fertile model and its creative uses, a paradigm, emerges and points the way toward an explosive "take off" ending the entrepreneurial phase. This "tipping point" unleashes the *corporate stage* of development characterized by ever increasing energy efficiency, economies of scale, standardization and the wide diffusion of new technologies. All energy systems possess physical limits. As those limits are approached the energy cost of advancing technology outstrips gains in effectiveness and efficiency. Technological innovation begins to slacken, signaling that the promise inherent in the existing energy system is nearing its horizon. On such an occasion, the energy system may be said to be reaching a state of *exhaustion*.[4]

When the exhaustion of an existing energy system combines with the appearance of a novel change in one or more of the structures of an existing energy system, a vision of life full of innovative and exciting possibilities and opportunities emerges. On such an occasion a discontinuity is formed. This discontinuity embraces the exhaustive stage of one epoch and the experimental stage of a new one and ushers in a clash in civilization. Western civilization is today confronted with just such a combination. It is a contemporary clash in civilization and it is every bit as stunning and extensive as was the change from classical to medieval and from medieval to modern life.

A *clash in civilization* is both profoundly different from, and more than, war or revolution, though both may be entwined in the process. A clash in civilization, rather than deciding *who* shall rule, determines *what* shall be the vital nature of a civilization yet to come, including what it means to rule in the first place. It is a struggle *within* a civilization over competing ways of using an emerging energy system for organizing the basic character of a community's system of security, its physical safety, the form of its wealth and productive arts, and the foundation of its core cultural symbols and ideological precepts.

A clash in civilization is a conflict between life as it is and life as it might be lived. It is the process by which one epic narrative of Western civilization is transformed into another. Such a clash evokes a struggle between the hearts and minds of an exhausted and dying epoch and a new and vibrant one struggling to be born. Constitutive of all security institutions to evolve in the ensuing epoch, such clashes are struggles over very different understandings of what it means to be civilized. It is a time when the very nature of Western civilization is itself altered in profound and irrevocable ways. It is happening again today which is why the West is once more in for the choice of its life.

A word of caution is in order. A change in the basic energy system of an epoch is not the *cause* of a transformation in civilization; it is a fundamental *condition* that makes change possible; it does not make change *necessary*. When combined with imagination, a new energy system begins to envision civilized living in previously unimagined ways. It is a new energy system that makes that *vision* possible and the *choice* to pursue that vision which imparts direction. The combination of the two challenges the prevailing order and induces a clash in civilization.

The dynamics of a clash in civilization

Despite the myriad of processes involved in the replacement of one epoch with another, patterns do emerge. A summary review of the shift from classical to medieval and from medieval to modern highlights the process.

From classical to medieval life

Classical life was an age of imperial conquest and colonization. Wealth resided in various forms of slavery. Because only simple tools were available, economic advance in the classical epoch was primarily geographic not technological. Progress could come only through an expansion of territory and an ever increasing supply and replenishment of slaves. The necessity of geographic expansion was met through imperial conquest by a military formation comprised primarily of heavy infantry. As a consequence, military valor and economic progress were tightly interwoven within a cultural narrative that extolled the glories and virtues of physical prowess and bravery exhibited in war.

Spanning the fifth through the eighth centuries CE, the classical life of sword, slave and citizen was transformed into the medieval life of lance, aristocrat and serf. When the stirrup, horse collar, horseshoe and heavy plow were introduced into Europe during the eighth and ninth centuries, a new energy system arose as the horse and oxen proved far more efficient power systems than human muscle. The change was expressed initially in new weapons technologies. The exhaustion of the primary form of physical safety, the human being (phalanx and legion), together with the appearance of a new form of power, the horse (cavalry), defeated the classical army.

When classical armies were no longer victorious, imperial conquest ceased (Dacia was Rome's last conquest and was abandoned in 270 CE), economic production stagnated and cultural life disintegrated. The costs of maintaining the state and imperial defense spiraled while the tax base shrank; the ability to pay for civil services collapsed. Huge internal migrations took place as Romans fled to the countryside seeking not only protection from the barbarians but escape from confiscatory economic policies, tax collectors and military conscription. Unable to protect themselves, villages and small land holdings fell under the patronage of great land barons (barbarian chieftains). Land ownership replaced slavery as a new form of wealth as Romans gave themselves into serfdom in return for security.

Communications collapsed and, as a consequence, so too did Roman culture. Out of touch with the urban centers of authority and power, Roman culture disintegrated. Expatriate Romans discarded their heritage and adopted the myriad pagan rituals and symbols of their protectors. The introduction of the religion of a single deity irrevocably changed the cultural life of the West as one god replaced the multiplicity of gods of classical culture. Loyalty shifted from the city-state to the lord of the manor who, sanctified by Christ and his earthly disciples, became a link in a divinely sanctioned hierarchy. Classical art, which had depicted gods, heroes, and warriors, gave way to displays of stories from the

Christian Bible. Cathedrals replaced temples and the religious imagery of their magnificent stained glass windows became the primary way of educating an illiterate peasantry. The center of power shifted to Byzantium and the Middle East. Medieval feudal life was firmly established, and a new epoch opened in Western civilization as Europe entered the "dark ages."

From medieval to modern life

Life in the middles ages was religious, royal and rural. Physical safety depended upon the aristocratic heavily armored knight and his castle walls. Productive life was dominated by large rural estates worked by serfs; trade was conducted by and large through barter. Religious life centered on large cathedrals accompanied by monasteries. Living was painful, miserable and cruel. Hope resided not in life as it was lived but in the vision of an afterlife.

Commencing with the Hundred Years War (c.1337–1453) and extending through the Thirty Years War (c.1618–1648), medieval Europe experienced a second military, economic, and cultural disaster and renaissance. Missile weapons unseated the heavily armored knight and brought down his castle walls. Physical safety, provided by knight and castle, was replaced by gunpowder armies. When in 1494 Charles VIII marched into Italy at the head of a combined arms force (infantry, artillery, cavalry), the military system organized around heavily armored cavalry and walled castle collapsed. The siege of Constantinople (1453) proved decisive. Lepanto (1571) reflected the corresponding changes in naval warfare as cannonading replaced ramming. Productive well-being, established through the working of land and barter, surrendered to capitalism. The culture of faith, divinely carved into the sacred and profane, was replaced by reason, as scholars recovered the work of the ancient Greeks from their Arab sanctuary. Medieval Europe underwent yet a second military, economic and cultural awakening, transforming the medieval life of lance, aristocrat and serf into the artillery,[5] subject/citizen and laborer of modernity.

Gunpowder and the combined arms formations they created proved devastating to the medieval political economy. Armies rapidly increased in size and the new weapons systems were expensive. The logistics of mobilizing such a force and maintaining it in the field were staggering. Greater manpower and wealth than that which could be extracted from the feudal estate demanded a new form of wealth together with a new form of wealth distribution. Capital (credit) replaced land as the primary form of wealth and private property replaced the royal beneficence and aristocratic grant. A system of wealth distribution (interest, wages and taxation) was created through large scale industry, banking, investment, joint stock companies and insurance. Towns displaced monasteries and feudal fiefdoms as centers of economic and cultural activity. City life was reinstated and the rural life of Medieval Europe was converted into a rustic, pastoral refuge.

The importation of movable type and the invention of the printing press ripped knowledge from the cloistered clerics and broke the Church's monopoly on literacy and knowledge. New knowledges exploded and with them new values. The *Renaissance* provided for the *dignity* of all human beings; the *Reformation* inserted the idea of religious and legal *equality*. The *Enlightenment* provided for the replacement of faith by *reason*. "The book of nature," wrote Galileo, "is written in the language of mathematics and is open to any one." From these new ideas grew a belief in the capacity of human beings to manage their own religious, political and economic affairs and to understand the natural world in which they lived. The underlying narrative that supported the authority of the Church and its associated political structure collapsed. It was neither accident nor coincidence that Protestantism, capitalism, democracy, and modern science were born and flourished together.

The requirements for managing the new gunpowder based army and the bureaucracy that supported it (administration, taxation) vastly expanded the role and size of royal authority. The new military technology and combined arms formations demanded tactical skill and command knowledge beyond those exercised by typical civic militias led by the local *burgermeisters*. Like the Romans before them, the towns turned to mercenaries to maintain their safety. Eventually the towns agreed to make a monetary contribution to the crown in return for immunity from certain feudal obligations and protection against depredation from unemployed mercenaries. Such monetary contributions provided the revenue necessary to sustain the bureaucracy of a professional standing army.

As a consequence, the balance of power between crown, aristocracy and church underwent drastic change. After competition with other forms of political organization, most notably the city-states bordering the Mediterranean and the city-leagues of northern Europe, the absolutist state (the embryonic form of the nation state) successfully centralized political authority in the crown. The Treaty of Westphalia brought an end to the political-religious conflict of the Thirty Years War (1618–1648), recognized the sovereignty of the nation state, and ended the medieval epoch.

The process of change

The dynamics of a clash in civilization can be summarized as follows. Primary is a change in the basic energy system. In the classical epoch, energy was converted into human muscle power. Although the source and process of conversion remained the same in the medieval epoch, biomass and metabolism, horsepower was exchanged for that of human muscle. The medieval epoch gave way to the modern when the source of energy shifted to fossil fuels, combustion replaced metabolism, and steam driven machines took the place of horsepower.

A change in energy is reflected in new weapons systems. Thus, the citizen based heavy infantry of the classical epoch gave way to barbarians employed as mercenary cavalry which became the aristocratic heavy cavalry of the medieval epoch. In turn the aristocratic cavalry gave way to mercenary armies employing gunpowder weapons, which eventually became the professional armies of the contemporary nation state. In each instance, the narrative on war acquired an entirely new meaning.

The cost of the new system of physical safety necessitated a new form of wealth and system of wealth distribution. Slavery as the form of wealth gave way to land held and distributed by the crown and aristocracy. Land gave way to capital (credit) held by a new business oriented elite and distributed by market forces. The new form of wealth and system of wealth distribution created greater wealth and provided a foundation for new directions in productive well-being.

Cultural fragmentation follows the development of a new system of communication. Greek and Roman experience and reason give way to religious faith in the Bible when the network of medieval monasteries replaced Roman roads. Pagan honor, virtue and city-states gave way to homage, fealty, and divinity arranged in a religious pyramid paralleled by a feudal hierarchy. When movable type and printing emerged, literacy became widespread. Ideas of equality, reason, science and utility replaced Christian divinity and morality, paving the way for the university, corporation, nation state and democracy, and the shift from serf and subject to citizen. With each transformation, the West came to regard the world in a very different way and to live accordingly.

A clash in civilization is reflected in a shift in the geographic focus of military power, commercial activity, and cultural life. Rome, the jewel of the central Mediterranean and center of classical life, gave way to Byzantium and the Arabian peninsula in the east, which, in turn, gave way to the Atlantic, the center of the modern epoch. This shift in geographical focus signals that transformation is underway and is unlikely to be effectively resisted.

Such are the dynamics of the fall of ancient and rise of new epochs in the historical narrative of Western civilization. On such occasions everything changes, and it is a new form of energy that makes it all possible—but not necessary. Whether the possibilities promised in a new energy system are undertaken at all and the extent and fervor with which they are pursued is a subject of human choice arising from dreams of a new future as it clashes with the present (Beattie, 2009). It is enough to note that in two instances in the history of the West the possibilities of a new form of civilized life were recognized and vigorously pursued while other civilizations facing the same opportunity chose differently or failed to choose altogether. More than geography, weather, ethnicity, or economic self-interest, it was the choice to pursue a fossil–steam–machine nexus that gave rise to modern Western civilization.[6]

The contemporary clash in civilization

The received narrative on the twentieth century relates the drama of titanic struggles between great powers fielding vast military forces armed with ever more devastating weapons and competing ideologies. On this view, the century encompassed two world wars followed by a Cold War, the last consisting of a series of threats and counter-threats, diplomatic confrontations and negotiations, a succession of military non-confrontation confrontations ("proxy" wars), a series of aid programs designed to purchase alliances, and a propaganda war in which each side painted the other as the very personification of the "evil empire"

The epochs		Classical		Medieval		Modern	
		(Greco-Persian Wars) 500 BCE	(Adrianople) 378 CE	(Charles Martel) 712	(Hundred Years War/ Constantinople, 1453) 1337–1453 CE	(Treaty of Westphalia) 1648	(Michelson–Morley Experiments) 1875
Communal institutions	Safety	Infantry	Clash in civilization I	Cavalry	Clash in civilization II	Artillery	Clash in civilization III
	Productive well-being	Slavery		Feudalism		Capitalism	
	Cultural identity and continuity	Virtue		Divinity		Utility	
Energy system	Source	Biomass				Fossil fuels	(Renewables?)
	Conversion	Metabolism				Combustion	(Direct?)
	Power	Human	Animal			Steam	Electricity

Figure 2.1 The epochs of Western civilization.

on Earth. During the Cold War, the armed forces of the two antagonists never engaged in direct military combat with one another. In the end, one side collapsed primarily as a result of a brittle, ideologically driven political tyranny, an ineffectual and incompetent economic system unable to satisfy the material needs of its people, and the unwillingness to integrate its subjugated populations.[7] The end of the Cold War now engulfs the globe, yet the peace that has followed is imperfectly known. Why should this be the case?

Attempts to characterize the post-Cold War world are legion and varied. The competition for power, the search for common values and institutions, and the xenophobic narratives of nations are the standard set of explanations for events in the international arena and they are being applied with great insight and rigor to the events of the post-Cold War world. Fukuyama sees in the end of the Cold War the "end of history" and the triumph of the Western liberal values of democracy and capitalism. Huntington reminds us that it does not follow from the "triumph of the West" that no alternatives to liberal capitalist democracy exist or that such alternatives will not provide seedbeds for future conflict. In the current conglomeration of international issues and quarrels, he foresees a "clash *of* civilizations." Friedman extols the economic benefits to be derived from "globalization" while Kennedy points out that globalization impacts different nations and cultures in different ways; there are still winners and losers in the game of global economics. Singer and Wildavsky describe the international scene as composed of "zones of peace; zones of turmoil." Barnett combines Freidman and Singer/Wildavsky and sees a "core of connectivity/gap of disconnectedness and that the process of globalization will not necessarily be a peaceful one. Mearshimer sees a return to great power politics. Krauthammer holds out a "unipolar moment" and Bacevich writes of an "American empire" and its eventual decline. Zakaria envisions the "rise of the rest." Then there are those who foresee a "spreading anarchy." In short, international life will carry on with business as usual (great power struggles/rich nations versus poor nations) or as a brave new world (American empire/globalization) or end in total collapse (clashes of civilizations/anarchy). The difficulty is not that these global characterizations are wrong; they are not. It is that they are treated as alternative views of global conditions rather than as complementary pieces of a shared but as yet unrecognized puzzle (Fukuyama, 1992; Huntington, 1997).[8]

The puzzle confronting the West is not so much the shape of the contemporary world as it is a dimly perceived contour of a world yet to come. An inquiry into that future world suggests that the combination of an exhausted energy system (electricity generated by fossil fuel combustion) coupled with the emergence of a novel energy system (renewable energy sources) now provides the West with new possibilities and the opportunity to once again undertake the task of transforming itself. The scientific revolution spanning the nineteenth and twentieth centuries has brought forth a myriad of electronic devices for exploring space, developing artificial intelligence, exploiting the ideas of quantum electronics, machines employing nanotechnology, and synthetic design biologies— all of which are altering the shape of communication, production, transportation, administration and the appliances of everyday living in very fundamental ways. Contemporary events as described by the scholars noted above are but surface waves on an ocean of tectonic change. They are reverberations unleashed by movements in the energy plate of Western civilization. This underlying seismic activity is a *clash in civilization*.

The first piece: energy exhaustion and novel energy

The burning of fossil fuels (oil, coal and natural gas) to boil water to generate steam to drive machines marked the origins of the modern epoch. The contemporary clash in civilization began in the last third of the nineteenth century with the discovery and development of an entirely new energy system: electricity. By the mid-twentieth century, electricity had replaced steam as the energy of choice. Fossil fuels are now employed to produce heat to boil water to create steam to turn the turbines to generate the electricity sent down the wires to run the machines and appliances in the factories and houses that Jack and Jill built. Today electricity is employed in every sector—safety, production, culture—and dominates everyday life in the West.

Where is the fuel to create the electricity to drive the new electronic technology to come from? Electricity exists in nature only in the form of lightning. If it is to be made to do the work of an electrified civilization, a constant flow must be generated. Prevailing methods of generating electrical power through fossil fuel combustion cannot produce the quantities of electricity sufficient to sustain the invention, evolution, implementation and diffusion of new and expanding electronic technologies (Klare, 2008). The contemporary process for *generating electricity* is rapidly reaching a stage of exhaustion. Substituting a critical mass in place of fossil fuels—nuclear energy—may well extend the life of the current system although the consequences of a nuclear accident are indeterminate and could be enormous while nuclear waste disposal remains problematic. Although there is significant disagreement as to whether peak oil production has been reached, expectations are that there will be sufficient oil, natural gas and coal to meet the ever increasing demand through the year 2050. Nevertheless, in the end fossil fuels are finite.

The growing cost of extracting the resources required is increasing the expense of supplying the electricity demanded by an ever expanding global demand for access to the new technologies. The price of electricity is increasing apace. A significant security threat exists from the fact that 80 percent of the world's proven reserves of oil and natural gas are concentrated in two regions not consistently friendly to the West: the Middle East and Russia. Control of resources is a powerful weapon for waging economic warfare, as threats to deny access to oil can effectively blackmail a nation. In addition, there are numerous choke points along the distribution network furnishing lucrative targets for terrorists and other insurgent groups. Energy wars are more than a distinct possibility.

The burning of fossil fuels to meet the demand for electricity and combustion driven transportation systems are primary sources of CO_2 and other "greenhouse" gases with wide ranging impacts on the environment. Scientific opinion has coalesced around the conclusion that the hydrocarbons generated by the burning of fossil fuels are a primary source of dramatic changes in the Earth's climate with predictably devastating consequences for life on Earth. These downsides to the contemporary process of generating electricity demand a fundamental change in the fuel source used to generate electricity.

Yet constraints on developing alternative fuel sources exist. The technology of such alternatives is only in its infancy and the pace of its development is unpredictable. No significant effort has yet been undertaken to develop an entirely new infrastructure for the generation and distribution of electrical energy or the technologies it is capable of sustaining (e.g. electronic transportation systems including highways). Estimates for the cost of financing new fuel sources (including the necessary infrastructure conversion) range up to an astronomical $26+ *trillion* through 2030, a staggering $1.6 trillion a year. However, in the final analysis, the cost of conversion is not the only or even the primary cost to be considered. That cost must be compared with the cost of the failure to convert. The ultimate—and greater—cost for failing to recognize and pursue the opportunities offered by a new energy system would be the collapse of the West into a new "dark age" not unlike that of the medieval epoch.

The second piece: military stalemate and the crisis in military affairs

Western civilization is rapidly approaching the limits of combustion-based military systems.[9] Electricity made possible the development of nuclear weapons and their marriage to missiles. New combat technologies centered on electronic warfare are creating what has been called a "revolution in military affairs" (RMA).[10] Nations lacking a nuclear capacity and the ability to wage conventional war have resorted to various forms of asymmetrical war. These developments collectively signal the end of the modern epoch's conventional military organizations and operations.

Nuclear weapons brought with them the ever present danger of total devastation. No "hot" war between great powers erupted during the Cold War. In effect, strategic thought about the conduct of nuclear warfare was stillborn. The evolution of strategic thought throughout the Cold War was, by and large, a history of the failure to conceive a nuclear war-fighting strategy that did not result in mutual annihilation. In the final analysis, no one could conceive of a realistic way of fighting, prevailing *and surviving as a viable community* in the event of an all-out nuclear exchange. After the near-run confrontation that was the Cuban Missile Crisis, neither side was willing to risk a direct military face-off for fear of escalation into a nuclear exchange. A policy of mutually assured destruction (MAD) was the result. Confrontations shifted to "proxy wars" in the "Third World." While nuclear weapons have not rendered war between nuclear powers, or the one-sided use of a nuclear weapon impossible, obsolete, or even "unthinkable," nevertheless their use has rendered *victory politically and rationally problematic if not utterly meaningless.* Nuclear warfare is thus stalemated.

Military victory as conceived in the style of the end of World War II is an archeological fossil. Where the tradition of non-use of nuclear weapons prevails, a conventional conflict between powers with relative equal military strength and industrial capacity is unlikely to produce a military victor (Korea (1950–1953) and the Iran–Iraq War (1981–1989) are examples). Only when gross inequality exists between the warring parties can a military victory in a war waged with conventional weapons be expected (United States against Iraq (1991 and 2003) and Great Britain and Argentina (1982) are cases in point). Even if military victory is possible, it is likely that the prevailing party will face a significant and prolonged struggle for political control of the conquered territory. Accordingly, conventional war between equals is as stalemated as nuclear war.

A military stalemate generates two responses. The first is the search for new weapons technology; the second is a turn toward asymmetrical war.[11] Waging warfare with the use of electronic weapons, including robots, is the contemporary approach of the capital-intensive West (Ramo, 2011; Singer, 2009). However, the tools and the skill sets required for such operations are not yet standard in the table of organization and equipment of conventional militaries, though many are in a testing phase. Lacking the appropriate skills and tools for waging electronic warfare, communities are turning, as they have throughout history, to mercenaries (including the modern day "military-industrial complex").

Labor-intensive asymmetrical war has been the approach undertaken by the weak (the rebel, the insurgent, the terrorist) against the strong. Strength as military capability gives way to strength as popular support and will as the primary determinant of political triumph. Under such a circumstance, a curious paradox arises. Short of total annihilation of the enemy, the strong while capable of achieving tactical military victories nevertheless appear incapable of converting such military victory into political success. The weak, on the other hand, while incapable of achieving tactical military victory nevertheless have attained significant political achievements. Thus, the importance of *military* victory is altered: *in asymmetric war* tactical, operational, or even strategic *military victory is no longer a precondition to political success*.[12] The clash of these alternative approaches to waging war, novel technological weapons versus popular will expressed though insurgency and terror, constitutes the basic ingredient of asymmetrical warfare at the strategic and policy levels. Asymmetrical war, typical of a clash in civilization, is rapidly becoming the "conventional" war of today.

Although originating as a crisis in military affairs, w*hat happens to the warrior sooner or later engulfs the entire community*. Why should the warrior play such a central role in the transformations in Western civilization? The warrior and the art of war are part of an intimately interwoven communal mosaic that far exceeds the meaning of the military as the mere executor of force and *ultima ratio* of political dispute. As a consequence, military stalemates and asymmetrical war call into question not only the traditional practice of the military art but the entire complex of assumptions, institutions and processes in which that art is intimately embedded. If the close combat tactics of the Roman warrior, symbolizing the bravery, glory and virtue that is classical civilization, is constantly defeated by barbarians on horseback employing hit and run tactics, then the very foundation of classical civilization, the glory of Rome, comes into question. If the foot soldier using missile weapons, and who plays only a minimal role in the divine scheme of medieval warfare, constantly defeats the armored knight, the instrument of God's justice on Earth, then feudal political and religious institutions are seriously undermined. If a rag-tag force of farmers and shepherds armed with outdated weapons can forestall the two greatest military forces on the planet, then the underpinnings of the civilization that produced those military forces are covertly emasculated. The supreme question for the warrior waging combat under such circumstances is no longer how best to fight and win but rather *just what it means to fight and what constitutes victory in the first place.* Such reflections by warriors are a sure indicator of a clash in civilization, for eventually that question translates into a profound community-wide consideration of just what does it to mean to live, work, love and play as well as fight.

The third piece: market failure and the crisis in productive well-being

The foundation of productive well-being in the modern epoch, the steam–machine nexus, has collapsed. The computer and robot, progeny of an electrical energy system, are transforming production, communication, transportation, service, and entertainment processes. The introduction of new skill sets less reliant upon brute force or the skilled labor of craftsmanship is increasing the emphasis upon understanding the direction and programing of the electronic control of machines and administrative processes. The processes of daily living are undergoing elemental change.

When—in previous clashes in Western civilization—a novel energy source was introduced and a new vision of civilized life emerged, the existing form of wealth (slaves, land) and system of wealth distribution (war, inheritance) obstructed the transition. In the event they were altered to sustain the transformation: slaves gave way to land, which, in turn, gave way to money based on precious metals. In the contemporary epoch, the form of wealth, under the exegesis of the Great Depression of the 1930s, has been altered.

Throughout the course of the twentieth-century nations gradually weaned themselves from paper money backed by precious metal. Instead, they now rely on the capacity of the government to enforce the acceptance of paper as representative of and payment for all public and private obligations. The effect of this change is to make wealth infinitely expandable. Today, the amount of capital available to a community is limited only by a government's willingness to introduce additional money based on the potential for economic growth and constrained only by fears of unemployment, inflation, or deflation—and the willingness of other nations to accept it in exchange for trade. Nevertheless, a severe constraint on developing alternative fuel sources and the civilization it promises remains.

Conflicting ideas about the method for distributing new wealth underlie the conflict over productive well-being in previous transformations; it lies at the heart of the contemporary clash in civilization as well. The primary system of wealth distribution in the contemporary West is the market. Under a rational market system, the distribution of new wealth is based upon return on investment. However, new energy alternatives and technologies are only in their infancy and the pace of their development is unpredictable. Contemporary attempts to generate electricity by means other than the combustion of scarce fossil fuels are fraught with missteps, blind alleys, and difficulties in achieving economies of scale and appear inefficient when compared with existing fossil fuel systems. Investment in new energy sources is heavily risk-laden and unattractive to investors resulting in market failures. As a result, those seeking capital in order to research, innovate, scale and commercialize the new energy enterprises necessary to support its associated technologies are starved for capital.

Development of new energy and technological possibilities is blunted by the market system of distribution. This raises anew the conflict over the proper balance to be struck between private and public interest in providing for the productive well-being of the community. If the market forces of the familiar prevail over the new and untried, if the ideology of the free market prevents the government from playing a role in guiding change, and if peaceful continuation of the existing epoch appears dearer than the violence necessary to overthrow the old order, Western civilization will stagnate.

The fourth piece: cultural disillusionment and the crisis in identity

Whether expressed as law, literature, art, drama, music, or scholarship, a library of narratives expresses a community's cultural identity. These narratives are the epics of Western civilization. Narratives express the ways a community responds to life's existential conditions of ambiguity, uncertainty, and a socio-historical existence. Through whatever medium, the tales a community tells itself establishes an understanding of the origins of the community, its concepts of good and evil, precepts of harmony and conflict, and its dreams of future possibilities.[13] The heroic myths of the classical epoch, the books of the Bible, and the philosophies, sciences and dramatic tales of the modern age provided the foundations of order within their respective epochs.

The foundation narratives of modern Western culture originated in the heritage emerging from the intellectual turmoil set off by the Renaissance, Reformation and Enlightenment. Those movements gave birth to the ideas of dignity, equality and reason as the precious possession of all human beings. The dynamic at the heart of this heritage is the idea of *action guided by reason available to all* and finds its most potent expression in modern science and the democratic spirit. Today, the ideas of dignity as honor, equality as human, science as reason and democracy as decision are the subject of an unrelenting onslaught threatening disintegration.

Dignity: the honor of the West

War is a horror orchestrated through the killing of human beings, the maiming of the human spirit and the destruction of the works of civilization. The cultural honor of Western civilization resides in the belief that war is irrational and is, at best, an occasionally necessary evil. This narrative reflects the principle of a just war, justly fought (*jus ad bellum* and *jus in bello*). The result is an effort to avoid war and, if that is not possible, to restrict the extent of its horror.

In the modern epoch the idea of a just war was initially expressed as state sovereignty and was confined to self-defense; aggressive war was regarded as unjust. Commencing with the end of World War II, this principle has been steadily eroded. The evolution of the Western concept of "human rights" now justifies intervention (war) in the name of "human rights." This newly emerging doctrine clashes with the original impulse behind the idea of a just war as reflected in the concept of sovereignty.

A second dilemma confronting the West's honor is the idea that there are unjust ways of engaging in combat, the concept of a just war justly fought. A justly fought war is one in which the killing is confined to those who participate in war as combatants; the killing of noncombatants is unjust. Technological developments throughout the modern epoch have placed this distinction at risk. The development of the doctrine of *strategic air power* together with the technology to execute it regards the home front (the traditional residing place of noncombatants) as a legitimate target thereby blurring the distinction between combatant and noncombatant. *Weapons of mass destruction*, as their name implies, are indiscriminate and altogether incapable of making the distinction between warrior and noncombatant. They cannot be precisely targeted to inflict damage only on those who are combatants. *Asymmetrical war* further obliterates the distinction and, like strategic bombing, positively targets the home front and noncombatant as crucial to its strategy. Given these trends, what then of the distinction between just and unjust wars, between just and unjust ways of waging war? Different cultural conceptions of "human rights" have become a pretext for war. Everywhere and everyone is a target, thereby challenging the West's concept of a justly fought war or negating it altogether.

Equality: economic depravation

Capitalism, regardless of its "socialist" appendages (e.g. government services), is the primary economic system of the West. In order to work, two forms of inequality must exist. The first form of inequality must be in either the command of resources or a desire to consume. In the absence of an inequality in either, there is no rational way of deciding between potential purchasers—that is, rationally allocating resources. Throughout history, various forms of prejudice—religious, racial, ethnic—have provided a basis for depriving one group or another of the resources necessary to participate equally in the market while simultaneously discouraging such groups for one reason or another (e.g. lack of ability, status, etc.) as unworthy of the goods and services available. For the current system of wealth distribution to work, an inequality of opportunity (resource or desire) must prevail in derogation of one of the West's basic source of cultural identity—equality.

The second form of inequality resides in the distribution of payments between the sectors of the wealth distribution system. Consider the four sectors in this system: (1) wealth holders, (2) wealth distributors (banks, investment firms, various other forms of credit institutions, etc.), (3) industrialists and entrepreneurs (the makers and sellers of goods and services), and (4) wage earners (those who actually make the goods and provide the services). If those holding wealth are to distribute that wealth through the system, then the amount distributed (investment, credit, wages) must be less than the amount returning to the wealth holders (profit, interest, return on investment). If this relationship does not hold, then there is no incentive for those holding wealth to make investments, loans, or sales. Over time, the result of such a system (the business cycle) must be a growing inequality between wealth holders and wage earners. In a time when labor is being replaced by robots and computers, structural change exacerbates the inequality through permanent unemployment. In a civilization whose cornerstone is one of equality, an increase in inequality and immobility is a leading indicator of movements promising social unrest and the potential for a violent eruption (Hacker, 2008; Krugman, 2003).

Reason: science

The results provided by the modern scientific enterprise as well as the methods by which it provides them have contributed to an assault on reason. The relativity, uncertainty, and complementarity principles of twentieth-century science undermined the confidence in the absolute certainty that was the hallmark of Newton's physics. The results yielded by relativity and quantum physics have produced a weird particle zoo scattered through multiple dimensions and an unlimited number of universes. "Life," as Alice observed and was later quoted by Mr. Spock somewhere in the Third Quadrant, got "curiouser and curiouser." The world painted by modern science has turned out to be not only stranger than we thought, but stranger than we might even imagine. That confusion has provided a launching pad for an assault on reason (Jacoby, 2008; Mooney, 2005).[14]

The assault on reason arises from three sources. The first arises internally from the limits science places upon itself. The second and third arise externally. The internal limits of science are those imposed by scientists themselves. Science confines itself to an instrumental study of the world of experience, the *is*. Science qua science rejects the *scientific* study of the *ought*. While science can establish what is, can, or might be, it can provide no answer to the question of which among a multitude of what can or might be "which ought to be." Yet it is precisely the question "to what purpose" that dominates intellectual activity during a clash in civilization. By declining consideration of "what ought to be," science places itself, and by implication scientific reasoning, outside the struggle while simultaneously providing the knowledge that makes the question of what ought to be unavoidably essential.[15]

The Romantic Movement, an external critique and the progeny of nineteenth-century literature, was not a critique of reason per se; it merely suggested that reason, while essential, is not sufficient to explain human existence. Thus, many sought to supplement reason with various romantic ideas attempting to provide the missing ingredient. In the romantic world the individual provided the central foundation. The singularity of each human life reflected the dignity of life. The notion that a single life was more and other than one atom among a collection of otherwise indistinguishable atoms all subject to and responding alike to the same forces defied the canons of scientific reason. In short, science emphasized the equality of life while the romantics defended the dignity of each individual life. The conflict between dignity and equality has remained a basic tension in Western philosophical thought ever since.

The third and most damaging assault on reason, however, arises from the distorted applications of science, the most tragic of which was the misapplication of the science of evolution in "Social Darwinism." That school of thought, "scientifically" grounded human nature and social relations in a biological evolutionary scheme characterized as "the survival of the fittest." Throughout the latter half of the nineteenth century, the principles of evolution were used to convert religious discrimination into a "scientifically grounded" racial and ethnic hatred that found its ultimate outlet in the Holocaust perpetrated by the Nazi regime. While the deaths and suffering of the victims of that genocide were horror enough, Nazism through its use of "science" profoundly undermined the West's faith in reason. Reason had long been thought the antidote to evil, superstition, and arbitrary and capriciousness rule. Its highest political expression was thought to be that of the state bureaucracy rationally applying the laws of the state. What the Nazi regime did in the name of a pseudo-science of racial purity, it executed through the relentless application of a rational bureaucratic process.[16] This proved devastating for it did not suggest the necessity of a mere supplement to reason as did the romantics. Rather it exposed reason itself as capable of evil. In so doing, it shattered the West's faith in reason as a guardian against evil.[17]

In the final analysis we are left with Gerald Holton's observation on contemporary science extended to the community as a whole. The scientist (and by implication "we") are trapped in "the labyrinth with the empty center, where the investigator meets only his own shadow, and his blackboard with his own chalk marks on it, his own solutions to his own puzzles" (Holton, 1973: 36). How, then, do we respond to such an existential void of ambiguity and uncertainty within the context of a social existence? The answer is a profoundly democratic one.

Reason: the democratic spirit

If the existential conditions of ambiguity, uncertainty, and social existence preclude ultimate "scientific" answers to the ought,[18] then by what manner can rational decision about the "good life" be achieved?[19] The answer is unavoidable:

the world of human action is, always has been, and always will be *profoundly* democratic. The people will decide—with their feet or bullets if necessary. If this proposition is not accepted, then we are left with no way to explain history. Without this proposition it would be impossible to understand either change or resistance. We would have no way to explain such events as the birth of the American republic, the collapse of the Union of Soviet Socialist Republics, or the contemporary "Arab Spring."

Profound democracy must be distinguished from administrative democracy. Historically, two ways of administratively coping with the existential state of human existence evolved. The first typically regards substantive answers as the province of an elite endowed with a special character (blood, special knowledge, physical prowess, etc.) while the second converted *profound democracy* into a process referred to as the "rule of law." The latter form of administrative democracy adopts a process of reasoned discussion among the people for arriving at substantive answers rather than accepting the knowledge presumably possessed by some elite endowed with some special access to absolute knowledge. Administrative democracy as the rule of law reflects the point of view adopted by the West. The Western practice of administrative democracy by rule of law exhibits a myriad of different institutional arrangements. What unites the West culturally, however, is the *democratic spirit* underlying the various administrative democratic arrangements.

Regardless of various institutional expressions, the democratic spirit entails four attitudes toward political, economic and moral decision derived from the basic Western values of dignity, equality and reason: an open agenda, consensus decision-making, temporary decisions and respect for the minority. Together these attitudes allow the widest latitude for dealing peacefully with the vicissitudes of the human condition in the absence of known or permanently agreed upon ultimate principles.

An *open agenda* means that all alternatives are open to the people as a whole. There exists no special "vanguard" in sole possession of the truth. *Consensus decision-making* rejects top down (elite) decision in favor of the peaceful resolution of issues through rational debate and compromise. *Temporary decision-making* accepts the idea that what may be right for one time may be wrong for another; any issue can be revisited. Reconsidering decisions allows for corrections and adjustments as knowledge increases and norms change. It thereby encourages the minority to accept a decision and forestalls a resort to violence. Finally, *respect for the minority* means that those opposing the decision are not stupid, corrupt, or evil (or, most likely, all three) but represent a legitimate alternative to the prevailing viewpoint. (What is meant here by minority is not race, ethnic, or religious status but simply those who lost the last vote.) The democratic spirit allows for choice from a "market place of ideas." Together this collection of decision-making attitudes reflects the West's cultural response to a social existence saturated with ambiguity and uncertainty. It accepts such conditions and rather than attempting to alter them seeks to ameliorate their consequences.

Today the West undermines its own case for democracy in two ways. First, through unmitigated hubris, it believes that all administrative democracies will enshrine those values common to the cultural identity of Western civilization. As a consequence, the democratic spirit is not only resisted but is under attack in many parts of the globe. Second, as a consequence of the unbridled pursuit of partisan and individual interest at the national and local level, legislative and executive deadlock is undermining the people's trust in existing forms of administrative democracy as currently practiced in the West. The infuriated voices of contemporary political debate, the powerful and the weak, left and right, reflect a rejection of the democratic spirit and are little more than thinly disguised claims for allowing an elite to implement their own absolutist ideas of political, economic and social justice—or anarchy. The result in both cases is an increasing turn toward the last resort of profound democracy, the alternative to administrative democracy—violence.

Each of the cornerstones of the West's cultural identity in the modern epoch—dignity, equality and reason—is disintegrating under the onslaught of the clash in civilization. Yet no new construction of a cultural identity capable of producing the values for a new Western civilization has yet arisen. Nor is there any indication that when one does appear it will do so peacefully.

A magnificent challenge

A clash in civilizations is characterized by chaos. The new elements of community security are only partially established, unstable and temporary as alternative ideas and rapid technological change overtake old ventures and new conjectures with the speed of light. New ideas and processes are not completely understood until the clash is resolved. This has been the dynamic path of the two previous clashes in Western civilization.

Yet historical analogy is fraught with peril. The process of forming an analogy highlights certain aspects of the subject while casting others into deep shadow. The risk is this: that which is out of sight may embrace those very features that render the analogy inappropriate. Hence, a word of caution is again in order. There are significant differences between the contemporary clash in civilization and those of the past, and these differences highlight the extraordinary complexity confronting the West.

Historically, the West faced a clash in civilization in splendid geographic isolation. Today that clash is entangled in a global mélange of scientific, political, economic and social interconnectedness. The new form of energy and its technologies are available to all.[20] Competition between visions of a future will not involve Western ideas alone. Visions springing from the dust of the Soviet Union, the rise of the "New China" and the "rest," and the promises sought in the "Arab Spring" will blaze different trails into the future, generated from a multitude of historical starting points. The future is more than a clash in Western civilization; it involves a clash in civilization for all the communities of the globe and is only incidentally a clash *of* civilizations. Competition for the future is globalized.

The chaotic clash of different visions, the core of a clash in civilization, was in the past resolved through a *profoundly democratic* process. This highlights a second difference between the previous clashes in Western civilization and the current one. Prior to the twentieth century the tools of violence were equally available to the forces of change and resistance. That relative equality was altered dramatically during the twentieth century. Today vested interests command and administer tools of violence far beyond the reach of the general populace. Yet the general populace also has access to tools of violence than can ensure a continual low grade level of constant violence. Should the process devolve into the *ultima ratio* of profound democracy, the contemporary clash of life as it is and a vision of life as it could be lived might well result in destruction on a scale dwarfing that of all twentieth-century wars.[21]

New electronic technologies also energize resistance as new processes of pro-ductive well-being threaten the existing structure of privileges. Those who hold large measures of the existing form of wealth may find themselves relegated to the fringes of the new system of productive well-being and cultural identity. Moreover, a chief characteristic of new technology is that it is typically a labor saving device. Structural unemployment develops as old skills are rendered obsolete and induces additional resistance. Finally, the general population may not be "ready" for the changes implied by the new technologies. Planes flown by robots in the cockpit (thereby eliminating the expense of a pilot and reducing the cost of air travel) may not sit at all well with passengers in the cabin. Thus, the market (private interest), while well designed to distribute resources in an estab-lished market where increasing efficiencies are obvious (faster assembly), may not operate effectively in a period of fundamental transformation (steam power replaces horsepower). The forces of change may not be sufficient to overwhelm resistance.

The central question of our time is this: which of the world's communities is best able to engage the contemporary clash and seize the future. Which has the combination of the capacity to generate new ideas, the willingness to access the material and financial resources required to implement them, and the institutions (including that of civil society) with the will to overcome deeply entrenched vested interests? Is the route to the future a movement from authoritarian to more democratic forms of governance or is the path one of democratic governance assuming greater responsibility for creating the future? The answers to these and other questions like them will be decisive in fashioning the West of tomorrow.

These differences suggest that the path to tomorrow will not be easily tread. Nevertheless, the future cannot be avoided. The difficulty is the West's capacity and desire to shape tomorrow to its own yearning and its willingness to do so. Historically the path to new technologies originated in weapons, moved to the scientific laboratory, emerged as entertainment and toys, and finally spread throughout the entire processes of communal life. Throughout the first half of the twentieth century, the West conducted a romance with technology. World War II introduced the dark side of that relationship and a break up ensued. The West must reengage that liaison. Various forms of communication (iPhones, etc.) may signify the time of toys and indicate a rekindled romance. But the West must move beyond playthings.

The West can successfully engage the future through a policy of *sustainment.* It must sustain the genius and industry of those who light the bonfires of the future and keep them burning brightly. Education, research, design, fabrication and infrastructure development must be encouraged. Simultaneously, if chaos and its offspring violence are to be avoided, we must moderate the consequences for and sustain those whose knowledge and skills will be displaced and whose lives would otherwise be left smoldering on the ash heap of history. So, too, the growth in global population and its impact upon the planet must be confronted. Governments will have to assume these responsibilities as economic markets will be neither willing to take the risks nor able to provide the necessary sustenance. In the early stages of development, as in times of war, the public interest must be conceived as something greater than the sum of individual interests. If the West is to avoid returning to living patterns long shed, it must give full voice to the search for the good life while reaffirming the basic Western values of dignity, equality and reason. Although implemented in different ways, these core values characterize the cherished foundations of a Western way of life.

We can no more escape the future than we can ignore history. The future will in time be accomplished; the past already is. The primary concern must be whether the West will accomplish for itself the future which is open to it. If it does not, the future will be imposed upon it through circumstance or, worse still, inflicted upon it from outside. Neither would necessarily be to the West's liking.

The primary hazard lies inside not outside the West. Through the cartoon Pogo, Walt Kelly observed, "We have met the enemy and they is us." The peril confronting the West is the fear generated by the uncertainty that always accompanies thoughts of the future. Out of fear the West may reject the opportunity. Overcoming that fear is the first step. The ultimate—and greater—cost for failing to recognize and pursue the opportunities offered by a new energy system would be the collapse of the West into a new "dark age." The West need only remember that the future is not to be feared but to be embraced, that "the only thing we have to fear is fear itself." This is the *magnificent challenge.*

Notes

1 The global demand for electricity is enormous—and growing exponentially. By the year 2030 the population of the Earth is predicted to expand by two billion, most of which will be concentrated in the already highly populated developing regions of the world. Over the same period the corresponding demand for electricity is expected to grow by 45 percent over the current demand level.
2 The quantum world of the microscopic once thought irrelevant to the macroscopic appearance of everyday life is now taken to extend throughout the universe. *Scientific American* (June, 2011), online, available at: http://www.scientificamerican.com/article/living-in-a-quantum-world.
3 Selection of the term "epic narrative" warrants explanation. To be sure, the epics of Western civilization are not narratives in the style of Homer, *Beowulf,* the *Epic of Gilgamesh* or the Arthurian legends. Historical style changes with the intellectual

currents of the time. Thucydides introduced a "rational" reconstruction to the study of history. Nevertheless, just as those heroic narratives that preceded him were historical reconstructions, his historical reconstruction of the Peloponnesian Wars is likewise a narrative, albeit a rational rather than heroic one.

4 *Exhaustion* has multiple meanings. The one employed here refers to the limits of the possible where relative increases in energy input are greater than the relative gains in power output. When that stage is reached it is appropriate to say that the energy system is nearing exhaustion—its limits.

5 By artillery is meant all missile weapons driven by human or mechanical power from the crossbow to the Predator.

6 Recent studies on the history of the West and its current predicament underemphasize the role of a change in the basic energy system as it affects the development of Western civilization while overemphasizing the role of far more stable factors or far less stable factors without accounting for the instability in the history of human civilization. See Morris (2010) and Ferguson (2011).

7 Kennan (1947) outlined the factors that would lead to the fall of the Soviet Union. Nevertheless, US policy proceeded on the basis that the Soviet Union would always be with us.

8 The subject first appeared in article in the summer 1993 volume of *Foreign Affairs*. See Friedman (2000, 2003, 2005); Kennedy (1993); Singer and Wildavsky (1993); Barnett (2004); Mearshimer (1994); Layne (1994); Krauthammer (1990/1991); Bacevich (2002); Zakaria (2011); and Kaplan (2000). It is instructive for the discipline of international relations that, with the exception of George Kennan, no scholar predicted the end of the Cold War. At least one group of theorists made the case that it was apt to end—with the *other side* as the "victor." Moreover, no one has yet explained how it ended, though ideological struggles are being waged over who was responsible for bring it to a conclusion.

9 Reviewing the limits of mechanical energy as applied to contemporary weapons systems, John Bodnar has observed: "all technology is ultimately limited by some physical law; while performance improves in successive generations of hardware, the rate of increase slows as the technology approaches its physical limits." He goes on to conclude,

> By any measure, the platforms employed in Desert Storm were not very different in their speed, range, maneuverability, and ability to inflict or absorb (non-nuclear) damage, from those that fought in Vietnam and, in most cases, not significantly better than those that fought in Korea. [Accordingly] One can look at the "cutting edge" of virtually every area of military weaponry and see that the hardware today pushes physical limits so closely that the next generation would require "redesigning" Newton's laws, chemical bonds, or the human body.
>
> (Bodnar, 1993)

10 The idea of a "revolution in military affairs" was first advanced by Parker (1988); but see also Black (1991). Toffler and Toffler (1993) advanced the idea. Military writers swarmed to the idea publishing dozen of articles in the various military journals. For a sampling see Gongora and von Riekoff (2000). The flood has yet to abate.

11 The basic concept underlying asymmetric combat is to pit strength against weakness. In conventional terms this means pitting standard military strength against standard military weakness (e.g. armor against infantry). As used here, asymmetric warfare pits different concepts of strength against one another.

12 Summers, Jr. (1982) wrote the following in the introduction to his book *On Strategy: A Critical Analysis of the Vietnam War*: "'You know you never defeated us on the battlefield,' said the American colonel. The North Vietnamese colonel pondered this remark a moment. 'That may be so,' he replied, 'but it is also irrelevant.'"

13 Consider that the fiction of Jules Verne and H.G. Wells and their science fiction followers set forth a set of possibilities, many of which are now standard practice.

14 See especially chapter 9 "Junk science" in Jacoby (2008).

15 The case of the physicists whose efforts brought nuclear power into existence is illustrative. Although they entered the policy debate on the use and handling of nuclear weapons, they did not do so as scientists but as advocates of a policy position free of scientific backing for their arguments. They could not provide a scientific answer to the question is it "better to be red or dead." In that debate they could offer no better foundation for their position than the non-scientist citizen. Science qua science could not provide an answer to the issue. The ultimate irony, then, is that science cannot even rationally justify itself as an end worthy of pursuit. The issue is a particularly poignant one in the field of political studies. See Strauss (1972).

16 The genocide of the Nazi regime should be clearly distinguished from the slaughter in such place as Kosovo and Rwanda. What took place in Kosovo and Rwanda was simply the unleashing of pure emotion for the purposes of slaughter. They demonstrated what happens when reason is set aside. In that sense they did not challenge reason so much as verified what could happen in its absence. What took place in Germany prior to and during World War II was the ruthless application of reason. The Holocaust challenged the very foundation of the West's belief in the efficacy of reason itself. To the same effect was the modernization of the Soviet Union by Stalin. The slaughter of millions of human lives in the name of "scientific" planning intensified the revolt against reason. The attitude of "how do you feel" rather than "what do you think" expresses the anti-rational bias of contemporary life.

17 Additional examples include the rejection of climate science, stem cell research, and the extolling of "intelligent design" as a substitute for evolutionary science.

18 Either they do not exist or, if they do, they are unknowable or, if known, are not agreed upon by all.

19 Economists are fond of saying that the fundamental economic questions are what products will be produced, how they will be produced, and how will they be distributed. The more fundamental question is *who* will decide the answers to these questions.

20 So, too, was the new energy in previous clashes. But the non-Western world chose not to pursue the possibilities. Hence the West enjoyed its dream in seclusion.

21 The destruction of administrative democracy and authoritarianism and the resort to unbridled violence and anarchy is the final answer of profound democracy. The conflict in Libya and the current fighting in Syria are examples resulting from the change in the balance of power. Egypt is an example of profound democracy falling short, for the most part, of its *ultima ratio*—violence—although as of this writing the case is not settled.

References

Bacevich, A. (2002) *American Empire: the Realities and Consequences of US Diplomacy.* Cambridge: Harvard University Press.

Barnett, T. (2004) *The Pentagon's New Map: War and Peace in the Twenty-first Century.* New York: Berkley Books.

Beattie, A. (2009) *False Economy: a Surprising Economic History of the World.* New York: Riverhead Books.

Black, J. (1991) *A Military Revolution? Military Change and European Society, 1500–1800.* Atlantic Highlands: Humanities Press International, Inc.

Bodnar, J. (1993) "The Military Technology Revolution." *Naval War College Review.* Vol. 46. No. 3:7–21.

Ferguson, N. (2011) *Civilization: The West and the Rest.* New York: Penguin Press.

Friedman, T. (2000) *The Lexus and the Olive Tree.* New York: Random House.

Friedman, T. (2003) *Longitudes and Attitudes: Exploring the World after September 11.* New York: Farrar, Straus & Giroux.

Friedman, T. (2005) *The World is Flat: A Brief History of the Twenty-first Century.* New York: Farrar, Straus & Giroux.

Fukuyama, F. (1992) *The End of History and the Last Man.* New York: Free Press.

Gongora, T. and von Riekoff, H. (2000) *Toward a Revolution in Military Affairs: Defense and Security at the Dawn of the Twenty-First Century.* Westport: Greenwood Press.

Hacker, J. (2008) *The Great Risk Shift: the New Economic Insecurity and the Decline of the American Dream.* New York: Oxford University Press.

Holton, G. (1973) *Thematic Origins of Thought: Kepler to Einstein.* Cambridge: Harvard University Press.

Huntington, S. (1997) *The Clash of Civilizations and the Remaking of World Order.* New York: Simon and Schuster.

Jacoby, S. (2008) *The Age of American Unreason.* New York: Pantheon Books.

Kaku, M. (2008) *Physics of the Impossible: A Scientific Exploration into the World of Phasers, Force Fields, Teleportation, and Time Travel.* New York: Doubleday.

Kaplan, R. (2000) *The Coming Anarchy: Shattering the Dreams of the Post-Cold War.* New York: Random House.

Kennan, G. (1947) "The Sources of Soviet Conduct." *Foreign Affairs.* Vol. 25. No. 4: 566–592.

Kennedy, P. (1993) *Preparing for the Twenty-first Century.* New York: Random House.

Klare, M. (2008) *Rising Powers, Shrinking Planet: the Geopolitics of Energy.* New York: Henry Holt & Company.

Krauthammer, C. (1990/1991) "The Unipolar Moment." *Foreign Affairs: "America and the World 1990."* Vol. 70. No. 1: 22–33.

Krugman, P. (2003) *The Great Unraveling: Losing Our Way in the New Century.* New York: W.W. Norton & Company.

Layne, C. (1994) "The Unipolar Illusion: Why New Great Powers Will Arise." Lynn-Jones, S. and Miller, S. eds. *The Cold War and After: Prospects for Peace.* Cambridge: MIT Press: 244–290.

Mearshimer, J. (1994) "Back to the Future: Instability in Europe after the Cold War." Lynn-Jones, S. and Miller, S. eds. *The Cold War and After: Prospects for Peace.* Cambridge: MIT Press: 141–192.

Mooney, C. (2005) *The Republican War on Science.* New York: Basic Books.

Morris, I. (2010) *Why the West Rules-For Now: the Patterns of History and What They Reveal About the Future.* New York: Farrar, Straus, & Giroux.

Parker, G. (1988) *The Military Revolution: Military Innovation and the Rise of the West, 1500–1800.* New York: Cambridge University Press.

Ramo, S. (2011) *Let Robots Do the Dying: the Coming Partnership of Men and Robots in the US Military.* Los Angles: Figueroa Press.

Singer, M. and Wildavsky, A. (1993) *The Real World Order: Zones of Peace/Zones of Turmoil.* Chatham: Chatham House Publishers.

Singer, P. (2009) *Wired for War: The Robotics Revolution and Conflict in the 21st Century.* New York: Penguin Books.

Strauss, L. (1972) "Political Philosophy and the Crisis of Our Time." Graham, Jr., G. and Carey, G. eds. *The Post-Behavioral Era: Perspectives on Political Science.* New York: David McKay.

Summers, Jr., H. (1982) *On Strategy: A Critical Analysis of the Vietnam War*. Novato: Presidio Press.

Toffler, A. and Toffler, H. (1993) *War and Anti-War: Survival at the Dawn of the 21st Century*. Boston: Little, Brown & Company.

Zakaria, F. (2011) *The Post American World: Release 2.0*. New York: W.W. Norton & Company.

3　The illicit and sovereign free international political economies

Yelena A. Tuzova

With the dramatic expansion of world trade over the past few decades, there has been a rise in cross-border economic activities. "Goods, services, money, people, and ideas, in no particular order, have become increasingly mobile across space, time, and political boundaries" (Gilman *et al.*, 2011: 6). A substantial reduction in international as well as *intra*-national trade costs, availability of new technologies, and financial liberalization have made it possible to trade a wide variety of goods and services that in the past were difficult or impossible to trade. This includes purchases and sales of prohibited products. For example, the high-speed Internet not only boosts the speed and efficiency of all legal trades, but it also hosts an online market for pirated software, knock off clothes, cosmetics, compact disks, counterfeit medicine, labor in the form of coerced sex, psychoactive substances (such as cocaine, cannabis and heroin), weapons, and many other banned or stolen commodities (Naim, 2006). As financial liberalization has given money new mobility, money laundering, tax evasion and capital flight have expanded dramatically. More and more businesses use offshore zones to lower taxes and amass profits. The amount of money laundered every day varies considerably from case to case, from a few hundred to several million US dollars daily.[1] This, in turn, erodes a government's ability to collect taxes and social security contributions, provide for military defense and deliver other public goods and services.

This chapter aims to provide a comprehensive picture of the underground economy. First, it elucidates the concept of illicit economies and "off the books" activities, also known as "sovereign free" or "active financing exception" activities. Second, it provides empirical estimates of the magnitude of the underground economy across countries, emphasizing the growing nature of this phenomenon in recent years. It lists the major factors that affect individuals' and firms' decision to go underground and explains why some markets are prone to develop shadow economies. Finally, it outlines the major initiatives that have taken place to establish more effective governance in dealing with corrupt markets.

The underground economy

The term "underground economy" has been used to describe a wide spectrum of economic activities that are deliberately concealed from public authorities. There are plenty of terms in the existing literature (underground, subterranean, shadow, informal,[2] hidden, parallel, clandestine, etc.) that are used to describe ways to defy detection and get around government controls. Each of these terms represents a particular segment of the underground economy. Despite numerous research studies by Alderslade *et al.* (2006), Bovi and Dell'Anno (2009), Feige (1997), Frey and Schneider (2000), Giles (1999), Gylys (2005), Öğünç and Yilmaz (2000), Smith (1994), Tanzi (1998), there is presently no single or uniform definition for the "underground economy" in the economic literature. To dispel the ambiguity and conceptual confusion, I first propose a new topology that is consistent with many theoretical and empirical studies (see Figure A3.1), and then provide a brief description of each diverse form of the total economic activity.

In theory, total economic income is comprised of officially measured production of legal goods and services, usually referred to as the official gross domestic product (GDP), and economic activities that are left out of the official statistics. The official GDP is defined as the market value of domestically produced goods and services, which are legal under criminal law, within a period of time. By accounting conventions, the official GDP excludes goods and services produced by households for their own consumption (e.g. meals at home, food grown and consumed on a farm, household work, etc.) This is simply because there is no systematic way to measure such activities with sufficient reliability. Therefore, they are excluded from fiscal income. In our analysis household, or "do-it-yourself," work and voluntary activities are classified as an unproductive subset of the black economy and, therefore, subsumed within the category called "non-monetary, or barter transactions."

On the other hand, the "underground economy" is that part of the economy, where "market production of goods and services, legal and illegal, are sold or purchased illegally" (Lemieux, 2007: 8). These are "all economic activities that contribute to the officially calculated (or observed) gross national product but are currently unregistered" (Schneider and Enste, 2000: 78). The underground economic activities, because they are concealed from the tax authorities, are not subject to taxes, and, therefore, escape the conventional income measure. For example, in the United States, such activities include trade in stolen goods, illegal drug dealing, clandestine movement of migrants, money laundering, currency exchange in the black market, illegal gambling, smuggling, prostitution and pornography.

As displayed in Figure A3.1, two kinds of the "underground economy" can be distinguished. The first subcategory is called the "irregular economy" (also referred to as the "legal economy" or "sovereign free economy"). This is the production and consumption of legal goods and services that are exchanged under illegal conditions. "They would generally be taxable were they reported to the tax authorities" (Schneider and Enste, 2000: 79). An example would be smuggling or illegal sales of goods that would otherwise be legal, unlicensed or undeclared employment, etc. The second subcategory is known as the "illicit economy," which I will also refer to as either the "illegal economy" or "productive black markets." The illicit economy is comprised of transactions in goods and services that are forbidden by law. Productive markets are ones where the buyer and the seller "receive benefits from their trades, and neither of them nor any third party has any interest in stopping the transactions" (Lemieux, 2007: 7). An example of "productive black markets" would be the sale of illegal drugs, prostitution, pornography, trade in protected species, etc. Unlike "productive black markets," "unproductive black markets" are ones where no net value is created. Therefore, they are not counted as part of GDP. Criminal activities, such as robbery, trade in stolen goods, extortion, or hiring a killer simply represent "a transfer of wealth from one person or group to another" (Lemieux, 2007: 7). In our analysis, an unproductive subset of the black economy is subsumed within the category called "nonmonetary, or barter transactions."

Tax evasion represents an important part of officially unmeasured economic activities. It is defined as either a reckless failure to pay taxes or deliberate concealment of taxable income or overstatement of allowable deductions from revenue authorities. The concept of tax evasion is regarded as a much wider concept than the "underground economy" itself. It applies to income from legally or illegally produced goods and services as well as income not generated from production, such as taxes on interest payments and capital gains. "These incomes would be coextensive with the underground economy if they originated only in production" (Lemieux, 2007: 8). Tax havens, generally known as territories with low-tax jurisdictions, provide foreign companies opportunity to defer on their tax obligations. Most of the companies registered in tax havens conduct no or very limited local business activity. Typically, owners of such enterprises (the clients of tax havens) cannot own or rent real property. Nor can they locally reside or use the local currency in their business operations. However, companies established in tax havens are partly or wholly exempted from paying taxes. Tax havens also offer secrecy so that the identities of those who own or control the business are kept confidential. Secrecy legislation and zero tax policies attract many business owners who want to conceal their earnings and increase returns. The number of businesses (known as exempted companies or international business companies (IBCs)) being registered in tax havens is much greater per capita than in most industrial and financial centers. For example, in the British Virgin Islands with a population of about 27,800 inhabitants, more than 800,000 companies are incorporated. Allingham and Sandmo (1972), Yitzhaki (1974), Falkinger (1988), Klepper *et al.* (1991), Das-Gupta (1994), Pestieau *et al.* (1994), Caballe and Panades (1997), Sandmo (2005) have made significant contributions to the literature on tax evasion and tax compliance behavior.

What drives individuals and firms underground?

It is not surprising that everything we do, from the considerate to the heroic, we do ultimately for our own benefit. In some cases the personal gain is obvious, in others—it is not. Nevertheless, what appears to be altruistically motivated behavior is really only self-interest in disguise. "It is not from the benevolence of the butcher, the brewer, or the baker that we expect our dinner, but from their regard to their own interest," wrote Adam Smith in his famous book *Wealth of Nations* (1776). Thus, when an individual makes a decision (for instance, to pay or hide taxes), his decision depends upon expected costs and benefits, which are, in turn, also affected by government policies and regulations.

Empirical research shows that high tax burdens, weak banking systems, high intensity of business regulations and prohibitions, inefficiency of government institutions, high incidence of bribery, a weak rule of law, and high unemployment rate bear primary responsibility for driving a number of individuals and businesses into the underground economy. Indeed, when strict prohibitions and regulations are imposed, individuals start seeking ways to circumvent such constraints, even if this means becoming actively engaged in alleged practices, "under-the-table" trades and "off the books" activities. If the expected marginal benefits of doing so equal the risk-adjusted expected marginal costs, an economic agent is likely to choose to operate in the unofficial economy. Here I will describe some major factors that affect the size of the underground economy.

Almost all studies ascertain that high direct and indirect taxes appear to be the most important determinants of the shadow economy. The tax burden decreases the net monetary reward of the taxpayers and hence reduces their incentives to work in the official economy. For instance, in the United States, a 1-percentage point increase in the marginal federal personal income tax rate, other things being equal, enlarges the underground economy by 1.4 percentage points (Schneider and Enste, 2000: 85). "The bigger the difference between the total labor cost in the official economy and after-tax earnings (from work), the greater is the incentive to reduce the tax wedge and work in the shadow economy" (Schneider, 2011: 9). Countries with a tax burden around 35 percent, like Japan, the United States, or Switzerland, tend to have an underground economy that stands at about 10 percent of GDP, while in countries with a tax burden over 65 percent, like Scandinavia, the underground sector is more than 15 percent of GDP.

Another major cause of the underground economy is increased intensity of government regulations (i.e. labor market regulations, trade barriers and immigration laws). According to Bajada and Schneider (2005), "54 percent of the variance in the size of the shadow economy can be explained by labor market regulations." Strict government policies lead to a substantial increase in labor costs in the official economy, borne, primarily, by entrepreneurs. This unequivocally affects labor market outcomes. It is clear that a decrease in demand for official labor leaves some groups of workers unemployed. Unable to find jobs, some workers start looking for work outside the official economy. For instance, in the United States and the United Kingdom—countries with lower labor regulations—the size of the shadow economy accounts for about 10 percent of GDP, while in countries with heavy regulation, such as Iceland and Greece, an underground economy is around 25 percent (Lemieux, 2007: 11). Extreme regulations lead to an increase in the costs of official production, a decrease in supply, an increase in price, and a decrease in quantity demanded. As a result, this will generate underground markets with much higher prices (to compensate for risk taken by suppliers) than official ones. Johnson *et al.* (1997), and Friedman *et al.* (2000) report empirical evidence supporting the fact that countries with high government regulation tend to have a higher share of the unofficial economy in total GDP.

A slow and extensive bureaucracy, complex and at times nonsensical rules, submission of copious amounts of paperwork, and unnecessary formalities inevitably lead to corrupt practices. Several weeks, or even months, may elapse before one can access the decision-making stage, which costs firms large sums of money. High levels of regulations lead to a significantly high incidence of bribery.

> Rather than going through an exhaustive and possibly costly legal process to ensure that all the rules have been followed to the letter, there will often be the temptation bypass them by placing money in a brown envelope which benefits only the recipient.[3]

Based on the survey of 75 Ukrainian nonstate small and medium-sized firms, Kaufmann and Kaliberda (1996) provided a summary table of the unofficial "fees" that were to be paid in 1994 by Ukrainian enterprises to get around various administrative difficulties. For instance, in Kiev firms spent on average nearly $12,000 a year to get around licensing and permit requirements. In addition, to acquire greater security, 70–80 percent of businesses had to pay 10–20 percent of their profits for an organized criminal protection group, known as "krysha."

Quality of public institutions has recently been considered as another key factor of the development of the informal economy. There is an old Russian proverb saying, "A fish rots from the head down." Countries with a weak rule of law, where politicians and government officials in high positions commit white-collar crime with impunity, or where criminals don't go to jail if they have money for legal appeals, have larger shadow economies.

According to Feld and Frey (2007), tax morale may also influence the size of the shadow economy. The willingness of individuals to pay or evade taxes is highly correlated with whether they consider taxation to be fair or unfair. Paying taxes becomes a moral obligation only if there exists demand from the citizens for publicly provided goods and services, and if those goods and services are provided efficiently (Kirchgässner, 2010). Friedrich Schneider has summarized this as follows:

> Tax morale is not only increased if taxpayers perceive the public goods received in exchange for their tax payments to be worth it. It also increases if political decisions for public activities are perceived to follow fair procedures

or if the treatment of taxpayers by the tax authorities is perceived to be friendly and fair. Tax morale is thus not exogenously given but is influenced by deterrence, the quality of state institutions, and the constitutional difference among states.[4]

In contrast, there is surprisingly little evidence from empirical literature on the impact of deterrence on undeclared income. Andreoni *et al.* (1998), Blackwell (2009), Feld *et al.* (2007), Feld and Larsen (2005, 2008, 2010), and Pedersen (2003) conducted experimental studies to see whether deterrence has any effect on the size of the shadow economy. They found that deterrence matters for tax evasion but does not have a strong and consistent effect on the shadow economy.

Methods of measurement

In recent years, economists and policy makers have developed several methods to measure corruption and the overall level of underground activities. There are two different types of approaches widely used in a number of countries: direct approaches and indirect approaches. They are briefly discussed below.

Direct approaches

Direct approaches are primarily based on well-designed surveys, interviews and questionnaires, based on voluntary participation. Given the illegal nature of any underground activity, obtaining reliable information is not an easy task. Therefore, the results of such research methods greatly depend on the participants' willingness to reveal their true actions. "Most interviewed hesitate to confess a fraudulent behavior and quite often responses are rarely reliable so that it is difficult, from these types of questionnaires, to make a real estimate—in monetary terms—of the extent of undeclared work" (Schneider and Enste, 2000: 30). For this reason, direct methods are rarely used in practice.

In the United States, direct approximations of the level of tax compliance come from the Internal Revenue Service (IRS) Taxpayer Compliance Measurement Program (TCMP) survey and the National Research Program (NRP). Having information on the reported individual tax returns and "amounts deemed 'correct' following the audit,"[5] social scientists are able to calculate the unreported income and identify tax gaps[6] (Clotfelter, 1983: 366). These are "the most careful and comprehensive estimates of the extent and nature of tax noncompliance anywhere in the world" (Slemrod, 2007: 26). For instance, in 1981 the IRS published an estimate of $34.2 billion of illegal income, which included income from drugs, illegal gambling and prostitution (Cebula and Feige, 2012: 268). In 1988 the IRS estimated that $449.1 billion of legal source income was unreported as a result of misreporting of filed returns and delinquencies of non-filers (Cebula and Feige, 2012: 267). On average, "for every dollar of income detected in TCMP, another $2.28 went undetected" (Internal Revenue Service, 1988: A-31). However, despite the fact that these surveys obviously reveal more details about the structure of the shadow economy, there are some serious gaps. For example, the TCMP survey does not contain information about individuals who did not file their tax returns. It also fails to measure the underreported income by taxpayers, such as income from moonlighting or cash-only businesses. "Beyond wage and salary withholding information, the only other independent income data available to auditors ... were information reports on interest and dividend income filed by payers" (Clotfelter, 1983: 366). In addition, the last IRS TCMP and IRS NPR estimates for the US tax gap were undertaken for the years of 1988 and 2001, respectively, which make it impossible to assess fraudulent behavior for the current years. Thus, more and more often researchers use indirect methods to estimate tax compliance behavior.

Indirect approaches

There are three major indirect methods currently used to measure the size of the informal economy: currency demand approach, electricity demand approach, and the multiple indicators multiple causes (MIMIC) model. These methods are mainly macroeconomic, as they use various macroeconomic indicators to estimate the growth of the shadow economy. Let us briefly describe the method- ology of these approaches.

The currency demand approach

The general currency demand, or currency-ratio, approach is the most commonly used of the so-called indirect macroeconomic approaches. It was first developed by Cagan (1958), who "calculated a correlation between the currency demand and the tax pressure (as one cause of the shadow economy) for the United States over the period 1919–55" (Schneider and Enste, 2000: 33). It was later refined by Gutmann (1977), who looked at the ratio between currency and demand deposits (for the United States) over the years 1937–1976 (Schneider and Enste, 2000: 33). Their interest was stimulated by some apparent market anomalies. They all witnessed a considerable growth of currency in the United States over time despite the advent of credit cards and other financial instruments.[7] Assum- ing that most underground transactions were conducted in cash, they believed that individuals used cash rather than checks to acquire goods and services pro- duced outside the official economy. Feige (1989) provides a detailed specifica- tion of a general currency demand model. Let us take a look.

Let Y_u be unreported income[8] of the general currency-ratio model defined as follows:

$$Y_u = \frac{1}{\beta} Y_o \frac{(k_u + 1)(C - k_o D)}{(k_o + 1)(k_u D - C)}, \tag{1}$$

where Y_o is the observed income,[9] C is the total amount of currency in circula- tion (both observed and unobserved), D is the actual stock of demand deposits,[10]

$k_0 = C_o/D_o$ is the ratio of currency to demand deposits in the observed sector, $k_u = C_u/D_u$ is the ratio of currency to demand deposits in the unobserved sector, and $\beta = \dfrac{Y_o / (C_o + D_o)}{Y_u / (C_u + D_u)} = \dfrac{v_o}{v_u}$ is the ratio of observed sector income velocity, v_o, to unobserved sector income velocity, v_u Clearly, the unobserved sector is a function of the observed variables Y_0, C and D, as well as three exogenous parameters or functions β, k_0, and k_u.

The general currency-ratio approach (GCR) has been applied to many countries to estimate the size of the hidden economy, although this approach has limitations. There are three restrictive assumptions: (1) currency is the only medium of exchange for unreported transactions, meaning that unreported transactions are paid only with cash and never by check, that is, $k_u \rightarrow \infty$; (2) the currency deposit ratio, k_0, remains constant over time except for changes induced by the growth of unreported income[11]; (3) the amount of unreported income produced by a dollar of currency transacted in the unreported sector is the same as the amount of reported income produced by a dollar of currency transacted in the reported economy, that is, $\beta = 1$. With the imposed restrictions, the relative size of the unreported economy takes the form:

$$\frac{Y_u}{Y_o} = \frac{(C - k_o D)}{(k_o + 1)D},$$

(2)

where C is currency, D is checkable deposits, and $k_0 = (C_0/D_0)$ is the ratio of currency to demand deposits in the observed sector, which is assumed to be constant over time.

Cebula and Feige (2012) reapplied the currency demand approach to empirically estimate the magnitude, growth, and determinants of tax noncompliance behavior in the United States. Figure A3.2(a) displays the dynamic path of the ratio of unreported (both legal and illegal) income to reported income, $(Y_u/Y_o)_t$, for the United States from 1940 until 2010. It is derived from the highly restrictive currency demand approach (C/D model), specified by Equation 2.[12] Assuming no unreported income in 1940, the ratio $(Y_u/Y_o)_t$ increases above 12 percent of reported income during World War II, then declines to a low of 3 percent in the mid-1960s, and then gradually grows until the early 1990s, after which it accelerates to peak at roughly 46 percent in 2007 (Feige, 1989: 40; Cebula and Feige, 2012: 269).

The currency-ratio method traditionally employs all US currency in circulation held both domestically and overseas. Cebula and Feige (2012) relaxed this assumption and only used estimates of *domestic* currency holdings (C_{dom}). As one can see from Figure A3.2(b), there is a significant reduction in the magnitude of estimated noncompliance in the mid-1960s but an apparent increase in the 1990s. The authors also accounted for sweeps programs in their definition of checkable deposits (D_{adj}). Figure A3.2(c) shows that the noncompliance rate, assumed to be zero in 1940, rises to a peak of 9 percent in 1980, declines to a low of 5 percent in 1987, and then rises again to 10 percent in 2007. Figure A3.3

displays the time series of unreported income with two new, 1988 and 2001, benchmarks. The new audit 1988 benchmark raises the initial 1940 noncompliance rate from zero to 9.19 percent, and the 2001 benchmark to 10.76 percent. By 2010, the noncompliance rate estimates totaled 18–19 percent, almost double those based on the 1940 base year model. The tax gap appears to have picked up in 2007, accounting for \$475.9 billion as shown in Figure A3.4.

Tanzi (1980, 1983) "econometrically estimated a currency demand function for the United States for the period 1929–80 in order to calculate the shadow economy" (Schneider and Enste, 2000: 33). The basic econometric model proposed by Tanzi (1983) is given by:

$$\ln\left(\frac{C}{M_2}\right)_t = \beta_0 + \beta_1(1+TW)_t + \beta_2 \ln\left(\frac{WS}{Y}\right)_t + \beta_3 \ln(R)_t + \beta_4 \ln\left(\frac{Y}{N}\right)_t + u_t,$$

where $\beta_1 > 0$, $\beta_2 > 0$, $\beta_3 < 0$, $\beta_4 < 0$. Here C/M_2 denotes the ratio of cash holding to current and deposit accounts, TW is a weighted average tax rate, WS/Y is the proportion of wages and salaries in national income, R is the interest rate paid on savings deposits, and Y/N is the per capita income. The model shows that an increase in the direct and indirect tax burden makes individuals and businesses hold more cash, and thereby increases the size of the total shadow economic activities. Thus, a recent growth in currency stocks and payments might be a good indicator of the growing size of the shadow economy. "This simple currency method has been applied in many countries as a first approximation of the size of the 'underground' economy" (Feige, 1989: 37).

Tanzi's currency demand approach has been widely criticized. For instance, Garcia (1978), Park (1979), and Feige (1996) disagreed that the excess increase in currency was primarily caused by the hidden activities. They explained that "increases in currency demand deposits [were] due largely to a slowdown in demand deposits" (Schneider and Enste, 2000: 35). There were also many questions raised about the initial assumption of no shadow economy in 1940, a baseline year, and of the same velocity of money in both the official and hidden economies. "There is already considerable uncertainty about the velocity of money in the official economy; the velocity of money in the hidden sector is even more difficult to estimate" (Schneider and Enste, 2000: 35). Moreover, the fact that the model considers only one particular factor, the tax burden, as a cause of the shadow economy and since other factors, such as the impact of regulation or tax morality, are not included, this might lead to misleading results. With these other factors that also have a strong effect on the size of the underground economy, the overall level of underground economy might be even higher.

Electricity demand approach

In 1996, Kaufmann and Kaliberda launched a new "macro-electricity consumption" method, which they used to measure the size of the unofficial economy in

16 states (including Ukraine) of the former Soviet Union (FSU) and Central and Eastern European countries (CEE). They collected data on both official GDP and electricity power consumption from 1989 until 1994 provided by the World Bank and its FSU Statistical Unit. They considered official GDP figures as a reliable measure of official economic activity in an economy. But to measure overall (official and unofficial) economic activity in an economy they used electricity power consumption. They made their calculations based on the assumption that the unofficial economy accounted for 12 percent of overall economic activity in 1998, a baseline year, and that the electricity-to-GDP elasticity was closer to one throughout the world. The growth of the unofficial economy was derived from the difference between the growth of total electricity consumption and the growth of registered (official) GDP.

This method has also been criticized by some researchers. The opponents believed that there were some other factors that could cause either an upward or a downward bias in utilizing electricity consumption as a proxy for overall GDP. The upward-biasing factors are the following: (1) higher overhead and fixed electricity use per unit of output; (2) some technological redress due to the lack of basic maintenance; and (3) substitution of electricity for other energy sources. The downward-biasing factors are the following: (1) improved efficiency in electricity use; (2) an increase in electricity prices; (3) a shift in output mix away from electricity-intensive industries; and (4) an increase in underreporting of electricity consumption.[13] Thus, only a part of the hidden economy can be captured by using the electricity demand approach.

The MIMIC approach

The standard MIMIC, or "multiple indicator multiple cause," model explains the relationship between observable variables ("causal" variables and "indicator" variables) and an unobservable variable by minimizing the distance between the sample covariance matrix and the covariance matrix predicted by the model. Zellner (1970), Goldberger (1972), Frey and Weck-Hannemann (1984), Giles (1999), Giles and Tedds (2002), Bajada and Schneider (2005), Dell'Anno and Schneider (2003) have applied this model to derive estimates of the size and development of the underground economy over time in various countries. The hidden output (or income) of the underground economy is represented by a simple unobservable latent variable, or index, whose values are inferred from observable data on "causal" variables and "indicator" variables. The fitted index then provides a time-series estimate of the size of the underground economy.

Formally, the MIMIC model consists of two parts: the structural equation model and the measurement model. The structural equation model is defined as:

$$\eta_t = \gamma' x_t + \xi_t, \tag{3}$$

where $\gamma' = (\gamma_1, \ldots, \gamma_q)$ is a $(1 \times q)$ vector of unknown coefficients describing the "causal" relationships between the unobserved latent variable η_t (scalar) and a

$(q \times 1)$ vector $x_t = (x_{1t}, \ldots, x_{qt})'$ of causal variables for all $t = 1, \ldots, T$. Each time series x_{it}, $i = 1, \ldots, q$, represents a potential cause of the latent variable η_t. The variables in the model are measured as deviations from their means, which are given by:

$$E(\eta_t) = E(x_t) = E(\xi_t) = 0.$$

The error term ξ_t (scalar) represents the unexplained component with a zero mean, as shown earlier, and the variance of ξ_t is defined as:

$$\mathrm{var}(\xi_t) = \psi.$$

In the MIMIC model, the error term is not correlated with the causes, that is:

$$E(x_t \xi_t) = E(\xi_t x_t) = 0,$$

and the covariance matrix of the causes x_t is denoted by a $(q \times q)$ matrix Φ.

The measurement model is specified as follows:

$$y_t = \lambda \eta_t + \varepsilon_t, \tag{4}$$

where $y_t = (y_{1t}, \ldots, y_{pt})'$ is a $(p \times 1)$ vector of indicator variables of the latent variable η_t (scalar), a $(p \times 1)$ unknown parameter vector λ describing the magnitude of the expected change of the respective indicator for a unit change in the latent variable and a $(p \times 1)$ vector of disturbances, where each ε_{jt}, $j = 1, \ldots, p$, is a white noise for all $t = 1, \ldots, T$ with a zero mean and variance θ_j, $j = 1, \ldots, p$. The covariance matrix, denoted by Θ, is given by:

$$\Theta = diag(\theta_1, \ldots, \theta_p).$$

The MIMIC model assumes that the error terms in the measurement model are not correlated either to the causes x_t or the latent variable η_t, that is:

$$E(x_t \varepsilon_t') = E(\varepsilon_t x_t') = 0 \text{ and } E(\eta_t \varepsilon_t') = E(\varepsilon_t \eta_t') = 0.$$

As in the structural equation model, all variables are represented as deviations from their means, given by:

$$E(y_t) = E(\varepsilon_t) = 0.$$

The MIMIC model also assumes that the error terms ε_t and ξ_t are uncorrelated with each other, that is:

$$E(\varepsilon_t \xi_t') = E(\xi_t \varepsilon_t') = 0.$$

To determine the scale of all parameters, Giles and Tedd (2002) set the first element of λ to be 1, that is, $\lambda = (1, \lambda_1, \ldots, \lambda_2, \ldots, \lambda_p)'$. Expressing this model in term of covariance gives:

$$\Sigma = \begin{pmatrix} \text{var}(y_t) & \text{cov}(y_t, x_t) \\ \text{cov}(x_t, y_t) & \text{var}(x_t) \end{pmatrix} = \begin{pmatrix} \lambda(\gamma'\Phi\gamma + \psi)\lambda' + \Theta & \lambda\gamma'\Phi \\ \Phi\gamma\lambda' & \Phi \end{pmatrix}.$$

This matrix describes the relationship between the observed variables (the observed "causes" x_t and "indicators" y_t) in terms of their covariance. The parameters of the model are estimated using the links between the observed variables' variances and covariance. The goal is to find values for the parameters λ and γ and covariance contained in Φ, Θ, and ψ that produce an estimate for Σ that is as close as possible to the sample covariance matrix for the observed causes and indicators (Schneider and Buehn, 2008: 8). For example, consider the case of two "indicator" variables, that is, $p = 2$. Equations 3 and 4 can be written as:

$$y_t = \Pi x_t + v_t,$$

where $\Pi = \lambda\gamma'$ and $v_t \sim (0, \Omega)$ and $\Omega = \lambda\lambda'\psi + \Theta$. The reduced form regression equations become:

$$y_{1t} = \gamma'x_t + v_{1t} \tag{5}$$

$$y_{2t} = \lambda_2\gamma'x_t + v_{2t}, \tag{6}$$

where $v_t = [v_1, v_2]' \sim (0, \Omega)$ and

$$\Omega = \text{var}(v_t) = \text{var}([v_{1t}, v_{2t}]') = \begin{bmatrix} \Psi + \theta_1 & \lambda_2\psi \\ \lambda_2\psi & \lambda_2^2\psi + \theta_2 \end{bmatrix}.$$

Multiply Equation 6 by λ_2 and subtract from Equation 5 to get:

$$y_{2t} = \lambda_2 y_{1t} = v_{2t} - \lambda_2 v_{1t}.$$

Let $u_t = v_{2t} - \lambda_2 v_{1t}$. The two-equation linear simultaneous model can be written as

$$y_{2t} = \lambda_2 y_{1t} + u_t$$

$$y_{1t} = \gamma'x_t + v_{1t},$$

where

$$\text{var}([u_t, v_{1t}]') = \begin{bmatrix} \lambda_2^2\theta_1 + \theta_2 & -\lambda_2\theta_1 \\ -\lambda_2\theta_1 & \psi + \theta_1 \end{bmatrix}.$$

The primary use of the MIMIC model is to estimate the latent variable η_t, that is the measure of the size of the underground economy. Since

$$E(\eta_t \mid x_t) = E(\gamma' x_t + \xi_t \mid x_t) = \gamma' x_t$$

and

$$E(y_{1t} \mid x_t) = \gamma' x_t,$$

the estimate of the latent variable is equal to the predicted value of the first indicator variable

$$E(\eta_t \mid x_t) = E(y_{1t} \mid x_t).$$

The two reduced form equations are estimated using generalized least squares (GLS).[14]

The use of MIMIC modeling has its critics. Helberger and Knepel (1988) claimed that any "minor changes in either the data period or the group of countries studied" might lead to unstable results (Breusch, 2005c: 1). Smith (2002) and Hill (2002) questioned the relevance of the "causal" and "indicator" variables used in the model.

Empirical estimates of the shadow economies around the globe

It is estimated that about 230 million people, or 5 percent of the world adult population used either heroin, or cocaine, or other illicit drugs at least once in 2010 (UNODC, 2012). In 2010, the International Organization of Migration estimated that 25.5 to 32.1 million people of a total 214 million international migrants are unauthorized immigrants. According to the Small Arms Survey, in 2010 there were around 650 million weapons around the world that were in the hands of civilians while only 225 million guns and firearms were in the hands of military, policy, and other government officials.[15] Illicit trade brings misery for thousands of families and intensifies violence, crime and economic instability.

Economists and policy advisors strive to estimate the size of the underground economy, which is without doubt a challenging task. In 1996, Kaufmann and Kaliberda estimated the size of the informal economy in the FSU and CEE, using the electricity consumption method. Table A3.1 displays the dynamics of the unofficial economy for the Ukraine from 1989 to 1994, presented in index numbers. As one can see, in 1989 (the baseline year), the size of the unofficial economy accounted for 12 percent of overall economic activity and continued to rise over the next five years.

In 2000, Friedrich Schneider and Dominik Enste published two articles that have since become the most-cited references on the underground economy. Using the various computational methods described above, the authors presented numerical estimates of the size of the underground economy (as a percentage of official GDP) for different countries at different times along with a discussion of the causes and consequences of a shadow economy. It should be no surprise that during times of financial crisis the size of the underground economy was on the rise. Data shows that the average size of the shadow economy of all 31 European countries (27 EU-members and four non EU-members) constituted 19.9 percent of official GDP in 2009 (see Figure A3.5). "In 2009, there were almost 1.8 billion people employed in the shadow economy," (Freakonomics, 2011).[16] But after 2009, due to an economic recovery, it fell to 18.5 percent in 2012 (see Figure A3.5). Schneider argues that "the most important reason for this decrease is that if the official economy is recovering or booming, people have less incentive to undertake additional activities in the shadow economy and to earn extra 'black' money." For instance, in 2012 the largest average size of the shadow economy (as a percentage of official GDP) of 31 European countries were in Bulgaria (31.9), Croatia (29.0), Cyprus (25.6), Estonia (28.2), Greece (24.0), Hungary (22.5), Italy (21.6), Latvia (26.1), Lithuania (28.5), Malta (25.3), Poland (24.4), Romania (29.1), and Slovenia (23.6). The lowest size and thus development of the shadow economy was observed in Austria (7.6), Luxemburg (8.2), Netherlands (9.5), and Switzerland (7.6). Among highly developed non-European countries, the lowest level of economic informality was in Australia (9.8), Canada (11.5), Japan (8.8), New Zealand (8.8), and the United States (7.0).

Trevor Breusch (2005d) highly criticized Schneider and Enste's work, questioning the provenance of their numbers. Breusch found that a few estimates originally presented by the authors as "own calculations" were in fact attributed to other scholars. In some instances, the authors referred to works with no quantitative information, or to unpublished (working) papers, which were presumably less authoritative than published ones, or to secondary references. Sometimes the cited works contained no quantitative information at all, which made Schneider and Enste's work seem obscure and fallacious to some extent.

Why has the illicit economy continued to expand and grow?

Why has the illicit economy continued to expand and grow so fast? There is no simple answer to this question. Here, I will highlight three reasons that might explain the persistence and expansion of the illicit economy in most countries. The first reason is that some economies experience so-called "jobless growth." If not enough jobs are created for those who seek work, frustrated job seekers, mostly low-skilled, will continue working in the informal economy. The second reason has to do with economic restructuring and economic crisis. It is well documented that during financial and economic turmoil, many public and private companies either shut down or downsize. Retrenched workers facing financial difficulties are forced to move into the informal economy. The third reason is related to global trade and investment. Today, more and more large companies in pursuit of minimizing costs shift their production to labor abundant countries with low labor costs, or shift to informal employment arrangements with no minimum wages and benefits. Unable to migrate easily or at all, domestic low-skilled workers have nothing to do but to compensate a loss in earnings by moving into the informal economy.

Entrepreneurs also repeatedly affirm that the removal of extreme administrative controls, the presence of a stable and moderate tax structure, and political and economic stability may reverse the continuing flight to the unofficial economy and motive people to stay and work officially. But even if all reforms were implemented, people would not immediately switch toward operating officially. For some, it might take a few years before they come back. For others, especially for those who lost their belief in government's ability to carry out sustained liberalization reforms, the time may never come.

Positive and detrimental effects of the shadow economy

A shadow economy may have both positive and negative effects on the official economy. On the one hand, a growing shadow economy creates competition. Workers, who feel overburdened by high taxes and social security and who choose to go underground, create competition for official firms (domestic and foreign). Income generated in the underground economy is spent in the official economy, which stimulates consumer demand. Mironov (2012) examined the relationship between propensity to corrupt (PTC) and firm performance. Using micro-level data on traffic accidents and traffic violations in the city of Moscow and the Moscow region from 1997 until 2007, he developed an individual measure of propensity to corrupt for 3,136,839 Muscovites (Mironov, 2012: 3). He found that firms with corrupt entrepreneurs grow much faster than those with non-corrupt management. "A one standard deviation increase in PTC of tax agency corresponds to a decrease in firms' annual revenue growth by 0.65 percent" (Mironov, 2012: 1). On the other hand, a growing level of shadow economy may further erode public revenues, deepen the nation's debt burden, lead to a larger increase in tax rates, and mislead the government by providing incorrect economic indicators. A growth of unrecorded economic activity that escapes NIPA (National Income and Product Accounts) measurement creates systematic discrepancies between what is recorded and what is actually taking place in the economy. In less developed countries with corrupt governments, closed legislative systems, and constant changes in legislation, the hidden economy appears to be more uncontrolled, more complicated, and more likely to have detrimental effects on the official economy. It deprives the state budget from income and creates serious problems for the establishment of a market economy.

Over the last decade, the problem of shadow economy has received a lot of attention from international political institutions. In 1998, the Organisation for Economic Co-operation and Development (OECD), an international organization made up of representatives from 34 countries, began publishing "blacklists" of countries actively engaging in harmful and unfair tax competition (Maurer,

2010: 219). The focus was primarily on jurisdictions of tax haven countries and offshore financial service centers (for instance, the Cayman Islands, the British Virgin Islands, and the Isle of Man). The OECD identified two types of harmful activity offshore: classic tax havens and the so-called "harmful preferential tax regimes" (Maurer, 2010: 222). Classic tax havens are applied to states or countries "with no or only nominal tax on business entities" (Maurer, 2010: 222). Tax offshores with "harmful preferential tax regimes" refer to states that grant tax privileges to nonresidents and denies the same ones to residents. The 34 OECD member countries and five non-member countries—Argentina, Brazil, Bulgaria, Russia, and South Africa—have adopted the OECD Anti-Bribery Convention that entered into force on February 15, 1999. At the end of 2005, the United Nations Convention against corruption was adopted. In 2007, the World Bank launched its Strengthening World Bank Group Engagement on Governance and Anticorruption (GAC). However, most countries have a long way to go in adopting comprehensive laws and enforcement measures against illicit activities, which should be addressed soon before it can turn into something more dangerous.

Conclusion

Illicit trade permeates rich and poor societies and developing and developed countries, and the volume of these trades becomes larger, more complex and more sophisticated every day. To address the challenges posed by a wide range of illegal activities, academic scholars, policy makers, politicians, foreign advisors, journalists and state institutions have been trying to enhance the effectiveness of law enforcement agencies. But, in order to make the right policy recommendations and come up with the solution to the underground economy, it is crucial to acknowledge the importance of the illicit economy, understand its causes, examine its nature, and estimate the extent of the "off the books" activities that have increasingly emerged from an unrecognized problem to an issue now taken seriously by governments. This chapter has provided a brief overview at what exists in the theoretical and empirical literature on the shadow economy. It has emphasized the main characteristics and determinants of the unofficial economy, reviewed the empirical methods used to measure the size of the unofficial economies, and provided numerical estimates of the underground economy in selected countries.

There exist a number of theoretical and empirical studies on the unofficial economy. However, disagreements persist about definitions and estimation procedures. The underground activities appear to mean very different things to labor economists, criminologists, fiscal experts, macroeconomics and national income accountants. The continuous growth in unrecorded/unreported economic activities is influenced by a number of factors, such as inefficient government policy, high taxes and regulation, a trust crisis between the people and the government, low quality of public services, and corrupt and closed legislative systems. Being hidden by nature, underground economic activities are not easy to observe and measure. "Gathering information about underground economic activity is difficult, because no one wants to be identified" (Schneider and Enste, 2000: 17). Unofficial activities are not always small and invisible. In fact, they may be large and visible. But, since many unofficial activities take place within large corporate structures operating partly in the official economy and partly unofficially, it becomes difficult to recognize the unofficial nature of certain activities. The anonymity of market players, new information systems, and an inability to perfectly monitor activity makes this task hard to accomplish, which allows the illicit trade to continue being a large, ominous and global reality.

Economists have devised a number of methods, direct and indirect, to estimate the overall level of the underground economy. However, different methods produce different results. Lemieux (2007) writes, "the estimates of the Canadian underground economy with five different methods in the period 1986–1990 produced estimates ranging from 1.4 percent and 21.2 percent of the official economy." The existing literature has successfully established that underground economic activities exist everywhere. Moreover, one would expect that a country would have a particularly large shadow economy where there is a weak legal institutional framework, high and volatile tax rates, a lack of economic and political stability, and a high level of corruption. For instance, in countries like Azerbaijan, Ukraine and Russia, the size of the unofficial economy is greater than, say, in Poland, Estonia and the Czech Republic (Kaufmann and Kaliberda, 1996).

Despite massive financial appropriations, strict judicial laws, enforcement efficacy, and sophisticated technology, the fact remains that in some countries (for instance, the FSU states) no governments can yet show any significant, durable progress in the fight against illicit trade. The main reason is that governments themselves are part of the problem. State officials are often linked to informal activities in order to generate private income flows and gain political power. Governments boost illicit trade by criminalizing new activities. For example, in Russia, organized crime has forged alliances with members of political elite turning into, as Louise Shelley says, a "political criminal nexus." The interests of the state and mafias occasionally become one. "In regions where the mafia is efficiently run, problems of law and order and public hazards are kept under control," argues Diego Gambetta.[17] The lack of capacity of weak governments to respond adequately, and the unwillingness of corrupt governments to take decisive action against criminal organizations may lead to severe problems for governance and for national security. Criminalizing activities for which high market demand exists inflates their profitability and encourages new market entrants. If not addressed in a timely manner, this may potentially lead to a much bigger threat to a global society, fueling conflicts among nations and damaging the world economy.

Appendices

Table A3.1 Evolution of the official and unofficial economy (unitary elasticity scenario)

Index type	1989	1990	1991	1992	1993	1994
Official economy index	88.0	84.7	73.3	60.5	51.5	38.9
Unofficial economy index	12.0	16.3	25.5	32.2	34.0	36.6
Overall economy index	100.0	100.0	98.8	92.7	85.4	75.4

Source: Kaufmann and Kaliberda (1996).

Table A3.2 Size of the shadow economy of 31 European countries over 2003–2012 (in % of official GDP)

Country	2003	2004	2005	2006	2007	2008	2009	2010	2011	2012
Austria	10.8	11.0	10.3	9.7	9.4	8.1	8.5	8.2	7.9	7.6
Belgium	21.4	20.7	20.1	19.2	18.3	17.5	17.8	17.4	17.1	16.8
Bulgaria	35.9	35.3	34.4	34.0	32.7	32.1	32.5	32.6	32.3	31.9
Cyprus	28.7	28.3	28.1	27.9	26.5	26.0	26.5	26.2	26.0	25.6
Czech Republic	19.5	19.1	18.5	18.1	17.0	16.6	16.9	16.7	16.4	16.0
Denmark	17.4	17.1	16.5	15.4	14.8	13.9	14.3	14.0	13.8	13.4
Estonia	30.7	30.8	30.2	29.6	29.5	29.0	29.6	29.3	28.6	28.2
Finland	17.6	17.2	16.6	15.3	14.5	13.8	14.2	14.0	13.7	13.3
France	14.7	14.3	13.8	12.4	11.8	11.1	11.6	11.3	11.0	10.8
Germany	17.1	16.1	15.4	15.0	14.7	14.2	14.6	13.9	13.7	13.3
Greece	28.2	28.1	27.6	26.2	25.1	24.3	25.0	25.4	24.3	24.0
Hungary	25.0	24.7	24.5	24.4	23.7	23.0	23.5	23.3	22.8	22.5
Ireland	15.4	15.2	14.8	13.4	12.7	12.2	13.1	13.0	12.8	12.7
Italy	26.1	25.2	24.4	23.2	22.3	21.4	22.0	21.8	21.2	21.6
Latvia	30.4	30.0	29.5	29.0	27.5	26.5	27.1	27.3	26.5	26.1
Lithuania	32.0	31.7	31.1	30.6	29.7	29.1	29.6	29.7	29.0	28.5
Luxemburg (Grand-Duché)	9.8	9.8	9.9	10.0	9.4	8.5	8.8	8.4	8.2	8.2
Malta	26.7	26.7	26.9	27.2	26.4	25.8	25.9	26.0	25.8	25.3
Netherlands	12.7	12.5	12.0	10.9	10.1	9.6	10.2	10.0	9.8	9.5
Poland	27.7	27.4	27.1	26.8	26.0	25.3	25.9	25.4	25.0	24.4
Portugal	22.2	21.7	21.2	20.1	19.2	18.7	19.5	19.2	19.4	19.4
Romania	33.6	32.5	32.2	31.4	30.2	29.4	29.4	29.8	29.6	29.1
Slovenia	26.7	26.5	26.0	25.8	24.7	24.0	24.6	24.3	24.1	23.6
Spain	22.2	21.9	21.3	20.2	19.3	18.4	19.5	19.4	19.2	19.2
Slovakia	18.4	18.2	17.6	17.3	16.8	16.0	16.8	16.4	16.0	15.5
Sweden	18.6	18.1	17.5	16.2	15.6	14.9	15.4	15.0	14.7	14.3
United Kingdom	12.2	12.3	12.0	11.1	10.6	10.1	10.9	10.7	10.5	10.1
27 EU-countries/average	22.3	21.9	21.5	20.8	19.9	19.3	19.8	19.5	19.2	18.4

Source: Friedrich Schneider (2011).

Table A3.3 Size of the shadow economy of four European countries (non EU-members) over 2003–2012 (in % of official GDP)

Country	2003	2004	2005	2006	2007	2008	2009	2010	2011	2012
Croatia	32.3	32.3	31.5	31.2	30.4	29.6	30.1	29.8	29.5	29.0
Norway	18.6	18.2	17.6	16.1	15.4	14.7	15.3	15.1	14.8	14.2
Switzerland	9.5	9.4	9.0	8.5	8.2	7.9	8.3	8.1	7.8	7.6
Turkey	32.2	31.5	30.7	30.4	29.1	28.4	28.9	28.3	27.7	27.2
Non EU-countries/ average	23.2	22.9	22.2	21.6	20.8	20.2	20.7	20.3	19.9	19.5
Average of all 31 European countries	22.4	22.1	21.6	20.9	20.1	19.4	19.9	19.7	19.3	18.5

Source: Friedrich Schneider (2011).

Table A3.4 Size of the shadow economy of five highly developed non-European countries over 2003–2012 (in % of official GDP)

Country	2003	2004	2005	2006	2007	2008	2009	2010	2011	2012
Australia	13.7	13.2	12.6	11.4	11.7	10.6	10.9	10.3	10.1	9.8
Canada	15.3	15.1	14.3	13.2	12.6	12.0	12.6	12.2	11.9	11.5
Japan	11.0	10.7	10.3	9.4	9.0	8.8	9.5	9.2	9.0	8.8
New Zealand	12.3	12.2	11.7	10.4	9.8	9.4	9.9	9.6	9.3	8.8
United States	8.5	8.4	8.2	7.5	7.2	7.0	7.6	7.2	7.0	7.0
Other OECD countries/ average	12.2	11.9	11.4	10.4	10.1	9.6	10.1	9.7	9.5	9.2

Source: Friedrich Schneider (2011).

Table A3.5 Size of the shadow economy of various averages over 2003–2012 (in % of official GDP)

Country	2003	2004	2005	2006	2007	2008	2009	2010	2011	2012
27 EU-countries/average	22.3	21.9	21.5	20.8	19.9	19.3	19.8	19.5	19.4	18.4
4 non EU-countries/average	23.2	22.9	22.2	21.6	20.8	20.2	20.7	20.3	20.0	19.5
5 other OECD countries/ average	12.2	11.9	11.4	10.4	10.1	9.6	10.1	9.7	9.5	9.2
All 36 countries/average	19.2	18.9	18.4	17.6	16.9	16.3	16.9	16.5	16.3	15.7

Source: Friedrich Schneider (2011).

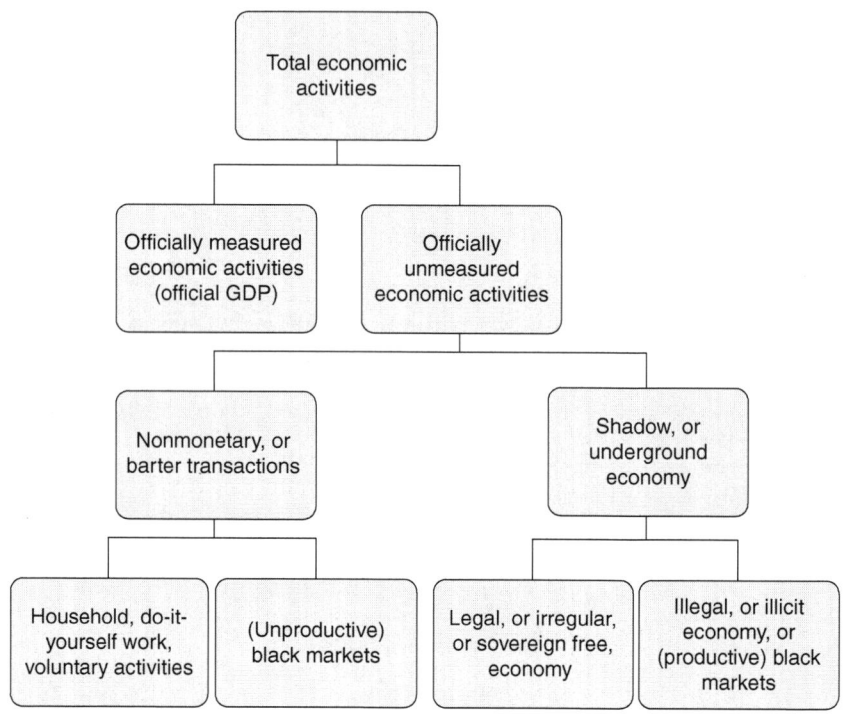

Figure A3.1 Topology of economic activities (source: own methodology).

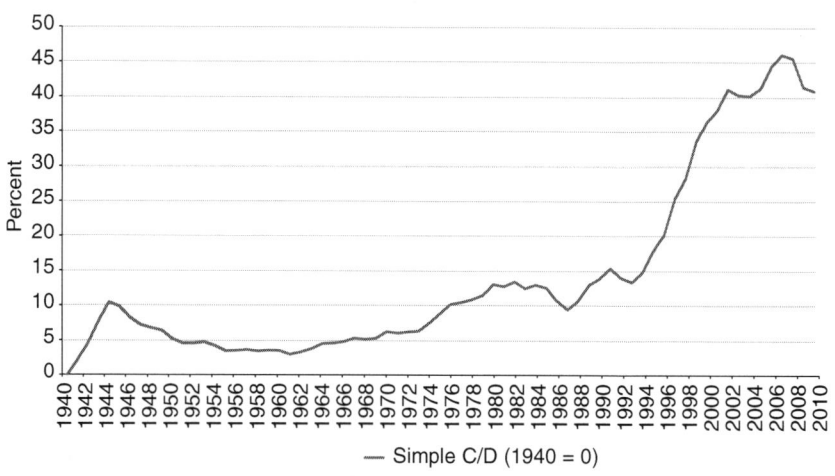

Figure A3.2(a) Estimated noncompliance rates (source: Cebula and Feige, 2012).

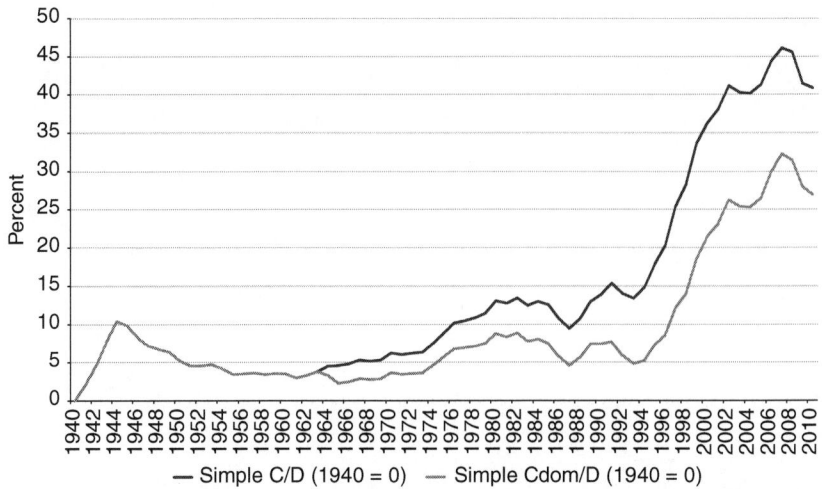

Figure A3.2(b) Estimated noncompliance rates based on the 1940 benchmark (incl. simple C/D and simple Cdom/D) (source: Cebula and Feige, 2012).

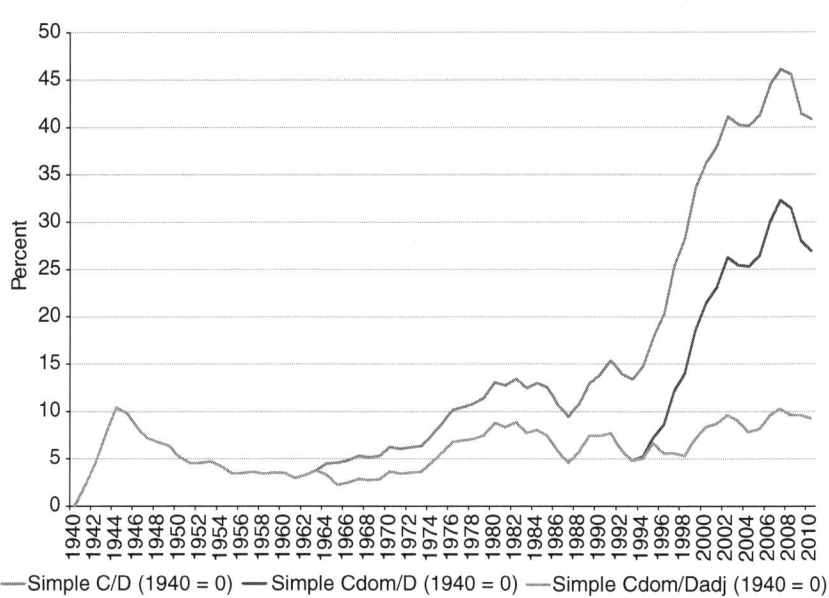

Figure A3.2(c) Estimated noncompliance rates based on the 1940 benchmark (incl. simple C/D, simple Cdom/D and simple Cdom/Dadj) (source: Cebula and Feige, 2012).

Figure A3.3 Estimated noncompliance rates based on the 1940, 1998 and 2001 benchmarks (in percentages) (source: Cebula and Feige, 2012).

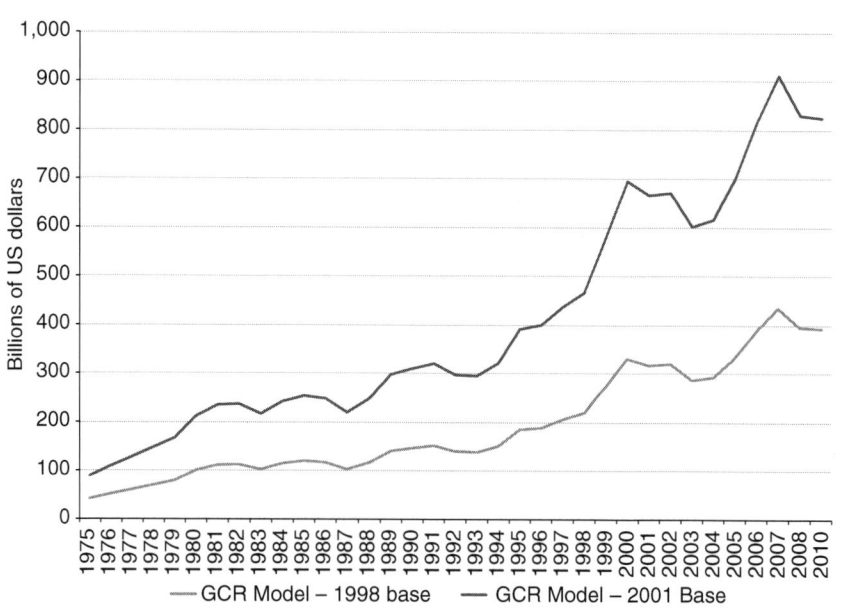

Figure A3.4 Estimated noncompliance rates based on the 1998 and 2001 benchmarks (in billions of U.S. dollars) (source: Cebula and Feige, 2012).

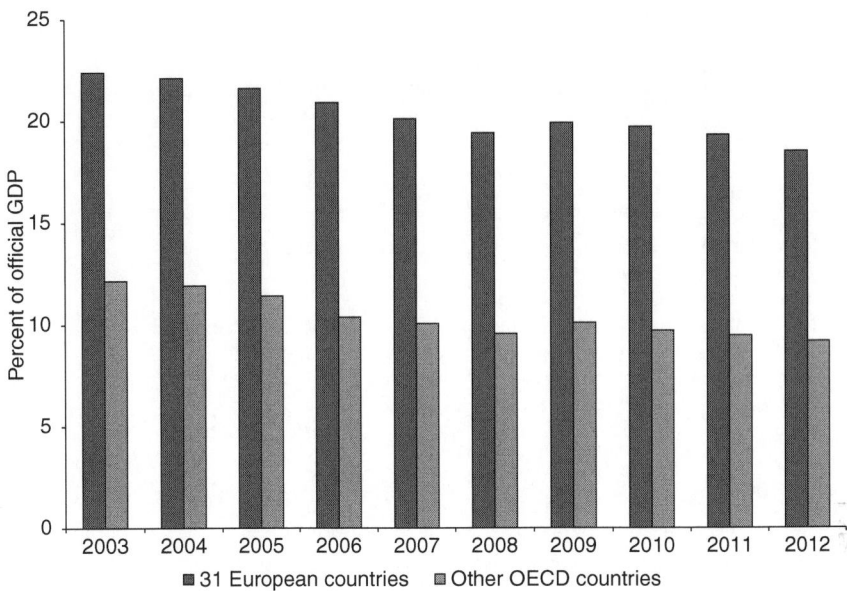

Figure A3.5 The size of the shadow economy in all 36 countries/average (in % of official GDP) (source: Schneider, 2011).

Notes

1 See *Money Laundering Using New Payment Methods*, FATF Report, October 2010.
2 Keith Hart (1973), a social anthropologist, was the first to bring the term "informal sector" in a Third World context into the academic literature. He introduced the concept of the "informal sector" as a part of the urban labor force, which takes place outside of the formal labor market. Hart considered the "informal sector" as almost synonymous with the categories of small self-employed.
3 See Dalziel, S. (2010) "Russian bureaucracy leads to corruption." April. Online, available at: www.telegraph.co.uk/sponsored/russianow/business/7564203/Russian-bureaucracy-leads-to-corruption.html.
4 See Schneider, F. (2011: 7).
5 These "corrected" amounts may not necessarily be true but just represent the IRS's opinion.
6 The tax gap is defined by the IRS

> as the aggregate amount of true tax liability imposed by law for a given tax year that is not paid voluntarily and timely. It is important to emphasize that IRS estimates of the tax gap are associated with the legal sector of the economy only.
>
> (IRS, 2007: 6)

7 US currency in circulation amounted to more than $950 per capita by the end of 1986 and roughly $2,900 per capita by the end of 2010.
8 Unreported income is defined as the difference between the total amount of income that should be reported to the tax authority under the tax code and the amount actually reported. The size of the unreported economy is measured by the magnitude of unreported income.

9   The empirical counterpart of observed income is adjusted gross income.
10 *D* is defined as demand deposits plus other checkable deposits. These are funds deposited in accounts that people can quickly access without any restrictions or limitations. The majority of demand deposits are checking and savings accounts.
11 Cagan (1958) and Gutmann (1977) thought that prior to the introduction of the income tax, there were no incentives to not properly report earnings and assumed $k_{ot} = k_o = (C_o/D_o)_{1940} = (C/D)_{1940}$ for all *t*, the year of 1940 was chosen to be the benchmark year.
12 See "Simple C/D (1940 = 0)" dynamic path.
13 See Kaufmann and Kaliberda (1996).
14 See Bühn, A. and Schneider, F. (2008) for further details.
15 See Louis Charbonneau (2012) "National Rifle Association Vows to Fight Arms Trade Treaty at UN." Reuters, December 28.
16 See Freakonomics website. Online, available at: www.freakonomics.com/2011/11/01/the-black-market-is-the-second-largest-economy-in-the-world/.
17 See Benedick, *Ozone Diplomacy*, 91; see also Brack, D. (1996) *International Trade and the Montreal Protocol*. London: Earthscan: 67–69.

References

Alderslade, J., Talmage, J. and Freeman, Y. (2006) *Measuring the Informal Economy: One Neighborhood at a Time*. Washington, DC: Brookings Institution, Metropolitan Policy Program.

Allingham, M. and Sandmo, A. (1972) "Income Tax Evasion." *Journal of Public Economics*. Vol. 1. No. 3: 323–338.

Andreas, P. (2004) "Illicit International Political Economy: The Clandestine Side of Globalization." *Review of International Political Economy*. Vol. 11. No. 3: 641–652.

Andreoni, J., Erard, B. and Feinstein, J. (1998) "Tax Compliance." *Journal of Economic Literature*. Vol. 36: 818–860.

Bajada, C. and Schneider, F. eds. (2005) *Size, Causes and Consequences of the Underground Economy: An International Perspective*. London: Ashgate Publishing Company.

Becker, K. (2004) *Fact Finding Study: The Informal Economy*. Stockholm: Sida. Online, available at: http://rru.worldbank.org/Documents/PapersLinks/Sida.pdf.

Blackwell, C. (2009) "A Meta-Analysis of Incentive Effects in Tax Compliance Experiments." Alm, J., Martinez-Vazquez, J. and Torgler, B. eds. *Developing Alternative Frameworks Explaining Tax Compliance*. London: Routledge, 164–181.

Blades, D. (1982) "The Hidden Economy and the National Accounts." *OECD (Occasional Studies)*. Paris: 28–44.

Bovi, M. and Dell'Anno, R. (2009) "The Changing Nature of the OECD Shadow Economy." *Journal of Evolutionary Economics*. Vol. 20: 19–48.

Breusch, T. (2005a) "Australia's Cash Economy: Are the Estimates Credible?" *Economic Record*. Vol. 81: 394–403.

Breusch, T. (2005b) "Fragility of Tanzi's Method of Estimating the Underground Economy." Acton: The School of Economics, The Australian National University.

Breusch, T. (2005c) "Estimating the Underground Economy using MIMIC Models." Acton: The School of Economics, The Australian National University.

Breusch, T. (2005d) "Shadowy Figures? An Investigation of Some Estimates of the Underground Economy." Acton: Centre for Social Research, Research School of Social Sciences and School of Economics, The Australian National University.

Breusch, T. (2006) "Size, Causes, and Consequences of the Underground Economy: An International Perspective." Bajada, C. and Schneider, F. eds. *Economic Record, The Economic Society of Australia.* Vol. 82. No. 259: 492–494.

Bühn, A. and Schneider, F. (2008) "MIMIC Models, Cointegration and Error Correction: An Application to the French Shadow Economy." IZA Discussion Paper No. 3306.

Caballe, J. and Panades, J. (1997) "Tax Evasion and Economic Growth." *Public Finance/ Finances Publiques.* Vol. 52. Nos. 3–4: 318–340.

Cagan, P. (1958) "The Demand for Currency Relative to the Total Money Supply." *Journal of Political Economy.* Vol. 66. No. 4: 303–328.

Cebula, R. and Feige, E. (2012) "America's Unreported Economy: Measuring the Size, Growth and Determinants of Income Tax Evasion in the US." *Crime, Law and Social Change.* Vol. 57: 265–285.

Clotfelter, C. (1983) "Tax Evasion and Tax Rates: An Analysis of Individual Returns." *Review of Economics and Statistics.* Vol. 65. No. 3: 363–373.

Cowell, F.A. (1990) *Cheating the Government: The Economics of Evasion.* Cambridge: MIT Press.

Das-Gupta, A. (1994) "A Theory of Hard-to-Get Groups." *Public Finance/Finances Publiques.* Vol. 49 (Supplement): 28–39.

Dell'Anno, R. and Schneider, F. (2003) "The Shadow Economy of Italy and Other OECD Countries: What do We Know?" *Journal of Public Finance and Public Choice.* Vol. 21. No. 203: 97–120.

Desai, M., Foley, C. and Hines, J. (2006) "The Demand for Tax Haven Operations." *Journal of Public Economics.*" Vol. 90. No. 3: 513–531.

Enste, D. (2005) "The Shadow Economy in OECD and EU Accession Countries— Empirical Evidence for the Influence of Institutions, Liberalization, Taxation and Regulation." Bajada, C. and Schneider, *F. eds. Size, Causes and Consequences of the Underground Economy.* Farnham: Ashgate: 123–128.

Falkinger, J. (1988) "Tax Evasion and Equity: A Theoretical Analysis." *Public Finance/ Finances Publiques.* Vol. 43. No. 3: 388–395.

Feige, E. (1989) *The Underground Economies: Tax Evasion and Information Distortion.* Cambridge: Cambridge University Press.

Feige, E. (1990) "Defining and Estimating Underground and Informal Economies: The New Institutional Economics Approach." *World Development, Elsevier.* Vol. 18. No. 7: 989–1002.

Feige, E. (1996) "Overseas Holdings of US Currency and the Underground Economy." Pozo, S. ed., *Exploring the Underground Economy: Studies of Illegal and Unreported Activity.* Kalamazoo: W.E. Upjohn Institute for Employment Research: 5–62.

Feige, E. (1997) "Revised Estimates of the Underground Economy: Implications of US Currency Held Abroad." Lippert, O. and Walker, M. eds. *The Underground Economy: Global Evidence of its Size and Impact.* Vancouver: Fraser Institute: 146–165.

Feige, E., ed. (2007) *The Underground Economies: Tax Evasion and Information Distortion.* Cambridge: Cambridge University Press.

Feige, E. and Cebula, R. (2011) "America's Unreported Economy: Measuring the Size, Growth and Determinants of Income Tax Evasion in the US." University Library of Munich. MPRA Paper 34781. Online, available at: http://ideas.repec.org/p/pra/ mprapa/34781.html.

Feld, L. and Frey, B. (2007) "Tax Compliance as the Result of a Psychological Tax Contract: The Role of Incentives and Responsive Regulation." *Law and Policy.* Vol. 29. No. 1: 102–120.

Feld, L. and Larsen, C. (2005) "Black Activities in Germany in 2001 and 2004: A Comparison Based on Survey Data, Study No. 12." Copenhagen: The Rockwool Foundation Research Unit.

Feld, L. and Larsen, C. (2008) " 'Black' Activities Low in Germany in 2006," News from the Rockwool Foundation Research Unit, March 2008: 1–12.

Feld, L. and Larsen, C. (2010) *Undeclared Work in Germany 2001–2007—Impact of Deterrence, Tax Policy, and Social Norms: An Analysis Based on Survey Data*. Berlin: Springer.

Feld, L., Schmidt, A. and Schneider, F. (2007) "Tax Evasion, Black Activities and Deterrence in Germany: An Institutional and Empirical Perspective." mimeo, University of Heidelberg.

Frey, B. and Schneider, F. (2000) "Informal and Underground Economy." Ashenfelter, O., *International Encyclopedia of Social and Behavioral Science*, Bd. 12 Economics. Amsterdam: Elsevier Science Publishing Company.

Frey, B. and Weck-Hannemann, H. (1984) "The Hidden Economy as an 'Unobservable' Variable." *European Economic Review*. Vol. 26: 33–53.

Friedman, E., Johnson, S., Kaufman, D. and Zoido-Lobatón, P. (2000) "Dodging the Grabbing Hand: the Determinants of Unofficial Activity in 69 Countries." *Journal of Public Economics*. Vol. 76: 459–493.

Garcia, G. (1978) "The Currency Ratio and the Subterranean Economy." *Financial Analysts Journal*. Vol. 69. No. 1: 64–66.

Giles, D. (1999) "Modelling the Hidden Economy and the Tax-Gap in New Zealand." *Empirical Economics*. Vol. 24: 621–640.

Giles, David E. and Tedds, L. (2002) *Taxes and the Canadian Underground Economy*. Toronto: Canadian Tax Foundation.

Gilman, N., Goldhammer, J. and Weber, S. (2011) *Deviant Globalization*. New York: Continuum International Publishing Group, Limited.

Goldberger, A. (1972) "Structural Equation Methods in the Social Sciences." *Econometrica*. Vol. 40. No. 6: 979–1001.

Gutmann, P. (1977) "The Subterranean Economy." *Financial Analysts Journal*. Vol. 34. No. 1: 26–27.

Gylys, P. (2005) "Economy, Anti-economy, Underground Economy: Conceptual and Terminological Problems." *Ekonomika*. Vol. 72: 1–11.

Hart, K. (1973) "Informal Income Opportunities and Urban Employment in Ghana." *Journal of Modern African Studies*. Vol. 11. No. 1: 61–89.

Helberger, C. and Knepel, H. (1988) "How Big is the Shadow Economy? A Re-Analysis of the Unobserved-Variable Approach of B.S. Frey and H. Weck-Hannemann." *European Economic Review*. Vol. 32: 965–976.

Helleiner, E. (1999) "State Power and the Regulation of Illicit Activity in Global Finance." Friman, H. and Andreas, P. eds. *The Illicit Global Economy and State Power*. Lanham: Rowman & Littlefield: 53–90.

Hill, R. (2002) "The Underground Economy in Canada: Boom or Bust?" *Canadian Tax Journal*. Vol. 50. No. 5: 1641–1654.

Internal Revenue Service (1983) "Income Tax Compliance Research: Estimates for 1973–1981." Washington, DC: Research Division, July 1983.

Internal Revenue Service (1988) "Income Tax Compliance Research: Supporting Appendices to Publication 7285." Publication 1415 (July), Washington, DC, 1988.

Johnson, S., Kaufmann, D. and Shleifer, A. (1997) "The Unofficial Economy in Transition." *Brookings Papers on Economic Activity*. Vol. 2: 159–221.

Kanniainen, V., Pääkönen, J. and Schneider, F. (2004) "Fiscal and Ethical Determinants of Shadow Economy: Theory and Evidence." *Helsinki Center of Economic Research, Discussion Paper, 30.*

Kaufmann, D. and Kaliberda, A. (1996) "Integrating the Unofficial Economy into the Dynamics of Post-Socialist Economies: A Framework of Analysis and Evidence." *World Bank Policy Research Working Paper, 1691.*

Kirchgässner, G. (2010) *Tax Morale, Tax Evasion, and the Shadow Economy.* St. Gallen: Department of Economics, University of St. Gallen.

Klepper, S., Nagin, D. and Spurr, S. (1991) "Tax Rates, Tax Compliance, and the Reporting of Long Term Capital Gains." *Public Finance/Finances Publiques.* Vol. 46. No. 2: 236–251.

Lemieux, P. (2007) *The Underground Economy: Causes, Extent, Approaches.* Montreal: Montreal Economic Institute.

Maurer, B. (2010) "From Anti-Money Laundering to … What? Formal Sovereignty and Feudalism in Offshore Financial Services." Clunan, A. and Harold, T. eds. *Ungoverned Spaces: Alternatives to State Authority in an Era of Softened Sovereignty.* Stanford: Stanford Security Studies: 215–231.

Mironov, M. (2012) "Should One Hire a Corrupt CEO in a Corrupt Country?" IE Business School, Spain. Online, available at: www.nhh.no/Files/Filer/institutter/for/seminars/finance/2012_fall/121012.pdf.

"Money Laundering Using New Payment Methods" (2010) *Financial Actional Task Force,* October.

Naim, M. (2006) *Illicit: How Smugglers, Traffickers and Copycats are Hijacking the Global Economy.* London: William Heinemann.

Nardo, M. (2011) "Economic Crime and Illegal Markets Integration: A Platform for Analysis." *Journal of Financial Crime.* Vol. 18. No. 1: 47–62.

Öğünç, F. and Yılmaz, G. (2000) "Estimating the Underground Economy in Turkey." *The Central Bank of the Republic of Turkey, Research Department: Discussion Paper.* September. Online, available at: www.tcmb.gov.tr/research/discus/dpaper43.pdf.

Park, T. (1979) "Reconciliation between Personal Income and Taxable Income, 1947–1977, mimeo." Washington, DC: Bureau of Economic Analysis.

Pedersen, S. (2003) *The Shadow Economy in Germany, Great Britain and Scandinavia: A Measurement Based on Questionnaire Service.* Study No. 10. Copenhagen: The Rockwool Foundation Research Unit.

Pestieau, P., Possen, U. and Slutsky, S. (1994) "Optimal Differential Taxes and Penalties." *Public Finance/Finances Publiques.* Vol. 49. (Supplement): 15–27.

Sandmo, A. (2005) "A Theory of Tax Evasion: a Retrospective View." *National Tax Journal.* Vol. 63. No. 4: 643–663.

Schneider, F. and Enste, D. (2000) "Shadow Economies: Size, Causes, and Consequences." *Journal of Economic Literature.* Vol. 38. No. 1: 77–114.

Schneider, F. and Enste, D. (2002a) "Hiding in the Shadows: the Growth of the Underground Economy." *Economic Issues.* No. 30. International Monetary Fund. Online, available at: www.imf.org/external/pubs/ft/issues/issues30/index.htm.

Schneider, F. and Enste, D. (2002b) *The Shadow Economy: An International Survey.* Cambridge: Cambridge University Press.

Schneider, F., Buehn, A. and Montenegro, C. (2010) "Shadow Economies all over the World: New Estimates for 162 Countries from 1999 to 2007." *Policy Research Working Paper, 5356.* Online, available at: www.econ.jku.at/members/Schneider/files/publications/LatestResearch2010/shadoweconomies_June8_2010_FinalVersion.pdf.

Schneider, F. (2011) "Size and Development of the Shadow Economy of 31 European and 5 Other OECD Countries from 2003 to 2012: Some New Facts. Available on the web." Online, available at: www.econ.jku.at/members/Schneider/files/publications/2011/Shad Econ31.pdf.

Schneider, F. (2012) "The Shadow Economy and Shadow Economy Labor Force: What do we (not) Know?" *IZA Discussion Paper, 6423*, ftp.iza.org/dp6423.pdf.

Sharman, J. (2010) "Shopping for Anonymous Shell Companies: An Audit Study of Financial Anonymity and Crime." *Journal of Economic Perspectives*. Vol. 24: 127–140.

Shelley, L. (1997) "The Criminal–Political Nexus: Russian Case Study." *Trends in Organized Crime*. Vol. 3. No. 1: 12–14.

Slemrod, J. (2007) "Cheating Ourselves: the Economics of Tax Evasion." *Journal of Economic Perspectives*. Vol. 21. No. 1: 25–48.

Smith, A. (1937 [1776]) *An Inquiry into the Nature and Causes of the Wealth of Nations*. New York: Modern Library, reprint.

Smith, P. (1994) "Assessing the Size of the Underground Economy: the Statistics Canada Perspective." No. 28. Online, available at: www.statcan.gc.ca/pub/13-604-m/13-604-m1994028-eng.pdf.

Smith, R. (2002) "The Underground Economy: Guidance for Policy Makers?" *Canadian Tax Journal*. Vol. 50. No. 5: 1655–1661.

Tanzi, V. (1980) "The Underground Economy in the United States: Estimates and Implication." *Banca Nazionale del Lavoro*. Vol. 135. No. 4: 427–453.

Tanzi, V., ed. (1982) *The Underground Economy in the United States and Abroad*. Lexington: Lexington Books.

Tanzi, V. (1983) "The Underground Economy in the United States: Annual Estimates, 1930:1980." *IMF Staff Papers*. Vol. 30. No. 2: 283–305.

Tanzi, V. (1998) "Corruption and the Budget: Problems and Solutions." Jain, A., ed., *Economics of Corruption*. Boston: Kluwer Academic Publishers: 111–128.

UNODC (United Nations Office on Drugs and Crime) (2010) *World Drug Report*. New York: United Nations Office for Drug and Crime Prevention (UDCCP).

Yitzhaki, S. (1974) "A Note on Income Tax Evasion: a Theoretical Analysis." *Journal of Public Economics*. Vol. 3. No. 2: 201–202.

Zellner, A. (1970) "Estimation of Regression Relationships Containing Unobservable Variables." *International Economic Review*. Vol. 11: 441–454.

4 Criminal enterprises, private military companies, smart robots and their implications for national sovereignty

T.X. Hammes

Surprisingly, this chapter will bring a bit of optimism to the *Dark Renaissance*. While the news is not all good—and often times is grim—there is reason for optimism concerning the intersection of PMCs, criminal armies, information systems and robots on international order, if not national sovereignty. This chapter will first examine criminal enterprises, PMCs, and information/robotics individually and then speculate on how the intersection of these three elements will impact both the international order and state sovereignty.

Criminal armies

For the purpose of this chapter, criminal armies are defined as personnel or organizations that execute violence on the part of a criminal enterprise purely for the paycheck. As such, criminal armies are much closer to the traditional concept of a mercenary than are PMCs. I specifically exclude tribal militias and gangs from the category of criminal armies even when they act violently in support of criminal activity. While remunerated in some fashion, members of tribal militias/gangs are fighting out of loyalty to the tribe or gang rather than purely for the paycheck. They generally live in the area where they fight to protect their control of their areas as well as to protect their criminal activities. The Sunni tribes of western Iraq that fight over smuggling routes are a good example of a militia fighting to protect tribal criminal enterprises.

In contrast, criminal armies that fight only to protect criminal activity and criminal enterprises will hire qualified personnel regardless of social affiliation or national origin. The key qualification is loyalty to the organization and willingness to commit violence to achieve its goals. Over the last decade, conflict among these organizations, primarily funded by narcotics profits, has led to casualty levels normally seen only in open warfare. Because of its particularly high levels of violence, Mexico became the public face of this phenomenon. From 2006 to 2012, 60,000 people died in Mexico due to drug related violence (*BBC News*, 2012). The average of 12,000 deaths per year vastly exceeds the minimum standard of 1,000 deaths needed for inclusion in the Correlates of War Database (COW).

To defend their territories and business, the Mexican drug cartels have become increasingly militarized over time. As early as 1999, rogue Mexican army commandos deserted and formed Los Zetas. They initially hired out to Osiel Cardenas Guillen, leader of the Gulf Cartel, as enforcers (Logan, 2009). In response to the professional skills, weapons, and violence the Los Zetas brought to the conflict, other cartels had to hire better trained and more violent enforcers. Over time, the original members of Los Zetas were eliminated, but the men they recruited and trained insured the Zeta organization and reputation lived on. By 2009, the Zeta organization had vastly expanded and begun to operate as its own cartel. It acquired an arsenal that included automatic rifles, 0.50 caliber Barrett sniper rifles, light armored vehicles, rocket and grenade launchers (Logan, 2000). In short, it had achieved the capabilities of a light infantry army.

The extreme violence employed by the drug cartels in Mexico led many observers to note that the cartels were actually challenging the state. In a speech on March 6, 2009, Senator John Cornyn stated the cartels were a threat to US national security and could muster 100,000 armed men compared to the Mexican army's strength of 135,000 (Roebuck, 2009). The senator was not alone in referring to the epidemic of drug violence as an insurgency. By 2010, the violence had escalated to the point that secretary of state Hillary Clinton publically referred to it as an insurgency. Although this characterization was immediately refuted by both President Obama and the Mexican government (Peter, 2010), there has been a significant discussion among police, government officials and academics concerning whether or not the actions of the drug cartels constitute an insurgency. A Google search of "Mexico insurgency" brings over three million hits.

In a more sophisticated analysis, Robert J. Bunker and John P. Sullivan (2010: 30) see the Mexican cartels as *criminal* insurgencies that are battling for dominance of the corridors for transshipment of drugs to the United States. They note that in alliance with other transnational criminal organizations such as Mara Salvatrucha (MS-13), they were challenging the Mexican government by creating enclaves the government cannot enter. While Mexico is the poster child for this form of conflict, Bunker and Sullivan note the emergence of these third phase cartels across the globe indicates that a new form of parallel criminal state is displacing legitimate governance (Bunker and Sullivan, 2010: 35). In particular, they list the *plazas* of Mexico, the *favelas* of Brazil, and Ciudad del Este, the capital of the Tri-border region of South America, as examples. They might well have added the functionally criminal state of Moldava. Of particular concern to Bunker and Sullivan was the cooperation between the third phase cartels and third generation gangs. There are trends that indicate a coalition of these interests is challenging the power of sovereign states.

In 2011, Rand Corporation's report *The Challenge of Violent Drug Trafficking Organizations* (VDTOs) noted that the full extent of the activities and challenges of these organizations and the best way to combat them remained unknown but noted that conditions were similar to earlier recorded insurgencies (Paul *et al.*, 2011). While Rand felt the best methods to combat such organizations remain unknown, it is known that the criminal armies the cartels employ are well funded. According to the United Nations Office on Drugs and Crime, in

2009 the global opiate market was valued at $68 billion and the global cocaine market was worth $85 billion (UNODC, 2011: 16–17).

Clearly, many of the techniques used by the criminal cartels to establish protection for their drug business are similar to those of insurgencies. The cartels intimidate or bribe government officials and civilians, assassinate those who refuse to cooperate, establish bases outside government control, and purchase weapons equal to or better than the police and sometimes the military. They do in fact control parts of some nations. However, this author does not see them as an insurgency since they do not strive to overthrow the government or even to establish government in the sections of the country they control. Rather, they are driven by the requirements of business. Thus Bunker and Sullivan's concept of a criminal insurgency is a more accurate depiction of the threat. Despite the fact the cartels do not have the traditional insurgent's goal of overthrowing the government, they remain a significant threat to state sovereignty. Their control of parts of states as well as the sense of insecurity they bring degrades the legitimacy of the government.

Further blurring the distinction between criminal and insurgent, some gang leaders do claim to be establishing alternative forms of government and many gang members feel they are working for the good of the people (Memmott, 2011). In fact, both gangs and cartels have made some efforts to improve the lot of the people in areas they control by providing clean water, community centers and protection from corrupt local government. Some of these efforts appear to reflect genuine concern for the population; others seem to be an effort to insure the people support the gang/cartel against government efforts. However, none have established fully functioning local governments nor attempted to establish a national government.

While the violence associated with the cartel's criminal armies in fact destabilizes local governance, Mexico, Columbia and Brazil have shown that with focused effort the government can restore order and drive the cartels underground if not completely out of a region. Over the last decade, governments have developed a process for regaining control. Much like counterinsurgency campaigns, the government first employs heavily armed police, paramilitary, and even military units to clear an area of gang members. This may well be the easiest part of the operation. The government then has to maintain its control over the area while it earns the trust and cooperation of the people. To do so, it must bring effective government services to the area.

Like historic counterinsurgency campaigns, government anti-cartel campaigns have a steep learning curve and often fail at first. There is even frequently a rise in crime immediately after the criminal organizations are driven out. While they were present in force, the criminal organizations maintained control over criminal activity and revenge killings. With their removal, it takes a while for government forces to achieve the same level of control. Complicating matters, the government should not employ the criminal approach of summary execution but must introduce an effective justice system to control crime. Even this is only one element of the effective local governance required to protect the population from exploitation by outside interests and gain its loyalty (Felbab-Brown, 2011: iv–vii). To succeed fully, the government must complete the difficult and lengthy process of clear, hold and build.

Mexico

As grim as things looked in 2009, Mexico has made great progress against the drug trafficking networks in the last three years. The city of Ciudad Juarez suffered 10,000 deaths in the last four years, but according to the University of San Diego's Trans-Border Institute, organized crime killings were down 32 percent for Mexico's six states that border the United States in 2012. Murders in Juarez fell from a high of 3,622 in 2010 to 797 in 2012—a drop of 78 percent (Johnson and Gomez, 2013). The dramatic turnaround is not attributable to any single factor but rather a combination of better policing, exhaustion of the drug cartels from their intramural wars, citizen militias, government, and business investment. It may also reflect cartel decisions to shift business to lower cost areas such as countries in Central America as well as the natural decline in cartel versus cartel violence that occurs when one achieves a monopoly in an area.

Colombia

Colombia represents another government success against narco-insurgents. While the *Fuerzas Armadas Revolucionarias de Colombia* (FARC) has been active since 1964, it was not until the mid-1990s that it took full advantage of the resources available from participating in the drug trade. In essence, the FARC formed an alliance with drug networks to provide both protection and production in exchange for a share of the profits. The sudden increase in wealth allowed the FARC to expand dramatically. By 1998, President Pastrana conceded sovereignty of 42,000 km of Colombian territory to the FARC by agreeing to stay out of that area. Nationwide the security situation had deteriorated so badly that rich Colombians were afraid to travel outside the capital city.

At this low point, a series of events occurred that completely reversed the situation. First, the army set about reforming itself as an institution. Senior leaders reviewed its performance, took corrective action and doubled the size of the professional army. It also focused on improving intelligence. Then in 2000, the United States funded Plan Colombia as a counternarcotic effort to provide helicopters and training for an army brigade. Initially specifically forbidden to support counterinsurgency efforts, the rules changed after 9/11 and US aid could be used more broadly.

In 2002, the Colombians elected Alvaro Uribe as president and he widened the reform to encompass much of his government. The ensuing counterinsurgency campaign reduced the FARC to the point that, in 2012, it unilaterally released all its hostages. Late that year, the FARC offered a unilateral two-month ceasefire and joined in peace negotiations with the government. At the time of this writing (February 2013), the FARC had declared the unilateral ceasefire over and that they would continue to attack government forces. However, the Colombian government and FARC peace talks continue. Despite the massive reduction in the power of the insurgency, elements of the narcotics network continue to operate in Colombia. But the narcos no longer challenge the government for control.

Brazil

By the mid-2000s, Brazil faced a seemingly intractable problem with the criminal armies that controlled Rio's *favelas* (slums). These areas were essentially no go areas for government officials, including the police (Sullivan, 2012: 21). Yet, in the last two years, government efforts have radically changed the situation. Local governments and the national government have focused efforts on wresting control of Rio's *favelas* from the drug gangs that have ruled them. Using a clear, hold, build approach, the government has demonstrated that it can remove the drug gangs and reestablish government control if it dedicates enough resources. However, it is still too early to see if Brazil will remain in control of these poor, congested areas. Cynics believe the major effort against the *favelas* is primarily driven by the approaching 2014 World Cup and 2016 Olympic Games (Fabres, 2013). Despite the cynicism, the progress is real and measureable in many of the *favelas*. Some have even become tourist destinations and *Business Week* states there is a developing middle class in what were previously no-go shantytowns (Biller and Petroff, 2012).

The government successes in Brazil, Colombia and Mexico have not destroyed the drug cartels. Rather, in response to the pressure, the cartels have moved to places with lower costs of doing business. In the last decade, Guatemala, Honduras and El Salvador have all seen Mexican cartels moving into their nations and their native drug transportation organizations expand into production for the global market as well as local distribution. In each nation, the cartels have made contact with third generation gangs to broaden their bases of power. The result has been a marked rise in drug related violence in the last few years. In 2011, the UN noted that San Pedro Sula, Honduras had become the world's most violent city, in the world's most violent country (Miroff, 2011). By March 2013, *The Economist* expressed concern that Honduras was on the verge of being a failed state but did not suggest the cartels would attempt to govern it if the government collapses.

These cases highlight one of the key differences between insurgencies and criminal enterprises. While criminals will fight for control of an area, they will withdraw if costs become too high. In contrast, most insurgencies are tied to their native countries and will continue the struggle to gain political control of their homes rather than shifting their effort to target another state. The fate of Honduras illustrates a key advantage that criminal cartels have over insurgencies. They can shift operations to weaker areas where it is less costly to do business.

State use of crime

A different threat comes from criminal states such as North Korea and Moldava. In these cases, the state itself either conducts or actively protects criminal activity. North Korea's most famous activity lies in the field of nuclear weapons and missile proliferation but is it also heavily active in counterfeiting US currency, distribution of drugs, money laundering and cigarette smuggling. Central Committee Bureau 39 of the Korean Workers Party is specifically tasked with conducting these illicit activities and funneling the profits to the government. Office #39 is not a new organization—it was formed in 1974 (Kan *et al.*, 2010: 1). Unlike most state officials that use state sovereignty to protect illegal activity, North Korean officials are not focused primarily on personal profit but rather on funding the state itself—although the ruling class are the primary beneficiaries. Obviously, this activity reinforces North Korea's ability to threaten South Korea and its allies.

In many other states, government officials or those warlords who are effectively the government make use of the sovereignty of their states to conduct illegal international activity but for personal profit. States such as Moldava, Afghanistan, Sierra Leone, Congo, Sudan and Myanmar make use of diplomatic pouches, control of customs and immigration, official airlines and the like to facilitate criminal activity. These states do not directly threaten other states but rather weaken the rule of law and thus distort international trade in negative ways. They have no interest in eliminating the crime within their borders but only in profiting from it. Thus, they will use state structures to facilitate the criminal organizations' efforts to move goods across international boundaries as well as to protect criminal elements from extradition and prosecution by other states.

States may also make use of criminal organizations to further state goals. Russia has used cyber-criminal networks to attack both Estonia and Georgia. The attacks against Estonia were in response to Estonia's movement of a Russian memorial out of a downtown park. There is agreement that most of the resultant cyber attacks originated in Russia. It is unclear whether they were officially sanctioned. Estonian officials have accused Russian government organizations of participating in the attack. The Russian government denies this and attributes the attacks to patriotic Russian citizens. While the attack on Estonia was reactive, the cyber attacks on Georgia coincided with the Russian invasion and therefore at least appeared to be preplanned. Once again, the Russian government denied official involvement. These two attacks illustrate several points. First, cyber attacks will clearly be a part of future conflict. Second, attribution of cyber attacks remains difficult and governments will make use of that uncertainty to obfuscate their participation. Finally, non-state cyber patriots will be a part of almost any future conflict. As early as 2004, terrorist groups responded to the activity of the Internet Haganah by threatening a beheading (Weinman, 2006: 199–200). Internet Haganah was an unofficial, loose affiliation of Internet activists who attempt to disable the websites of those groups they designated as terrorist—primarily Islamist groups. Apparently, it was effective enough to draw the beheading threat. We have seen Russian, Chinese, Japanese and American cyber activists attack websites either for patriotic or ideological reasons.

Thus, states do not have to pay for and sustain certain cyber capabilities. Rather they can draw on the resources that already exist as criminal enterprises, as well as mobilize cyber militias. Cyber attacks will not be limited to periods of conflict. Recently, US government officials admitted US companies have lost billions of dollars of value to cyber espionage. Both businesses and individuals have also lost significant sums to purely cyber criminal efforts—from the notorious and widely used "Nigerian" Internet letters to more subtle and often unreported financial losses to hacking. In testimony before Congress, Gordon M. Snow, assistant director, Cyber Division, Federal Bureau of Investigation noted cyber criminals have successfully conduct a wide range of attacks on businesses, governments, school districts, financial firms and individuals resulting in hundreds of millions in losses (Snow, 2011). At the same time, state sponsored cyber espionage has recently received high level attention in the United States.

In the same way that state actors have either paid for or intimidated criminal networks to attack other states, non-state actors will also use these assets in future conflicts. Cyber militias, cyber criminals, cyber contractors and government cyber organizations will be an essential factor in future conflicts.

In summary, criminal armies have not taken over states. Rather states have repeatedly demonstrated that they can defeat criminal cartels if they focus sufficient resources and political will. However, those criminal cartels do not go out of existence but simply move to a more business friendly location. As long as there is a profitable demand for their illegal services, cartels will either move to or emerge in new locations to meet those demands. The presence of these criminal organizations will adversely impact the state they choose to operate from, but does not directly threaten either the host nation government or other governments. They will export crime, and all its attendant problems, to any location where they can make a profit but remain focused on business not revolution.

While criminal organizations have not taken over states, states have found it useful to employ criminal organizations to execute tasks the states either do not want to do or do not want to be seen to do. In most weak states, such as Afghanistan, Nigeria and Honduras, criminal cartels have been content to simply disrupt the state in those regions they require for their criminal businesses but have not sought to actually seize control of the state. While criminal cartels have not yet taken over a state, in at least two cases—North Korea and Moldova—existing state governments have become criminal enterprises. Thus, while criminal armies degrade a state's legitimacy and have disputed state sovereignty in specific areas, they have not to date destroyed a state's sovereignty.

Private military companies

PMCs or private security companies, as they prefer to be called, have had a mixed impact on both international order and sovereignty. In most cases, these companies reinforce a state's capabilities, while in others they undercut state sovereignty. Often referred to as mercenaries, these companies argue with some merit that they are in fact different than the popular perception of mercenaries. Unfortunately, at the same time as these companies returned to the public consciousness, there has also been a rise in genuine mercenaries—those who fight only for the money with no regard for the legality or legitimacy of their actions. In contrast, most Western PMCs work for governments or international corporations. Thus, the actual role of such entities in conflict is somewhat blurred.

Over the last 50 years, contractors have played an increasing role in US military operations. The presence of contractors on the battlefield is not a new phenomenon but has dramatically increased from the ratio of one contractor to 55 military personnel in Vietnam, to 1:1 in Iraq (CBO, 2008) and 1:1.42 in Afghanistan (Schwartz, 2010: 5). By 2012, the secretary of defense directed military planners to assume that half of all forces deployed in a contingency will be contractors. However, the US Department of Defense counts both armed and unarmed contractors. Other states have also adopted the use of contractors for a wide variety of support and even combat activities. For the purposes of this chapter, we will focus on the impact of armed contractors on the sovereignty of a state.

The most prominent recent use of armed contractors has been in Iraq and Afghanistan. They have worked as personal security, convoy security, fixed point security and even quick reaction forces. In these roles, they have reinforced the power of the state and, often filled the vacuum where state power did not exist. While their actions in Iraq and Afghanistan have drawn the most attention, contractors have simultaneously executed these missions for a wide variety of nations, companies, NGOs and IGOs across the globe.

It can be argued that the United States could not have continued operations in either Iraq or Afghanistan without the presence of armed contractors. In Iraq, there was a serious national discussion of whether or not to surge 25,000 additional troops. The US army and marine corps had to extend the tours of those troops already in country in order to fulfill the surge. At the time, there were approximately 20,000 armed contractors in Iraq. There were also an additional 125,000 unarmed contractors doing jobs that uniformed forces would have had to do in their absence (Fainaru, 2007: 1). Quite simply, the United States could not have operated, much less surged, without them.

The contractors not only provided relief in terms of personnel tempo but also absorbed over 25 percent of the killed in action figure in Iraq. Contractors reported almost 1,800 dead and 40,000 wounded by the end of 2009 (iCasualties, no date; ProPublica, no date). For all practical purposes, these casualties were "off the books" in that they had no real impact on the political discussions about the war. As Peter Singer noted,

> there was no outcry whenever contractors were called up and deployed, or even killed. If the gradual death toll among American troops threatened to slowly wear down public support, contractor casualties were not counted in

official death tolls and had no impact on these ratings.... These figures mean that the private military industry has suffered more losses in Iraq than the rest of the coalition of allied nations combined.

(Singer, 2007)

Of course, it is difficult if not impossible to determine how many additional casualties were suffered by Third World nation contractors in either Iraq or Afghanistan. The United States tracks such casualties only when the individual, his survivors, or his firm file an insurance claim with the US Department of Labor. While we have partial records for US citizens, there is less clarity about non-US citizens working for US firms, and almost none for those working for firms from other nations.

With the failure of Iraq and the United States to sign a Status of Forces Agreement, the United States had to turn to PMCs to provide security for the US government personnel who would remain after the withdrawal of US forces. By supporting US advisory and assistance efforts, these PMCs are increasing the power of the Iraqi state.

While the support of these armed contractors has been essential to the operations of host and allied nations in these counterinsurgencies, they have also caused four distinct operational problems. First, the government did not control the quality of the personnel the contractor hired. Second, unless it provided a government officer or NCO for each convoy, personal security detail or facilities protection unit, it did not control their daily interactions with the local population. Third, contracting firms often cannibalized the armed forces of the host nation. Finally, the population held the government responsible for everything the contractors did or failed to do. Since insurgency is essentially a competition for legitimacy between the government and insurgents, this factor elevates the issue of quality and tactical control to the strategic level.

In addition to undercutting its legitimacy, the use of contractors actually undercut local government power. In Afghanistan, security and reconstruction contracts have resulted in significant shifts in relative power between competing Afghan qawms as well as allegations of corruption. Dexter Filkins, writing in the *New York Times* notes that the power structure in Orugzan Province, Afghanistan changed completely when the US government selected Mr. Matiullah Khan to provide security for convoys from Kandahar to Tirin Kot:

> With his NATO millions, and the American backing, Mr. Matiullah has grown into the strongest political and economic force in the region. He estimates that his salaries support 15,000 people in this impoverished province.... This has irritated some local leaders, who say that the line between Mr. Matiullah's business interest and the government has disappeared.... Both General Carter and Hanif Atmar, the Afghan interior minister, said they hoped to disband Mr. Matiullah's militia soon—or at least to bring it under formal government control.... General Carter said that while he had no direct proof in Mr. Matiullah's case, he harbored more general worries

that the legions of unregulated Afghan security companies had a financial interest in prolonging chaos.

(Filkins, 2010)

There are also a number of indirect consequences of employing armed contractors. First, it opens the door for local organizations to build militias under the cover of being a security company. It is difficult to object to other elements of a society hiring security contractors when the government is doing so. This is particularly true when the government is hiring both locals and foreign nationals to provide security. If the government needs private contractors to feel safe, the citizens, local businesses or even local political organizations can certainly argue that they do too. This aspect created significant problems for ISAF in Afghanistan in 2010: "Because PSCs are under the control of powerful individuals, rather than the Afghan National Security Forces, they compete with state security forces and interfere with a government monopoly on the use of force" (Forsberg and Kagan, 2010). In addition, private security companies can compete directly with host nation attempts to recruit and retain military and police personnel. In January 2010, Major General Michael Ward stated that Afghanistan's government was considering capping the pay of private security firms because Afghan police were deserting in large numbers for the better pay and working conditions associated with private companies (CPB Wire, 2010). This created significant problems for ISAF. Major General Nick Carter, UK Army and Commander, ISAF Regional Command-South told reporters:

> private security companies and militias are a serious problem ... they are paid a great deal more than our Afghan security forces, which in itself is counterproductive because, of course, the temptation for a soldier in the ANP is to go across to a private security company because he might earn double in pay.

(Carter, 2010)

Contract hiring also competes directly with the host nation civil government. In both Iraq and Afghanistan, educated professionals took jobs as drivers or clerks with contractors and NGOs simply because the jobs paid more than they could earn working for their own governments. In effect, ISAF and NGO hiring has created an internal "brain drain." This is of particular concern in Afghanistan where human capital is a major limitation on the ability of the government to function.

While their efforts in Iraq and Afghanistan have been well documented, contractors have provided a much broader range of services literally across the globe. The failure of the Bahraini security forces to disperse the rioters led to the deployment of Saudi Arabian troops to shore up the unpopular Bahraini government. This failure of local troops to suppress their own population was not unnoticed in the region:

The crown prince of Abu Dhabi has hired the founder of the private security firm Blackwater Worldwide to set up an 800-member battalion of foreign troops for the United Arab Emirates, the New York Times reported Sunday.

The Times said it obtained documents that showed that the unit being formed by Erik Prince's new company, Reflex Responses, with $529 million from the UAE would be used to thwart internal revolt, conduct special operations and defend oil pipelines and skyscrapers from attacks.

(Reuters, 2011)

In short, Abu Dhabi contracted with Blackwater to insure it had a politically reliable force to protect the ruling family from potential dissidents.

Armed contractors support to extraction companies and charities

In other areas of the world, armed contractors are providing protection for charitable/development organizations and extraction industries. In some areas, this benefits the people. In other areas, it benefits the government and in others it appears only the extraction company and corrupt officials benefit.

By necessity, many charitable NGOs and IGOs operate in areas where there is no government presence. In order to continue their charitable work, they often have to hire armed contractors—either local or international companies. While these companies fill the security vacuum left by the absence of a state in places like Somalia, the resources they transfer to local gunmen also undercut efforts to reestablish the state. Thus charities are faced with the tradeoff of attending to immediate, critical humanitarian needs at the expense of long-term stability. Even longer term development projects often have to be protected from a variety of threats. In the absence of government protection, development agencies hire armed contractors.

Under similar conditions, armed contractors have also filled the security void for resource extraction companies. As demand for natural resources—particularly energy—has continued to increase, resource extraction companies are forced to prospect in ever more dangerous and unstable locations. In many of these regions, the host nation simply cannot provide effective security for the business operations and therefore business has turned to private security companies.

Typical of the situation extraction companies deal with is oil extraction in Nigeria and the Gulf of Guinea. In 2006, the Movement for the Emancipation of the Niger Delta (MEND) announced it was responsible for the kidnapping of four oil executives in Nigeria (Hanson, 2007). This was the beginning of an insurgency that has continued, with varying levels of intensity, until today. Throughout this period, the insurgents have conducted attacks on oil company personnel and facilities. In addition to the insurgent attacks, there have been regular criminal attacks in the form of kidnapping, oil "bunkering," and pipeline ruptures. The Nigerian government has made repeated efforts against the insurgents and criminals but for a variety of reasons has been unable to provide effective security for the oil industry. Private security companies have filled the gap by providing security for facilities and personnel both onshore and offshore. Despite the companies' best efforts, MEND has conducted successful attacks as far as 64 km offshore. The global oil market has responded to the repeated attacks with brief price spikes until it is reassured that Nigeria's light sweet crude will continue to flow (O'Neill, 2007). It is the presence of the PMCs that insure the oil workers are protected and thus production continues. Without the PMCs, Nigeria's export of over two million barrels per day (CIA WFB, n.d.) would be problematic at best. Thus the entire globe's economy benefits from their presence. While PMCs have clearly usurped Nigeria's monopoly on violence, they have also insured the continued flow of oil revenue to the government.

PMCs provide similar security services to a full spectrum of customers in a wide range of countries. For instance, in the last year, piracy has declined by 65 percent off the coast of Somalia. Two factors seemed to drive the decline—increased operations by international naval forces and the addition of armed contractors and anti-boarding measures to commercial ships (Smith and Chonghaile, 2012). In another example of crime moving to more favorable conditions, we have seen a rise in attacks on shipping in the Gulf of Guinea even as piracy dropped precipitously off Somalia (ICC CCM, 2012). When costs rise enough, shipping companies will make arrangements for armed security off of this coast too.

However, PMCs' efforts against piracy have also created problems. In 2010, Sterling Corporate Services, a private security company, obtained funding from the United Arab Emirates to develop the Puntland Maritime Police Force. Sterling was to recruit, equip and train a force of 1,000 men to combat the pirates operating out of Puntland. Unfortunately, after forming, arming and partially training the force, Sterling withdrew its trainers. No other contractors were willing to take on the project. This left the trainees unpaid and unsupported but well-armed in Puntland (Mazzetti and Schmitt, 2012). In its fragile condition as an emerging state, Puntland did not need more well-armed but unemployed men dumped inside its boundaries.

The complexity of the relationships between states, companies, charities, and armed contractors defies drawing simple conclusions. In some cases, state's control has been increased by the presence of contractors even as the state's legitimacy has been reduced. Similarly, by protecting the delivery of aid, contractors have assisted the development of the state. In at least the case of Abu Dhabi, contractors signed on as the ultimate protection of the ruling family. While the protection of resource extraction has often undercut local authority and legitimacy, it has added to global stability by reducing the cost and uncertainty in the supply of critical resources. Armed contractors' impact on sovereignty and stability is clearly mixed with effects tied directly to the local political, economic and social conditions.

Information and robotics

The marriage of robotics and information technology is going to have massive impacts across societies. Inevitably, these changes will impact states in different ways. Information systems have, and will continue to, vastly increase the government's ability to track individuals or groups—and thus reinforce a state's security infrastructure. At the same time, they will increase the ability of non-state groups to gather information on individuals, organizations and governments for their own purposes. When married with robotics (drones), information systems have allowed governments to conduct precision strikes at long ranges. They will soon provide non-state actors the same capabilities. This will allow smart small groups or individuals to challenge state authority even as the state's ability to monitor the masses of its people increases. Robotics and information technology will combine with advances in nanotechnology and biology to reinforce the decades-long trend of providing much greater potential power to smaller and smaller political entities.

However, the biggest impact of information married to robotics will be their disruptive effect on the labor market with downstream impacts on societies as a whole. As always, periods of great economic change will produce winners and losers. Some of the losers will be angry or desperate enough to turn to violence. They will be aided in doing so by the same technologies that took their jobs.

State surveillance

It is clear that modern information systems allow governments to know more about their citizens than any time in history. For instance, London is known as a city with intense surveillance video coverage. Some of it is government installed and controlled but most of it is not. For the government's part, every vehicle entering the congested zone in London is noted and recorded so its owner can be billed the congestion fee. While the intent of gathering this information is for traffic control and revenue, obviously it provides a wealth of information on the movement of people and vehicles around the city. The government also maintains closed circuit TV coverage of many high crime or trouble spots in the community.

Yet these cameras represent only a fraction of the video systems blanketing London. Many public spaces, transport systems and local businesses use video cameras for their own security. More and more of these are tied to the Internet and thus their feeds can be compiled and searched to track the movement of individuals.

As early as 1999, when BBC reporter Jill Dando was murdered on her doorstep, investigators were able to manually compile and edit video footage from security cameras along her route of movement. They succeeded in tracing every step of her day up to the point she stepped out of sight in the alcove of her front door and was murdered. The videos used were not intended for tracking individuals moving through the city but rather to protect specific locations. But the police were able to tie those static locations together into a continuous coverage of her movements, indoors and out, across the city through the day of her murder.

While this was revolutionary and labor intensive in 1999, subsequent developments in digital video technology, Internet connectivity, optical recognition technology and the explosion in the number of cameras makes the task much easier today. Police are employing license plate recognition technology, and enforcement and traffic monitoring videos at an ever increasing rate. Toll bridge and tunnel cameras provide a record of every vehicle that passes—often with enough clarity to identify at least some of its occupants. As remarkable as this coverage is, it represents only a fraction of the coverage provided by commercial surveillance and security systems.

It is widely known that using drones police and intelligence agencies can track a targeted individual. As anyone who has watched *Law and Order* knows, police can even track a person in real time via the electronics he or she uses— such as cell phone, automobile, etc. They can often even recreate an individual's movements after the fact by requesting digital records. What will be different in the future is that a combination of massive increases in computing power, face recognition and ubiquitous video surveillance will allow police not only to trace a person after the fact but to acquire and track that person in real time as he or she moves about the city. Intelligence programs will be able to tie together the digital information collected by the entire range of government and business systems—surveillance, point of sale, bank card withdrawals, traffic cameras and so on. Clearly, information technology is rapidly increasing the power of the state to track its citizens.

Robotics will further increase such power. From self-driving vehicles to insect-sized mobile surveillance devices, these systems will feed enormous amounts of data to government agencies. Some will be designed specifically to follow individuals without being detected. Others will provide continuous surveillance of a location for days, weeks, and possibly months, at a time. As we have seen with the massive increase in data available from surveillance systems in Iraq and Afghanistan, the key issue for intelligence and police agencies will be sorting through the masses of data to find the information needed. As we also saw in Iraq and Afghanistan, the ability to track an insurgent remotely allows the security forces to follow foot soldiers back to their leaders or bomb factories and thus roll up the network. What will be new is the ability to track and kill, or even capture, a single individual remotely without causing any collateral damage.

Non-state use of technology

At the same time, robotics will enhance the ability of small groups and even individuals to gather information and conduct attacks. As early as 2003, a hobbyist created a drone that auto-piloted itself across the Atlantic to a point where it was captured by a ground controller at the assigned rendezvous and guided to a landing (Wicks, n.d.). In 2012, university students used additive manufacturing to "print" a drone (Senese, 2012). The autopilot that took the 2003 drone across the ocean could be combined with accurate GPS technology to deliver a cheap, printed drone to a specific target. While intercontinental ranges are still difficult, short range drones created with additive manufacturing are a relatively inexpensive reality.

At the same time, nanotechnology is increasing the power of explosives. Soon they will be an order of magnitude more powerful than TNT. This can drive two paths of development. First, it will make conventional warheads more destructive. Second, it can make truly miniature warheads deadly:

> Illinois University Prof D. Scott Stewart is postulating how to scale weapon systems down by a factor of 100 to 1000 which would essentially become micro attack devices. These new weapons will be cheaper due to their size and amount of material used. The affordability and capability of such weapons will ensure their proliferation and worldwide availability.
>
> Small enhanced explosive systems will be more easily hidden than traditional explosives. Adversaries will take advantage of their size, lethality and portability. Enhanced concealment will pose a significant challenge to militaries and law enforcement. There is no limit to the creative ways of disguising nEM explosive charges. Another second order effect of smaller more lethal weapons is shrinking delivery vehicles. Smaller warheads require less support structure. These smaller structures will contain nano alloys for enhanced characteristics yielding lighter mass and less volume. Smaller structures and lighter warheads require less propellant to get to the intended target. MICs will have a radical effect on rocket and gun propellants.
>
> (Yarbrough II, 2010: 9–10)

By combining robotics (drone), information (GPS and flight controls), nano-explosives, and a self-forging projectile, it will be possible to create precision weapons with devastating power. Worse, it will be possible for a non-state actor to make lots of them. With the addition of optical recognition technology, such weapons could literally hunt mobile targets such as armored vehicles, ships, or aircraft taxiing from shelters to runways. The absence of metal and very small heat signature of such weapons will make them difficult to detect and defeat. The very long loiter times will enhance their ability to attack even fleeting targets.

The rapid advance in each of these fields will converge to make a reality of the swarm concept predicted by Professor John Arquilla. Of more concern, the swarm capability will not be limited to nation states. As a technology becomes more widely used, it inevitably becomes cheaper and easier for anyone to obtain. Even more alarming, the radical reduction of cost in additive manufacturing technology means hobby printers now sell for under $1,000 while laser sintering systems are now under $10,000. The range and quality of products hobbyists can make is increasing exponentially. Innovators have already learned to 3D print a handgun (Coldewey, 2012). More sophisticated weapons will quickly follow along with widespread dissemination of the technology.

The marriage of information systems and robotics will revolutionize the intelligence and military capabilities of both state and non-state actors. But it is in the arena of industry that the combination will have the greatest impact.

Robotics and information as destabilizers

The primary destabilizing impact of robotics will be the destruction of jobs. In March 2013, the *Washington Post* reported "A wave of new robots, affordable and capable of accomplishing advanced human tasks, is being aimed at jobs that are high in the work force hierarchy" (Kang, 2013: 1). Although information systems and robots have been filling jobs for decades, combining artificial intelligence with robotics is deepening the penetration of the labor market. In the recent past, information systems plus robots greatly reduced the number of people needed to run businesses by replacing bank tellers, grocery checkouts, fuel station attendants, receptionists and factory workers. Today companies are letting smart systems handle the back office tasks that as little as a decade ago were being off-shored to India and other low cost locations. While the tasks are returning to Western high tech companies, the jobs are not. A January 2013 report in *The Economist* noted "One telecoms company … replaced 45 offshore employees, costing a total of $1.35m a year, with ten of Blue Prism's software robots, costing $100,000." More recently, smart systems started moving into the fields of radiology, accounting, oncology, and stock trading.

This trend is accelerating. The marriage of information systems with flexible robotic systems is going to rapidly replace a wide range of workers. Many of these jobs will be in fields previously beyond robot capabilities. Today robots are cooking, maintaining wind turbines, stocking warehouses and grocery shelves, and wrapping and shipping fragile items. At the same time, they are replacing more manufacturing workers—even in low wage countries. In August 2011, Taiwan-based Foxconn, the world's largest maker of computer components, announced its intention to replace 500,000 mainland Chinese workers with 1,000,000 intelligent robots over the next three years (Cap Falcon, 2011). Follow on reports indicated it had started the process and received 30,000 robots by November 2012. Robot prices are dropping sharply, with the Foxconn robots reported to be only $25,000–$30,000 each (Musil, 2012). According to the International Federation of Robotics, mainland China increased the number of robots in use by 42 percent during 2011 alone (Nan and Yanrong, 2012). While the concept of dark factories replacing manufacturing jobs has been developing for years, robots are now replacing workers more rapidly and in a much wider range of jobs. The job replacement is not limited to factories or warehouses. Robots are now capable of harvesting fruit and even tending crops (Fletcher, 2012).

The marriage of robotics and computer power will mean much higher productivity for companies and the creation of new jobs requiring more education or skills. At the same time, it will mean the massive destruction of jobs ranging from low to high skill. High skill workers may have the resources and education to retrain themselves for a different career. Unfortunately, low skill or poorly educated laborers will have fewer resources to retrain for high skill jobs even as more and more low skill jobs are automated. Increasing the pressure on all workers is the fact that this revolution in robotics is taking place just as the youth bulge is reaching maturity in many underdeveloped nations.

The volatility of the youth bulge will be aggravated by the decades-long revolution in sex selection. While long noted in China and India, the problem is emerging in other nations as sex selection procedures become widespread and less expensive. The planet-wide natural ratio of female to male babies is 105 males for every 100 females. Modern medical science has altered that ratio dramatically in some nations. In March 2011, the *Canadian Medical Association Journal* noted:

> with the advent of ultrasounds that enable sex-selection, the sex ratio at birth in some cities in South Korea climbed to 125 by 1992 and is over 130 in several Chinese provinces from Henan in the north to Hainan in the south.
>
> In 2005 in China, "it was estimated that 1.1 million excess males were born across the country and that the number of males under the age of 20 years exceeded the number of females by around 32 million," writes Professor Therese Hesketh, UCL Centre for International Health and Development, London, United Kingdom with coauthors.
>
> In India, similar disparities exist, with sex ratios as high as 125 in Punjab, Delhi and Gujarat in the north.
>
> (*Science Daily*, 2011)

The simultaneous pressure of fewer jobs and little prospect for marriage will create a situation ripe for instability. Two of the states most challenged—India and China—are already struggling with the issue of creating jobs for current cohorts coming of age. While China's 15–29-year-old population has started to decline (*The Economist*, 2012), China still has a massive unemployment and underemployment issue. India's working population will continue to grow for at least a decade. While today's Indian leaders are counting on the youth bulge to provide a competitive advantage for Indian industry, the rapid advent of intelligent robotic systems may well turn that to a disadvantage.

Clearly, one of the key challenges for all nations will be to manage the impact of improved robotics on their work forces. The revolution will create a large number of new jobs, but most will require well-educated people who are comfortable with technology. Unfortunately, the combination of rising expectations, fewer opportunities for employment, and reduced probability of marriage will be concentrated in those countries with the fewest resources available to assist its people in transitioning to the new economy.

Convergence of trends

The convergence of trends will be a cause for instability, while simultaneously improving the state's security capabilities, as well as potential insurgents'/terrorists' disruptive capability. Smart robots tied to information and surveillance systems will obviously be a major benefit to police departments trying to monitor illegal activity in their jurisdictions. However, these systems are already generating resistance from civil liberty groups who are concerned with the ability of such systems to accumulate huge amounts of information on citizens who have committed no crimes. They note that, in the past, governments have often used such information to control populations. Criminal organizations face no such resistance to their acquisition and the use of smart robotics, surveillance and information systems. In addition to keeping track of police activity, such systems may allow criminal or intelligence organizations to accumulate damaging information on key government officials and use that to influence their activities.

For the same reasons Foxconn is purchasing robots to replace laborers, PMCs will purchase robots and surveillance systems to replace people. As the basic security jobs are covered by robots, such companies will allow resource rich but technologically challenged governments to accrue all the control benefits of the advanced technologies. This will include remote targeted killing.

One of the more disturbing possibilities is the destructive power that a combination of emerging technologies will make available to non-state actors. Hobbyists are using desktop printers to produce cheap drones. More advanced private researchers built a drone that crossed the ocean autonomously. It used only about 1.5 gallons of fuel for power and an inexpensive GPS system to navigate. This provides a clear path to creating relatively cheap drones that can fly to a specified point—in essence a poor man's precision weapon. Iraqi insurgents showed the power of IEDs using self-forging projectiles. If one combines these capabilities, one can build relatively cheap but powerful (remember the images of armored vehicles hit by a self-forging projectile) smart weapons. The combination of small size, absence of metal, and little heat signature will make such drones difficult to acquire and destroy despite the fact they can defeat armored vehicles. The rapid advance in both digital imagery and target recognition software means these systems could be adapted to attack mobile targets too. Finally, research into nano-explosives is steadily improving the power of weapons. Thus smaller vehicles will be able to deliver higher levels of destruction.

Summary

This chapter has focused on the impact of criminal armies, armed contractors and emerging technologies on both state sovereignty and international stability.

Criminal armies

While criminal enterprises will continue to raise and support criminal armies to protect their activities, they will not take over states. Their pattern has been to seize as much control over a specific territory as necessary to protect their businesses and persons from the government and competitors. A state may develop the political will to overcome internal corruption; historically, governments have repeatedly demonstrated the capability to drive criminal enterprises either under-ground or out of their territory. Criminal cartels are fundamentally businesses and will seek areas with lower costs to maximize their profits. While individual criminals may fight—and often die or be imprisoned—to protect a specific place, most cartels will simply move when the pressure becomes too intense. Those governments that are corrupt will receive support from the cartels. Both the cartels and government officials will exploit the wealth generated by the combi-nation of illicit trade and government power. In these cases, the lack of legiti-macy and security will reduce economic growth and make the states vulnerable to genuine insurgencies.

Private military companies

For decades, armed contractors have compensated for the lack of government security available to the extraction industry and NGOs/IGOs. In the last decade, full-fledged PMCs have filled gaps in government capabilities in war zones. In the last few years, they have also protected shipping in pirate infested waters. While their very presence may undercut the legitimacy of a single state by aug-menting government capabilities and replacing them, many PMCs are providing support both for individual states and the international order.

At the same time, contractors, such as Viktor Bout before his arrest, provide support to state or non-state actors—essentially anyone who can pay. Everything from functioning air forces to logistics to cyber attacks have been and will con-tinue to be available. In some cases, these contractors will reinforce a state's capability. In others, they will directly challenge it. If current trends continue, the role of armed contractors will continue to expand while the impact on inter-national stability will be mixed. For democracies, one impact of contractors is to reduce the political capital necessary to commit forces to war; potentially redu-cing the legitimacy and perceived morality of the war effort. This is particularly damaging in protracted conflicts.

Converging technologies

The convergence of information, robotics, nanotechnology and additive manu-facturing will provide robots with exceptional capabilities across the range of economic and military activities. The low cost of such systems will provide unheard of power to smaller and smaller organizations. At same time, these tech-nologies will vastly increase the ability of the state to track, control and, if neces-sary, attack its opponents and its citizens. A key variable that will determine the outcome of the struggle between emerging non-state actors and states is the form of government of the state involved. Totalitarian states will feel free to use the full power of the new technologies against its citizens. While daily control will increase, it will also be more brittle. Any form of organized insurgency or revolution will become more difficult—as long as the security services stay loyal to the state. However, as we saw in the Arab Spring, if security services choose not to support the state, the technology will allow for rapid organization of insurgencies and perhaps the rapid downfall of the state. Unfortunately, as we have also seen in the Middle East, it will not ease the process of developing a legitimate government to fill the vacuum created.

For their parts, democratic states will have to carefully balance the perceived need for security against the people's demand for privacy. It is essential that governments get this balance right. While increased surveillance and intelligence will initially provide more security, in the long run it may undercut the state's legitimacy. If the people feel the state is intruding into areas it does not belong, they will remove the administration from office.

In short, like major technological advances throughout history, the increasingly rapid technological change will interact with the political, economic and social structures of each society. For good or bad, populations will learn by trial and error how to deal with these simultaneous technological advances.

References

BBC News (2012) "Q&A: Mexico's Drug Related Violence." December 24. Online, available at: www.bbc.co.uk/news/world-latin-america-10681249 (accessed February 11, 2013).

Biller, D. and Petroff, K. (2012) "In Brazil's Favelas, a Middle Class Arises." *Business Week.* December 20. Online, available at: www.businessweek.com/articles/2012–12–20/in-brazils-favelas-a-middle-class-arises (accessed February 13, 2013).

Bunker, R. and Sullivan, J. (2010) "Cartel Evolution Revisited: Third Phase Cartel Potentials and Alternative Future for Mexico." *Small Wars and Insurgencies.* March, Vol. 22. No. 1: 30–54.

Cap Falcon (2011) "Workforce: Foxconn to Replace 500,000 Workers by 1,000,000 Robots over the Next 3 Years." November 8. Online, available at: www.capfalcon. net/2011/11/08/workforce-foxcon-to-replace-500000-workers-by1000000-robots-over-the-next-5-years/ (accessed February 7, 2013).

Carter, MajGen. N. (2010) "Defense Department Briefing via Teleconference from Afghanistan." May 26.

CBO (Congressional Budget Office) (2008) "Contractors' Support of US Operations in Iraq." Table 2. Washington, DC. Online, available at: www.cbo.gov/ftpdocs/96xx/doc9688/MainText.3.1.shtml (accessed February 12, 2013).

CIA WFB (Worldfactbook) (n.d.) "Nigeria." Online, available at: www.cia.gov/library/publications/the-world-factbook/geos/ni.html (accessed February 17, 2013).

Coldewey, D. (2012) "3-D Printed Gun Fires 6 Shots—Then Falls Apart." *NBC News.* December 3. Online, available at: www.nbcnews.com/technology/futureoftech/3-d-printed-gun-fires-6-shots-then-falls-apart-1C7404226#/technology/futureoftech/3-d-printed-gun-fires-6-shots-then-falls-apart-1C7404226 (accessed March 1, 2013).

COW (Correlates of War) (n.d.) Online, available at: http://correlatesofwar.org (accessed February 15, 2013).

CPB (Canadian Press-Broadcast) Wire (2010) "Afghan-Cda Security Firms." January 25, 06:42. Document BNW0000020100126e61p00011.

Fabres, R. (2013) "Pacifying the Favelas of Rio de Janeiro." *Time.* January 30. Online, available at: http://lightbox.time.com/2013/01/30/pacifying-the-favelas-of-rio-de-janeiro/#1 (accessed February 12, 2013).

Fainaru, S. (2007) "Private War: Convoy to Darkness." *Washington Post*. July 29: 1+.

Felbab-Brown, V. (2011) "Bringing the State to the Slum: Confronting Organized Crime and Urban Violence in Latin America." Washington, DC: Brookings. December. Online, available at: www.brookings.edu/research/papers/2011/12/05-latin-america-slums-felbabbrown (accessed February 13, 2013).

Filkins, D. (2010) "With US Aid, Warlord Builds Afghan Empire." *New York Times*. June 6. Online, available at: www.nytimes.com/2010/06/06/world/asia/06warlords.html (accessed June 7, 2010).

Fletcher, O. (2012). "Agricultural Robots Face the Next Frontier: Harvest." *Wall Street Journal*. October 11. Online, available at: http://online.wsj.com/article/SB1000087239 6390444273704577637461944396668.html (accessed February 7, 2013).

Forsberg, C. and Kagan, K. (2010) "Consolidating Private Security Companies in South Afghanistan." Institute for the Study of War. May 28. Online, available at: www.understandingwar.org/files/BackgrounderPSC.pdf (accessed June 4, 2010).

Hanson, S. (2007) "MEND: the Niger Delta's Umbrella Guerrilla Group." Council of Foreign Relations Backgrounder Paper. March 22. Online, available at: www.cfr.org/nigeria/mend-niger-deltas-umbrella-militant-group/p12920 (accessed February 18, 2013).

iCasualties (n.d.) "Iraq Coalition Casualty Count." Online, available at: http://icasualties.org (accessed December 29, 2009).

ICC CCM (Commercial Crime Services) (2012) "IMB Reports Drop in Somali Piracy, but Warns against Complacency." October 22. Online, available at: www.icc-ccs.org/news/811-imb-reports-drop-in-somali-piracy-but-warns-against-complacency (accessed February 15, 2013).

Johnson, K. and Gomez, A. (2013) "Mexico's Commerce Crawls Back from Drug Wars Chaos." *USA Today*. February 6. Online, available at: www.usatoday.com/story/news/world/2013/02/05/mexico-drug-war-bloodbath-is-receding/1894933/ (accessed February 19, 2013).

Kan, P., Bechtel, Jr., B. and Collins, R. (2010) *Criminal Sovereignty: Understanding North Korea's Illicit International Activities*. Carlisle: US Army War College, Strategic Studies Institute. March. Online, available at: www.strategicstudiesinstitute.army.mil/pdffiles/pub975.pdf (accessed February 28, 2013).

Kang, C. (2013) "Job Creators—or Terminators?" *Washington Post*. March 7: 1+.

Logan, S. (2009) "Los Zetas: Evolution of a Criminal Organization." *ISN: International Relations and Security Network*. March 11. Online, available at: www.isn.ethz.ch/Digital-Library/Articles/Detail//?lng=en&id=97554 (accessed February 19, 2013).

Mazzetti, M. and Schmitt, E. (2012) "Private Army Formed to Fight Somali Pirates Leaves Troubled Legacy." *New York Times*. October 4. Online, available at: www.nytimes.com/2012/10/05/world/africa/private-army-leaves-troubled-legacy-in-somalia.html?pagewanted=all&_r=0 (accessed February 21, 2013).

Memmott, M. (2011) "In El Salvador: Gang Leaders Who Say They're Social Workers." June 2. Online, available at: www.npr.org/blogs/thetwo-way/2011/06/02/136858037/in-el-salvador-gang-leaders-who-believe-theyre-social-workers (accessed February 17, 2013).

Miroff, N. (2011) "Grim Toll as Cocaine Trade Expands in Honduras." *Washington Post*. December 26. Online, available at: www.washingtonpost.com/world/americas/grim-toll-as-cocaine-trade-expands-in-honduras/2011/11/08/gIQAYVvOJP_story.html (accessed February 19, 2013).

Musil, S. (2012) "Foxconn Reportedly Installing Robots to Replace Workers." November 13. Online, available at: http://news.cnet.com/8301-1001_3-57549450-92/foxconn-reportedly-installing-robots-to-replace-workers/ (accessed February 7, 2013).

Nan, Z. and Yanrong, Z. (2012) "The Rise of the Robots." *China Daily*. October 5. Online, available at: http://usa.chinadaily.com.cn/weekly/2012-10/05/content_15797110.htm (accessed February 8, 2013).

O'Neill, T. (2007) "Curse of the Black Gold: Hope and Betrayal on the Niger Delta." *National Geographic Magazine*. February. Online, available at: http://ngm.national geographic.com/2007/02/nigerian-oil/oneill-text/1 (accessed February 17, 2013).

Paul, C., Schaefer, A. and Clark, C. (2011) *The Challenge of Violent Drug Trafficking Organizations*. Santa Monica: Rand Corporation. February. Online, available at: www.rand.org/content/dam/rand/pubs/monographs/2011/RAND_MG1125.pdf (accessed February 17, 2013).

Peter, T. (2010) "Mexico Denies Hillary Clinton's 'Insurgency' Comparison." *Christian Science Monitor*. September 9. Online, available at: www.csmonitor.com/World/terrorism-security/2010/0909/Mexico-denies-Hillary-Clinton-s-insurgency-comparison (accessed February 17, 2013).

ProPublica (n.d.) "Disposable Army: Civilian Contractors in Iraq and Afghanistan." September 9. Online, available at: www.propublica.org/series/disposable-army (accessed December 29, 2009.

Reuters (2011) "UAE Prince Hires Blackwater Founder to Set up Foreign Security Force." *Washington Post*. May 15. Online, available at: http://articles.washingtonpost.com/2011-05-15/world/35232758_1_foreign-troops-uae-blackwater-guard (accessed February 18, 2013).

Roebuck, J. (2009) "Drug Cartels 100,000 Strong, Senator Says." March 6. Online, available at: www.cornyn.senate.gov/public/index.cfm?p=InNews&ContentRecord%09_id=ecfee62c-802a-23ad-4b53-f051f6d9a1df&ContentType_id=f6c645c7-%099e4a-4947-8464-a94cacb4ca65&Group_id=bf378025–1557-49c1-8f08-%09c5df1c4313a4&MonthDisplay=3&YearDisplay=2009, (accessed February 13, 2013).

Schwartz, M. (2010) "Department of Defense Contractors in Iraq and Afghanistan: Background and Analysis." July 2. Online, available at: http://fpc.state.gov/documents/organization/145569.pdf (accessed February 13, 2013).

Science Daily (2011) "The Impact of Sex Selection and Abortion in China, India and South Korea." March 15. Online, available at: www.sciencedaily.com/releases/2011/03/110314132244.htm (accessed February 17, 2013).

Senese, M. (2012) "Want a Flying Drone? These Students Printed Their Own." November 28. Online, available at: www.wired.com/design/2012/11/3d-printed-autonomous-airplane/ (accessed February 7, 2013).

Singer, P. (2007) "The Dark Truth about Blackwater." *Salon*. October 2. Online, available at: www.salon.com/news/feature/2007/10/02/blackwater/print.html (accessed January 29, 2013).

Smith, D. and Chonghaile, V. (2012) "Somali Pirates Hijacking Fewer Merchant Ships." *Guardian*. October 25. Online, available at: www.guardian.co.uk/world/2012/oct/23/somali-piracy-declines (accessed February 17, 2013).

Snow, G. (2011) "Statement before the House Financial Services Committee, Subcommittee on Financial Institutions and Consumer Credit." September 14. Online, available at: www.fbi.gov/news/testimony/cyber-security-threats-to-the-financial-sector (accessed February 18, 2013).

Sullivan, J. (2012) "From Drug Wars to Criminal Insurgency, Vortex Working Paper No. 6." Bogota: Vortex Foundation. March. Online, available at: www.scivortex.org/6From DrugWarsCriminalInsurgency.pdf (accessed July 11, 2013).

The Economist (2012) "China's Labour Force: One Billion Workers." January 23. Online, available at: www.economist.com/blogs/freeexchange/2012/01/chinas-labour-force (accessed February 18, 2013).

The Economist (2013a) "Rise of the Software Machines." January 19. Online, available at: www.economist.com/news/special-report/21569573-attractions-employing-robots-rise-software-machines (accessed February 7, 2013).

The Economist (2013b) "Central America: Out of Control." March 9. Online, available at: www.economist.com/news/americas/21573108-first-two-reports-threat-rampant-violence-central-americas-small (accessed July 11, 2013).

UNODC (United Nations Office on Drugs and Crime) (2011) *Estimating Illicit Financial Flows Resulting from Drug Trafficking and other Transnational Organized Crimes.* Research report. Online, available at: www.unodc.org/documents/data-and-analysis/Studies/Illicit_financial_flows_2011_web.pdf (accessed February 7, 2013).

Weinman, G. (2006) *Terror on the Internet: The New Arena, the New Challenges.* Washington, DC: US Institute of Peace Press.

Wicks, F. (n.d.) "Legend Pilots a Radio-controlled Model Airplane across the Atlantic Ocean." *Progressive Engineer.* Online, available at: www.progressiveengineer.com/profiles/maynardHill.htm (accessed February 14, 2013).

Yarbrough II, A. (2010) "The Impact of Nanotechnology Energetics on the Department of Defense by 2035." *Air War College.* Online, available at: www.au.af.mil/au/awc/awcgate/cst/bh2010_yarbrough.pdf (accessed February 28, 2013).

Part II

Criminal and sovereign free change and conflict

5 The reconfiguring of institutions by illicit networks in Colombia, Guatemala and Mexico

Luis Jorge Garay Salamanca and
Eduardo Salcedo-Albarán

Current illicit networks across the western hemisphere involve both private and public, lawful and unlawful agents participating in diverse social interactions, ranging from traditional methods of corruption such as bribery to sophisticated forms of political agreements. As a result, formal institutions are infiltrated, manipulated and sometimes modified through co-optation established by agents operating inside and outside the state. In the present chapter, SNA is applied in order to model and understand cases of criminal infiltration, co-optation and institutional reconfiguration in Colombia, Guatemala and Mexico.

The present document consists of seven sections. In the first, the concepts of StC and co-opted states' reconfiguration are discussed, as well as methodological elements regarding social networks analysis. In the second, third, and fourth sections, some cases of institutional reconfiguration in Colombia, Guatemala and Mexico are discussed. In the fifth section, a comparative analysis is presented, as a preamble for conclusions in the final section.

Traditional state capture and co-opted state reconfiguration

In the framework of public policy, corruption has been usually defined as the abuse of public function to obtain private and exclusive benefits (World Bank, 1997). Analyses regarding corruption have mainly focused on bribery and the interaction between public and private individuals pursuing economic interests. However, across the western hemisphere, Africa and Eastern Europe, the intervention of criminal and even violent groups using coercive means to replace or complement bribery are features justifying the qualifiers of what in Colombia is defined as "violent corruption" (Mockus, 2008), "armed corruption" (Flores, 2008), or "narco-corruption" (Cepeda, 1997). In this sense, the participation of drug traffickers and other unlawful organizations is a distinctive feature of emerging types of corruption with implications for security and global criminal trends.

Studies on StC carried out in the late 1990s in countries of Eastern Europe during their transition to a market economy, focused attention on bribery by economic groups to influence legislative processes, resulting in tax or administrative benefits (Pesic, 2007). Even though those countries exhibited strong mafia activity, encompassing prostitution and trafficking of nuclear weapons amongst others, studies of corruption and StC for that period and region do not consider the action of unlawful and violent agents: "the connections between international criminal organizations, and between them and their host governments, in the post-Cold War period remain poorly understood" (Greenhill, 2009: 96).

A distinctive feature of the traditional analysis on StC consists of omitting the intervention of unlawful groups and methods of coercion complementing and sometimes substituting for bribery. Therefore, StC is usually defined as the intervention of the private sector (Olsen *et al.*, 2010) in the drafting of laws, decrees, regulations and public policies, to obtain long-lasting benefits, mainly of an economic nature, usually through bribery (Hellman and Kaufmann, 2001, 2000; Hellman *et al.*, 2000).

In a situation of StC, social interactions are usually established in one direction: from agents outside the state towards agents inside the state. This means lawful agents outside the state, such as firms and economic groups, manipulate legislative and regulatory institutions. In other cases, when unlawful agents intervene in the process, situations of StC and also of advanced stage StC (AStC) can be configured and social interactions established from unlawful toward lawful agents. Both cases are strictly in line with the literal sense of "State Capture" as a process originating outside the state, carried out by an external agent or group capturing officials or formal institutions.

On the other hand, a subsequent process, CStR, happens when it is observed that: (i) there is participation of lawful and/or unlawful groups; (ii) the benefits sought are not only economic but also judicial, political and those related to social legitimacy; (iii) the use of coercive methods and/or political alliances complement or substitute for bribery; and (iv) the sphere of influence takes place in different branches of public power and at different levels of public administration.

Therefore, considering those characteristics, CStR is defined as:

> The action of lawful and unlawful organizations, which through unlawful practices seek to systematically modify from inside the political regime and to influence the drafting, modification, interpretation, and application of the rules of the game and public policies. These practices are undertaken with the purpose of obtaining sustained benefits and ensuring that their interests are validated politically and legally, as well as gaining social legitimacy in the long run, although these interests do not follow the founding principle of social welfare.
>
> (Garay and Salcedo-Albarán, 2012a: 179)

The definition of "co-opted reconfiguration" implies that co-optation happens in any direction, for instance when lawful agents—candidates or officials—co-opt unlawful agents—paramilitary or subversive groups—and vice versa. In a CStR situation the legal and illegal interests are coordinated. In this sense, the co-opted reconfiguration of a state must be carried out through officials that are co-opting or being co-opted. Coordination of interests is sometimes also observed as an inter-corporative co-optation (Burt *et al.*, 1980).

The concept of CStR allows the understanding that individuals inside and outside the state can establish different social interactions that "in our new so-called flattened world, ... provide Transnational Criminal Organizations with novel economic and political opportunities to exploit as well as with a prominence that allows them to threaten both national and international security in myriad ways" (Greenhill, 2009: 97).

The market of institutional functions

In a CStR situation, agents inside and outside of the state cooperate to fulfill their interests. Therefore, a CStR process is initiated by *agents inside of the state* (AiS), or *agents outside of the state* (AoS). Any AiS or AoS can have the initiative for co-opting and it does not matter if they are public or private. When this coordination happens, a self-stabilizing process is established, promoted and reproduced at the institutional nucleus of the state.

The coordination of interests is the first step in a CStR process: co-optation happens because AiS or AoS realize that they need each other to accomplish their interests. This mutual collaboration applies for each agent "using" the institutional capacities provided by *the other* agent, whether lawful or unlawful, private or public. The capacities provided and needed by each agent consist of a set of institutional functions:

a   AiS (Institutional Capacities$_{A.IS}$) = {Institutional Function$_1$, Institutional Function$_2$, ... Institutional Function$_n$}
b   AoS (Institutional Capacities$_{A.OS}$) = {Institutional Function$_1$, Institutional Function$_2$, ... Institutional Function$_n$}

Each agent has a set of institutional functions to promote or to hinder law enforcement, and these functions may be traded in a market. The first agent recognizing that their own set of institutional capacities is incomplete for realizing their interests, will offer their set of institutional capacities, or some of their institutional functions, in trade for the other agent's institutional set of capacities or functions. If AiS is the first agent realizing their lack of institutional functions, then, *ceteris paribus*, they will be the first agent demanding AoS' institutional capacities or some of the AoS' functions, and vice versa.

In the second stage, after establishing equilibrium of supply and demand in the market of institutional functions, by identifying the price that each agent is willing to pay, a temporary win/win collaboration scenario is proposed and established through an informal contract based on the following conditions:

1   AoS' capacities are useful for the realization of AiS' interests.
2   AiS' capacities are useful for the realization of AoS' interests.

3   Agents involved provide their institutional capacities and functions until the moment when full payment, expressed also in institutional functions provided, is complete. If one of the agents stops paying before completing the payment, even if the demand is fulfilled, the contract is broken and the scenario switches toward a lose/lose situation that consists, mainly, in the filtration of information. Since this scenario is configured for realizing criminal interests, information provided to lawful authorities will configure a lose/lose situation.

Social Network Analysis

The market of institutional functions implies establishing durable social interactions that can be modeled and analyzed as a network in the sense of "a pattern of interconnections among a set of things" (Easley and Kleinberg, 2010: 1). If a situation of CStR is defined as a social network, the following characteristics can be observed: (i) types of agents and interactions; (ii) flows and levels of information; and, therefore, (iii) quality of social capital (Degenne and Forsé, 1999; Wasserman and Faust, 1994; Easley and Kleinberg, 2010).

In the current analysis, each point in a social network, defined as a *node*, represents an agent, which is a unit with moral agency. It uses the concept of node/agent when referencing an agent. On the other hand, each line connecting two nodes, defined as an *edge* or an *arc*, represents a social interaction, while the arrow in the arc shows the direction of that interaction. For instance, in the social interaction "John speaks to Charlie," there is an arrow from the node/agent "John" towards the node/agent "Charlie."

A finite set of *n* nodes connected through arcs or arrows comprises a graph representing social interactions (Degenne and Forsé, 1999: 63). Graphs have been used in social sciences for representing individuals interacting in groups (Degenne and Forsé, 1999; Bornholdt and Schuster, 2003). In criminology, graphs have also been used to identify structural features of illicit networks (Morselli, 2008) and situations of corruption (Baker and Robert, 1993).

It is thereby possible to identify the *central* nodes/agents, which are relevant in a network. Two indicators of centrality are calculated herein to identify (i) the most connected node/agent and (ii) the node/agent concentrating the capacity to arbitrate information. Both are cases of *central* agents/nodes even though such centrality has two different meanings (Everett and Boratti, 2005).

According to the first sense of centrality, the *degree of direct individual centrality* allows the identification of the most connected node/agent (Degenne and Forsé, 1999: 132). Additionally, to find the relative centrality through the degree of individual centrality, it is possible to calculate an *"index of relative or weighted centrality for each node, ... by dividing the absolute degree centrality by the maximal possible centrality ... 0 denotes an isolated node, while 1 designates"* a highly connected node (Degenne and Forsé, 1999: 133). The node with a highest degree of individual centrality within a network is referenced as a *hub*, which represents a privileged position of influence within the network.

The second sense of centrality is based on the concepts of *structural holes* and *structural bridges* (Burt, 1992, 1997, 1998, 2000, 2005). Strong social relationships are a source of social trust (Coleman, 1988); nevertheless, after several interactions, each node/agent can get connected with every other node/agent and the information within the network becomes redundant. When this happens, there is no hub *because each node has the same amount of connections* (Figure 5.1).

In this case, the *degree of direct individual centrality* does not provide information about how relevant a node/agent is; it is therefore necessary to evaluate the capacity to intervene, through the indicator of *betweenness*. This indicator determines if a specific node intermediates among other nodes/agents. The node/agent with the highest indicator of *betweenness*, known as a *structural bridge*, has the highest potential to arbitrate information:

> Such an individual can easily influence the group by withholding and/or distorting information that passes through her hands. She is also in a better position to coordinate information for the entire group. From all of the above, she clearly occupies a central position.
>
> (Degenne and Forsé, 1999: 136)

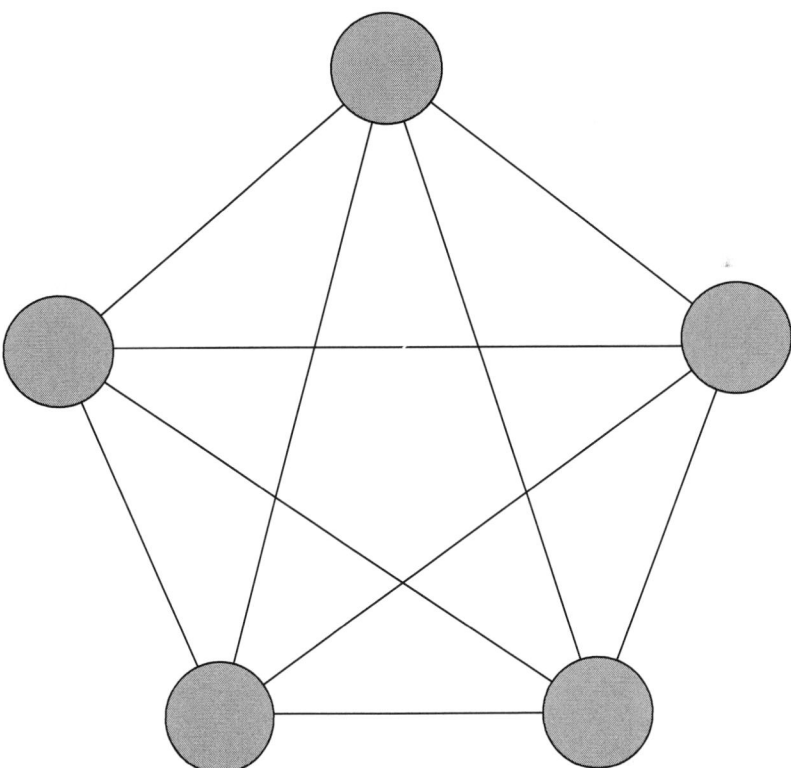

Figure 5.1 A clique.

The structural bridge therefore concentrates information and social capital and, even more important, is able to arbitrate information. This is a powerful node/agent, even if it is not highly connected, because "the greater an individual's actual or potential intermediary value to all members of a network, the greater his control over communication flow and independence of others to communicate" (Degenne and Forsé, 1999: 136). The following figure illustrates a node acting as structural bridge.

Situations of StC and CStR can therefore be analyzed and visualized through SNA, which allows understanding patterns of co-optation and collaboration among lawful and unlawful agents and, therefore, types of impacts on formal institutions. In some cases, CStR has long-term endemic effects on democratic formal institutions due to the manipulation of the rules of the social game, distorting the fundamental pillar of any modern state: the rule of law. For instance, when CStR affects lawmaking, laws consequently lose their required social legitimacy, affecting the rule of law and the basic notion of any modern democratic state.

Considering the tools of SNA and the concept of StC and CStR, cases from Colombia, Guatemala and Mexico are presented below in order to understand different patterns of capture and co-optation between lawful and unlawful, private and public nodes/agents.

Institutional reconfiguration in Colombia

Paramilitary groups were established in Colombia around the region of *Puerto Boyacá* at the beginning of 1980s, apparently with the initial purpose of protecting farmers against kidnappings committed by guerrillas (Romero, 2002, 2006; Duncan, 2005, 2006). Later, some of those paramilitary and self-defense groups were legalized by Colombian legislation also during the 1980s, and defined as "vigilante groups" known as "*Convivir*" (De León-Beltrán and Salcedo-Albarán, 2008; Gutiérrez and Barón, 2007; Romero, 2002; González *et al.*, 2003). In the 1990s as guerrilla activity intensified, a declaration of war against leftist subversive groups became almost generally accepted in Colombia, which

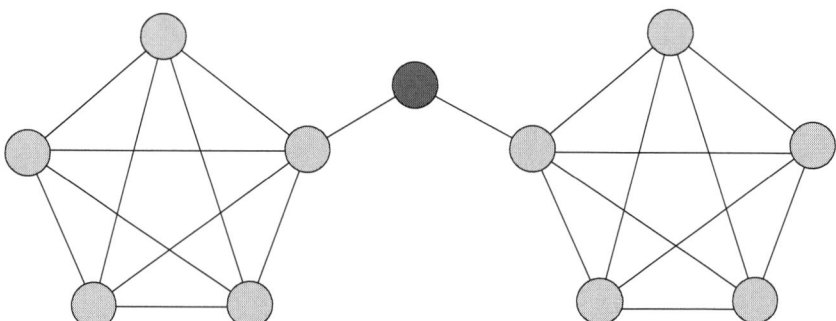

Figure 5.2 Two cliques connected through a single node.

increased the popularity of self-defense and paramilitary groups. Between 1997 and 1998, several paramilitary and self-defense groups were consolidated under an umbrella command known as *Autodefensas Unidas de Colombia* (AUC, United Self Defense Forces of Colombia).

According to testimonies and judicial investigations, during the decades of the 1990s and 2000s, the AUC infiltrated both the executive branch at the local and regional level, and the legislative branch and some other institutions at the national level. Agreements and interactions between paramilitary agents, landlords, entrepreneurs, candidates and public officials, among others, was known in Colombia as "para-politics"—which implied the final purpose of creating a new social order under a new set of rules in Colombia through illegitimate but still "legal" and "formal" democratic procedures. The massive intervention of paramilitary groups in public administration across Colombian municipalities and provinces strengthened criminal activity and worsened situations of corruption that were already present.

The AUC affected the legislative branch at the national level through agreements with candidates who became congressmen during the legislative period 2002–2006. As an additional effect of "para-politics," the AUC and other paramilitary groups infiltrated investigative bodies of the judicial branch—such as the Attorney General's Office at the local level and the National Intelligence Agency[1] at the national level.

Situations of paramilitary infiltration and co-optation were observed in Colombian provinces such as Bolivar, Atlántico, Magdalena, Sucre and Córdoba, with interaction between politicians, paramilitary and private nodes/agents. Those provinces, located at the Colombian Atlantic coast, were analyzed through judicial information resulting from prosecutions against public servants.

In the case of the Atlantic coast network, which consists of 131 nodes/agents and 309 interactions, the hub was the AUC commander Rodrigo Tovar Pupo, aka "Jorge 40," identified in Figure 5.3 (online, available at http://scholarship. claremont.edu/cgu_facbooks/27/) with the code AUCRTP. This node/agent concentrates 11.6 percent of the interactions, which is roughly twice that of the node/agent with the second highest direct centrality indicator: Salvatore Mancuso Gómez, another AUC commander, identified with the code AUCSMG, accounting for 6.6 percent of the connections.

On the other hand, the hub "Jorge 40," AUCRTP, is also the node with highest *betweenness* indicator (Figure 5.4, online, available at http://scholarship. claremont.edu/cgu_facbooks/27/). Salvatore Mancuso, AUCSMG, is the node/ agent with the second highest *betweenness* indicator, which explains why during declarations before Colombian courts Mancuso identified interactions with a great number of mayors and congressmen who benefited from paramilitary groups' support in the elections (*Verdad Abierta*, 2009). In fact, a couple of congressmen organized the visit and allocution of Salvatore Mancuso and other two paramilitary commanders to the Congress of the Republic of Colombia (*Semana*, 2007). Without any doubt, Mancuso was able to intermediate in great many interactions of the network, both with lawful and unlawful agents.

The Atlantic coast network and other regional cases (Garay and Salcedo-Albarán, 2012b; *Semana*, 2010) reveal important characteristics of the narco-paramilitary's operation across Colombia. In its local expressions, a *bottom up* scheme was carried out. Specifically, local political nodes/agents facilitated coordination between lawful and unlawful interests, and were also responsible for (i) allowing the manipulation of decisional local instances, (ii) providing apparent legality in terms of formal democracy, and (iii) allowing the manipulation also of informal institutions, for instance, within civil society. However, in its provincial and national expressions, the hub and the structural bridge is no longer a political agent, but a paramilitary commander. In this sense, the process requires the participation of political agents playing an organizationally lawful role but at the same time an institutionally unlawful role. Therefore, at least in Colombia, it can be expected that gray agents carry out CStR processes developed under the *bottom up scheme*; processes consisting mainly of gray agents operating under some legal rules for electoral and political processes, and dark agents promoting criminal interests and coordinating the process.

Institutional reconfiguration in Guatemala

The present section describes an illicit network focused on massive money laundering in Guatemala consisting of 46 nodes/agents who established 85 social relations.

This illicit network also results from interactions between drug traffickers, Guatemalan public servants and private bankers. The Guatemalan drug trafficker Byron Berganza provided the judicial authorities of the United States information used for elaborating the present network model, which describes the relationships between Jose Armando Llort, former director of a semipublic bank, and the then president of Guatemala, Alfonso Portillo. Berganza provided this information before a court in the United States when he was captured in El Salvador. By that time, Berganza was collaborating with DEA agents in Guatemala and had been captured in El Salvador when performing unreported activities.

When Alfonso Portillo was elected president of Guatemala, he appointed Llort as the president of Banco de Crédito Hipotecario Nacional (CHN), as a result of their close relationship. This appointment was questioned because Llort lacked the experience to assume such a position. However, following the appointment in CHN, Llort took advantage of both his discretional power and the access to privileged information to authorize financial operations aimed at laundering money that, according to the judicial evidence, came from drug trafficking activities. Llort's privileges also included the opportunity to handle the safety keys and codes of the bank vaults, which allowed him to deposit and withdraw large amounts of money in order for it to be laundered through complex financial movements that included foreign currency operations, before returning the monies to their respective owners. Llort also authorized illegal movements, such as overdrafts, for companies owned by his friends and relatives. Salomón Medina Girón, CHN's deputy director, facilitated most of the frauds carried out by Llort,[2] along with Jose Ricardo Rodas, who was the legal representative of several companies, including a money exchange agency that was used to carry out risky financial operations.

According to Berganza, Llort facilitated the laundering of money coming from drug trafficking activities. Berganza also pointed out that Llort not only facilitated the money laundering, but also directly took part in drug trafficking activities. In fact, when DEA agents captured Berganza, he assured them that he was going to meet Llort to arrange a drug trafficking operation. While the consulted judicial information to which we had access does not allow confirmation of such a statement, it is possible to suppose such interactions between Llort and Berganza, since the latter provided to the DEA important detailed information about Llort.

Although President Portillo does not appear in the documents as a direct participant in drug trafficking, his closeness to Llort has made him subject to international accusations of facilitating and allowing money laundering. After being requested for extradition by the Prosecutor's Office of the New York District, the Guatemalan government agreed to move him for trial in the United States, in the midst of threats against the judges in charge (López, 2010). Several family members of former president Portillo also have been investigated for money laundering (*La Nación*, 2010; *El País*, 2010).

After calculating the indicator of *direct centrality*, it was found that three core nodes/agents concentrate the largest percentage of direct interactions (Figure 5.5, online, available at http://scholarship.claremont.edu/cgu_facbooks/27/):

- *Hub*, with the highest indicator of direct centrality: NPBNJAL, Llort, with 15.9 percent out of the total interactions.
- Second highest indicator of direct centrality: ICBB, Byron Berganza, with 9.4 percent out of the total of interactions.
- Third highest indicator of direct centrality: FSFBESAM, with 8.2 percent out of the total of the interactions. This node/agent represents Salomón Abraham Molina, a chief of the International Division of Banco Empresarial SA, who facilitated the execution of international financial operations.

A difference of 6.5 percent is observed between the hub and core node 2, which implies that the *hub* had a high capacity to establish social relations. This is consistent with the fact that Llort would have known people involved in legal as well as illegal activities. The core/node with the fourth highest indicator of *direct centrality*, Alfonso Portillo, FUNPREAP, who interacts with Llort, especially through retired general Luis Francisco Ortega Menaldo, concentrates 4.7 percent out of the total direct relations.

After calculating the betweenness indicator, it was found that NPBNJAL, Llort, is the node/agent with the highest percentage of this indicator: 38.8 percent, which means that he operated as a *structural bridge* in the network and, therefore, as the node/agent with the highest capacity to arbitrate information. In Figure 5.6 (online, available at: http://scholarship.claremont.edu/cgu_facbooks/27/), the nodes' distribution according to the betweenness indicator can be observed: the node/agent with the highest indicator of betweenness is located in the nucleus and this indicator decreases towards the concentric external orbits.

Only 12 nodes/agents have some capacity for arbitrating information. The other nodes/agents, showing a betweenness indicator of 0 (zero), only receive or produce information and, therefore, lack any capacity for arbitration. Below are listed the three nodes/agents with the highest *betweenness* indicators:

- Structural bridge, or node/agent with the highest indicator of *betweenness*: NPBJAL, Jose Armando Llort, intervening in 38.8 percent out of the total of interactions.
- Second highest indicator of *betweenness*: ICBB, trafficker Byron Berganza, intervening in 22.3 percent out of the total of interactions.
- Third highest indicator of *betweenness*: FSFBESAM, Salomón Abraham Molina, chief of the International Division of Banco Empresarial SA, intervening in 14 percent out of the total of interactions.

President Portillo, FUNPREAP, is core node 6, with a betweenness indicator of 3.4 percent. This means that President Portillo intervenes only in 3.4 percent out of the total interactions. In Figure 5.6 (online, available at http://scholarship.claremont. edu/cgu_facbooks/27/), the node/agent FUNPREAP is identified with the color red.

Thanks to Llort's role as a *structural bridge*, drug trafficker Byron Berganza appears to have aligned an important public servant with his interests. The interaction starting in the nucleus begins with Jose Armando Llort, which then passes by PGRLFOM, retired general Luis Francisco Ortega Menaldo, and reaches President Portillo, who relates directly with FSFBESAM, chief of the International Division of Banco Empresarial SA. The interaction between Llort and Berganza is bidirectional, which means that probably Llort knew and was informed about the objectives and interests of drug trafficker ICBB. On the other hand, President Portillo only receives information from Llort, especially through Ortega Menaldo, which means that probably Portillo did know about the objectives and interests of drug trafficker ICBB, arbitrated and handled by Llort.

Institutional reconfiguration in Mexico

This section analyzes a social network corresponding to the Mexican cartel known as "La Familia Michoacana" (the Michoacana Family). This network, consisting of 284 agents with 880 interactions, is based on Mexican judicial files containing facts that occurred until 2009. A witness who was an active member of "La Familia Michoacana" provided to authorities the facts used as sources for the present analysis. Some of those facts date to the time when the Michoacana Family was joined to the "Golfo Cartel."

As discussed below, "La Familia Michoacana" mainly operated by bribing public servants of municipalities to facilitate the drug movement within *Michoacán* and other Mexican States. *Lázaro Cardenas* is one of the municipalities where, according to the information, official cars and local officers support the movement of illegal drugs.

Since 2005, there has been observed an establishment of agreements and interactions of mutual collaboration between members of "La Familia" and municipal presidents. The witnesses providing information to authorities stated that they knew that several municipal presidents facilitated actions carried out by "The Family."

Figure 5.7 (online, available at http://scholarship.claremont.edu/cgu_fac-books/27/) presents the distribution of the first six core nodes with the highest centrality indicator. Codes starting with letters NAR reference drug traffickers and those starting with letters FUN reference agents who are public servants.

- *Hub,* or node with the highest indicator of direct centrality: NARFADI-OLTI, aka "El Tío," with a direct centrality indicator of 4.7 percent. Some of the NARFADIOLTI's task consisted of (i) articulating to authorities the three levels of public administration, (ii) offering large amounts of money to public servants, (iii) coordinating different politicians, and (iv) selecting candidates and collaborators of "The Family" in Michoacán and other states.
- Second highest indicator of direct centrality: NARGOLTUT, aka "La Tuta," with a direct centrality indicator of 4.3 percent.
- Third highest indicator of direct centrality: FUNPRIC, a local judicial police form the Michoacán state, with a direct centrality indicator of 3.8 percent.
- Fourth highest indicator of direct centrality: NARFATEM, aka "Emilio," with a direct centrality indicator of 3.3 percent.
- Fifth highest indicator of direct centrality: NARFAJEMEC, aka "El Chango Méndez," with a direct centrality indicator of 3.1 percent.
- Sixth highest indicator of direct centrality: NARFANAMOG, aka "El Chayo," with a direct centrality indicator of 2.6 percent.

It is interesting to notice that among the first ten core nodes/agents with the highest concentrations of direct social relationships, the third one is a public servant who belongs to a security agency of the Michoacán state.

On the other hand, by calculating the *betweenness* indicator, there is observed a similar structure to that observed in Figure 5.8 (online, available at http://scholarship.claremont.edu/cgu_facbooks/27/). The agent/node identified as a *structural bridge* is NARGOLTUT, with 11 percent, while the second is NARFADIOLTY, with an indicator of 7.9 percent, which means that there is a distance of 3.1 percentage points between the *structural bridge* and the second core node. It is also found that just 89 out of the 284 nodes/agents of the network register some potential capacity to arbitrate information. Figure 5.8 presents the structure of the network when observed and analyzed in terms of the capacity to arbitrate information.

The *structural bridge*, having the highest *betweenness* indicator, is the second core node in terms of direct centrality; the *structural bridge* is not the most connected node/agent in the network. In contrast, the *hub* is the second core node in terms of capacity to arbitrate information. The most important nodes/agents in terms of capacity to arbitrate information are:

*   *The structural bridge*, or node/agent with the highest indicator of *between-ness*: NARGOLTUT, a.k.a. "La Tuta," who intervenes in 11 percent of all the interactions, is the second most important regarding the quantity of social direct interactions and at the same time, has the highest capacity to arbitrate information. This capacity may account for the fact that "La Tuta," on its own, has formed and led an autonomous fraction of "The Family," currently known as "Los Caballeros Templarios," which, in turn, has become a military target for the Mexican state. Considering the foregoing, the capture of "El Chango" Mendez, on June 21, 2011, explains the apparent dismantling of one fraction of "The Family," which had had clashes with another fraction led by "La Tuta." According to the mass media, the capture of "El Chango" Mendez happened because the latter was running away from both "La Tuta" and the "Cartel del Golfo" (*Milenio*, 2011).
*   The node/agent with the second highest indicator of *betweenness*: NAR-FADIOLTI, which intervenes in 7.9 percent of total interactions in the "Michoacana Family" network.
*   The public servant with the highest capacity to arbitrate information ranks in the sixth highest indicator of *betweenness*: FUNPRIC, which appears in 5.1 percent of the interactions. This node, a municipal president, has the greatest capacity among the involved public servants to arbitrate information. The other nodes with *betweenness* indicators higher than 5.1 percent are drug traffickers.

Comparative results

Interactions

In the case of the Llort network, the most important type of interactions are those related to political or administrative arrangements for money laundering (see Table 5.1).

The pattern of interactions is coherent with the participation of important public servants, drug traffickers and private bankers working together to accomplish money laundering purposes. The Llort network is therefore a good example of a CStR situation in which political and administrative agreements between unlawful agents and high-level public servants allowed a massive and systematic process of money laundering. This shows how paying bribes or exercising coercion does not allow stability in the fluxes of information and communication required for committing high-scale or systematic crimes such as those involving public, private, domestic and international banks in Guatemala.

The second most important interaction, related to intra-agency relationships, describes those relationships established only between lawful officials pertaining to the Drug Enforcement Administration (DEA) in Guatemala and Honduras;

Table 5.1 Social relationships in the Llort network

Social relationship in the Llort network	%
Political or administrative arrangements for money laundering	47
Intra-agency	11
Requesting for information	9
Providing information	8
Testifying against	4
Family	3
Interfering in the custody of money laundering	3
Business acquisition	2
Criminal complaint	2
Drug trafficking	2
Friendship	2
Marital relationship	2
Owning company	2
Blackmail	1
To know	1

therefore it does not provide relevant information about the network structure. However, the other important interactions do provide information regarding the modus operandi and purposes of the network. For instance, it can be observed that the direct exchange of information between lawful and unlawful agents involved was important. Additionally, it can be observed that the network carried out procedures of interfering in the keeping of money laundering and the acquiring of firms. It is also found that familiar relationships were important in the exchange of direct information providing, at the same time, a background of confidence between agents.

On the other hand, regarding the Michoacana Family network, the full list of interactions is presented presented in Table 5.2.

Political collaboration is not as important as bribes or homicides, which means that this social network is largely articulated through bribes and coercion, which are typical mechanisms of illicit networks whose functionality is relatively concentrated in purely criminal activities and still does not configure a sophisticated form of CStR. Although in the "Michoacana Family" network, the political and administrative agreements do not have the relevance observed in the case of the Llort network, it has reproduced a process of AStC at the local level. Also, it can be inferred that there is the beginning of a process towards a CStR at the local level. This network contrasts with the Colombian narco-paramilitary case, in which, instead of bribes and coercion, political and administrative agreements were the mechanisms that allowed long-term commitments. In fact, the "Michoacana Family" network also contrasts with the Llort network, in which bribery or violence is not even registered as a type of interaction. In short, the social situation observed in the "Michoacana Family" network configures a scenario that could be interpreted as a form of advanced state capture (AStC) evolving towards CStR, especially at the local level.

Table 5.2 Social relationships in "the Michoacana Family" network

Social relationships in "the Michoacana Family" network	%
Intra-organization	37
To know (generic)	18
Collaboration (generic)	11
Bribe	10
Brothers	4
Collaboration for protection	4
Works for "the family"	3
Homicide	3
Support and political management commitment (agreements with political agents)	2
Collaboration for drug distribution	2
Collaboration for providing information	1
Family relationship	1
Intermediation	1
Intra-organization to carry out a rescue	1
Sentimental relationship	1
Collaboration with the Golfo Cartel	1
Participation in homicides	1
Friendship relation	1

Finally, in the Colombian case, the social relationships are observed in Table 5.3.

In general terms, in the Mexican case there is not observed a great intervention, infiltration, or manipulation of electoral and political institutions, which means that situations of traditional corruption are mainly established through bribes. However, in the Colombian case, there is observed the intervention and manipulation of political institutions. The absence of bribery is an additional indicator that allows interpreting the Colombian network as an evident case of CStR, not only at the local level but also at the national level.

Node/agents

The concentration of nodes/agents of the Colombian narco-paramilitary network (Atlantic coast network) allows inferring a CStR process because: (i) it registers at all the administrative levels, which means that, at a certain point, some

Table 5.3 Social relationships in Colombian narco-paramilitary network

Social relationship in the Colombian narco-paramilitary network	%
Agreements for political support	40
Agreements to establish vigilante groups	30
General collaboration and unidentified agreements	18
Coercion	7
Unlawful favoritism	3
Administrative collaboration	2

instances of the executive, legislative and judicial institutions were functional to the AUC's criminal interests, and (ii) the political and administrative agreements were a relevant type of interaction between politicians, public servants and AUC members. In this sense, it is inferred to be a structure in which public servants from different administrative branches established long-term political and administrative agreements with the AUC.

The Atlantic coast network is an extreme situation of CStR with an impressive concentration of agents in charge of the legislative branch and candidates for public office by popular vote in every level of the Colombian public administration. When all the public servants appearing in the network are categorized, according to their local/regional, departmental/provincial and national/federal administrative levels and according to their executive, legislative, security or political branches and sectors, it is observed that the legislative branch and the national/federal level account for 49 percent of the total public servants of the network.

The more perverse structural effects arise when the CStR takes the form of direct manipulation of lawmaking institutions; therefore, considering the important participation of legislators in the Colombian network, this can be defined as a CStR situation with deep and long-term institutional effects. The establishment of close relationships between public officials at the national level with commanders of the AUC exemplifies the cooperation that allowed candidates, public officials and members of the AUC to set the goal of "Re-fund the Colombian State."

The Llort case is also a good example of a CStR situation at the highest administrative levels of Guatemalan public administration. Even though this network does not have the complexity of types of nodes/agents observed in the Atlantic coast network, this was a *top down* process of CStR from the presidency of Guatemala. In fact, when the public servants in the network were classified as was done in the Colombian case, it was found that, beginning with the most affected: the public banking sector, the security sector and the executive branch were affected in each case at the national level. No other administrative level is registered as involved in the network, which means that basically the presidency, the Semi-State Bank of Credit, and public servants in charge of the bank security were used to accomplish objectives mainly related to money laundering.

The "Michoacana Family" network, when modeled with information including facts until 2005, shows a concentration of agents belonging to agencies of the judicial and security branches, mainly at the local level (58 percent). Given the low participation of political, administrative and electoral agreements until the year 2005, the "Michoacana Family" network affected institutions in charge of security and judicial functions at the local level of the Mexican state consolidating a process of StC at the municipal level and to a much lesser extent, at the provincial level. However, when calculating the concentration of nodes/agents with information including facts until 2009, there is found a change in the administrative level of the public servants participating in the network. For instance, in 2009 there is registered a participation of public servants at the national/federal level, specifically at the executive and judicial branches, of only 1 percent and 7 percent, as well as the security sector, 7 percent. In 2005, no public servants at the national/federal level were registered. Also, in 2009 there was observed an important participation of public servants belonging to the executive branch at the local level, with 28 percent, while in 2005 the public servants at the local level of the executive branch accounted for only 2 percent.

Considering the high percentages of nodes/agents belonging to both the executive branch and the security agencies sector at the municipal level in 2009, operating either throughout mutual agreement or coercion, there can be inferred the advancement of a CStR process under a *bottom up* scheme; which contrasts with the *top down* scheme observed in the Llort case in Guatemala. This means that there is a high risk that executive branch institutions and security agencies at the local level in Mexico were used for accomplishing the "Michoacana Family" interests, facilitating a reconfiguration of those branches. The same trend, although to a lesser degree, is observed for the case of the state/provincial level, with the additional burden of the legislative branch affectation, which implies the risk that the "Michoacana Family" interests influence some legislative decisions at the provincial level.

Given the fact that the legislative branch was not affected at the national/ federal level, at least from the available judicial evidence, a situation of CStR in the Mexican institutions at the national/federal level cannot be inferred. Only through additional evidence that (i) sustains the establishment of bi-directional agreements, of mutual benefit, between criminals and public servants at the national/federal level, as well as (ii) affectation of the national legislative branch, among others, such as observed in Colombia, could it be inferred that there is the existence of an ongoing solid process towards CStR at the national level of the Mexican state.

Conclusion: active processes of CStR occurring in the analyzed networks

The information presented and discussed herein suggests a variety of interactions, mechanisms and procedures among paramilitaries, drug traffickers, public officers, candidates for elected office, lawmakers and private sector agents in all the social networks modeled and analyzed. The data regarding amounts of social interactions and nodes/agents allows inferring the presence of intense processes of institutional capture and reconfiguration, and therefore a diversity of scenarios of StC, AStC and CStR, at different levels, instances and sectors of the public administration in Colombia, Guatemala and Mexico. Those processes affect different institutions and different administrative levels; therefore, some common but also differential measures are required in each one of these states.

Low institutional capacity and corruption levels are conditions configuring "generous environments" for the illicit networks, including those related with drug trafficking, a criminal activity which currently catalyzes various other criminal activities and illegal markets. For reasons not discussed in the present document, the most representative producers/suppliers and consumers of the illegal drug trafficking market are rarely matched in the very same country. Such a situation has required not only the permanent transnational movement of nationals of the different countries, but also the international transport of input shipments and associated illegal drugs. In other words: the main consumers of cocaine and marijuana are not located in Colombia and Mexico, nor the main producers of cocaine located in the United States. In addition, amid the most representative producer and consumer countries, neither are those countries serving as transit routes for these transnational movements, thanks to their institutional weakness, social vulnerability, geographical location and/or lack of effective institutional instruments specifically designed to fight drug trafficking.

In addition to the above, the process of money laundering resulting from illegal drug trafficking activities must be added. Increasing taxes and financial controls to prevent money laundering are imposed in those countries where the main producers of illicit drugs may be located, almost always as a result of the United States' demands, so it can be expected that much of the drug trafficking profits are incorporated into the legal transnational economic system through operations carried out in those countries with reduced controls. That is, those countries that have not been commonly known for concentrating the production of illicit drugs become target locations for carrying out asset laundering operations. For example, Chile has not traditionally been interpreted as an attractive country for the production of drugs due to its geography. However, its relative passivity has been signaled regarding the controls on the transport of chemical inputs used for the production of cocaine paste in Bolivia and Peru. Therefore, while the international pressure is focused on Peru, because of its increasing relevance as a pass-through in the chain of cocaine production, Chile becomes an attractive environment because its maneuver margin is still easy for the social agents dealing with drug trafficking. In this sense, the traffic and transportation of chemical inputs from Chile to other bordering countries has been recognized as a growing problem in that country. It is easy to understand why. In countries such as Chile and Argentina, that have not captured the world's attention as typically indispensable countries for drug trafficking, no criminal, judicial, tax, financial, or political controls have been imposed such as those adopted in Colombia and that, to an increasing extent, will be adopted over the coming years in Mexico and other countries in Central America as a result of both the political pressure from countries such as the United States,[3] and explicit needs in the affected countries themselves. Thus, Chile, for example, during the last decade has seen the enactment of laws and instruments aimed not only to prevent and control the physical movement of illegal money through the financial system, but also the movement of money through its ports.

Such dynamics eventually allow for the assumption that some countries of the western hemisphere, that traditionally have not faced CStR processes brought about by drug trafficking networks, could in the coming years show similar processes related to the transnational activity of those networks. In this sense, initiatives against drug trafficking and other means of transnational crime will be more urgently required to integrate and harmonize initiatives and mechanisms among countries.

Those states failing in guaranteeing security at various administrative levels—with high levels of corruption, poor management of the public budget, with very fragile democratic systems and citizenship participation, and lacking effective information systems, accountability and tax inspection—generate an environment that facilitates the development of illicit networks such as those linked to drug trafficking and other forms of crime. In turn, these illicit networks, by their corrupt and coercive power, have the ability for exacerbating such initial institutional failures. Specifically, it has been found that high levels of public corruption are an institutional condition associated with drug trafficking development (Beltrán and Salcedo-Albarán, 2007).

Drug trafficking in the western hemisphere enhances the convergence of criminal activities that are directly or indirectly required to produce and transport psychotropic substances, to market them in bulk, to distribute and sell them retail, and to launder and invest the resulting capitals in illegal and legal markets. The successful commission of all these tasks requires, for example, bribes or the use of violence by the drug dealers' networks, not only to subjugate those public servants responsible for the prevention and prosecution of drug traffickers, but also to: (i) regulate the market through the protection of territories and production routes used for transportation and distribution, (ii) establish entrance barriers against the competition, and (iii) reinforce the established agreements with lawful and unlawful sectors of society.

On the other hand, corruption generates an institutional and social space providing opportunities for the drug traffickers and other criminals to gain favor not only from the public servants at different levels and branches of the public administration—from local security authorities to governors, deputies or congressmen—but also from diverse social agents such as politicians and candidates for positions of public responsibility, among others.

Situations such as those currently observed with drug trafficking and criminal networks of Colombia, Guatemala and Mexico, that carry out criminal actions across borders, even with the collaboration of national agents of those other countries, can be interpreted as transnational crime (Shelley, *et al.*, 2005). Such a transnational nature causes serious difficulties in pursuing, investigating, judging and punishing criminal activities across differing countries and takes advantage of the varying institutional weakness among countries in order for them to gain a larger operating environment.

In addition to the transnational integration of individuals, interests, networks and operations, there is observed another process that, at least in Mexico, appears so important in both the strengthening of illegality and the described weakening process: the appearance of markets and illegal activities, additional to and different from those of drug trafficking that also generate important economic profits. For the particular case of the "Michoacana Family," at least, the following illegal activities complementary to but integrated with drug trafficking are identified: (i) production and trafficking of the illegal substances other than cocaine and marijuana, such as the synthetic drugs, (ii) extortion with economic purposes, (iii) piracy, (iv) arms trafficking, (v) illegal marketing of natural resources and by-products, and (vi) narco-retail or domestic micro-traffic. In this sense, the illegal network of the "Michoacana Family" shows a certain capacity to replicate and innovate illegal technologies that, although they are initially applied to drug trafficking activities, also are used to commit other crimes. Techniques such as the exercise of violence, the extortion and international transportation, and the marketing of illegal products also are susceptible to being replicated for the development of piracy markets or for the illegal trafficking of other drugs and products and natural resources, as is the case with the export of the above described ferrous material.

Therefore, drug trafficking and corruption are mutually strengthening, to the extent that higher levels of drug trafficking, due to their economic and coercive power, ceteris paribus, tend to increase the corruption risks, and vice-versa. This perverse causal circle tends to strengthen the generalized environment of criminality. This is further exacerbated when advancing to the CStR, given the reproduction of agreements with illegal groups promoted from within the state—and by institutional instances of the state—so as to take advantage of the capabilities of such unlawful agents and groups in order to obtain individual illicit interests, even of an openly criminal nature, at the expense of the collective well-being. This is, for instance, what happened in Colombia when candidates and active public servants proposed pacts to narco-paramilitary groups such as AUC, to accomplish electoral or economic interests through violence.

Notes

1 Departamento Administrativo de Seguridad, DAS.
2 Jose Armando Llort also has been under investigation for making illegal financial operations with the minister of defense of Guatemala. In some of these operations about 30 million quetzals, equivalent to approximately $10 million, were compromised.
3 Even those countries in the region with certain institutional strength, and low levels of corruption, as is the case with Chile, would call the attention of drug traffickers because of the lack of both legal technologies and institutional arrangements specifically designed for drug trafficking control.

References

Baker, W. and Robert, R. (1993) "The Social Organization of Conspiracy: Illegal Networks in the Heavy Electrical Equipment Industry." *American Sociological Review.* Vol. 58. No. 6: 837–860.

Beltrán, I. and Salcedo-Albarán, E. (2007) *Entornos generosos para el crimen: Análisis del narcotráfico en Colombia.* Método: Bogotá.

Bornholdt, S. and Schuster, H. (2003) *Handbook of Graphs and Networks: From the Genome to the Internet.* Berlin: Wiley-Vch.

Burt, R. (1992) *Structural Holes: the Social Structure of Competition.* Cambridge: Harvard University Press.

Burt, R. (1997) "The Contingent Value of Social Capital." *Administrative Quarterly*. Vol. 42. No. 2: 339–365.

Burt, R. (1998) "The Gender of Social Capital." *Rationality and Society*. Vol. 10. No. 1: 5–46.

Burt, R. (2000) "The Network Structure of Social Capital." *Research in Organizational Behavior*. Vol. 22: 345–423.

Burt, R. (2005) *Brokerage and Closure: an Introduction to Social Capital*. New York: Oxford University Press.

Burt, R., Christman, K. and Kilburn, H. (1980) "Testing a Structural Theory of Corporate Cooptation: Interorganizational Directorate Ties as a Strategy for Avoiding Market Constraints on Profits." *American Sociological Review*. Vol. 45. No. 5: 821–841.

Cepeda, F. (1997) *La Corrupción en Colombia*. Bogotá: Fedesarrollo y Universidad de los Andes.

Coleman, J. (1988) "Social Capital in the Creation of Human Capital." *American Journal of Sociology*. Vol. 94: S95–S121.

De León-Beltrán, I., and Salcedo-Albarán, E. (2008) *Narcotráfico y parapolítica en Colombia, 1980–2007: Evolución del Capital Social Perverso*. Bogotá: Metodo.

Degenne, A. and Forsé, M. (1999) *Introducing Social Networks*. London: Sage Publications.

Duncan, G. (2005) *Del Campo a la Ciudad: La infiltración urbana de los señores de la guerra*. Universidad de los Andes, Cede. Bogotá: Universidad de los Andes.

Duncan, G. (2006) *Los Señores de la Guerra*. Bogotá: Planeta.

Easley, D. and Kleinberg, J. (2010) *Networks, Crowds and Markets: Reasoning about a Highly Connected World*. New York: Cambridge University Press.

El País (2010) "Guatemala decreta el estado de sitio en el norte del país para combatir al cartel Los Zetas." December 19 (accessed January 12, 2011). Online, available at: www.elpais.com/articulo/internacional/Guatemala/decreta/estado/sitio/norte/pais/combatir/cartel/Zetas/elpepuint/20101219elpepuint_8/Tes.

Everett, M. and Boratti, S. (2005) "Extending Centrality." Carrington, P., Scott, J. and Wasserman, S. eds. *Models and Methods in Social Network Analysis*. Cambridge: Cambridge University Press: 57–76.

Flores, J. (2008) "La corrupción armada." Gonzales, B., ed., *Diez Años de Transparencia por Colombia*. Bogotá: Diez Años de Transparencia por Colombia: 133–140.

Garay, L. and Salcedo-Albarán, E. (2012a) "Institutional Impact of Criminal Networks in Colombia and Mexico." *Crime, Law and Social Change*. Vol. 57. No. 2: 177–194.

Garay, L. and Salcedo-Albarán, E. (2012b) *Narcotráfico, Corrupción y Estados: Cómo las redes ilícitas reconfiguran instituciones en Colombia, Guatemala y México*. Mexico City: Random House Mondadori.

González, F., Bolivar, I. and Vásquez, T. (2003) *Violencia política en Colombia: De la nación fragmentada a la construcción del Estado*. Bogotá: CINEP.

Greenhill, K. (2009) "Kleptocratic Interdependence: Trafficking, Corruption, and the Marriage of Politics and Illicit Profits." Rotberg, R., ed., *Corruption, Global Security, and World Order*. Cambridge: World Peace Foundation, Harvard Kennedy School Program of Intrastate Conflict, American Academy of Arts and Sciences & Brookings Institution Press: 96–123.

Gutiérrez, F. and Barón, M. (2007) "Estado, control territorial paramilitar y orden político en Colombia: Notas para una economía política del paramilitarismo, 1978–2004." Sánchez, G. and Gutiérrez, F. eds. *Nuestra Guerra sin Nombre*. Bogotá: IEPRI—Norma: 267–312.

Hellman, J. and Kaufmann, D. (2000) *Intervention, Corruption and Capture: the Nexus between Enterprises and the State.* London: European Bank for Reconstruction and Development.

Hellman, J. and Kaufmann, D. (2001) "La Captura del Estado en las economías de Transición." *Finanzas and Desarrollo.* September: 31–35.

Hellman, J., Jones, G. and Kaufmann, D. (2000) *Seize the Day: State Capture, Corruption and Influence in Transition.* Washington, DC: World Bank.

La Nación (2010) "Aprueban extradición del ex Presidente Portillo a EEUU." March 18 (accessed December 12, 2010). Online, available at: www.lanacion.cl/aprueban-extradicion-del-ex-presidente-portillo-a-eeuu/noticias/2010-03-18/084000.html.

López, J. (2010) "Deciden extradición de Portillo entre amenazas" (from *BBC Mundo*). March 17 (accessed November 15, 2010). Online, available at: www.barrigaverde.net/?q=node/8679.

Milenio (2011) "El Chango huía de La Tuta y el Golfo al ser aprehendido." June 23 (accessed June 23, 2011). Online, available at: www.milenio.com/cdb/doc/impreso/8980265.

Mockus, A. (2008) "Colombia en los últimos diez años, avances en probidad y mutación hacia una corrupción violenta." Gonzales, B., ed., *Diez Años de Transparencia por Colombia.* Bogotá: Transparencia por Colombia: 111–122.

Morselli, C. (2008) *Inside Criminal Networks.* Montreal: Springer.

Olsen, W., Petrowski, D. and Greenhalgh, S. (2010) "Case for Collective Action: the World Bank Initiative." Olsen, W., ed., *The Anti-Corruption Handbook: How to Protect Your Business in the Global Marketplace.* New Jersey: John Wiley & Sons, Inc.: 143–156.

Pesic, V. (2007) *State Capture and Widespread Corruption in Serbia.* CEPS Working Document No. 262.

Romero, M. (2002) *Paramilitares y autodefensas: 2998–2003.* Bogotá: IEPRI-Planeta.

Romero, M. (2006) "Paramilitares, narcotráfico y contrainsurgencia: una experiencia para no repetir." Leal, F., ed., *En la encrucijada: Colombia en el siglo XXI.* Bogotá: Norma.

Semana (2007) "La Fiscalía llama a la ex congresista Rocío Arias para que responda sí recibió respaldo de los paras." October 24 (accessed December 27, 2010). Online, available at: www.semana.com/noticias-on-line/fiscalia-llama-ex-congresista-rocio-arias-para-responda-recibio-respaldo-paras/107189.aspx.

Semana (2010) "La saga de mal." December 4 (accessed December 24, 2010). Online, available at: www.semana.com/noticias-nacion/saga-del-mal/148389.aspx.

Shelley, L., Picarelli, J., Irby, A., Hart, D., Craig-Hart, P., Williams, P., *et al.* (2005) *Methods and Motives: Exploring the Links between Transnational Organized Crime and International Terrorism.* Washington, DC: US Department of Justice.

Verdad Abierta (2009) "El paramilitarismo en Sucre, un proyecto armado por su clase política." February 4 (accessed December 25, 2010). Online, available at: www.verdadabierta.com/component/content/article/59-introduccion/845-el-paramilitarismo-en-sucre-un-proyecto-armado-por-su-clase-politica.

Wasserman, S. and Faust, K. (1994) *Social Network Analysis: Methods and Applications.* New York: Cambridge University Press.

World Bank (1997) *Helping Countries Combat Corruption: the Role of the World Bank.* Washington, DC.

6 Public looting for private gain

Predatory capitalism, MNCs and global elites, and plutocratic insurgency

Robert J. Bunker

We love capitalism. But can capitalism be made to love us?

The end of the Cold War represented the climactic finish to a 40-year-old global struggle between competing ideologies derived from adversarial forms of political and economic organization. This struggle, albeit with minimized direct confrontations due to the rise of nuclear arms, reflected the twilight of the wars between industrialized states as a vestige of the modern Westphalian era. At its conclusion, we witnessed the economic implosion of the USSR and its subsequent partition and the rejection of a centrally planned economy by China that gave rise to its extensive market economy reforms. These events proved to unequivocally exorcise the nineteenth-century legacy of Marx, Engels, and their adherents by discrediting a school of political and economic thought at whose basis was that of a class struggle between the owners of production (the bourgeoisie; *the propertied class—the capitalists*) and the oppressed workers (the proletariat; *the propertyless class*) (Marx and Engels, 1886).

Still, recent concerns over class conflict—even warfare—have been espoused by capitalist scholars whose work is far removed from the tenets of historical materialism. In hindsight, it would be accurate to state that the victory of capitalism over Marxism in many ways resulted in the seeds of its own demise—at least in the sense of the continuing existence of a moderated capitalism subordinate to the needs of the Western states and their peoples.[1] The advent of globalization has in many respects gone sideways—a condition that has been commented on by a number of authors (Hertz, 2001; Stiglitz, 2003; Gilman *et al.*, 2011; Rodrik, 2012). Back in the early 1990s, however, few individuals—be they scholar, policymaker, or common citizen—would have bet on these dark horses of globalization to even finish, much less sweep the competition, in what was then viewed as the start of bright new era.[2] Still, this "trifecta of dark globalization" derived from the rise of predatory capitalism, the increasing wealth accumulated by multinational corporations and global elites; the proverbial 1 percent controlling them, and the resulting emergence of a "plutocratic insurgency" endangering the Western states and their peoples is winning out. Each of these components of this trifecta, symptomatic of the rise of a new and aberrant form of post-modern political economy, will be addressed in turn in this chapter, and the public looting—that is the extraction of wealth from the middle classes and public institutions of the United States and United Kingdom—that has ensued will be addressed. Further, a comparison of plutocratic insurgency to the earlier recognized construct of criminal insurgency will be highlighted, as will some thoughts on the intersection between the extra sovereign and illicit economies upon which they are linked.

Predatory capitalism

Capitalism can be defined as "an economic and political system in which a country's trade and industry are controlled by private owners for profit, rather than by the state" (*Oxford Dictionaries*, 2013a). Implicit in such a system is the duality of the free-market—"an economic system in which prices are determined by unrestricted competition between privately owned businesses" (*Oxford Dictionaries*, 2013b) and some sort of moderating state influence that ensures that its citizens—the majority of whom labor (workers) in the middle and lower classes—are not exploited by the owners of capital (e.g. national elites). This "political compromise" has been the traditional Western neo-liberal approach to capitalism following the excesses of the gilded age (1870–1900) and the gradual enshrinement of reformist labor laws and tax codes in the United States (Pizzigati, 2012) and in Western Europe (Maier, 1975). It resulted in the creation of a symbiotic partnership between big business and states, with the later the dominant partner in this relationship.

This political compromise began to breakdown by the 1980s and, with the advent of globalization, the process by which states function as a moderating force was increasingly besieged by the owners of capital who by then had become multinational and extra-sovereign in size and scope—representative of a new class of global elites (Rothkopf, 2008; Collins, 2012; Freeland, 2012) and indicative of what is being called a second gilded age by numerous writers (Fraser, 2008; Schulz, 2011; DeLong, 2012). A new form of capitalism befitting such elites—one with "predatory" attributes—has since emerged. Predatory capitalism—that is, capitalism that is exploitive and oppressive of others and given to bribery, corruption and coercion by its practitioners to achieve their profit seeking ends—is finding its way back into today's world or at the very least, as many scholars would argue that it never left the Global South, is now finding its way into the Western democracies; a brutish reality that is becoming increasingly recognized (Warner, 2007; Reich, 2012; Smith, 2013; Stiglitz, 2013). Such capitalism is reminiscent of European colonialism—who can forget the nineteenth-century British plundering of India via excessive levels of taxation (Naoriji, 1881) and the experience of Africa carved up like a holiday roast at the Berlin Conference of 1884–1885 (Rodney, 1972)? Yet, in this scenario, it is turned inwards, with cities like Detroit, with its $18 billion bankruptcy and 21,000 imperiled public pensioners, and other rust belt disasters becoming the poster children of this new reality (Reeves, 2013). These are poster children, by the way, further preyed upon by the ongoing looting of public pension funds via alliances between politicians, who gained sizeable campaign donations, and New York based hedge fund managers who profit from the back door deals (Taibbi, 2013). Juxtapose this middle American reality with "tomorrow economy" cities, such as San Francisco with their $900,000 median home sales, where the 1 percent and their retainers congregate and techies utilize private buses to commute to social media campuses in the Silicon Valley (Egan, 2013).

Part of this process is attributed to increasing globalization with the flight of investment capital away from the traditional centers of concentration and its flow into emerging markets where labor is cheap and profit margins are high. In fact, according to Richard Wolff:

> After 200 years of concentrating its centers in western Europe, north America, and Japan, capitalism is moving most of its centers elsewhere and especially to China, India, Brazil and so on...
>
> ...Among the social effects of capitalism's withdrawal from many old capitalist centers in the US are rapidly widening wealth and income inequalities there. These in turn provoke rising tensions within and between the two major political parties and a growing disaffection of the population with political leadership in general...
>
> ...The consequence of political dysfunction (on top of the crises that punctuate capitalism's withdrawal) is to reinforce that withdrawal. The October shutdown and the ongoing stalemate over the national debt ceiling and federal budgets are events that force corporations, wealthy individuals, and central banks to rethink the proportions of their portfolios held in US-based assets. Comparable rethinking affects the proportions allocated to Western Europe and Japan.
>
> (2013)

The above quote captures many of the concerns raised in this work. The changing nature of capitalism—one that allows CEOs to loot their companies with excessive bonuses while denying basic benefits to common workers and allowing corporations to pretend to be nationalistic companies until it is time to pay their taxes—is resulting in an implosion of both the Western middle class and the liberal state supporting it (Barnett, 2011; Faux, 2012; Rothkopf, 2012).

Descriptions of capitalism that have escaped the moderating influence of modern democratic (liberal) states is representative of both pre- and post-twentieth-century realities. Caricatures of Ebenezer Scrooge in his counting-house and the more ravenous robber barons of the nineteenth century can easily be juxtaposed with Gordon—"Greed is Good"—Gekko and his cohort of modern day Wall Street cronies at Goldman Sachs and related firms. Literally, the hard won social contract between the common citizen and the liberal state has been torn up and cast aside. Unfettered capitalism does not result in a utopian world—rather "self-regulating markets" are not regulated at all but result in concentrations of wealth in the hands of the few (Polanyi, 1944).

As a result, the twenty-first-century-market focuses on private gain and enrichment in an increasingly zero-sum and mercantilist-like struggle. Public good is of little consequence in a globalized economic system where anything goes—be it toxic waste dumping off the coast of Somalia, doctored baby formula produced in China, or small arms illicitly being smuggled into contested states—with caveat emptor being the new watch word of the day. It should be noted, however, that this privatized, and many times pseudo-dynastic, onslaught is not representative of some monolithic or centralized conspiracy. Quite the opposite—rather it is an evolutionary and structural response by massive corporations and holding conglomerates, and the elites who own them, to an evolving and hypercompetitive globalized economy. Identifiable elements of this response—in essence predatory capitalistic activities—are as follows:

- *Stress profit and equity gain at all costs.* The *raison d'être* of predatory capitalism is the accumulation of wealth by all means possible—especially preying on the misfortunes of others because this helps to maximize profits. Disaster capitalism (Klein, 2007) is ideal, utilizing complexity, anonymity, secrecy and conspiracy is prudent *(The Economist,* 2013b), and the use of "unconscionable" practices, such as what foreign companies are doing in Africa's mining sector (Annan, 2013), represent acceptable operating procedures. As of March 2013, Moody's estimated that US linked multinationals had $1.45 trillion in cash reserves, with 68 percent of it held overseas to avoid taxation (Semuels, 2013).
- *Follow the principals of hyper-rationalism.* The overreliance on the use of cost–benefit calculations makes this form of capitalism amoral and soulless. If a few percentage points of profit can be squeezed out by altering a design, changing suppliers, or moving a factory, the principals of hyper-rationalism will be followed. Further, the creation of substandard goods or engineered defects, known points of failure, which result in expensive parts replacements or shorten the lifecycle of a product also follows this logic *(Engineer,* 2008). Other examples include renouncing US citizenship in order to gain preferable tax treatment prior to a corporate IPO launch (Wolverson and Walt, 2012) and the creation of ever quicker (in the low milliseconds) networks that allow high-frequency traders to pull boatloads of pennies out of the market via each transaction with zero market exposure at the end of the day (Adler, 2012).
- *Show no loyalty to workers, suppliers, customers, or even nations.* Another tenet of predatory capitalism is to have no affinity or sense of responsibility to anyone but yourself, family and close allies (cronies). This zero-sum world view and lack of emotional attachment allows for high capital mobility—to quickly take advantage of profit making opportunities in a globalized economy. It results in a 24/7 "it's just business" philosophy that replaces the social contract with a business contract that includes fine print prejudicial to anyone who signs it. A favored game of those engaging in this form of capitalism is playing laborer (employee and contract), city, region-state and

sovereign against their peers in a multilevel and global bidding war focused on lowering operating costs and gaining concessions (*The Economist*, 2013a; Inman, 2007; Reich, 2013).

- *Increasingly operate within a sovereign free economy.* This form of economy —also known as "off the books"—represents an attempt by multinational corporations and global elites to gain freedom from the oversight, regulation and taxation of sovereign states, especially Western ones. Essentially, a parallel supra-national economy is being constructed by global elites to facilitate predatory capitalist endeavors. Techniques include the use of the "active financing exception," which "is the main tool GE uses to avoid nearly all US corporate income tax" (Carney, 2013) and the use of offshore tax havens with potentially $32 trillion in offshore accounts in 2010 (Hsu, 2012). The efforts of Apple computers to profit from such chicanery have been well publicized (Neate, 2012; McCoy, 2013a, 2013b).

- *Utilize corruption, co-option and coercive force as required.* Another component of this form of capitalism is using subtle and targeted "carrot and stick" tactics to manipulate the political environment and market in which global elites are operating. These tactics include corrupting and co-opting congressional members in the United States who gain from "abnormal" stock profits while in office, benefit from big money campaign donations, and after leaving office look forward to being invited to become members of high salaried corporate boards (Richardson, 2011; Schweizer and Boyer, 2011; Palmer and Schneer, 2013). Such "crony capitalism" found in the United States (Stockman, 2013) of course also extends to Europe and across the globe where plutocratic collaborators hold public office. At the other extreme, we see the use of legions of lawyers—legal "hitmen"—who can stall and manipulate a judicial system where actual innocence of a crime is less important than having the economic resources to purchase a court ruling of such innocence. For this reason, *¿Plata O Abogado?* (Silver or Lawyer) might become the new catchwords of predatory capitalism. Outside of Western societies, though, nothing matches the coercive capability of hiring a private military corporation (PMC) to do your bidding (Project Censored, 1999).

- *Have a willingness to profit from the informal, and even the illicit, economy.* Global firms such as Proctor and Gamble, Colgate-Palmolive, and Unilever have for some time now learned how to reach past the formal economy into "System D" transactions. These are all cash micro-level transactions and even include the bartering of goods and services via street vendor distribution in the developing world (Kostigen, 2012; Neuwirth, 2012). Multinationals disposing of commercial vessels to be broken up on the shores of Gujarat, India and bulk recycling of precious metals from old computers and electronics systems in Agbogbloshie, Ghana by masses of underpaid workers represent other aspects of semi-informal transactions, which by the way, create high levels of unregulated pollution (UNESCO, 2000; PBS, 2009). On the illicit side, major banks and brokerages have readily involved themselves with "Black Market Peso Exchanges" in the Americas and currency debt swaps as in the case of Goldman Sachs in 2002 conspiring with national officials to hide actual debt levels in Greece (Martinuzzi, 2010; Martinuzzi and Petrakis, 2010). These linkages appear to be just the tip of the iceberg.

The last bullet takes us to an interesting component of the rise of the predatory capitalism; that is its relationship to the illicit economy. The pioneering work of Ed Vulliamy, author of *Amexica* (2010), discusses this phenomenon from both the micro and macro perspectives. On a city level in northern Mexico, we see that:

> Juarez has imploded into a state of criminal anarchy—the cartels, acting like any corporation, have outsourced violence to gangs affiliated or unaffiliated with them, who compete for tenders with corrupt police officers. The army plays its own mercurial role … Juarez is also a model for the capitalist economy. Recruits for the drug war come from the vast sprawling *maqui-ladora*—bonded assembly plants where, for rock-bottom wages, workers make the goods that fill America's supermarket shelves or become America's automobiles, imported duty-free. Now, the corporations can do it cheaper in Asia, casually shedding their Mexican workers, and Juarez has become a teeming recruitment pool for the cartels and killers. It is a city that follows religiously the philosophy of a free market.
>
> (Vulliamy, 2011b)

We are getting a blurring effect between predatory (mostly formal) capitalism, and the participating extra sovereign entities, and illicit capitalism, and the participating subnational entities. These capitalist forms are where the profit margins lie—state moderated capitalism, on the other hand, saddled with both bureaucratic rules and ethical guidelines, is not only noncompetitive with these emergent forms of capitalism but vulnerable to their co-optive power. For instance, at the global level, stemming from the Wachovia bank and Sinaloa cartel money laundering scandal (in the hundreds of billions of dollars)—it was determined that this may have only been one of numerous illegal transactions:

> At the height of the 2008 banking crisis, Antonio Maria Costa, then head of the United Nations office on drugs and crime, said he had evidence to suggest the proceeds from drugs and crime were "the only liquid investment capital" available to banks on the brink of collapse. "Inter-bank loans were funded by money that originated from the drugs trade," he said. "There were signs that some banks were rescued that way."
>
> (Vulliamy, 2011a)

According to this same author:

> Antonio Maria Costa, who was executive director of the UN's office on drugs and crime from May 2002 to August 2010, charts the history of the

contamination of the global banking industry by drug and criminal money since his first initiatives to try to curb it from the European commission during the 1990s. "The connection between organised crime and financial institutions started in the late 1970s, early 1980s," he says, "when the mafia became globalised."

Until then, criminal money had circulated largely in cash, with the authorities making the occasional, spectacular "sting" or haul. During Costa's time as director for economics and finance at the EC in Brussels, from 1987, inroads were made against penetration of banks by criminal laundering, and "criminal money started moving back to cash, out of the financial institutions and banks." Then two things happened: the financial crisis in Russia, after the emergence of the Russian mafia, and the crises of 2003 and 2007–2008.

"With these crises," says Costa, "the banking sector was short of liquidity, the banks exposed themselves to the criminal syndicates, who had cash in hand."

(Vulliamy, 2011a)

While the relationship between predatory capitalism and the darker illicit economy is of great interest, other matters are also of significance. The concern now is to focus on the extra sovereign entities, and elites behind them, who are participating in the demise of the Western democracies. The next, necessary short overview, strives to understand whom they and the powerful individuals associated with those corporations are, now that their predatory motives have become clear.

Multinational corporations and global elites

Multinational corporations—which can also now be considered extra sovereign entities—have grown in size over the last half a century to become economic behemoths. Corporations such as Exxon Mobil have greater revenues than most states, and have become laws unto themselves (Coll, 2012). In fact, such corporations have sterling AAA credit ratings that are higher than many sovereign states, and as a result, have become preferred investment options over sovereign bonds in many instances (Pertuno, 2011; Foroohar, 2012a). Walmart, for example, is: "the world's largest private organization, has a bigger population than several United Nations member countries. Its revenue base is larger than many of the world's economies. And its borders extend far beyond the US" (Heskett, 2013). Various lists exist that show the power rankings of these corporations against those of states (revenues vs. GDP). For instance, in one list Proctor and Gamble is wealthier than Libya, Bank of America is wealthier than Vietnam, and ConocoPhillips is wealthier than Pakistan. Walmart would now rank as the world's twenty-fifth most powerful country and Exxon Mobil as its thirtieth if we went by these revenue indices. In fact, of the top 100 economic entities, half are states and the other half are now corporations (Hertz, 2001;

Trivett, 2011). Another list put out by *Forbes* determines the world's largest corporations by determining their ranking via a composite score of their sales, profits, assets and market value (Decarlo, 2013).

Increasingly, we only half-jokingly ask if a massive corporation like a JPMorgan Chase or a Royal Dutch Shell were to get into a full blown conflict with a sovereign like Angola or even Greece, where the smart money bets would go. A number of books and studies have emerged in this regard, recognizing the increasing power and size of these non-sovereign entities and the threat that they now represent to sovereign states. Earlier works include David Korten's *When Corporations Rule the World* (2001), John Cavanagh's *Alternatives to Economic Globalization* (2004), and Joel Bakan's *The Corporation* (2005).

Additionally, research into the rise of these corporations by a team of researchers in Zurich has focused on the relationships between 43,000 individual business entities. The findings of this network analysis suggest that a core of 1,300 companies with interlocking ownerships control most of the global economy via their possession of the majority of shares of multinational blue chips and manufacturing firms. At the core of these companies was a "super-entity" of 147 even more closely linked corporations composed mostly of financial institutions such as JPMorgan Chase, Goldman Sachs and Barclays Bank (Coghlan and MacKenzie, 2011; Vitali *et al.*, 2011).

In tandem with the rise of these super corporations is the increasing wealth of their masters. Terms for these ultra-rich individuals varies; superclass, global power elite, new global super-rich, plutocrats, new robber barons, the 1 percent, the 0.1 percent, the 0.01 percent, with the list ongoing. Awareness of the rise of this privileged economic class has grown increasingly over the last decade. Numerous reports, news stories and commentaries have highlighted their excesses and the growing concentration of wealth that they hold—such as the title of this article from the *Guardian*: "The new robber barons: how taxpayers subsidize CEOs' multimillion salaries: A new report finds many top executives are taking home more than their corporations pay in taxes—at our expense" (Chatterjee, 2012). Even the internal financial documents pertaining to these groups recognize this new reality. In what has become an infamous Citigroup "Equity Strategy" industry note from 2005, the following wording is used:

The World is dividing into two blocs—the Plutonomy and the rest. The US, UK, and Canada are the key Plutonomies—economies powered by the wealthy...

...We will posit that: 1) the world is dividing into two blocs—the plutonomies, where economic growth is powered by and largely consumed by the wealthy few, and the rest...

...2) We project that the plutonomies (the US, UK, and Canada) will likely see even more income inequality, disproportionately feeding off a further rise in the profit share in their economies, capitalist-friendly governments, more technology-driven productivity, and globalization.

...The usual analysis of the "average" US consumer is flawed from the start. To continue with the US, the top 1 percent of households also account for 33 percent of net worth, greater than the bottom 90 percent of households put together. It gets better (or worse, depending on your political stripe)—the top 1 percent of households account for 40 percent of *financial* net worth, more than the bottom 95 percent of households put together...

(Kapur *et al.*, 2005)

Each scholar and research group addressing this issue provides its own metric of who these new plutocrats are and the estimated amount of wealth and power that they control. David Rothkopf analyzes a micro focused population of six thousand individuals as representative of this superclass. He focuses on the international influence, rather than simply wealth or achievements, of this group that has moved beyond borders and has become part of an exclusive global community. At the time of his analysis, 95,000 ultra-high-net-worth individuals (UHNWIs) with assets in excess of $30 million controlled $13 trillion. About a thousand or so billionaires also existed—though the superclass was by no means highly correlated with the former grouping (2008). Chrystia Freeland, on the other hand, focuses on the 0.1 percent of globe's individuals as representative of the new super-rich. She provides overviews of these new working rich, alpha geeks, and citizens of the world and how "the billionaire's circle" transformed the global banking business (2012). Jeff Faux is more limited in his analysis, with a focus on America's elite creating a servant economy in that nation (2012) while Sam Pizzigati also focuses on America's rich (2012). Another more recent study characterizes the global plutocratic grouping, based on UHNWIs whose cohort has since grown in size, as follows: "There were nearly 200,000 people worth $30 million or more globally in 2013, with a combined wealth of $27.8 trillion. Wealth-X predicts that figure will exceed $40 trillion by 2020" (Zeveloff, 2014). These global elites, in what can be considered a gilded age redux, would make Mark Twain feel quite at home. In 1871, Twain penned the satirical "Revised Catechism" in the *New York Tribune* as a response to the excesses of Tammany Hall under "Boss" Tweed:

Q: What is the chief end of man?
A: To get rich.
Q: In what way?
A: Dishonestly if we can; honestly if we must.
Q: Who is God, the only one and true?
A: Money is God—gold and greenbacks and stocks—father, son, and the ghost of the same—three persons in one: these are the true and only God, mighty and supreme; and William Tweed is his prophet.

Twain would readily recognize this new plutocratic offensive except for the fact that the conspirators have become far more sophisticated, now operate on a globalized level, and have achieved supra-national status outside of the confines of state moderated capitalism. This new offensive has been gradually developing since the 1970s and 1980s and represents what David Rothkopf terms, via the subtitle of *Power, Inc.*, as "The Epic Rivalry Between Big Business and Government—and the Reckoning That Lies Ahead" (2012). Basically, the thesis is that private power is now concentrated in a few thousand global corporations held by wealthy elites and their families. These plutocrats—via their corporations and trusts—now wield more power than a majority of modern states. One of the more recent factors that are leading to the creation of this powerful class of global "super-citizens" is how the legal status of corporations has changed in America. This can be viewed in the recent *Citizens United v. FEC* 558 US 310 (2010) decision. Corporations are now considered to be artificial—albeit immortal—people given the same rights as US citizens. Politically, this has helped to undermine the democratic process by opening up free speech and campaign donations to corruptive influences by corporations seeking to gain special economic and legal concessions (Rothkopf, 2012). Some years ago—back in 1997—Jessica Mathews identified the "power shift" that was taking place between such corporations and nations. Her perceptions were that:

> National governments are not simply losing autonomy in a globalizing economy. They are sharing powers—including political, social, and security roles at the core of sovereignty—with businesses, with international organizations, and with a multitude of citizens groups, known as nongovernmental organizations (NGOs). The steady concentration of power in the hands of states that began in 1648 with the Peace of Westphalia is over, at least for a while.
>
> (Mathews, 1997)

This power shift also extends to elite American, and to a slightly lesser extent British, educational institutions—which means unbiased research and analysis concerning what is taking place within the IPE may at some point also become co-opted. Look at FY2013 endowments for the most prestigious and elite colleges in the United States; Harvard has a $32.7 billion endowment, Yale has a $20.8 billion endowment, and Stanford has an $18.7 billion endowment (*Harvard Magazine*, 2013; *Yale News*, 2013; *Stanford News*, 2013). Cambridge comes in at a paltry £4.9 billion and Oxford at £3.7 billion for a prior FY (Dent, 2014). Student tuition is now basically meaningless for these and other hugely endowed universities, though they still readily seek it, while they continue to pull down sizeable donations from their elite alumni and corporate gift programs, with Stanford adding $1 billion by such means to its FY2013 endowment (Lewin, 2013). Harvard, in fact, has been characterized as a massive hedge fund that now engages in teaching on the side. Emphasis is now fully placed on fund management and those financial elites that oversee it:

> Harvard's Division of Arts and Sciences—the central core of academic activity—contains approximately 450 full professors, whose annual salaries

tend to average the highest at any university in America. Each year, these hundreds of great scholars and teachers receive aggregate total pay of around $85 million. But in fiscal 2004, just the five top managers of the Harvard endowment fund shared total compensation of $78 million, an amount which was also roughly 100 times the salary of Harvard's own president. These figures clearly demonstrate the relative importance accorded to the financial and academic sides of Harvard's activities.

(Unz, 2012)

Further, if the affluent family of a lackluster student seeks to be admitted they can make a donation to the university known as the "Harvard Price" now estimated to be $10 million (Golden, 2007; Unz, 2012). While at first glance a steep price, it represents quite a deal for the heir apparent of a global fortune. Attending prestigious colleges is extremely critical because they facilitate a closed loop cycle of educating plutocratic elites—and their retainers, as members of an administrative meritocracy—whose associations with each other continue on for a lifetime and are beginning to extend to their children and grandchildren as the new social classes of the 1 percent and beyond begin to solidify. These serve to cement early functional relationships as does the yearly World Economic Forum (WEF) meeting in Davos, Switzerland and the Aspen Institute gathering in Colorado for the networking of older plutocrats who descend via hundreds of private jets to these locales to cut their backroom deals and then once again scatter across the globe (Rothkopf, 2008; Freeland, 2012).

These globetrotters behave much like swarms of predators looking for fresh business opportunities in order to squeeze out additional profits for their portfolios. It can be said that the new world that they are helping to create is one of *Evil Paradises* (Davis and Monk, 2008) and dark and deviant realms (Heine and Thakur, 2011; Gilman *et al.*, 2011) free of state moderated capitalism and built upon skewed perceptions of social and political organization. We have begun to see the erection of the plutocratic playgrounds of the future, already now upon us, in which anything or anyone can be bought or sold—or at least rented or timeshared—built upon masses of Filipino maids, Indian laborers, and other miserably paid developing world workers. Throw in a stratum of European or American expats for their technical skills and expertise, who can't find such lucrative contracts back home and desperately need to provide for their families, and you have the makings of an emerging world gone very bad indeed.

For the elites who are building these playgrounds no *noblesse oblige* exists—rather, as an Apple executive recently quoted said, "We sell iPhones in over a hundred countries … We don't have an obligation to solve America's problems. Our only obligation is making the best product possible" (Duhigg and Bradsher, 2012). The rest of his thinking surely went something like this, "We just want you to purchase our products, make us fat and rich, and then you and your petty states are to just leave us alone and allow us to live in our own enclaves and cities." As US corporations and their jobs have moved beyond the national interest so others in the Western democracies follow—though London and New

York still make for some of their favorite abodes (Foroohar, 2012b; *Telegraph*, 2013; Zeveloff, 2014).

Plutocratic insurgency

Building upon our explorations and analysis of predatory capitalism and the global elites and their corporations who promote it, we come to the emergence of what is known as plutocratic insurgency. That insurgency form is a derivative of the "commercial insurgency" construct first articulated by Steven Metz in 1993. The *raison d'être* of commercial insurgency draws upon psychological factors affecting discontented individuals:

> *Commercial Insurgency and the Search for Wealth.* In the pursuit of personal meaning in the developing world, there is an alternative to violent nativism or other forms of spiritual insurgency. When the discontented define personal meaning by material possessions rather than psychic fulfillment, they create the environment for commercial insurgency. This was made possible when Western materialism penetrated nearly every corner of the Third World via electronic communications and widespread travel. Commercial insurgency is a quasi-political distortion of materialism.
>
> (Metz, 1993)

Another, and better known, derivate of this insurgency construct is that of the "criminal insurgency" form first developed by John Sullivan in 2008. That form is illicit economy based and was developed to better describe the conflict being waged by the gangs and cartels in Mexico and Central America (Sullivan, 2008). Plutocratic insurgency, on the other hand, is somewhat counter-intuitive vis-à-vis the initial commercial archetype. It is not meant to be descriptive of "personal meaning in the developing world" but rather is directed towards the developed world and the hyper-materialistic individuals within it who already hold great wealth and power. The term was first coined in 2011 by the author in an attempt to characterize rising inequalities in the United States and Western Europe with the advent of the 1 percent and is viewed as a natural complement to the earlier identified criminal insurgency form (Bunker, 2012). The construct was further developed for this book project via what was initially a private exchange in 2012 with Nils Gilman, who was asked to periodize and further comment on it vis-à-vis his *Deviant Globalization* research (Gilman *et al.*, 2011).

Just as criminal insurgency is derived from interaction between the illicit economy and increasingly politicized—either intentional or de facto—violent non-state actors (e.g. gangs, organized crime and cartels), plutocratic insurgency emerges from interaction between the sovereign free economy, with its predatory capitalist behaviors, and the multinationals (and the global elites controlling them). To better understand the plutocratic insurgency construct and place in context the threat that it represents to the Western states, it is compared to the criminal insurgency construct in Table 6.1. This table compares and contrasts these two constructs in the categories of actors involved, relationship to formal IPE, orientation to public goods, economic effect on the state, military (crime) effect on the state, citizen threat perceptions when facing such an insurgency, TTPs (tactics, techniques and procedures) involved, and the types of capitalism represented.

A brief summary of what a plutocratic insurgency looks like goes like this. Multinational corporations and a segment of the global elites (the 0.1 percent and 0.01 percent) are distancing themselves from the rest of humanity by the amount of wealth and power that they hold. This elite includes foreign royalty—autocrats—controlling sovereign wealth funds such as the Saudi ruling families. These vast corporations and important individuals are considered the "winners" of globalization and hold high legitimacy. They are global insiders and power-brokers. Because of their immense wealth and status, these individuals retreat to exclusive and privatized spaces protected by private security (mercenary) forces and high walls. These elites also see a different Internet than the rest of us (Fertik, 2013). They have no need for public goods—they can directly purchase anything that they need—and in fact eschew collective societal risk strategies in favor of individual and family based ones. States suffer that come in contact with these individuals and their business interests due to a denial of tax revenues—a bevy of lawyers and lobbyists ensure that they pay as little taxes as feasible via accounting tricks, special privileges and other concessions gained. Middle class families suffer via loss of formal economy jobs due to outsourcing and corporate economies of scale making their small business endeavors non-competitive. At best, such families end up servicing the elites in a servant economy relationship (Faux, 2012). The plutocrats engage in rampant cronyism, with white collar crime becoming institutionalized—family and friends simply come first. Individuals showing high competency become their retainers. This meritocracy, composed of skilled knowledge workers and armed guards, protect these global elites and help to ensure that they enjoy impunity from the laws of sovereign states.

The political effect on the state is pronounced. Public goods are both privatized and defunded and, in essence, just become another commodity to be bought and sold. This extends to the criminal justice and courts system whose scales are weighted in favor of those with the most wealth. Democratic governance is further undermined by elite campaigns to rewrite social contacts or, at a minimum, have them narrowly interpreted. This results in a crisis of legitimacy for the state as democratic consensus within the political process is lost and polarization of viewpoints becomes entrenched. At some point, the election process can become almost meaningless. Ultimately, the state slowly becomes reconfigured to plutocratic values. The average citizen on the street does not understand the larger context of what is taking place but feels the effects. They become fearful, and rightly so, of seeing their middle class lifestyle imperiled, have personal debt concerns as they try to maintain that lifestyle, and recognize a lack of future social mobility for their children. This adds to societal stress levels and tensions. Police state-like behaviors can also manifest themselves when the bureaucracies of a state get mixed signals from polarized governance. Without a policy consensus, those bureaucracies turn in on themselves and, as a result, create greater and greater levels of efficiency with regard to domestic policing and homeland security. These measures may ultimately promote draconian policies with zero-tolerance for non-compliance.

The tactics, techniques and procedures (TTPs) of plutocratic insurgency are one of *¿Plata O Abogado?* (Silver or Lawyer). Lawyers and lobbyists are used in generous measure and elected officials are selectively co-opted by means of campaign and party donations in order to gain special privileges. Lucrative corporate board deals come later as rewards for collaboration with plutocratic interests. Offshore financial schemes and the use of tax havens and other tax avoidance measures help promote the extra sovereign economy, which goes hand-in-hand with the extra sovereign (resident non-citizen) non-domicile status that the 1 percent (and more exclusive groupings) seek to achieve in the political communities within which they live. Ultimately, plutocratic insurgency is representative of a supra-national globalized form of predatory capitalism that is attempting to move beyond the confines of mere sovereign states.

The plutocratic and criminal insurgency forms tie back into broader strategic concerns discussed in the overview to this book, specifically, that we are seeing a "Dark Renaissance" taking place as an outcome of globalized capitalism and information technologies that is incrementally leading to a process of Westphalian state deconstruction. Quite possibly, the intersection of these two insurgency forms can best be summed up as follows by a *Forbes* reporter looking back at tweets about Mexico in 2012—"Mexico is 'a contradictory situation—economy is doing relatively well, but security = problem.'" (Flannery, 2013). This tweet only tells us part of the story, however. While it is agreed that the criminal insurgencies are now well advanced in that state, with over 10 percent of Mexico—or 2,437 cities—now under gang and cartel control (Reyes, 2013), the formal economy itself is not doing well. Criminal control over cities in Mexico means that local populations and businesses in their areas of control pay extortion and street taxes before governmental taxes and fees. Also, the aging and underperforming state oil monopoly—PEMEX—which represents a major share of federal revenues has now seen over 1,300 incidents of pipeline thefts (via breaches) by criminal organizations in 2011 alone, resulting in over 3.35 million barrels of fuel stolen (Reuters, 2012). Rather the illicit—as seen above with the addition of tens of billions of dollars of narcotics revenues—and sovereign free economies, via multinational production (e.g. the maquiladoras) and sales in Mexico and segments of the tourism industry, are the ones prospering. Thus money from the illicit economy, and to a far more limited extent the sovereign free one, are helping to prop Mexico up and make the overall economy appear to be doing well.

Fortunately, such criminal insurgencies as seen in Mexico—which also are taking place in other parts of Latin America—have not, as of yet, gained a significant foothold in the Western democracies. Still, with an estimated 1.4 million

Table 6.1 Plutocratic insurgency and criminal insurgency constructs

	Plutocratic insurgency	Criminal insurgency
Actors	Multinational corporations (MNCs) and a segment of the global elites (1.00–0.01 percent); includes foreign royalty controlling sovereign wealth funds (SWFs).	Criminals, gangs, organized crime (domestic and transnational), and other violent non-state actors (VNSAs).
Relationship to the IPE (formal)	Insiders ("winners"); high wealth and legitimacy.	Outsiders ("losers"); mostly low wealth (kingpin and group exceptions) and illegitimacy.
Orientation to public goods	Public spaces replaced by gated/private communities; police replaced by private security/mercenaries; collective societal risk replaced by individual/family risk strategy.	Public spaces replaced by "no go zones"; police replaced by armed gangs and private armies; collective societal risk replaced by tribal risk strategy.
Economic effect on the state	Denial of tax revenues; increasingly knowledge and service oriented economy polarization.	Denial of tax revenues—extortion (street taxation) of businesses/individuals; theft of governmental assets/property.
Military (crime) effect on the state	Rampant cronyism; white collar crime becomes institutionalized; elites enjoy impunity.	Impunity of criminal activities (assaults, killings, etc.); danger of corruption of police/courts.
Political effect on the state	Defunding or privatizing of public goods (and institutions); social contracts rewritten/narrowly interpreted; loss of democratic consensus/polarization; state reconfiguration to plutocratic values.	De facto loss of governmental control in areas; public goods co-opted by criminals; environmental modification/ resocialization of citizens (narco cultural); state reconfiguration to criminal values.
Citizen threat perceptions	Middle class lifestyle imperiled; personal debt concerns; no social mobility for children; government is draconian (police state-like).	Safety and security of individuals imperiled; children are suffering (PTSD); government is ineffective and/or corrupt.
Tactics, techniques, and procedures (TTPs)	¿Plata O Abogado? (Silver or Lawyer); use of lawyers, lobbyists and elected officials (co-opted); campaign/party donations for special privileges; offshore finance; promote extra-sovereign (off-the-books) economy.	¿Plata O Plomo? (Silver or Lead); use of terrorism; suppression/control of journalists/media; smuggling activities; money laundering/co-option of formal businesses.
Type of capitalism	Predatory (formal based); supra-national globalized.	Criminalized (illicit based); sub-national globalized.

Sources: Steven Metz (1993) *The Future of Insurgency*. Carlisle: Strategic Studies Institute, US Army War College, December 10, (for the original "commercial insurgency" construct); John P. Sullivan and Robert J. Bunker (2011) "Rethinking Insurgency: Criminality, Spirituality and Societal Warfare in the Americas." Special Issue: Criminal Insurgencies in Mexico and the Americas: The Gangs and Cartels Wage War. *Small Wars and Insurgencies*, Vol. 22. No. 5: 742–762; Nils Gilman (and Robert J. Bunker) (2012) "Plutocratic Insurgency." *Small Precautions*, September 5, online, available at: http://smallprecautions.blogspot.com/2012/09/pluto-cratic-insurgency.html; preface and postscript information from this book project and additional discussions between John P. Sullivan, Nils Gilman and the author.

gang members (street, prison and outlaw motorcycle) now existing within the United States, we should at least be cognizant of such potentials as these numbers grow (NGIC, 2011). Additionally, Western Europe is also plagued by its own gang member radicalization concerns in Britain (Peachy, 2013), the 751 *Zones Urbaines Sensibles* (Sensitive Urban Zones) in France alone (Pipes, 2013 [2006]), and 3,600 organized crime groups now operating throughout the larger continent (Europol, 2013). Still, for the West, the plutocratic insurgency underway may now represent more of a threat; albeit a subtler (and cognitive dissonance based) one given the celebrated Horatio Alger mythos—now spread by Hollywood imagery—of idolizing the rich from humble origins who are able to enjoy the monetary successes of their hard work.

Public looting for private gain

The outcomes of this "trifecta of dark globalization"—predatory capitalism, the rise in dominance of multinational corporations and the elites (1 percent) behind them, and the emergence of what can be termed plutocratic insurgency—are undermining both Western states and the middle classes found within them. The economic erosion is readily evident when Western governmental and household (family) debt levels are viewed. US governmental debt recently crossed over the $17 trillion threshold and now represents 73 percent of US GDP (National Debt Clocks, 2013; Schroeder, 2013). Far less known is that US state and local governmental debts levels are also climbing:

> Across America, elected officials, taxpayer groups, and other researchers have launched a forensic accounting of state and municipal debt, and their fact-finding mission is rewriting the country's balance sheet. Just a few years ago, most experts estimated that state and local governments owed about $2.5 trillion, mostly in the form of municipal bonds and other debt securities. But late last year, the States Project, a joint venture of Harvard's Institute of Politics and the University of Pennsylvania's Fels Institute of Government, projected that if you also count promises made to retired government workers and money borrowed without taxpayer approval, the figure might be higher than $7 trillion.
>
> (Malanga, 2013)

Further, it was determined that within the United States "States often manipulate their accounting rules to show a balanced budget, when in actuality a deficit exists" and that "Federal fiscal stimulus to states has ended. As a result, states have faced budget gaps totaling $55 billion in FY2013" (Harvard Institute of Politics, 2012). European governmental debt levels are also significant. For example, the United Kingdom's basic debt level is £1 billion or 70 percent of its GDP. The national debts (and GDP percentages) of Spain, France and Italy are €.615 trillion (77 percent), €1.83 trillion (95 percent), and €1.99 trillion (141 percent), respectively (National Debt Clocks, 2013).

Such excessive national debt levels raises concerns of credit downgrades—such as the August 2011 Standard and Poor's US downgrade from AAA (outstanding) to AA+ (excellent) and the more recent February 2013 Moody's UK downgrade from Aaa (highest quality) to Aa1 (high quality/very low risk) (O'Toole, 2013; Standard and Poors, 2011). Fitch, in April 2013, also downgraded the United Kingdom from AAA to AA+ rating and, in October 2013, put the United States on its downgrade watchlist (McGarth, 2013; Patnaude, 2013). These downgrades can ultimately increase the costs of borrowing for a state if its prime investment grade ratings are lost. Excessive national debt levels also signal the potential dysfunction of national economies due to the strains placed upon them by large interest servicing payments, a reduction in internal influence, and ultimately raise the specter of sovereign bankruptcy (Buchhelt *et al.*, 2013; Neu *et al.*, 2013). End of FY2013 US national debt payments were $227.75 billion (6.23 percent of all federal outlays), which has been manageable only because of the Federal Reserve's aggressive policy of ensuing that the "US government is paying historically low rates on its debt," which is presently at 2.43 percent and is not sustainable (Desilver, 2013).

We should also turn our attention to household and family debt in the United States and the United Kingdom. For the United States, aggregated family net worth suffered a 40 percent drop between 2007 and 2010—from $126,400 to $77,300—which is the equivalent of 18 years of family savings and investments (Riley, 2012). These figures are misleading, though, because wealth is polarized within American society, with the elites holding stocks and bonds while the rest of America, those with any form of savings (20 percent of Americans have $0 or negative net worth), generally have it tied to the equity of their homes—an asset that suffered a greater drop in values than financial investments during that period (Mishel *et al.*, 2012). Factored into the aggregate net worth figures is the fact that one year later—in 2011—median household debt had increased to $70,000 (Gottschalck *et al.*, 2013), which suggests that family debt levels in the 2010–2011 period were slightly below 50 percent of assets. A sizeable chunk of this debt comes from student debt that has doubled since 2007 and crossed the $1.2 trillion threshold (Denhart, 2013; Flores, 2013).

Based on the median US family income of $51,000 in December 2011 (Davidson, 2012), this would place family debt levels to income at 137 percent, which, while not a national debt to GDP equivalent, provides insights into the economic health of families. Such family to income debt levels would of course be skewed with easily over 50 percent of American society—including 45 million individuals on food stamps (the Supplemental Nutrition Assistance Program; SNAP) (Ellis, 2011)—having much higher rates and the upper 1 percent having little to no family debt to income levels. The lower class situation is likely even graver given that, in June 2013, the food stamp situation further deteriorated with a "record 23,116,928 American households" enrolled—more than the entire number of estimated households that exist in the entire Northeastern United States (Jeffrey, 2013). This can be contrasted to the "sucking money pit" the greater DC metro region has become. It contains half of the top

20 median income counties in the United States flush with governmental contractors—many of which support homeland security and intelligence agencies—tied to big business interests (Ferguson, 2012).

In the United Kingdom, family wealth and debt level variances are also very pronounced. A full 10 percent of British households are said to now hold assets of £1 million, derived primarily from the value of sky high London properties, a surge in stock prices, and the future valuation of occupational pensions. Though the future valuation of public pensions—in one example set at £1.3 million for a career police inspector—is speculative as it assumes municipal solvency in the face of underfunded public retirement programs (Clark, 2013). For example, the police pension fund in Britain was underfunded by £481 million in 2007–2008, more than twice that of 2006–2007 (Doward, 2009). These concerns are warranted given that by 2008 the United Kingdom had become the biggest debtor of the developed world, even more so than debt laden Japan, and in 2011 was at 492 percent of GDP when all "aggregate indebtedness of the UK is considered" (Peston, 2013). Thus less than 10 percent of British households can be considered truly wealthy, while at the other extreme: "The bottom 50 percent of households in Britain have just £4,400 of cash, property and pensions ... according to an Office for National Statistics report which lays bare the vast disparities in wealth across the UK" (Collinson, 2012). As a result, British society is very much mimicking the have and have-not character of American society, with a shrinking middle class and ongoing governmental debt spending to sustain social welfare programs (e.g. public goods) for increasing numbers of households that exist within the lower classes. At the same time, as discussed earlier in this chapter, the net worth of global elites has been accelerating, with the global elite (1 percent) now controlling 46 percent of the world's wealth (Kharpal, 2013). In the United States, the 1 percent took home about 22 percent of the income earned by Americans (Lowrey, 2013) while in Britain "The share of the top 1 percent of income earners increased from 7.1 percent in 1970 to 14.3 percent in 2005" (Ramesh, 2011) with additional yearly gains expected.

Conclusion

Drawing upon a Western capitalist—and post-Marxist—interpretation of these developments, we must accept that we are witnessing a "civil war" amongst ourselves (e.g. the capitalists). We have a supra-bourgeoisie composed of transnational elites—that new global class super-rich according to Freeland (2012)—in a class struggle with the petty-bourgeoisie—middle class shop owners, small business people and moderately skilled professional workers. An example of this conflict can be readily seen each time a Walmart, Costco, or similar big box store is sited in a small city or urban neighborhood within the United States or Western Europe. Local shops and businesses in city downtowns and strip malls are unable to compete, and as a result go under. Additionally, the part-time replacement jobs generated by these mega-stores do not meet "living wage" standards—at least in the sense of adult workers providing for dependent children. This can be juxtaposed with the fact that high-end "ritzy" malls catering to the elite are flourishing in the United States—not so, of course, for the lower end "middle class" malls, which are struggling to generate profits in the face of growing vacancies (Matthews, 2012).

Another example of this conflict is that of major insurance companies and networks becoming the middlemen of health care. Medical doctors are seeing their incomes falling, with independent general practitioners becoming a legacy of the past—while quality of service is going down (increased waiting times, scripted care, and use of nurse practitioners) and medical insurance premiums are going up. Once again, both incomes and expenses for the petty-bourgeoisie are negatively impacted. In both examples, and numerous others not provided, savvy corporations and multinationals—drawing upon their bevy of lobbyists, lawyers and accountants—are able to maximize shareholder profits for the economic elites.

Resulting from such a changing global economy, with its predatory underpinnings, and coupled with a massive recession, many American workers have been hit hard. However, America has had the resources to extend federal unemployment benefits and provide welfare and aid payments, during and after the great recession of December 2007 to June 2009 (US BLS, 2012). Ongoing US federal budget deficits and the recent governmental shutdown, however, are putting a strain on the governmental system and causing intense bipartisan schisms. Presently, 1.3 million long-term jobless Americans are set to lose their benefits at the end of 2013 if a congressional compromise can't be reached (Green, 2013).

The focus on the importance of having a secure job in order to be considered part of the middle class can be seen in a 2012 PEW Research report. In the 2012 report, 86 percent of the adults surveyed considered a secure job the most important attribute, while, in a 1991 survey, 70 percent of adults surveyed said that home ownership was more important (Drake, 2013). This shift portrays the partial devolution of the US petty-bourgeoisie away from capital accumulation (home ownership) into more of a proletariat (renter) mindset. This comes at the same time that a Cornell and Stanford University study found that "Fewer people are living in middle class neighborhoods in America as people increasingly dwell in areas segregated by income extremes" (Li, 2013). The study found that in 1970 about 65 percent of American families lived in middle class neighborhoods— a level in 2009 that dropped to 42 percent. Extreme types of neighborhoods, with either well-off or poor residents, increased during these periods from 15 percent to 33 percent of American families (Li, 2013). By 2007, this already resulted in a shift in which more Americans below the poverty line could be found in the suburbs rather than in US inner cities (Tyre and Philips, 2007). Further exacerbating this trend is the fact that the institution of marriage is receding for the less affluent in the United States. These concerns were expressed by Bradford Wilcox who led a university research team looking at this subject:

He ... is concerned that marriage is "withering" among middle and lower social groups, with potentially disastrous effects on American society and the economy.

I think we are moving towards a classically Latin model, where the powerful and the privileged have strong, stable families and access to decent income and assets. And everyone who is not in that upper third is worse and worse off.

(Wheeler, 2012)

The United Kingdom is also becoming a nation of renters, with housing stock being purchased by the global elites and their wealth funds (Warner, 2012), and is suffering its own erosion of the institution of marriage in its working classes, making marriage more of an elite and surviving middle class phenomena (*Guardian*, 2010; Marsden, 2013). Across Western Europe—writ large—the issue of retrograde social mobility is also now a very real concern. While the lower population Baltic states (Norway, Sweden, Finland and Denmark) have done better than the United Kingdom and other larger states such as Spain, France and Italy, the overall trending in what is known as the "Great Gatsby Curve" is not promosing.[3] This graph portrays the relationship between genera-tional social mobility (y) and income inequality (x) with high levels in both ratings indicative of states in which the poor are likely to remain poor and the income gap between the elites and the poor is sizeable. The score is derived from a 1985 Gini coefficient (Greeley, 2013). Bottom rankings are evident in the United Kingdom (0.5 and 0.3) and France (0.41 and 0.27). A score of (0.18 and 0.21) for Finland is reflective of a low ranking (Krueger, 2012; Bloomberg, 2013). Per the *White House Blog*:

The curve shows that children from poor families are less likely to improve their economic status as adults in countries where income inequality was higher—meaning wealth was concentrated in fewer hands—around the time those children were growing up.

(Vandivier, 2013)

Needless to say, the United States has fared even worse with its Gatsby score than the European states with a score of (0.47 and 0.34) and a further sizeable increase into 2010 (Bloomberg, 2013). Children born into low-income house-holds, in essence, remain have-nots throughout their lives and have little chance of joining the dwindling ranks of the middle class. It is of little wonder then that mass Occupy and related anti-1 percent protests (e.g. #Occupy, *We are the 99 percent*) should sweep the United States and areas of Europe where the middle class was imperiled, and many other regions of the globe from September 2011 through February 2012 (Castells, 2012; Wolff and Barsamian, 2012).[4] Protests broke out in hundreds of cities including the major Western centers of Rome, Madrid, London, New York and Los Angeles. Such protests are reminiscent of the sixteenth-century Peasant's War in Germany, when the free peasants were forced into serfdom via increased taxation; however, in this modern incarnation, bloodshed was kept to a minimum even though the outcome was very much the same, with victory going to the elites. In the case of the European Union, the winners were appointed (not democratically elected) technocrats and allied multinational business interests, and in the United States were global elite investors hidden behind the trappings of liberal democracy.

Still, we are only in the mid-phases of this plutocratic onslaught and conditions have the potential—via either the enactment of police state-like policies (via over centralization) and/or state failure (via fragmentation)—to become far more severe. These potentials can be seen in Juarez, Mexico where the extra sovereign and illicit meet at a dystopian—feral and criminal city—level (Bunker and Sullivan, 2012). The bloodshed with nearly 10,000 deaths (Dudley, 2013) over the last half dozen years has not been moderated. The reason for this is twofold: Mexico has lost control over parts of the country to criminal forces, in addition it does not have the resources—based on how its state institutions are designed—to "buy off the populace" via a social safety net (as in the United States and the United Kingdom) because the resources simply do not exist. As a result, destitute and unemployed individuals have no choice but to hit the streets and work for the gangs and cartels that dominate the illicit economy. Formerly autocratic states, such as a transitioning Mexico, are thus being hit even harder by both the plutocratic (supra-national) and criminal (sub-national) insurgencies coming together in a vice-like grip compressing state institutions. Nils Gilman and Michael Costigan would call this process "the arbitrage of the nation-state" (2012). From an Epochal Warfare theory perspective, this is the ultimate expression of the process by which the era of dominance of Westphalian states is coming to a close. For the United States and Western Europe, a level of state stability and civility within the populace still exists. The question we must now ask is for how long. Quite possibly, the answer will be until the public and formerly middle class family monies run out.

Notes

1 See the Nils Gilman foreword to this work concerning the nurturing of industrial workers—both capitalist and communist based—during the high social modernist era (1945–1971).

2 Instead, the post-Cold War honeymoon period was just beginning with only one superpower still standing after a decades-long ideological slug fest. Francis Fukuyama's "The End of History" (1989, 1992) heralded the triumph of neo-liberalism and democracy and became the watchwords of this era.

3 It should be noted that Germany is mid-range on the Gatsby curve and with its population of 82 million is lessening the effects in Europe. Still, from 1985 to 2008, it had a significant increase on the curve along with notable increase in the Baltic states highlighted. See the "Gini coefficients of income inequality, mid-1980s and late 2000s" (OECD, 2011: 24).

4 In a sense, these protests resembled developing world food riots as a reaction to mandated International Monetary Fund (IMF) during the late 1970s and 1980s. In this instance, it was not the very poor rebelling against the inequalities of predatory capitalism but the Western middle and lower classes. See Davis (2007: 161).

References

Addler, J. (2012) "Raging Bulls." *Wired*. September: 116–125.

Annan, K. (2013) "Foreword." *Equity in Extractives*. Africa Progress Panel. Online, available at: www.africaprogresspanel.org/wp-content/uploads/2013/08/2013_APR_Equity_in_Extractives_25062013_ENG_HR.pdf.

Barnett, T. (2011) *America's False Recovery: The Coming Sovereign Debt Crisis and Rise of Democratic Plutocracy*. Jacksonville: Merit & Justice Press.

Baskan, J. (2005) *The Corporation: The Pathological Pursuit of Profit and Power*. New York: Simon & Schuster.

Bloomberg Visual Data (2013) "The Great Gatsby Curve: Declining Mobility." November 8. Online, available at: www.bloomberg.com/infographics/2013-10-08/the-great-gatsby-curve-explained.html.

Buchhelt, L., Beatrice Weder di Mauro, Anna Gelpern, Mitu Gulati, Ugo Panizza, Jeromin Zettelmeyer (2013) "Revisiting Sovereign Bankruptcy." *Vox*. November 12. Online, available at: www.voxeu.org/article/revisiting-sovereign-bankruptcy.

Bunker, R. (2012) "Plutocratic Insurgency." *Small Wars Journal*. September 6. Online, available at: http://smallwarsjournal.com/blog/plutocratic-insurgency.

Bunker, R. and Sullivan, S. (2012) "Integrating Feral Cities and 3rd Phase Cartels/3rd Generation Gangs Research: the Rise of Criminal (Narco) City Networks and Black-For." Bunker, R., ed., *Criminal Insurgencies in Mexico and the Americas: The Gangs and Cartels Wage War*. Routledge: London, 765–787.

Carney, T. (2013) "How Corporate Tax Credits got in the 'Cliff' Deal.'" *Washington Examiner*. January 2. Online, available at: http://washingtonexaminer.com/tim-carney-how-corporate-tax-credits-got-in-the-cliff-deal/article/2517397.

Castells, M. (2012) *Networks of Outrage and Hope: Social Movements in the Internet Age*. Cambridge: Polity Press.

Cavanagh, J. (2004) *Alternatives to Economic Globalization: A Better World Is Possible*. San Francisco: Berrett-Koehler Publishers.

Chatterjee, P. (2012) "The New Robber Barons: how Taxpayers Subsidise CEOs' Multi-million Salaries." *Guardian*. August 19. Online, available at: www.theguardian.com/commentisfree/2012/aug/19/new-robber-barons-how-taxpayers-subsidise-ceos.

Clark, T. (2013) "One British Household in 10 has £1m Assets." *Guardian*. May 21. Online, available at: www.theguardian.com/money/2013/may/21/british-household-1m-assets.

Coghlan, A. and MacKenzie, D. (2011) "Revealed—the Capitalist Network that Runs the World." *New Scientist*. October 24. Online, available at: www.newscientist.com/article/mg21228354.500-revealed-the-capitalist-network-that-runs-the-world.html.

Coll, S. (2012) *Private Empire: ExxonMobil and American Power*. New York: Penguin Press.

Collins, C. (2012) *99 to 1: How Wealth Inequality Is Wrecking the World and What We Can Do about It*. San Francisco: Berrett-Koehler Publishers.

Collinson, P. (2012) "Richest 10% of UK Households Own 40% of Wealth, ONS says." *Guardian*. December 3. Online, available at: www.theguardian.com/money/2012/dec/03/richest-10-uk-households-40-per-cent-wealth-ons.

Davidson, P. (2012) "US Median Household Income up 4% at End of 2011." *USA Today*. February 9. Online, available at: http://usatoday30.usatoday.com/money/economy/story/2012-02-09/income-rising/53033322/1.

Davis, M. (2007) *Planet of Slums*. London: Verso.

Davis, M. and Monk, D. (2008) *Evil Paradises: Dreamworlds of Neoliberalism*. New York: The New Press.

Decarlo, S. (2013) "The World's Biggest Companies." *Forbes*. April 17. Online, available at: www.forbes.com/sites/scottdecarlo/2013/04/17/the-worlds-biggest-companies-2/.

DeLong, J. (2012) "Inequality: Living in the Second Gilded Age." For the *San Francisco Chronicle*. October 28. Online, available at: http://delong.typepad.com/sdj/2012/10/inequality-living-in-the-second-gilded-age.html.

Denhart, C. (2013) "How the $1.2 Trillion College Debt Crisis Is Crippling Students, Parents and the Economy." *Forbes*. August 7. Online, available at: www.forbes.com/sites/specialfeatures/2013/08/07/how-the-college-debt-is-crippling-students-parents-and-the-economy/.

Dent, K. (2014) "Cambridge's Endowment Funds make it Britain's Richest University." *Cambridge Student*. January 16. Online, available at: www.tcs.cam.ac.uk/news/0030480-cambridges-endowment-funds-make-it-britains-richest-university.html.

Desilver, D. (2013) "5 Facts about the National Debt: What you should Know." Pew Research Center. October 9. Online, available at: www.pewresearch.org/fact-tank/2013/10/09/5-facts-about-the-national-debt-what-you-should-know/.

Doward, J. (2009) "Taxpayers in £481m Police Pension Top-up." *Guardian*. November 21. Online, available at: www.theguardian.com/politics/2009/nov/22/police-pension-funding-shortfall.

Drake, B. (2013) *Having a Secure Job Replaces Homeownership as the Key to being Middle-class*. August 9. Online, available at: www.pewresearch.org/fact-tank/2013/08/09/having-a-secure-job-replaces-homeownership-as-the-key-to-being-middle-class/.

Dudley, S. (2013) "How Juarez's Police, Politicians Picked Winners of Gang War." *Insight Crime*. February 13. Online, available at: www.insightcrime.org/juarez-war-stability-and-the-future/juarez-police-politicians-picked-winners-gang-war.

Duhigg, C. and Bradsher, K. (2012) "How the US Lost Out on iPhone Work." *New York Times*. January 21. Online, available at: www.nytimes.com/2012/01/22/business/apple-america-and-a-squeezed-middle-class.html?pagewanted=all.

Egan, T. (2013) "Dystopia by the Bay." *New York Times*. December 5. Online, available at: www.nytimes.com/2013/12/06/opinion/dystopia-by-the-bay.html?_r=0.

Ellis, B. (2011) "Food Stamp use Rises to Record 45.8 million." *CNN*. August 4. Online, available at: http://money.cnn.com/2011/08/04/pf/food_stamps_record_high/.

Engineer (2008) "Defective Body Armour." October 10. Online, available at: www.theengineer.co.uk/news/defective-body-armour/308333.article.

Europol (2013) *EU Serious and Organised Crime Threat Assessment (SOCTA 2013)*. March 19. Online, available at: www.europol.europa.eu/content/eu-serious-and-organised-crime-threat-assessment-socta.

Faux, J. (2012) *The Servant Economy: Where America's Elite is Sending the Middle Class*. Hoboken: John Wiley & Sons, Inc.

Ferguson, A. (2012). "Bubble on the Potomac." *Time*. May 28: 46–52.

Fertik, M. (2013) "The Rich See a Different Internet Than the Poor." *Scientific American*. February 18. Online, available at: www.scientificamerican.com/article.cfm?id=rich-see-different-internet-than-the-poor.

Flannery, N. (2013) "Looking Back at 2012: A Year of #Mexico #Drugwar Tweets." *Forbes*. January 4. Online, available at: www.forbes.com/sites/nathanielparishflannery/2013/01/04/looking-back-at-2012-a-year-of-mexico-drugwar-tweets/.

Flores, A. (2013) "Student Debt Nearly Doubles since 2007." *Los Angeles Times*. June 20: B4.

Foroohar, R. (2012a) "Stocks for Safety?' *Time*. January 9. Online, available at: http://content.time.com/time/magazine/article/0,9171,2103281,00.html.

Foroohar, R. (2012b) "Companies are the New Countries." *Time*. February 13: 21.

Fraser, S. (2008) "Tomgram: Steve Fraser, the Two Gilded Ages." April 22. Online, available at: www.tomdispatch.com/post/174922.

Freeland, C. (2012) *Plutocrats: The Rise of the New Global Super-Rich and the Fall of Everyone Else*. New York: Penguin Books.

Fukuyama, F. (1989) "The End of History." *National Interest*. Summer, Vol. 16. No. 3: 3–18.

Fukuyama, F. (1992) *The End of History and the Last Man*. New York: Free Press.

Gilman, S., Goldhammer, J. and Weber, S. (2011) *Deviant Globalization: Black Market Economy in the 21st Century*. New York: Continuum.

Gilman, N. (2012) "Plutocratic Insurgency." *Small Precautions*. September 5. Online, available at: http://smallprecautions.blogspot.com/2012/09/plutocratic-insurgency.html.

Gilman, N. and Costigan, M. (2012) "The Arbitrage of the Nation-state." *Breakthrough Journal*. February. Online, available at: http://thebreakthrough.org/index.php/journal/debates/against-cosmopolitanism-a-breakthrough-debate//the-arbitrage-of-the-nation-state/.

Golden, D. (2007) *The Price of Admission: How America's Ruling Class Buys Its Way into Elite Colleges—and Who Gets Left outside the Gates*. New York: Random House.

Gottschalck, A., Vornovytsky, M. and Smith, A. (2013) "Household Wealth and Debt in the U.S: 2000 to 2011." United States Census Bureau. Online, available at http://blogs.census.gov/2013/03/21/household-wealth-and-debt-in-the-u-s-2000-to-2011/.

Greeley, B. (2013) "The Gatsby Curve: How Inequality Became a Household Word." *Bloomberg Businessweek*. December 12. Online, available at: www.businessweek.com/articles/2013-12-05/obama-talks-inequality-and-mobility-going-full-gatsby.

Green, J. (2013) "Congress: 1.3 Million Americans are about to have a Terrible Christmas." *Bloomberg Businessweek*. December 9. Online, available at: www.businessweek.com/articles/2013-12-09/1-dot-3-million-americans-are-about-to-have-a-terrible-christmas.

Guardian (2010) "Marriage Rates in the UK." February 11. Online, available at: www.theguardian.com/news/datablog/2010/feb/11/marriage-rates-uk-data.

Harvard Magazine (2013) "Endowment Value Rises to $32.7 Billion." September 24. Online, available at: http://harvardmagazine.com/2013/09/harvard-endowment-up-2-billion-to-32-7-billion.

Harvard University Institute of Politics (2012) "Harvard's Institute of Politics, UPENN's Fels Institute of Government and AEF Produce US State Annual Reports." November 27. Online, available at: www.iop.harvard.edu/november-27-2012-harvard's-institute-politics-upenn's-fels-institute-government-and-aef-produce-us.

Heine, J. and Thakur, R. eds. (2011) *The Dark Side of Globalization*. New York: United Nations University.

Hertz, N. (2001) *The Silent Takeover: Global Capitalism and the Death of Democracy*. New York: The Free Press.

Heskett, J. (2013) "Is Walmart Defying Economic Gravity?" *Forbes*. December 5. Online, available at: www.forbes.com/sites/hbsworkingknowledge/2013/12/05/is-walmart-defying-economic-gravity/.

Hsu, T. (2012) "Wealthy May Hide as Much $32 Trillion Offshore, Report Says." *Los Angeles Times*. July 23. Online, available at: http://articles.latimes.com/2012/jul/23/business/la-fi-mo-tax-havens-20120723.

Inman, P. (2007) "Amicus Moves to Create Multinational 'Super-union.'" *Guardian*. January 1. Online, available at: www.theguardian.com/business/2007/jan/02/politics. tradeunions.

Jeffrey, T. (2013) "23,116,928 to 20,618,000: Households on Food Stamps Now Outnumber All Households in Northeast US." *CNS News*. September 17. Online, available at: http://cnsnews.com/news/article/terence-p-jeffrey/23116928-20618000-households-food-stamps-now-outnumber-all-households.

Kapur, A., Macleod, N. and Singh, N. (2005) "Equity Strategy: Plutonomy: Buying Luxury, Explaining Global Imbalance. Citigroup Equity Note. October 16: 1–32.

Kharpal, A. (2013) "Global Wealth Hit $241 Trillion, but Distribution Skewed." *CNBC News*. October 11. Online, available at: www.cnbc.com/id/101105809.

Klein, N. (2007) *The Shock Doctrine: The Rise of Disaster Capitalism*. New York: Metropolitan Books.

Korten, D. (2001) *When Corporations Rule the World*. San Francisco: Berrett-Koehler Publishers.

Kostigen, T. (2012) "Informal Economy: Huge and Growing." *MSN Money*. January 16. Online, available at: http://money.msn.com/investing/informal-economy-massive-and-growing-marketwatch.aspx.

Krueger, A. (2012) "The Rise and Consequences of Inequality in the United States: Charts." Charts prepared for a speech by A. Krueger, Chairman of the Council of Economic Advisers, on January 12 at the Center for American Progress. Online, available at: www.slideshare.net/whitehouse/the-rise-and-consequences-of-inequality-in-the-united-states-charts.

Lewin, T. (2013) "Report Says Stanford is First University to Raise $1 Billion in a Single Year." *New York Times*. February 20. Online, available at: www.nytimes.com/2013/02/21/education/stanfords-fund-raising-topped-1-billion-in-2012.html?_r=0.

Li, S. (2013) "Middle-class Neighborhoods Losing Residents." *Los Angeles Times*. October 18: B2.

Lowrey, A. (2013) "Top 1 Percent Take Record Share of US Income." *Seattle Times*. September 10. Online, available at: http://seattletimes.com/html/nationworld/2021795994_incomegapxml.html.

McCoy, K. (2013a) "Did Apple do Irish Jig around Taxes?" *USA Today*. May 21: 3B.

McCoy, K. (2013b) "Apple's Tax Ingenuity a Tough Sell." *USA Today*. May 22: 1B–2B.

McGarth, M. (2013) "Fitch Puts US On Credit Downgrade Watch." *Forbes*. October 15. Online, available at: www.forbes.com/sites/maggiemcgrath/2013/10/15/fitch-puts-u-s-on-credit-downgrade-watch/.

Maier, C. (1975) *Recasting Bourgeois Europe*. Princeton: Princeton University Press.

Malanga, S. (2013) "The Indebted States of America." *City Journal*. Summer, Vol. 23. No. 3. Online, available at: www.city-journal.org/2013/23_3_state-debt.html.

Marsden, S. (2013) "Job Insecurity Leaves Marriage the Preserve of Middle-class Couples—Study." *Telegraph*. August 13. Online, available at: www.telegraph.co.uk/news/politics/10238664/Job-insecurity-leaves-marriage-the-preserve-of-middle-class-couples-study.html.

Martinuzzi, E. (2010) "Goldman Sachs, Greece Didn't Disclose Swap Contract (Update1)." Bloomberg. February 17. Online, available at: www.bloomberg.com/apps/news?pid=newsarchive&sid=akqC4y5U7MnU.

Martinuzzi, E. and Petrakis, M. (2010) "EU Seeks Greek Swaps Disclosure after Ministry Probe (Update2)." *Bloomberg*. February 15. Online, available at: www.bloomberg.com/apps/news?pid=newsarchive&sid=a5MJFT2dMyIU.

Marx, K. and Engels, F. (1886) *Manifesto of the Communists*. London: International Publishing Co. Online, available at: www.bl.uk/learning/images/21cc/waves/large1745.html.

Mathews, J. (1997) "Power Shift: The Rise of Global Civil Society." *Foreign Affairs*. January–February. Online, available at: www.foreignaffairs.com/articles/52644/jessica-t-mathews/power-shift.

Matthews, C. (2012). "Ritz Retail: Why Shopping Developers are Catering to the Well-off." *Time*. September 17: 18.

Metz, S. (1993) *The Future of Insurgency*. Carlisle: Strategic Studies Institute, US Army War College. December 10. Online, available at: www.strategicstudiesinstitute.army.mil/pubs/display.cfm?pubID=344.

Mishel, L., Josh Bivens, Elise Gould, Heidi Shierholz (2012) *The State of Working America*. 12th edition. Ithaca: Cornell University Press. EPI digital edition overview. Online, available at: http://stateofworkingamerica.org/files/book/Chapter1-Overview.pdf.

Naoriji, D. (1881) *No. 3. Memorandum on a Few Statements in the Report of the Indian Famine Commission, 1880*. Posted July 28, 2013. Online, available at: http://sabhlokcity.com/2013/07/british-rule-in-india-was-plunder-of-an-unceasing-foreign-invasion-naorojis-1880-statement/#sthash.G0amJuiG.dpuf.

National Debt Clocks (2013) December 16. Online, available at: www.nationaldebtclocks.org.

National Gang Intelligence Center (NGIC) (2011) *National Gang Threat Assessment—Emerging Trends*. Washington, DC. Online, available at: www.fbi.gov/stats-services/publications/2011-national-gang-threat-assessment/2011-national-gang-threat-assessment-emerging-trends.

Neate, R. (2012) "Apple Paid Less than 2% Tax on Overseas Profits Last Year." *Guardian*. November 4. Online, available at: www.theguardian.com/technology/2012/nov/04/apple-paid-low-overseas-tax.

Neu, C., Mao, Z. and Cook, I. (2013) *Fiscal Performance and US International Influence*. Santa Monica: RAND. Online, available at: www.rand.org/pubs/research_reports/RR353.html.

Neuwirth, R. (2012) *Stealth of Nations: The Global Rise of the Informal Economy*. New York: Anchor Books.

Organisation for Economic Co-operation and Development (OECD) (2011) "An Overview of Growing Income Inequalities in OECD Countries: Main Findings." Paris. Online, available at: www.oecd.org/els/soc/49499779.pdf.

O'Toole, J. (2013) "Moody's Downgrades United Kingdom from Aaa." *CNN Money*. February 22. Online, available at: http://money.cnn.com/2013/02/22/news/economy/moodys-uk-downgrade/.

Oxford Dictionaries (2013a) Definition of "Capitalism." Oxford: Oxford University Press. Online, available at: www.oxforddictionaries.com/definition/english/capitalism.

Oxford Dictionaries (2013b) Definition of "Free Market." Oxford: Oxford University Press. Online, available at: www.oxforddictionaries.com/definition/english/free-market?q=free+market.

Palmer, M. and Schneer, B. (2013) "Capitol Gains: Retired Members of Congress and Corporate Board Directorships." Prepared for the Annual Meeting of the Southern Political Science Association, New Orleans, Louisiana. January 9–11, 2014. Online, available at: http://maxwellpalmer.com/files/capitol_gains.pdf.

Patnaude, A. (2013) "Fitch Downgrades UK Rating." *Wall Street Journal*. April 19.

Online, available at: http://online.wsj.com/news/articles/SB1000142412788732449370 4578432761463111892.

Public Broadcasting System (PBS) (2009) "Ghana: Digital Dumping Ground." June 23. Online, available at: www.pbs.org/frontlineworld/stories/ghana804/video/video_index. html.

Peachy, P. (2014) "Lee Rigby Murder: UK's Street Gangs 'are the Next Breeding Ground for New Brand of Extremist.'" *Independent*. January 7. Online, available at: www. independent.co.uk/news/uk/crime/lee-rigby-murder-uks-street-gangs–are-the-next-breeding-ground-for-new-brand-of-extremist-9016698.html.

Pertuno, T. (2011) "Corporate Power Grows as Government Wanes." *Los Angeles Times*. November 19: B1, B4.

Peston, R. (2011) "UK's Debts 'Biggest in the World.'" *BBC News*. November 21. Online, available at: www.bbc.co.uk/news/business-15820601.

Pipes, D. (2013 [2006]) "The 751 No-Go Zones of France." *Daniel Pipes Middle East Forum*. November 22 [November 14]. Online, available at: www.danielpipes.org/blog/2006/11/the-751-no-go-zones-of-france.

Pizzigati, S. (2012) *The Rich Don't Always Win: The Forgotten Triumph Over Plutocracy that Created the American Middle Class, 1900–1970*. New York: Seven Stories Press.

Polanyi, K. (1944) *The Great Transformation*. New York, Toronto, Farrar & Rinehart, Inc.

Project Censored (1999) "Mercenary Armies in Service to Global Corporations." Online, available at: www.projectcensored.org/16-mercenary-armies-in-service-to-global-corporations/.

Ramesh, R. (2011) "Income Inequality Growing Faster in UK than any Other Rich Country, says OECD." *Guardian*. December 5. Online, available at: www.theguardian. com/society/2011/dec/05/income-inequality-growing-faster-uk.

Reeves, J. (2013) "19 Shocking Facts about Detroit's Bankruptcy." *USA Today*. December 3. Online, available at: www.usatoday.com/story/money/personalfinance/2013/12/02/19-facts-about-detroit-bankruptcy/3823355/.

Reich, R. (2012) *Beyond Outrage: Expanded Edition: What has Gone Wrong with our Economy and our Democracy, and how to Fix It*. New York: Vintage.

Reich, R. (2013) "Global Capital and the Nation State." May 20. Online, available at: http://robertreich.org/post/50890974932.

Reuters (2012) "RPT-Theft on Mexico Fuel Pipelines Jumps 55 pct—Pemex." April 23. Online, available at: http://uk.reuters.com/article/2012/04/23/mexico-oil-idUKL2E8FNC6320120423.

Reyes, I. (2013) "El 10% del país en 'estado fallido.'" *24 Horas*. December 10. Online, available at: www.24-horas.mx/el-10-del-pais-en-estado-fallido/.

Richardson, V. (2011) "House Members in the Know Score 'Abnormal' Stock Profits, Study Says." *Washington Times*. May 25. Online, available at: www.washingtontimes. com/news/2011/may/25/house-members-stock-market-success-questioned/?page=all.

Riley, C. (2012) "Family Net Worth Plummets nearly 40%." *CNN Money*. June 12. Online, available at: http://money.cnn.com/2012/06/11/news/economy/fed-family-net-worth/.

Rodney, W. (1972) *How Europe Underdeveloped Africa*. London: Bogle L'Ouverture Press.

Rodrik, D. (2012) *The Globalization Paradox: Democracy and the Future of the World Economy*. New York: W.W. Norton & Company.

Rothkopf, D. (2008) *Superclass: The Global Power Elite and the World They Are Making*. New York: Farrar, Straus, and Giroux.

Rothkopf, D. (2012) *Power, Inc. The Epic Rivalry between Big Business and Government —and the Reckoning That Lies Ahead.* New York: Farrar, Straus, and Giroux.

Schroeder, R. (2013) "US on 'Unsustainable' Budget Course: CBO." *MarketWatch: Wall Street Journal.* September 17. Online, available at: www.marketwatch.com/story/cbo-issues-fresh-long-term-debt-warning-2013-09-17?link=MW_pulse.

Schulz, T. (2011) "The Second Gilded Age: Has America Become an Oligarchy?" *Spiegel Online International.* October 28. Online, available at: www.spiegel.de/international/spiegel/the-second-gilded-age-has-america-become-an-oligarchy-a-793896.html.

Schweizer, P. and Boyer, P. (2011) "The Wonk Who Slays Washington." *Newsweek.* November 21: 32–37.

Semuels, A. (2013) "US Firms' Cash Hoard: $1.45 Trillion." *Los Angeles Times.* March 21: B5.

Smith, H. (2013) *Who Stole the American Dream?* New York: Random House.

Standard and Poors (2011) "United States of America Long-Term Rating Lowered To 'AA+' Due To Political Risks, Rising Debt Burden; Outlook Negative." August 5. Online, available at: www.standardandpoors.com/ratings/articles/en/us/?assetID=1245316 529563.

Stanford News (2013) "Stanford Management Company Releases 2013 Results." September 25. Online, available at: http://news.stanford.edu/news/2013/september/stanford-management-company-092513.html.

Stiglitz, J. (2003) *Globalization and Its Discontents.* New York: W.W. Norton & Company.

Stiglitz, J. (2013) *The Price of Inequality: How Today's Divided Society Endangers Our Future.* New York: W.W. Norton & Company.

Stockman, D. (2013) *The Great Deformation: The Corruption of Capitalism in America.* New York: Public Affairs.

Sullivan, J. (2008) "Transnational Gangs: The Impact of Third Generation Gangs in Central America." *Air and Space Power Journal—Spanish Edition.* Second Trimester. Online, available at: www.airpower.maxwell.af.mil/apjinternational/apj-s/2008/2tri08/sullivaneng.htm.

Taibbi, M. (2013) "Looting the Pension Funds." *Rolling Stone.* September 26. Online, available at: www.rollingstone.com/politics/news/looting-the-pension-funds-20130926.

Telegraph (2013) "Energy Companies 'Turning their Noses Up' at Parliament and Consumers, says MP." October 29. Online, available at: www.telegraph.co.uk/earth/energy/10411192/Energy-companies-turning-their-noses-up-at-Parliament-and-consumers-says-MP.html.

The Economist (2013a) "Sweet Land of Subsidy." April 27: 27–28.

The Economist (2013b) "Subject: Asset Protection and Regime Change." May 11: 16.

Trivett, V. (2011) "25 US Mega Corporations: Where They Rank If They Were Countries." *Business Insider.* June 27. Online, available at: www.businessinsider.com/25-corporations-bigger-tan-countries-2011-6?op=1.

Twain, M. (1871) "The Revised Catechism." *New York Tribune.* September 27.

Tyre, P. and Philips, M. (2007) "Poor Among Plenty." *Newsweek.* February 12: 54.

United Nations Educational, Scientific and Cultural Organization (UNESCO) (2000) "Gujarat—Ship-Breaking and Coastal Pollution." May 29. Online, available at: www.unesco.org/csi/act/india/IndiaGujR.htm.

Unz, R. (2012) "Paying Tuition to a Giant Hedge Fund." *American Conservative.* December 4. Online, available at: www.theamericanconservative.com/articles/paying-tuition-to-a-giant-hedge-fund/.

US Bureau of Labor Statistics (US BLS) (2012) "BLS Spotlight on Statistics: The Recession of 2007–2009." February. Online, available at: www.bls.gov/spotlight/2012/recession/pdf/recession_bls_spotlight.pdf.

Vandivier, D. (2013) "What is the Great Gatsby Curve?' *White House Blog*. June 11. Online, available at: www.whitehouse.gov/blog/2013/05/28/great-gatsby-curve.

Vitali, S., Glattfelder, J. and Battiston, S. (2011) "The Network of Global Corporate Control." *PLOS One*. October 26. Online, available at: www.plosone.org/article/info%3Adoi%2F10.1371%2Fjournal.pone.0025995.

Vulliamy, E. (2010) *Amexica: War along the Borderline*. New York: Picador.

Vulliamy, E. (2011a) "How a Big US Bank Laundered Billions from Mexico's Murderous Drug Gangs." *Observer*. April 2. Online, available at: www.theguardian.com/world/2011/apr/03/us-bank-mexico-drug-gangs.

Vulliamy, E. (2011b) "Ciudad Juarez is all our Futures. This is the Inevitable War of Capitalism Gone Mad." *Guardian*. June 20. Online, available at: www.theguardian.com/commentisfree/2011/jun/20/war-capitalism-mexico-drug-cartels.

Warner, C. (2007) *The Best System Money Can Buy: Corruption in the European Union*. Ithaca: Cornell University Press.

Warner, J. (2012) "Britain is becoming a Nation of Renters as Overseas Investors Gobble up the Housing Stock." *Telegraph*. December 11. Online, available at: http://blogs.telegraph.co.uk/finance/jeremywarner/100021775/britain-is-becoming-a-nation-of-renters-and-overseas-investors-gobble-up-the-housing-stock/.

Wheeler, B. (2012) "Why is the US Marriage Rate Falling Sharply?' *BBC News*. January 9. Online, available at: www.bbc.co.uk/news/magazine-16274740.

Wolff, R. (2013) "US Political Dysfunction and Capitalism's Withdrawal." *e-International Relations*. October 27. Online, available at: www.e-ir.info/2013/10/27/us-political-dysfunction-and-capitalisms-withdrawal/.

Wolff, R. and Barsamian, D. (2012) *Occupy the Economy: Challenging Capitalism*. San Francisco: City Lights Publishers.

Wolverson, R. and Walt, V. (2012) "Take the Money and Run." *Time*. July 30: 13.

Yale News (2013) "Endowment Earns 12.5% Return." September 24. Online, available at: http://news.yale.edu/2013/09/24/endowment-earns-125-return.

Zeveloff, J. (2014) "Where the World's Super-Rich Spend Their Millions on Real Estate [MAP]." *Business Insider*. January 16. Online, available at: www.businessinsider.com/where-super-rich-spend-money-on-real-estate-map-2014-1.

Part III

Demise of the Western democracies

7 The demise of the American middle class and the rise of the police state

Tanya Buhler Corbin and Nicole Hendrix

When we think of governments that exercise power through coercion, we typically think of dictatorships, authoritarian regimes, and pseudo-democracies. The common feature of these regimes is corruption, and control over the government and the people by a select, elite group. In contrast, democratic government provides a potential inhibitor on corruption through constitutional checks and institutional arrangements that are intended to prevent the concentration of power among elites. However, democracy is at risk when these protections fail to provide adequate limitations on governmental power. The success of democracy depends on an active and educated citizenry to function as the watchdog over government.

Political thinkers since Aristotle have established an important relationship between the middle class and democracy. A large and robust middle class is both the harbinger and shepherd of democracy. Likewise, securing and protecting individual liberties from government intrusion is fundamental to ensure a free society. In recent decades, the United States has experienced a decline in the middle class, rising economic inequality, and a decrease in civil liberties and freedoms among citizens. We argue that these trends, if unabated, threaten the future of democratic government in the United States.

In this chapter, we explore the precarious position of the middle class, and the increased and often unchecked use of militaristic law enforcement strategies to combat crime and respond to global and domestic terrorist threats. First, we consider the decline of the middle class and increasing economic inequality in America. We argue that changes to the current economic and political trajectory are essential to preserve the middle class in America, and in turn, the republic. Next, we discuss the ways in which an American culture of fear has developed over several decades, and the ways in which the 9/11 attacks have exacerbated this fear. We examine the rise of the police state and the encroachment on Americans' civil liberties, and explore the ways in which our institutions have legitimized this shift. We conclude with some thoughts about the implications of these developments for the future, as well as strategies and recommendations for reforms to strengthen the middle class and check the power of the police state.

The ubiquitous American "middle class"

Although about half of all Americans purport to belong to the "middle class," when pressed to explain the term, few can do so with precision. Economists focus on income measures, while social scientists (e.g. sociologists and psychologists) have emphasized other characteristics that define the middle class, such as social status, identity, values and lifestyle. Some social scientists have aggregated occupation, income, education and other characteristics to create rankings of social standing and living standards (Gilbert, 2008; Nam and Boyd, 2004).

Defining the middle class with precision is difficult. Even relying solely on economic data, there are several different income measures used to define the middle class that vary depending on the data source and how the data are operationalized. Most economic analyses of the middle class use income as the defining measure (Frank, 2007; Isaacs *et al.*, 2008). However, some economic analyses use ranges based on absolute dollar-values, income levels relative to median household income, and income levels relative to the poverty line. The economic measure of middle class suggested by economist Robert Reich defines middle class as families with income levels ranging from 50 percent above and below the median income (Reich, 2012). This measure would put the 2012 middle class income range at $25,500–$76,500, with a median of $51,071 (Kamp, 2013). Another measure, more easily tailored to variations among individual families, is the Family Budget Calculator measure, constructed by the Economic Policy Institute (EPI), which calculates the amount of money needed for a family of four to live a modest and comfortable lifestyle. In 2013, according to this measure, a two-parent family in Wichita, Kansas, with both parents working and two children, would need to earn $64,250 to live the modest lifestyle that we typically equate with the middle class (Gould *et al.*, 2013). This number is close to the Pew Research Center's (Pew) analysis based on US Census Data of the median income for a family of four of $68,274. Public opinion closely mirrors these measures: public opinion estimates of income levels needed for a middle class lifestyle put the median at $60,000 in the Midwest, $70,000 in the South and West, and $85,000 in the East. Rural areas estimate $55,000 and suburban and urban areas estimate $70,000–$75,000 (Pew Research Center, 2012).

Sociologists address the wide income range used to define the middle class by breaking the middle class into subgroups. The upper middle class earns an above average income, ranging from $113,000–200,000 annually. The average-middles include occupations such as bank managers, teachers and high-skilled blue-collar jobs, and earn $49,000–112,000 annually. Lower middle or working class members earn $28,000–49,000 annually, and are more vulnerable to economic shocks and hardships (Macionis, 2012). Although these income groups have differences between them, they are all part of the "middle class" according to sociologists.

In addition to looking at an income median derived from government data, some measures, such as those used by the Pew Research Center, include survey respondents who self-identify as middle class. By this measure, based on a 2012 national survey of 2,508 adults, 49 percent describe themselves as middle class. This compares with 53 percent who defined themselves as middle class in a similar survey in early 2008. The 2012 survey finds an increase in those who self-identify as being in the lower or lower-middle class. In 2008, 25 percent categorized themselves as such, but by 2012, this number rose to 32 percent. Similarly, 17 percent now classify themselves as part of the upper or upper-middle class, down from 21 percent in 2008 (Pew Research Center, 2012). A summary of survey results in which people reported their income and class status indicated that the self-defined middle class included people with household incomes ranging from $40,000 to $250,000 (Cashell, 2008). For example, 40 percent of Americans with incomes below $20,000, and one-third of people with incomes above $150,000 categorize themselves as middle class (Pew Research Center, 2008).

However, we cannot adequately define the middle class solely by income, or even by measures of income and wealth combined. Being part of the middle class is as much a cultural identification as it is an economic one. While there is an income threshold associated with the middle class that is necessary to afford a modest and comfortable lifestyle, the middle class ethos is also about the cultural identification of the "American dream," achieved by hard work and education, and with the accompanying reward of economic stability. In fact, the majority of Americans (63 percent) agree with the statement "Most people can get ahead if they are willing to work hard." In contrast, 34 percent believe that "hard work and determination are no guarantee of success" (Pew Research Center, 2012). There is a strong belief in individual control over one's destiny amongst middle class Americans. An important value for the middle class is the value of equality of opportunity over equality of outcomes.

Middle class expectations about the American way of life include protection against hardships associated with poverty. They expect access to affordable health care, high quality education for their children, and the ability to own a home and maintain a savings account. The middle class has respect for the law, which they view as providing them protection from crime (US Department of Commerce Economics and Statistics Administration, 2010). For many years, a middle class life meant holding a "white collar job" and home ownership, but the Great Recession that began in 2007 and economic trends of the last three decades have shifted the priorities of the middle class to emphasize a secure job with health care benefits over home ownership. Having a secure job has replaced homeownership as the hallmark of the middle class, with 86 percent of Americans citing a secure job as the number one defining characteristic of the middle class (Drake, 2012). Middle class Americans and those aspiring to be part of the middle class seek economic stability, a secure retirement, affordable health care, and being able to send their children to college and take family vacations (US Department of Commerce Economics and Statistics Administration, 2010).

In sum, regardless of which measures economists and social scientists employ, most Americans self-identify as members of the "middle class."

Although attaining a place in the middle class requires an adequate income level, this is merely one part of the picture. Beyond income, those who seek to join or remain part of the middle class in America need equality of opportunity for social mobility that comes through affordable, high quality education, affordable and accessible health care, and the availability of jobs that can provide economic stability. The defining features of the middle class are economic stability and security, and the core belief in the "American dream" that if people work hard enough, they can improve their economic situation and class status.

Inequality, class and implications for democracy

The middle class is shrinking and losing ground. Using the Pew Research Center income measure, over 61 percent of Americans were part of the middle class in 1961. By 2011, this number had decreased by 10 percent, to include 51 percent of all adults (Pew Research Center, 2012). In addition to having fewer people in the middle class, social and economic measures of well-being indicate that the individuals in the middle class and those who hope to join the ranks someday are in a precarious position. For several decades, the middle class has experienced stagnant and declining incomes and net worth, and decreases in economic opportunities. In the cases where we see modest income gains among middle class families, this has come from working longer hours, moving from one to two adult labor force participants, and increasing household debt levels to compensate for wages that failed to keep pace with inflation (Boushey and Hersh, 2012).

Middle class incomes have remained stagnant over the past few decades, and in the last decade incomes have declined (Madland, 2012). Census Bureau data indicate that in 2012, the average American household earned $51,017, roughly the equivalent dollar amount of what the average household earned 25 years ago (Porter, 2013). When that number is adjusted for inflation using the CPI Inflation Calculator from the Bureau of Labor Statistics, the average earnings of $51,017 in 1988 translates to the equivalent of earning $99,013 in today's dollars. The net worth of middle-income families also took a hit during the past decade. According to data (2001 to 2010) from the Federal Reserve's Survey of Consumer Finances, the median net worth fell 28 percent, which eliminated two decades of gains (Bricker *et al.*, 2012). It would be difficult for any casual newspaper reader to miss the articles sounding the alarm about the declining middle class. A cursory search in LexisNexis returned 979 articles containing headlines about the middle class in the last five years, most of which discuss the perilous position or the alarming decline of the number of middle class Americans. The Great Recession of 2007 accelerated the trend of declining economic gains and economic security for the middle class.

At the same time that wages have stagnated and declined, the cost of three important middle class expenses have increased faster than income: college, healthcare and housing. This makes it is more difficult to attain a middle class lifestyle now than it was in past decades. The current family median income of $60,000 is woefully inadequate to achieve a middle class lifestyle. In fact, even families earning almost $81,000 in 2008 would have a much tougher time affording a middle class lifestyle compared to middle class families in 1990[1] (US Department of Commerce, 2010). As Porter notes:

> Incomes of these types of [middle class] families increased between 1990 and 2008. They were more educated and worked more hours, on average, and had children at a later age. Still, that was no match for the 56 percent jump in the cost of housing, the 155 percent leap in out-of-pocket spending on health care and the double-digit increase in the cost of college.
>
> (Porter, 2013)

"Americans may today benefit from cheap cell phones, inexpensive clothing, and Facebook, but they increasingly cannot afford their own homes, or health insurance, or comfortable pensions when they retire." (Fukuyama, 2012: 6).

The decline of the American middle class threatens the future of the republic, as a thriving middle class is fundamental for democracy to flourish. In fact, beginning with Aristotle, democratic theorists have consistently argued that a society must have few citizens living in poverty and a large, stable middle class to develop and sustain the habits that support democracy. As Aristotle notes:

> Thus, it is manifest that the best political community is formed by citizens of the middle class, and that those states are likely to be well-administered in which the middle class is larger, and stronger, if possible, than both other classes.
>
> (Aristotle, *Politics*, Book IV: 11)

Since Aristotle, political philosophers have written extensively about the importance of a large middle class to sustain democracy in the nation state. This has been one of the hallmarks of the American tradition.

In the United States, the government derives its legitimacy from the fundamental principle of popular sovereignty, as articulated by the American Founders. Popular sovereignty hinges upon both the secure protection of individual civil liberties and a large middle class, as these conditions ensure that the citizens are empowered to serve as watchdogs over the government. The Bill of Rights and US constitution establish a republican form of government. However, the primary mechanisms by which citizens check the powers of government require more than written documents. Consider the many examples around the world of other nations who have constitutions that often look surprisingly similar to the US constitution, yet in practice operate as pseudo-democracies.

To sustain democratic societies, vigilance on the part of citizens is required. Where does this citizen vigilance in guarding democracy come from, and what sustains it? Democratic theorists, ancient and modern, understand the crux of democracy to include active and engaged participation in political and civic affairs by educated, invested and empowered citizens with individual rights and liberties. Tocqueville refers to this as equality of condition. In Tocqueville's observations of American life from his travels to America, he reflected on Americans' equality and the resulting political and civil society that springs from this condition:

> No novelty in the United States struck me more vividly than the general equality of condition among the people. I readily discovered the prodigious influence that this primary fact exercises on the whole course of society; it gives a peculiar direction to public opinion and a peculiar tenor to the laws; it imparts new maxims to the governing authorities and peculiar habits to the governed. I soon perceived that the influence of this fact extends far beyond the political character and the laws of the country, and that it has no less effect on civil society than on the government; it creates opinions, gives birth to new sentiments, founds novel customs, and modifies whatever it does not produce. The more I advanced in the study of American society, the more I perceived that this equality of condition is the fundamental fact from which all others seem to be derived and the central point at which all my observations constantly terminated.
>
> (Tocqueville, *Democracy in America*, Author's Introduction)

The precarious position of the middle class threatens the equality of condition that Tocqueville references. In addition to a struggling and dwindling middle class, income inequality has steadily increased since 1970. In 2012, the top 10 percent of income earners took home more than half of all of the income earned in 2012. This is the highest percentage recorded since data collection began in 1917 (Saez, 2013). The United States has drastic income inequality when compared to other nations. According to the *CIA World Factbook*, the United States ranks forty-first in the world for income inequality. Countries with less inequality than the United States include countries such as Egypt, Pakistan, Russia, Iran and Yemen (*CIA World Factbook*).

Pervasive income inequality threatens the fabric of democracy. We have significant empirical evidence from economists and political scientists that a strong middle class and low levels of income inequality play an important role in supporting economic growth and democracy. High levels of inequality correlate with political polarization and partisan gridlock (McCarty *et al.*, 2006), which we see in the most recent example of the government shutdown for the first 16 days of October 2013. In addition to political gridlock and the failure to solve policy problems, inequality lowers social trust in society (Uslaner, 2012). Tocqueville identified this in his observations of early America:

> Equality of condition, while it makes men feel their independence, shows them their own weakness: they are free, but exposed to a thousand accidents; and experience soon teaches them that although they do not habitually require the assistance of others, a time almost always comes when they cannot do without it.... All the citizens of a democracy: they all feel themselves subject to the same weakness and the same dangers; and their interest,

as well as their sympathy, makes it a rule with them to lend one another assistance when required. The more equal social conditions become, the more do men display this reciprocal disposition to oblige each other.

(Tocqueville, *Democracy in America*, book iii, ch. 4)

As economic inequality increases in society, lower levels of political and communal efficacy and participation ensue (Uslaner, 2002). As Hacker and Pierson and others have argued, elites now wield extraordinary political power, and they have successfully used that power to extract policies that favor them at the expense of the American middle class (Domhoff, 2013; Hacker and Pierson, 2010). Widening inequality and a class of wealthy elites is associated with excessive rent seeking behavior.[2] Inequality and pessimism also reduce social cohesion in society. "Inequality makes people less likely to believe that what affects me affects you—and that ordinary people have the power to control the future or their political leaders." (Uslaner, 2012).

Trust in the government on the part of the American public is an important gauge on the legitimacy of the system. The public is generally more critical of government and skeptical of the motives of government actors when social trust is low (Dalton, 2005). While there has been a general decline in trust in the government since the 1960s, there has also been an increase in concerns about crime and increasing cynicism about government. Trust in the government was at the highest levels in 1966, with 61 percent of Americans indicating high levels of trust in government (ANES, 2008). By 2008, trust in the government hit a record low, with just 26 percent of Americans indicating high levels of trust in government (ANES, 2008). Following the terrorist attacks of 9/11 in 2001, cynicism focused on government's ability to address foreign threats and international issues (Chanley, 2002; Davis and Silver, 2004). At the individual level, Americans who indicate higher trust in the government are generally more conformist, follow the law, and participate in the political process and many other aspects of civic life (Chanley *et al.*, 2001). In contrast, individuals in the lower social classes and at the periphery of social groups are less likely to trust political processes and actors (Dalton, 2005). People with less social capital are more likely to bear the costs of government policy changes and are less likely to benefit from the machinations of large-scale change. Those in lower social classes feel most abandoned by their government and brutalized by the systems in place. Whether it is the tax regulations or changes in local law enforcement policies, those without the social capital to buffer themselves from the impacts of change will be the most affected, as they lack the political and social capital necessary to shape these policies (Domhoff, 2013).

While the level of trust in government is an important indicator of how social class might affect the rise of the police state, it is also important to understand citizen trust in police specifically. Slightly more than half (56 percent) of Americans trust the police in their communities a great deal. This is down slightly compared to past years (Maguire, 2012). Generally, individuals with higher education levels and incomes also have higher levels of confidence in the police and government generally.[3] Members of the middle and upper classes, who have more resources, are more likely to trust that those in power are protecting them and serving their interests (Uslaner and Brown, 2005; Cook and Gronke, 2005).

Rise of the American police state

In this section, we turn to the evolving role and increased power of the police in modern America. There has been unprecedented growth in the purview of law enforcement's ability to gather information about citizens in investigations at all levels of government in recent decades. Much of this growth is explained by the public's ongoing fear of crime and drugs and the focus on the global threat of terrorism. From the collection and use of information as evidence against offenders and suspected terrorists, to the transfer of military technology and strategies for crime control, the American system of justice is prepared to respond to the globalization of crime and terrorism, even at the local level.

The rise of the police state in America is best characterized as developing from quiet exceptions to the Constitution, in response to perceived threats of drugs, crime and terrorism. This has been coupled with the increasing use of militaristic technology and tactics in local and state law enforcement agencies. These developments are particularly concerning, because the constitutional concept of federalism means that the American local and state police are designed to be distinctly separate from federal military forces, and several protections are embedded in the American constitution to prevent the use of the federal military in civilian police matters. The American constitution and American political culture also protect an individual's right to privacy. The courts have supported Americans' right to privacy, despite the lack of such an explicitly stated right in the constitution, through a combination of several amendments, including the first, third, fourth, fifth, ninth, and fourteenth amendments. Although none of these amendments alone delineates a right to privacy, taken together they support the interpretation that the Founders intended privacy as part of Americans' individual liberty.

The courts have also expanded police powers of the state during wartime. Despite constitutional authority vested in Congress to declare and fund wars, the courts have rarely limited executive power in times of war. Public support for security is high when they are fearful of external threats (e.g. wars). Social problems like drugs, crime and terrorism have been framed as part of a "war" effort, which has increased police power at many levels of government. This expansion and development of local and state police agencies' powers has followed a deterministic trend, often relying on militaristic technologies and strategies (Maguire and King, 2004; Paul and Birzer, 2008; Kraska, 2007; Kraska and Kappeler, 1997; Davis, 1992). The militaristic police organization makes it an ideal partner with which to fight a war on any number of social issues, particularly where the diffusion of suspicion is high (Wisotsky, 2012).

From the earliest established watch systems, police departments were organized using the military model. With the passing of the Metropolitan Police Act in London in 1829, Sir Robert Peel established that efficiency and organization could be achieved by utilizing military-like authoritarian hierarchies (Hendrix, 2013; Paul and Birzer, 2008; Palmiotto, 1997). This persisted for nearly 200 years, as police often relied on traditional militaristic organizational structures and development to respond to community issues of crime and violence (Paul and Birzer, 2008). Over the past 40 years, the police partnership with the federal military has become more deliberate, as has thinking about police personnel as participants in a war. However, the enemy combatant is not always clearly identified or easily targeted, and may be difficult to differentiate from innocent citizens.

The Posse Comitatus Act of 1878 (18 USC § 1385, original at 20 Stat. 152) established limitations for federal military involvement in local law enforcement activities (Hammond, 1997). Originally developed following Reconstruction, *posse comitatus* translates to "power of the county" and refers to the general mistrust of governmental use of the military under English common law (Canestaro, 2003). In fact, Chief Justice Warren Burger referred to a "traditional and strong resistance of Americans to any military intrusion into civilian affairs." (*Laird v. Tatum*, 408 US., 15 (1972)). Another court argued, "Civilian rule is basic to our system of government. The use of military forces to seize civilians can expose civilian government to the threat of military rule and the suspension of constitutional liberties." (*Bissonnette v. Haig*, 776 F.2d 1384, (8th Circuit, 1985). Kopel and Blackman (1997) argue that the use of the military in domestic law enforcement has often led to disastrous outcomes for all involved. Modern examples include the Kent State University killings of student protestors and the BATF raid on the Branch Davidians (Kopel and Blackman, 1997). Originally, the Posse Comitatus legislation prevented the use of federal military forces to enforce state laws. However, its protections have been slowly dismantled as partnerships, including military training, availability of military grade weaponry, and access to federal resources and support, have been increasingly implemented (Canestaro, 2003).

Beginning in the 1980s, the power of police to seek out crime, particularly drugs, has expanded exponentially, much like the power of the federal military to collaborate with local and state law enforcement officials to combat crime. The Supreme Court has often come down on the side of the government, in many cases opening the door for increased police power. In cases involving drugs and crime generally, the courts often cite the unique nature of drug trafficking and the threats posed to the community as justification for violating constitutionally protected rights. The modern Supreme Court has routinely failed to act as a check on the power of the police to invade the privacy of individuals. Police are now permitted to obtain a search warrant based on an anonymous tip or to allow use of evidence obtained in "good faith" in order to use illegally obtained evidence pursuant to a defective warrant. (*United States v. Leon*, 468 US 897, 905 (1984); *Massachusetts v. Sheppard*, 468 US 981 (1984)). Law enforcement officials may also conduct a warrantless search of a home with the consent of individuals who do not have legal authority over the premises

(*Illinois v. Rodriguez*, 497 US 177 (1990)). The court has also authorized warrantless aerial surveillance over private property (*California v. Ciraolo*, 476 US 207 (1986); *Florida v. Riley*, 488 US 445 (1989)). The search of a public school student's purse on suspicion of drug possession was also upheld (*New Jersey v. T.L.O.*, 469 US 325, 333 (1985)).

The power of the police to stop and question individuals, on the street and in vehicles has also been found constitutional (*Terry v. Ohio*, 392 US 1 (1968); *United States v. Sharpe*, 470 US 675 (1985)). This includes: stopping vehicles on the highway with less than probable cause, or for no suspicious reason at roadblocks or checkpoints, warrantless searches of automobiles and secured containers, and the ability of police to place surveillance technology on vehicles or containers (*Texas v. Brown*, 460 US 730 (1983); *Michigan v. Sitz*, 496 US 444 (1990); *California v. Acevedo*, 111 S. Ct. 1982 (1991); *United States v. Knotts*, 460 US 276, 284 (1983); *United States v. Karo*, 468 US 705, 721 (1984)). There are some limitations on the use of technology, such as when the court found that the use of a thermal imaging device from a public vantage point constitutes a search under the fourth amendment. Thus, it required a search warrant (*Kyllo v. United States*, 533 US 27 (2001)). Many of these cases have divorced the search from requirements of suspicion. This allows surveillance because of the importance of the information that law enforcement are seeking. For example, the indiscriminate nature of the searches, such as those in a later case about roadblocks, was one of the redeeming features from a civil libertarian standpoint (*Illinois v. Lidster*, 540 US 419 (2004)). However, the indiscriminate nature of the search also means that many innocent individuals will be caught up in the intrusive search and subjected to government authority and invasion. Police entrenched in a war with citizens, potentially viewed as enemy combatants, threatens the autonomy of individuals and the democratic process. While local and state level police intrusion into citizens' lives is significant, it is the unchecked expansion of police powers at the federal level that poses an even greater threat to liberty of citizens.

The expansion of police power has been paralleled by an expansion of power wielded by the executive branch. Following the terrorist attacks on New York City and Washington, DC on September 11, 2001, several key cases defined the role of federal government in battling terrorism both abroad and on American soil. Many are familiar with the historically significant case of *Korematsu v. US*, which examined the relocation and internment of Japanese citizens during World War II. The court held that the need to protect the country against espionage outweighed the defendant's individual rights, and the rights of Americans of Japanese descent. The decision was limited to the validity of the exclusion orders, specifically,

> The provisions of other orders requiring persons of Japanese ancestry to report to assembly centers and providing for the detention of such persons in assembly and relocation centers were separate, and their validity is not in issue in this proceeding.
>
> (*Korematsu v. US*, 323 US 214 (1944))

Following the 2001 terrorist attacks on New York City and Washington, DC, the Supreme Court recognized the power of the federal government to detain enemy combatants, including American citizens. The court did rule that detainees who are US citizens must have the rights of due process, and the ability to challenge their status as enemy combatants before an impartial authority (*Hamdi v. Rumsfeld*, 542 US 507 (2004)). The court would go further a few years later, holding that—because of separation-of-powers concerns—Congress lacked the ability to deprive the federal courts of jurisdiction to review habeas petitions from noncitizens. Justice Kennedy explained this by stating, "Within the constitution's separation-of-powers structure, few exercises of judicial power are as legitimate or as necessary as the responsibility to hear challenges to the authority of the Executive to imprison a person." Access to the writ for the detainees "is a necessity to determine the lawfulness of their status, even if, in the end, they do not obtain the relief they seek." (*Boumediene v. Bush*, 553 US 723 (2008))

While only a brief review of these cases is possible here, it is important to document the failure of the courts to act as a check on the expansion of both civilian police power in the areas of search and seizure and the power of the federal government to use executive power to detain those suspected of terrorist activities. This has resulted in an expansion of the net of information gathering without suspicion and a reduction of the constitutional protections for those suspected of criminal activity, while simultaneously escalating the power of police to search and seize evidence against those individuals. Much of this has enjoyed societal support because of their fear of crime, violence and terrorism. However, trust in local police and the larger federal government is important to examine as crime has declined and the specter of terrorism has receded.

Much of the erosion of constitutional protection has occurred as American society has grappled with the war on drugs in the 1980s, the War on Crime in late 1980s and early 1990s, and the modern War on Terror that has increasingly been fought on American soil (Kraska, 1994). These have resulted in a growing police presence within American communities and increasingly militarized local law enforcement agencies (Paul and Birzer, 2008; Kraska, 1994, 2007; Kraska and Kappeler, 1997; Kraska and Cubellis, 1997; Kopel and Blackman, 1997; Davis, 1992). The threat of these three areas of policy development and public social concerns have opened doors to the use of military tactics in local communities, even as community policing was employed in neighborhoods and departments across the country.

Community policing is based on early work by George Kelling and James Q. Wilson, and is defined as "a collaborative effort between the police and the community to identify the problems of crime and disorder and to develop solutions." (Hendrix, 2013: 134). This shift in thinking about police is pushed forward by the idea of local law enforcement agencies collaborating with organizations, business, and individuals in the community to combat an array of social and justice issues (Kelling and Moore, 1988; Community Policing Consortium, 1994). Community policing solves problems within the neighborhood by relying on all available resources and takes a more holistic approach to reducing crime by focusing on social ills. These seemingly contradictory policy perspectives of militarism and community policing have worked in tandem to increase the use of paramilitary tactics and military hardware in neighborhood level drug and terror interdictions across the nation in communities large and small.

While community policing remains very much an influence, the shift in focus to problem oriented and intelligence led policing has in some instances been fueled by the responses to increased concerns about the threats of drugs in urban communities and the more recent focus on terrorism and homeland security. Intelligence led policing is more focused on the identification and response to threats using cooperative strategies that align information sharing both within law enforcement agencies and between members of the community, private sector, intelligence community and government. This concept helps law enforcement agencies at all levels to identify threats and develop responses to prevent threats in American communities (Carter and Carter, 2009). This focus on intelligence gathering has resulted in increased information collection and dissemination across law enforcement agencies, and sparked criticism from many. The slow historical development and implementation of these police powers offers insight into the nature of this expansion and the potential implications for the future.

Militarizing the police

The role of local and state police agencies in communities across the nation has changed over the past 200 years. While Sir Robert Peel saw the local constable as an emissary who served to keep citizens safe, modern law enforcement officials are more likely to think of themselves as soldiers on the front line of a local battle to reduce crime. This transition began in 1971, when Nixon declared drugs "public enemy no. 1" and identified a "war on drugs" that continues to be waged today. He established the federal DEA two years later to coordinate the efforts of all other agencies in fighting this war on drugs. Cooperation of the Bureau of Narcotics and Dangerous Drugs (the precursor to what would become the DEA) with local police agencies in combating the drug problem would begin in 1970, a year before Nixon established the DEA. A joint task force with the Bureau of Narcotics and Dangerous Drugs, New York State Police, and the New York City Police Department was developed in that year to combat drug problems in the city. Task forces like these were established across the nation using the model implemented in New York (DEA, 2013a, 2013b). This so-called "war on drugs" has offered unique opportunities for increased police presence in the private lives of American citizens, particularly those in lower class urban communities (Meeks, 2006; Davis, 1992). The militaristic manner in which our society exacts the control of crime and drugs has contributed to the acceptance of the use of high powered military style weapons and tactics in our communities as police and members of the community battle gangs and crime that are highly organized and well-funded (Kopel, 2000).

By 1981, Congress had passed the Military Cooperation with Law Enforcement Agencies Act that allowed military assistance for civilian police endeavors, including counterdrug operations, civil disturbances, special security operations, and similar activities. Efforts to combat the war on drugs has led five of the most recent presidents (Reagan, Bush, Clinton, Bush, and Obama) to encourage cooperation between federal military units and local law enforcement officials. Following the terrorist attacks of September 11, 2001, this connection was more firmly established through legislation, as federal agencies relied on local police personnel to help combat the newest threat, the War on Terror. The National Defense Authorization Act (NDAA) is a US federal law that specifies the budget and expenditures of the Department of Defense. The Act includes new and different provisions each year, including an authorization bill that determines the agencies responsible for defense, establishes funding levels, and sets the policies under which those resources will be used. The NDAA for Fiscal Year 2012 contains several controversial sections, the most contentious is §§ 1021–1022, which affirms provisions authorizing the indefinite military detention of civilians, including US citizens, without charges or trial. This provision is contained in the Authorization for Use of Military Force (AUMF).

Training and assistance from elite military personnel has become a cornerstone in local law enforcement agencies in order to prepare local personnel for this threat to security in their own backyards. The original SWAT team was formed in Los Angeles under chief Daryl Gates (Singh, 2000). In the 1990s, Congress made both training (at times conducted by non-active military personnel) and surplus military hardware available to local police agencies. While many of these developments identified the expansion of police power and the role of the military in local and civilian crime issues, it was not until September 11, 2001 that we welcomed a military era in modern policing with such open arms.

Police departments today are often outfitted with weapons, vehicles and uniforms more similar to the military than the night watchmen or local constable personnel of the past (Paul and Birzer, 2013). Most recently, legislation has encouraged the cooperation between federal military personnel and local police agencies in activities related to terrorism and homeland security. In fact, the Department of Defense released 42 pages of instructions entitled *3025.21 Defense Support of Civilian Law Enforcement Agencies*, on February 27, 2013. These instructions provide a list of exceptions where Department of Defense personnel may act alongside local law enforcement agencies, and firmly established the utility of federal military in activities in local communities (DHS, 2013). In 2013, more than $1.5 billion was available to various state and local agencies, including law enforcement agencies under the Department of Homeland Security Preparedness Grant programs. This money can be used to provide state and local law enforcement agencies with the latest technology to battle crime and prepare for potential terrorist attacks. In fact, this dedicated funding is given specifically to law enforcement and terrorism prevention activities "to prepare for and prevent and respond to pre-operational activity and other crimes that are precursors or indicators of terrorist activity."

Much of the expansion of police power has occurred with very little fanfare or attention. Local and state police agencies have established specialized units to aggressively combat crime. These teams are often trained by current or ex-military personnel, have military style uniforms (including battle dress uniforms, known as BDUs), and carry military grade weapons (Paul and Birzer, 2013). The establishment of paramilitary units typically identified as SWAT (special weapons and tactics) teams and their increasing use by local police departments is well documented by numerous scholars. The use of paramilitary units or SWAT teams has been increasing tenfold compared with their existence in the 1980s (Maguire and King, 2004; Kopel and Blackman, 1997; Kraska and Kappeler, 1997; Kraska, 1996; McCulloch, 2001; Weber, 1999). Kraska and Kappeler (1997) document the increase in departments that have established paramilitary units, and the increased use in local law enforcement and response to community crime. In 1997, the authors found that 89.4 percent of the departments in cities that serve more than 50,000 people and responded to their survey inquiry had a police paramilitary unit. Of the departments that did not have a unit, 20 percent were planning to establish one in the next few years (Kraska, 1997). At this time, many departments both large and small utilize the highly trained and skilled officers of these paramilitary units.

In addition to an overall increase in the existence of these units, a normalization of these units within modern policing has also occurred (Kraska, 2007). Early SWAT teams were used rarely, reserving their specialized skills for instances of significant community threats like hostage situations (Macko, 1997; Kraska and Kappeler, 1997). Several authors have noted that these units were increasingly working traditional response and reactionary police calls, with only about 10 percent of the units purely reactionary—by this, we and other authors mean saving their skills and specialized training for situations that require it, such as barricaded persons, hostage situations, terrorist activity and dangerous warrants. Instead, the units were participating in traditional crimes like robbery (Whitehead, 2013; Kraska and Kappeler, 1997; Macko, 1997; Kraska, 1999). Kraska (1999) found that 75 percent of the SWAT team missions across the nation were for high-risk warrant service. Slightly less than 5 percent were for hostage situations and/or riots, the most stereotypical situations where one might envision the necessity for SWAT skills. In Maryland, members of SWAT teams are sent out 4.5 times a day, with 94 percent of those deployments being for something as minor as serving search warrants (Whitehead, 2013). While one study found no difference in use of force by SWAT and non-SWAT officers, concerns about aggressive tactics, the use of military style raids and patrol within civilian communities abound (Williams and Westall, 2003). Though disconcerting, the increased use of SWAT teams for routine police activities may be the result of attempts to ensure or justify their continued existence within law enforcement agencies around the country, many of whom are experiencing relatively low levels of crime (Weber, 1997). Potentially expensive to operate and maintain, paramilitary units may be an additional resource that departments employ for patrol and routine crime control operations.

SWAT units and military style tactics, such as the use of armored personnel carriers (APCs), are being used in some departments for "aggressive, proactive patrol work." (Kraska, 2007: 507). The paramilitary units are often trained very differently than traditional patrol officers. In 2007, 275 instances were noted where SWAT raids on private residences had gone very wrong, with destruction of private property, the identification and inclusion of innocent individuals, or officers harmed in the line of duty (Kraska, 2007). Further research also identifies the transfer of technology (both weapons and strategic planning), information sharing, and the cooperative relationships developed to respond to drug control and terrorism security efforts (Kraska, 1997, 2007). The research identifies "a growing tendency by the police and other segments of the criminal justice system to rely on the military/war model for formulating crime/drug/terrorism control rationale and operations." (Kraska, 2007: 502) The use of this war model to battle issues in local communities may create additional concerns about the use of police power as these communities prepare themselves and train their officers to deal with the threat of terrorism (Pelfrey, 2007). Police are typically not at war with their communities. War is a unique set of circumstances that alter the expectations of how individuals engaged in the battle will respond. There is also little concern about protecting the rights of enemy combatants. The focus rather is on solving the overall conflict with whatever tool is necessary. In many instances, the response has been to gather as much evidence as possible to increase the amount and type of intelligence that law enforcement and homeland security personnel have to investigate threats to the community. The result is an enormous amount of information gathered about millions of Americans.

A nation under surveillance

In addition to the increased militarization of personnel, the government has also expanded its use of various forms of surveillance. From wiretaps to confiscation of records, the federal and state governments now have access to a vast array of technological tools with which to investigate crime and terrorism. In June of 2013, President Obama defended the National Security Agency surveillance programs by saying

> It's important to recognize that you can't have 100 percent security and also then have 100 percent privacy and zero inconvenience. We're going to have to make some choices as a society. And what I can say is that in evaluating these programs, they make a difference in our capacity to anticipate and prevent possible terrorist activity.
>
> (Jakes and Superville, 2013)

This was the president's response to national outrage at reports that information about phone calls by American citizens were being systematically and continuously collected in efforts to identify terror threats to national security. Following the infamous and tragic events of September 11, 2001, the federal government established the Department of Homeland Security (DHS) by consolidating 22 executive-level agencies into a single cabinet-level department (Hendrix, 2013).

This was the most significant transformation of the US government since 1947. President George W. Bush decided that the United States needed strategic coordination to address terrorist threats at home and abroad. The first priority of the DHS is to protect the nation from further terrorist attacks. The 233,000 men and women of the DHS analyze threats and intelligence, guard America's borders and airports, protect critical infrastructure, and coordinate the response of the nation for future emergencies. To this end, the DHS coordinates the collection of information and investigations into threats. (Hendrix, 2013) The development of the DHS, along with legislative developments like the Patriot Act, have hastened the rise of police and government power at the federal level.

The passage of the Patriot Act within six weeks of the 9/11 terrorist attacks initiated a dramatic increase in the power of the federal government to collect information and participate in the surveillance of American citizens (Levy, 2012). The ability to use roving wiretaps that follow people from device to device, rather than only those registered to a specific person and the identification of individuals as threats to national security has opened up an enormous amount of power to examine the personal and private communications of American citizens. On May 26, 2011, Congress passed a four-year extension of three expiring Patriot Act surveillance provisions (ACLU, 2013). Specifically, Section 215 authorizes the federal government to obtain "any tangible thing" related to terrorist investigations. This means that any materials that might give the federal government additional information may be seized as part of the ongoing investigations into terrorist activities. This has resulted in several newsworthy revelations that the American government was collecting massive amounts of sensitive data in order to investigate potential terrorist threats. Numerous concerned citizen groups, the American Civil Liberties Union (ACLU), and Congress have demanded information about the extent and nature of the surveillance of citizens, though they have had little success (ACLU, 2013).

Concluding thoughts

The decline of the American middle class and the increasing threats to our liberty are troubling developments in their own right. However, far more troubling is the convergence of these two developments, for this suggests that the United States could be traversing the path toward a permanent, Orwellian societal shift. The democratic safeguards of a large and stable middle class and individual liberties have been slowly eroded by the dual trends of a declining middle class and rising income inequality, coupled with the steady encroachment upon individual civil liberties. Although this erosion has been occurring for several decades, the Great Recession of 2007 and the terrorist attacks of September 11, 2001 exacerbated and accelerated these trends.

Based on the current economic and political conditions in America, we see an urgent need for reform to preserve the democratic tenets of the republic. Reform will not be easy to implement, since it requires a concerted effort on the part of the citizens to thwart the interests of the power elites. The elites have always enjoyed a disproportionate level of power and influence in society. However, the United States has historically been successful at mitigating the political influence of elites through adherence to constitutional safeguards, legislative reform, institutional checks and an increasingly inclusive participatory role of citizens in government. However, current trends, if unabated, threaten the continuation of democratic society. The United States is at risk of becoming a pseudo-democracy, where democracy exists only in its written documents, but in practice allows little or no power for the citizens. "A major characteristic of a pseudo-democracy is the capacity of a few to choreograph political outcomes" (National Development Institute, 2012). As the middle class declines, more power is concentrated with the elites of society, and the political system responds to their interests at the expense of the rest of the citizenry (Bartels, 2008), which threatens the future of democracy.

To mitigate the power of the elites, citizens must take an active, informed, and engaged role in their democracy; they must jealously safeguard their constitutional liberties. The middle class has historically been well equipped to participate in this way, as their economic security, leisure time and access to high quality education provided a supportive framework necessary to protect their ability to participate effectively in the political process. In addition, despite a wide range of rules and policies that tilt the field in the elites' favor, citizens still have the power of the vote. The middle class can and does make demands of government and can hold government accountable for political decisions, because they have the resources to do so. Historically, the power and influence of the elites was held in check by the power of the voters, which is, in democratic societies, widespread and protected. Without a robust middle class, popular sovereignty is at risk. Popular sovereignty requires an engaged citizenry, born from education that develops and nurtures the requisite civic and political habits and dispositions. Without the leisure time afforded by the economic security associated with being middle class, we may soon devolve into something more akin to a pseudo-democracy. We see this as a possibility for the United States if formal institutions and additional checks on political power secured through civil liberties (e.g. a free press) fail to provide adequate checks on governmental power.

One way to ensure the protection of democracy and liberty is for the nation to support and adopt policies that promote and sustain the middle class. Although many civil liberties, particularly those that fall under the purview of the criminal justice system, have been curtailed in the post Patriot Act world, we still enjoy strong first amendment free speech protections. This, combined with the right to vote, offers some power to the citizenry to reclaim their government and restore the American middle class. In addition, discussions of political reforms must move beyond class-based discussions, because this does not resonate with most Americans. Marxism does not resonate with Americans, because as capitalism matured, it generated middle class societies, not the working-class ones predicted by Marxism (Fukuyama, 2012). Middle class Americans enjoy the status of being the middle more than they have an interest in a class-based identity.

Rather, reforms need to emphasize policies that support equality of opportunity, rather than equality of outcomes, as these are more likely to resonate with Americans.

Developing economic opportunities that enable families to achieve a middle class lifestyle can improve the economy and increase their trust and faith in the government. Increasing the focus on civic education is vitally important. Several economic changes could encourage the development of a middle class. Lowering the cost of college and reducing the costs and barriers to job training will help more citizens to join and remain in the middle class. Boosting retirement security and stabilizing the economic markets will increase confidence and consumer spending. Reducing energy and transportation costs will promote entrepreneurship and build small business opportunities.

Economic policies that strengthen the economic middle class can constrain the police state. In addition, reforms should seek to reduce the militaristic nature of civilian law enforcement. The police serve a community of citizens protected by the Constitution who have rights that must be respected. They are not "enemy combatants," and viewing them in this manner will only result in further destruction of trust and confidence in police and government. Congress should strengthen the protections of the Posse Comitatus Act and repeal legislation that permits the use of military personnel in drug and crime control efforts (Kopel and Blackman, 1997). Military involvement in crime control should be limited to natural disasters, riots and other large-scale events.

The use of militaristic training and weapons technology should be limited to reactive situations where these assist in maintaining safety and security within the community. These innovations provide substantial advantages for the police when responding to serious crimes, but using these as a routine aspect of police interactions with the community is likely to result in disastrous consequences for police agencies and the community (Baker, 2011). Recent examples compiled by Balko (2012) demonstrate how disastrous these can be. From the killing of family pets to the terrorizing of local citizens mistaken for criminals, the use of military style force in local communities often results in embarrassing and devastating situations for all involved. Local and state agencies should exercise restraint in the use of paramilitary tactics and units in the local community.

We also advocate increasing the partnerships between police and members of the community, which will have positive effects for citizens. Whether through citizen review boards or increased transparency by police, it is important that police departments and other criminal justice agencies work with the communities they serve to solve crime and other social problems (Crank *et al.*, 2012). The use of militaristic tactics and policies decreases trust in the police and reduces the effectiveness of criminal justice professionals in the community. We recommend a shift to the community-policing model as a way to ameliorate the connection between citizens and their government, and reduce the police state approach to crime. Community policing relies on partnerships with those most likely to have the social capital in order to respond to problems in the neighborhood. Business owners and managers have the highest investment in outcomes within the community. These individuals have the resources to invest in the community and increase the safety and security of the neighborhood.

Other authors in this book explore the implications of the dark side of regimes that operate without adequate civil society controls to check their power. In this chapter, we have explored the dark side of the current state of American democracy. We have argued that the United States is at risk for becoming a pseudo-democracy without the restoration of the middle class and a return to our constitutional foundations. None of the reforms we have suggested will be easy to implement. Nonetheless, they are possible remedies to restore the middle class and stem the rise of the police state. Reducing the militarization of policing in America and strengthening the middle class are fundamentally important for restoring democracy in America.

Notes

1 Their definition of middle class is home ownership, a car or two in the garage, a vacation now and then, health care coverage, and enough savings to retire and contribute to the children's college education (US Department of Commerce Economics and Statistics Administration, 2010).
2 Rent seeking is the term economists use for the situation where people and corporations engage in tactics to manipulate politics as a way to obtain economic gains. In politics, an example of this is corporate lobbying of a congressional representative.
3 Levels of confidence and trust in police are complicated by issues of race and disadvantage, as well as the negative experiences individuals have with police personnel and agencies (Schuck *et al.*, 2008; MacDonald and Stokes, 2006).

References

American Civil Liberties Union (ACLU) (2013) *America's Surveillance Society.* Online, available at: www.aclu.org/sites/default/files/images/asset_upload_file381_37802.pdf.

American National Election Studies (ANES) (2008) *Trust in the Government Index 1958–2008.* Online, available at: www.electionstudies.org/nesguide/toptable/tab5a_5.htm.

Aristotle (no date) *Politics* 4.5.2057b 35–37.

Baker, A. (2011) "When the Police Go Military." *New York Times.* December 3. Online, available at: www.nytimes.com/2011/12/04/sunday-review/have-american-police-become-militarized.html?pagewanted=all&_r=0.

Balko, R. (2012) "Overkill: the Rise of Paramilitary Police Raids in America." Cato Institute. Online, available at: www.cato.org/publications/white-paper/overkill-rise-paramilitary-police-raids-america.

Bartels, L. (2008) *Unequal Democracy: the Political Economy of the New Gilded Age.* New York: Russell Stage Foundation.

Boushey, H. and Hersh, A. (2012) *The American Middle Class, Income Inequality, and the Strength of Our Economy: New Evidence in Economics.* Washington, DC: Center for American Progress. May. Online, available at: www.americanprogress.org/issues/2012/05/pdf/middleclass_growth.pdf.

Bricker, J., Kennickell, A., Moore, K. and Sabelhaus, J. (2012) "Changes in US Family Finances from 2007 to 2010: Evidence from the Survey of Consumer Finances." *Federal Reserve Bulletin.* Vol. 98: 1–80.

Canestaro, N. (2003) "Homeland Defense: Another Nail in the Coffin for Posse Comitatus." *Washington University Journal of Law and Policy*. Vol. 12: 99.

Carter, D. and Carter, J. (2009) "Intelligence-led Policing Conceptual and Functional Considerations for Public Policy." *Criminal Justice Policy Review*. Vol. 20. No. 3: 310–325.

Cashell, B. (2008) *Who are the Middle Class?* Report for Congress, Washington, DC: Congressional Research Service.

Central Intelligence Agency (no date) *CIA World Factbook Country Comparison: Distribution of Family Income*. Online, available at: www.cia.gov/library/publications/the-worldfactbook/rankorder/2172rank.html.

Chanley, V. (2002) "Trust in Government in the Aftermath of 9/11: Determinants and Consequences." *Political Psychology*. Vol. 23. No. 3: 469–483.

Chanley, V., Rudolph, T. and Rahn, W. (2001) "Public Trust in Government in the Reagan Years and Beyond." Hibbing, J. and Theiss-Morse, E. eds. *What is it about Government that Americans Dislike*, Cambridge: Cambridge University Press: 59–78.

Community Policing Consortium. (1994) "Understanding Community Policing: a Framework for Action." Washington DC: Bureau of Justice Assistance: 1–82.

Cook, T. and Gronke, P. (2005) "The Skeptical American: Revisiting the Meanings of Trust in Government and Confidence in Institutions." *Journal of Politics*. Vol. 67. No. 3: 784–803.

Crank, J., Iribeck, D., Murray, R. and Sundermeier, M. (2012) "Mission-based Policing: Rethinking the Relationship of Police to Crime." *Police Practice and Research*. Vol. 2: 103–120.

Dalton, R. (2005) "The Social Transformation of Trust in Government." *International Review of Sociology*. Vol. 15. No. 1: 133–154.

Davis, D. and Silver, B. (2004) "Civil Liberties vs. Security: Public Opinion in the Context of the Terrorist Attacks on America." *American Journal of Political Science*. Vol. 48. No. 1: 28–46.

Davis, M. (1992) "Fortress Los Angeles: the Militarization of Urban Space." Davis, M., ed., *Variations on a Theme Park*. New York: Hill and Wang: 154–180.

Department of Homeland Security (DHS) (2013) *DHS Announces Grant Guidance for Fiscal Year (FY) 2013 Preparedness Grants*. Online, available at: www.dhs.gov/news/2013/05/21/dhs-announces-grant-guidance-fiscal-year-fy-2013-preparedness-grants.

Domhoff, W. (2013) *Who Rules America? The Triumph of the Corporate Rich*. New York: McGraw Hill.

Drake, B. (2013) *Having a secure job replaces homeownership as the key to being middle-class*. August 9. Online, available at: www.pewresearch.org/fact-tank/2013/08/09/having-a-secure-job-replaces-homeownership-as-the-key-to-being-middle-class/.

Drug Enforcement Administration (DEA) (2013a) *State and Local Task Forces*. Online, available at: www.justice.gov/dea/ops/taskforces.shtml.

Drug Enforcement Administration (DEA) (2013b) *History of the Task Force*. Online, available at: www.justice.gov/dea/ops/taskforces.shtml.

Frank, R. (2007) *Falling Behind: How Rising Inequality Harms the Middle Class*. Los Angeles: University of California Press.

Fukuyama, F. (2012) "The Future of History: Can Liberal Democracy Survive the Decline of the Middle Class?" *Foreign Affairs*. January–February. Online, available at: www.foreignaffairs.com/articles/136782/francis-fukuyama/the-future-of-history.

Gilbert, D. (2008) *The American Class Structure in an Age of Growing Inequality*. Los Angeles: Pine Forge Press.

Gould, E., Finio, N., Sabadaish, N. and Wething, H. (2013) *Economic Policy Institute 2013 Family Budget Calculator: Technical Documentation.* July 3. Online, available at: www. epi.org/publication/wp297–2013-family-budget-calculator-technical-documentation/.

Hacker, J. and Pierson, P. (2010) *Winner-Take-All Politics: How Washington Made the Rich Richer—and Turned Its Back on the Middle Class.* New York: Simon and Schuster Printing.

Hammond, M. (1997) "The Posse Comitatus Act: a Principle in Need of Renewal." *Washington University Law Quarterly.* Vol. 75. No. 2.

Hendrix, N. (2013) *Experience Criminal Justice.* Columbus: McGraw-Hill Publishing.

Isaacs, J., Sawhill, I. and Haskins, R. (2008) *Getting Ahead or Losing Ground: Economic Mobility in America.* Washington, DC: The Brookings Institution.

Jakes, L. and Superville, D. (2013) *Obama Defends NSA, Says America Has To Make Choices Between Privacy and Security.* June 7. Online, available at: www.huffington-post.com/2013/06/07/obama-defends-nsa_n_3406448.html.

Kamp, K. (2013) *By the Numbers: the Incredibly Shrinking American Middle Class.* September 20. Online, available at: http://billmoyers.com/2013/09/20/by-the-numbers-the-incredibly-shrinking-american-middle-class/.

Kelling, G. and Moore, M. (1988) "The Evolving Strategy of Policing." *National Institute of Justice.* November. Online, available at: https://ncjrs.gov/pdffiles1/nij/114213.pdf.

Kopel, D. (2000) "Militarized Law Enforcement: the Drug War's Deadly Fruit." Kopel. D., ed., *After Prohibition: An Adult Approach to Drug Policies in the 21st Century.* Golden: Cato Institute.

Kopel, D. and Blackman, P. (1997) "Can Soldiers be Peace Officers—The WACO Disaster and the Militarization of American Law Enforcement." *Akron Law Review.* Vol. 30: 619–659.

Kraska, P. (1994) "The Police and Military in the Post-Cold War Era: Streamlining the State's Use of Force Entities in the Drug War." *Police Forum.* Vol. 4. No. 1: 1–8.

Kraska, P. (1996) "Enjoying Militarism: Political/Personal Dilemmas in Studying US Police Paramilitary." *Justice Quarterly.* Vol. 13. No. 3: 405–429.

Kraska, P. (1997) "The Military as Drug Police: Exercising the Ideology of War. Drugs, Crime and Justice: Contemporary Perspectives." *Justice Quarterly.* Vol. 13. No. 3: 405–429.

Kraska, P. (1999) "Militarizing Criminal Justice: Exploring the Possibilities." *Journal of Political and Military Sociology.* Vol. 27. No. 2: 205–215.

Kraska, P. (2007) "Militarization and Policing—Its Relevance to 21st Century Police." *Policing.* Vol. 1. No. 4: 501–513.

Kraska, P. and Cubellis, L. (1997). "Militarizing Mayberry and Beyond: Making Sense of American Paramilitary Policing." *Justice Quarterly.* Vol. 14. No. 4: 607–629.

Kraska, P. and Kappeler, V. (1997) "Militarizing American Police: The Rise and Normalization of Paramilitary Units." *Social Problems.* Vol. 44. No. 1: 1–18.

Levy, R. (2012) "The USA Patriot Act: We Deserve Better." Cato Institute. Online, available at: www.cato.org/publications/commentary/usa-patriot-act-we-deserve-better?print.

McCarty, N., Poole, K. and Rosenthal, H. (2006) *Polarized America: the Dance of Ideology and Unequal Riches.* Cambridge: Massachusetts Institute of Technology.

McCulloch, J. (2001) "Paramilitary Surveillance: S11, Globalization, Terrorists and Counter-terrorists." *Current Issues in Criminal Justice.* Vol. 13: 23.

MacDonald, J. and Stokes, R. (2006) "Race, Social Capital, and Trust in the Police." *Urban Affairs Review.* Vol. 41. No. 3: 358–375.

Macionis, J. (2012) *Society: the Basics.* Vol. 12. Upper Saddle River: Pearson Publishing.

Macko, S. (1997) *SWAT: Is It Being Used Too Much?* Emergency Services Report. Chicago: Emergency Response and Research Institute.

Madland, D. (2012) *Making Our Middle Class Stronger: 35 Policies to Revitalize America's Middle Class.* Research. Washington, DC: Center for American Progress.

Maguire, E. and King, W. (2004) "Trends in the Policing Industry." *Annals of the American Academy of Political and Social Science.* Vol. 593. No. 1: 15–41.

Maguire, K. (2012) *Sourcebook of Criminal Justice Statistics.* Albany: University of Albany. February 2. Online, available at: www.albany.edu/sourcebook/.

Meeks, D. (2006) "Police Militarization in Urban Areas: the Obscure War against the Underclass." *Black Scholar.* Vol. 35. No. 4: 33–41.

Nam, C. and Boyd, M. (2004) "Occupational Status in 2000: Over a Century of Census-based Measurement." *Population Research and Policy* Review. Vol. 23: 327–358.

National Development Institute. (2012) *Paper 71: Democracy vs Pseudo Democracy.* Sheffield. Online, available at: www.nd-i.org/?p=423.

Palmiotto, M. (1997) *Policing: Concepts, Strategies, and Current Issues in American Police Forces.* Durham: Carolina Academic Press.

Paul, J. and Birzer, M. (2008) "The Militarization of the American Police Forces: Critical Assessment." *Critical Issues in Justice and Politics.* Vol. 1. No. 1: 15–29.

Paul, J. and Birzer, M. (2013) "Images of Power: An Analysis of the Militarization of Police Uniforms and Messages of Service." *Free Inquiry in Creative Sociology.* Vol. 32. No. 2: 121–128.

Pelfrey, W. (2007) "Local Law Enforcement Terrorism Prevention Efforts: A State Level Case Study." *Journal of Criminal Justice.* Vol. 35. No. 3: 313–321.

Pew Research Center. (2008) "Inside the Middle Class: Bad Times Hit the Good Life." *Social and Demographic Trends.* April 8. Online, available at: www.pewsocialtrends. org/2008/04/09/inside-the-middle-class-bad-times-hit-the-good-life/.

Pew Research Center. (2012) "The Lost Decade of the Middle Class Fewer, Poorer, Gloomier." *Social and Demographic Trends.* August 22. Online, available at: www. pewsocialtrends.org/2012/08/22/the-lost-decade-of-the-middle-class/.

Porter, E. (2013) "America's Sinking Middle Class." *New York Times.* September 18. Online, available at: www.nytimes.com/2013/09/19/business/americas-sinking-middle-class.html?_r.

Reich, R. (2012) *Beyond Outrage: What Has Gone Wrong With Our Economy and Our Democracy, and How to Fix It.* New York: Vintage Books.

Saez, E. (2013) *Striking it Richer: The Evolution of Top Incomes in the United States.* Preliminary Estimates, California: UC Berkeley.

Schuck, A., Rosenbaum, D. and Hawkins, D. (2008) "The Influence of Race/Ethnicity, Social Class, and Neighborhood Context on Residents' Attitudes toward the Police." *Police Quarterly.* Vol. 11. No. 4: 496–519.

Singh, K. (2000) "Treading the Thin Blue Line: Military Special-operations Trained Police SWAT Teams and the Constitution." *William and Mary Bill of Rights Journal.* Vol. 9. No. 3: 673.

Tocqueville, A. (1988) *Democracy in America.* New York: Harper Perennial.

US Census Bureau (2013a) *Current Population Survey Annual Social and Economic Supplement: 2012.* Online, available at: www.census.gov/hhes/Online, available at: www/ poverty/publications/pubs-cps.html.

US Census Bureau (2013b) *Income, Poverty and Health Insurance Coverage in the United States: 2012.* September 17. Online, available at: www.census.gov/newsroom/ releases/archives/income_wealth/cb13-165.html.

US Department of Commerce Economics and Statistics Administration (2010) "Middle Class in America." *United States Department of Commerce.* Online, available at: www. commerce.gov/sites/default/files/documents/migrated/Middle%20Class%20Report.pdf.

Uslaner, E. (2002) *The Moral Foundations of Trust.* Cambridge: Cambridge University Press.

Uslaner, E. (2012) *Income Inequality in the United States Fuels Pessimism and Threatens Social Cohesion.* December 5. Online, available at: www.americanprogress.org/issues/economy/report/2012/12/05/46871/income-inequality-in-the-united-states-fuels-pessimism-and-threatens-social-cohesion/.

Uslaner, E. and Brown, M. (2005) "Inequality, Trust, and Civic Engagement." *American Politics Research.* Vol. 33. No. 6: 868–894.

Weber, D. (1999) *Warrior Cops: The Ominous Growth of Paramilitarism in American Police Departments.* Washington, DC: Cato Institute.

Whitehead, J. (2013) *A Government of Wolves: the Emerging American Police State.* New York: SelectBooks Inc.

Williams, J. and Westall, D. (2003) "SWAT and Non-SWAT Police Officers and the Use of Force." *Journal of Criminal* Justice. Vol. 31. No. 5: 469–474.

Wisotsky, S. (2012) *A Society of Suspects: the War on Drugs and Civil Liberties.* Washington, DC: Cato Institute.

Court cases

Bissonnette v. Haig, 776 F.2d 1384, (8th Circuit, 1985)
Boumediene v. Bush, 553 US 723 (2008)
California v. Acevedo, 111 S. Ct. 1982 (1991)
California v. Ciraolo, 476 US 207 (1986)
Florida v. Riley, 488 US 445 (1989)
Hamdi v. Rumsfeld, 542 US 507 (2004)
Illinois v. Lidster, 540 US 419 (2004)
Illinois v. Rodriguez, 497 US 177 (1990)
Korematsu v. US, 323 US 214 (1944)
Kyllo v. United States, 533 US 27 (2001)
Laird v. Tatum, 408 US, 1 (1972)
Massachusetts v. Sheppard, 468 US 981 (1984)
Michigan v. Sitz, 496 US 444 (1990)
New Jersey v. T.L.O., 469 US 325, 333 (1985)
Terry v. Ohio, 392 US 1 (1968)
Texas v. Brown, 460 US 730 (1983)
US v. Knotts, 460 US 276, 284 (1983)
US v. Karo, 468 US 705, 721 (1984)
US v. Leon, 468 US 897, 905 (1984)
US v. Sharpe, 470 US 675 (1985)

8 Crisis in Europe

The deconstruction of the Westphalian state

Pamela Ligouri Bunker

Europe—the birthplace of the Westphalian state—has experienced recent challenges to this state form at both the supra- and sub-state level. These challenges are both directly and indirectly linked to the deviant forces of globalization (Gilman *et al.*, 2011), which are putting pressure on the modern state from both the bottom up—with the advent of increasing criminality and growth of the illicit economy; and from the top down—with the concentration of wealth in a globalized plutocratic elite and the rise of what is being termed a sovereign free economy that is beyond the ability of the state to effectively tax, creating rising inequality between the social classes. Europe is not alone. Western states around the world are feeling the pressures of this deviant globalization, although their actual form and the responses have varied.

In Europe, a unique situation exists, however, in which a supra-national entity comes into the equation in the form of the European Union. The question follows whether this type of economic integration is a one-off, a product of its own specific *raison d'être*, or whether it is a step towards a new form of social and political organization. With regard to the forces of globalization, technological change, and accompanying predatory and "crony" capitalism, plutocracy guru Chrystia Freeland has been quoted as saying that, "We are living through an era of economic evolution comparable in scale to the industrial revolution" (*TED Blog*, 2013). T. Lindsay Moore likens the state form evolution resulting from such pressures more to an epochal change, a proverbial clash *in* civilization (2014). Just as city-states gave way to feudal states that gave way to the Westphalian states, perhaps then the European Union represents a sign of things to come. The late anthropologist Michel-Rolph Trouillot maintained over a decade ago:

> Once we see the necessity of the nation-state as a lived fiction of late modernity—indeed, as possibly a brief parenthesis in human history—we may be less surprised by the changes we now face and be able to respond to them with the intellectual imagination they deserve.
>
> (2001: 130)

Whether or not this is the case—and whether the European Union as currently conceived is the answer—the European Westphalian state form is ultimately being molded into something potentially unrecognizable in terms of its role as a sovereign entity that upholds the social contract between state and citizen. It is being essentially "deconstructed." On one hand, its sovereignty is at stake with the state experiencing mounting debt and loss of economic resources, a loss of control over decision-making, and—in some cases—threatened fragmentation of its national territory. On the other, its legitimacy is at stake as it moves towards a polarized "hourglass" society with a vanishing middle class, a public perception of decreased representation by decision-makers, and a lack of any national identity.

This chapter thus looks at the challenges currently facing the European Westphalian state and considers them in terms of these two main aspects: the crisis of state sovereignty and the crisis of legitimacy.

The Westphalian state and the European Union

In order to set the stage for understanding the responses to these challenges with regard to the European states, some background is in order. The Treaty of Westphalia of 1648 established the concept of sovereign states in Europe and the leadership of these fledgling nations became the legitimate representative of a people—united by history, language and culture—and ostensibly acted in their interest.[1] Over time, the Westphalian state form became dominant within the international system. These early states transitioned from dynastic, guild-based and mercantilist entities into national, industrialized and capitalist systems of political organization. The early-to-mid-twentieth century saw the additional developments of both a burgeoning "middle class"—a productive social strata, protected by labor laws, earning beyond a living wage—and a state-moderated capitalism that formed the basis of the modern welfare state.[2] This middle strata of society would come to enjoy a "comfortable" existence and could look forward to a secure retirement.

Experiences of two world wars and a partitioned Europe during the Cold War, however, called into question rampant nationalism and the prerogatives of those sovereign states. The formation of the European Coal and Steel Community (ECSC) in 1951 hoped to build on the power of joint economic interest between West Germany and France and later other western European nations as a bridge to lasting peace in the region, and led to the creation of the European Economic Community (EEC) in 1957. The closer economic integration of the region continued incrementally over the following decades. With the reunification of the German state looming as a possibility, the Treaty of Maastricht was signed in 1992, formalizing the European Union (EU) and setting the stage for the eventual adoption by many EU members of the common monetary unit, the euro, introduced in 2002. The EU now consists of 28 nations across Europe and continues to expand.[3] While proposed, further integration in the form of an EU constitution has yet to be unanimously approved, although the Lisbon Treaty of 2009 incorporates many of its provisions.

Begun then as a compact for peace, the continuing trend toward integration of the countries of Europe at the regional level shifted to one of practicality as nation states sought to leverage their individual strengths as a communal unit in the face of economic pressures. At first, this meant simply consolidating their respective positioning in relation to much larger trading entities such as the United States. Daniel Cohen notes that, with the breakup of their formerly hostile neighbor, the Soviet Union and the fall of the Berlin wall, it also meant the potential for EU expansion by incorporating countries of the former Eastern Bloc. As he puts it, "the idea of Europe as a protective 'fortress' was replaced by the idea, which had not been foreseen, of Europe as a gate to the world economy" (Cohen, 2009: 59).

In subsequent years, the existence of the EU as a supra-national entity that operates at a regional level has been seen as crucial to effectively respond to the pressures of a globalized world economy. As Jurgen Habermas has pointed out:

> For it is only through such new transnational steering capabilities that the *social* forces of nature that have been unleashed at the transnational level— i.e. the systemic constraints that operate without hindrance across national borders, today especially those of the global banking sector—can also be tamed.
>
> (2012: 10)

These transnational "social forces" to which he refers might be said to equate in large part with those deviant forces of globalization, particularly the concentration of wealth in a globalized plutocratic elite and the sovereign free economy, mentioned above.

Thus, in the context of an increasingly globalized world, an ever-increasing number of European states have, in fact, found themselves in the position that at least some of their interests are best served at the supra-national level. Primarily, this has been in the form of the single market, administered by a governing bureaucracy based in Brussels, which serves a growing and increasingly integrated union of European States, and the smaller but even more integrated monetary union of the Eurozone. The results of this regionalization, however, have been mixed.

The economic crisis, which began in the US banking sector in 2008, quickly spread to the nations of Europe, whose banking systems were closely intertwined. The resulting Europe-wide recession and subsequent Eurozone crisis— due to the near-default and necessary bailout of Portugal, Italy, Ireland, Greece and Spain—set in motion a series of events, including the implementation of conditions of austerity, that brought sharply into question the appropriate role for the EU governing bodies and cast a spotlight on their competence and legitimacy.[4] At the height of the crisis, the survival of the euro and indeed the European Union itself was uncertain.

Some see the fact that a number of states seem to be moving their economies forwards as evidence that the EU strategy is working. Others are convinced that any successes have occurred *despite* involvement by the EU, whose dedication to austerity without growth is seen as having hindered individual states' economic recovery from the crisis. A bigger issue, however, is a lack of consensus regarding the role that the European Union should play for the future. Amitai Etzioni views the institutional crisis in Europe as due both to national "policy and ideational conflicts" on globalization and related issues as well as "a major design flaw on the collective transnational level," in terms of the creation of the Eurozone and of the EU itself, which he describes as a "top down project" (2012: 109). This design flaw is found by many to lie in the fact that German chancellor Helmut Kohl's idea for the monetary union to be accompanied by fiscal and political union never got farther than the first—resulting in what Timothy Garton Ash has described as the conception of a "sickly child" (2012: 6). Vivienne Schmidt, however, assigns blame more pointedly to EU member states, finding the root of the problem lies in the fact that "the postwar visions of their countries in Europe, with all that means in terms of ideas about democracy as well as sovereignty and identity, no longer account for the new realities" (2006: 271–272). The next two sections will discuss these "new realities" and their effects on the Westphalian states and their citizens. In the process, they will also seek out where the regionalization of these states in the form of the European Union has had a positive or negative impact on states' abilities to deal with these effects. While it is recognized that the individual nations within the European Union are a heterogeneous grouping and factors are discussed that may not always be applicable to the same level in each country, it is contended here that general trends can be identified.[5]

The crisis of sovereignty

As outlined earlier, the sovereignty of the Westphalian state is currently at stake in terms of mounting debt and loss of economic resources, a loss of its control over decision-making, and, for some, in the threatened fragmentation of its national territory. While these factors are largely interconnected, this section will attempt to address them in turn. It will first consider EU member state debt levels.

Under the terms of the Maastricht Treaty's Stability and Growth Pact (SGP), EU member states cannot have a national debt that exceeds 60 percent of GDP. According to Eurostat data, as of the third quarter of 2013, of the 28 members, only 12 met this criterion—most of them in Eastern Europe (Eurostat, 2014b). Further, the more established EU democratic states with significant levels of government debt in percentage of GDP in 2013Q3 are: Germany with 78.4 percent, United Kingdom with 89.1 percent, France with 92.7 percent, Spain with 93.4 percent, Belgium with 103.7 percent, and Italy with 132.9 percent. Except for Belgium, all of the nations listed have seen marked expansion in their debt as a percentage of GDP since 2000Q1 (ibid.). Greece's financial woes, with debt at 176 percent of GDP, exceed its levels of 2012 when the EU deemed it was in need of a bailout (Matlack, 2013: 23).

These high levels of debt are influencing the credit ratings of the EU states and even of the larger EU itself. Since 2010, there have been a number of downgrades to the credit worthiness of European states, with some such as Greece, Ireland and Portugal being relegated early on to junk status by one or more of the big three credit rating agencies (Alessi *et al.*, 2013). Then, in 2012, nine Eurozone nations saw their ratings downgraded, including France, which lost its "AAA" rating in a mass action by Standard and Poors (Elliott and Inman, 2012). These downgrades have since spread. For instance, in February 2013 the credit rating of the United Kingdom was downgraded to "Aa1" by Moody's and in April to "AA+" by Fitch (*BBC News*, 2013a; Moody's, 2013). Further, in December 2013 the EU itself was downgraded by Standard and Poors to "AA+" to reflect the fact that the aggregate credit worthiness of the 28 EU member states has declined (Walter *et al.*, 2013). European sovereigns, and the EU itself, are extremely sensitive to these ratings because they can trigger investor votes of no confidence, raise the cost of bond offerings, and also aggravate financial crises. As a result, Eurozone officials have threatened actions against the three big rating firms for their rating policies (Fairless, 2013).

A nation's debt is composed of contributions from various parts of the economy: the government itself plus households and financial and non-financial institutions. *Businessweek* ranked the countries of Europe according to their 2012 gross external debt (public and private) per capita. The figures for Finland, Sweden, Belgium, Norway and the Netherlands, were more than double that of the United States, which has been long held to engage in high deficit spending at both a state and household level. The United Kingdom almost tripled the US figures at a massive $148,242 per capita. Even Germany, generally held to be fiscally responsible, weighed in higher than the United States with a figure of $67,621 (*Businessweek*, 2013: 74). Additionally, as of 2012, the overall private debt alone as a percentage of GDP ratio for the EU states remained high—at near 2008 levels (Eurostat, 2014c).

Across the Western states, major contributing factors to the increasing public and private debt burden were the easy availability of credit and the housing bubble that burst with the 2008 US banking crisis. A 2010 report by the office of the European Parliament Directorate General for Internal Policies addressed the issue of household indebtedness in the EU. While varying by country, for the EU as a whole the largest component of indebtedness was found accordingly to be mortgage debt (67 percent) followed by consumer credit (19 percent). Contributing factors driving rapid growth in indebtedness for the EU during the 2000s included the introduction of the euro, financial liberalization, the harmonization of financial services regulation, rises in house prices, and convergence by new member states. Other global factors included the emergence of China and the development of the Internet, which reduced the prices of certain goods (Lilico, 2010).

The major impact of the housing bubble collapse is reflected in the fact that countries without a strong reliance on leveraging from housing prices—like Germany—have recovered more quickly than those such as the United Kingdom, France, Italy, Spain and the Netherlands where housing prices continue to fall and therefore that aspect of deleveraging is only just beginning (McKinsey

Global Institute, 2012; *The Economist*, 2013a). The United Kingdom is also held up as an example of an instance where both government and households relied on credit debt to fund purchases prior to the bank crisis, which, along with mortgage debt, resulted in the scale of its current economic slump (*The Economist*, 2013b: 52). Remarkably, figures from 2012 have shown Eurozone household debt at 110 percent of disposable income—again higher than that of the United States—likely due to the fact that widespread defaults have yet to come to Europe (Tett, 2013). Household debt in the Netherlands, for example, is the heaviest in the Eurozone—at 285 percent of disposable income—with total mortgage debt exceeding its GDP (*The Economist*, 2013a; Chu, 2013: A9).

The question that must be then asked is what has facilitated the accumulation of this mortgage and household debt by states of the EU. The modern nation state suffers the stresses of globalization on a number of fronts but, two in particular stand out: the challenges of taxation and the workings of the IPE, both of which have contributed to state indebtedness. The first factor to be considered will be taxation. A key capability of a sovereign state is its ability to tax those residing and operating within its borders.[6] The increased mobility and global nature of firms have put constraints on the individual nation's ability to institute and control levels of taxation, the fruits of which help fund important public services in the modern welfare state. Phillip Genschel has looked at the transformation of the tax state and explains that globalization has "made transnational tax bases less of an exception," due in particular to "two developments: the ascendancy of multinational corporations and the emergence of electronic commerce" (2005: 8).

Multinational corporate strategies have often involved their movement (actual or in name only) to tax havens, regions where taxation is virtually non-existent, thus the term "sovereign free" economy. The international charitable organization Oxfam has found that two-thirds of the €13.5 trillion in global offshore wealth—amounting to more than €8.77 trillion—is "hidden in EU related tax havens such as Luxembourg, Andorra, or Malta," contributing to approximately €114 billion in lost tax revenue. Moreover, over a third of the total is found in British Overseas Territories and Crown Dependencies (Oxfam, 2013a, 2013b). Oxfam's head of Development Finance and Public Services, Emma Seery, has said:

> These figures put the UK at the center of a global tax system that is a colossal betrayal of people here and in the poorest countries who are struggling to get by, and put the government on the side of the privileged few.
>
> (Oxfam, 2013b)

Tax evasion has understandably even affected EU bailout of struggling nations. A 2012 request from Cyprus was greeted with concerns that nation was a tax haven for wealthy Russians who would be the ones who would stand to gain from such measures (*Telegraph*, 2012). In a major UK whistleblowing scandal, more than 100 of Britain's wealthiest individuals were implicated in a cross-border tax evasion investigation (Neate and Ball, 2013). A potential issue is that of the arbitrary prosecution of offenses. Crime correspondent Martin Evans reports that, while prosecutions for tax evasion more than doubled in the United Kingdom in 2012–2013, Her Majesty's Revenue and Customs (HMRC) has focused on middle class white-collar businesspersons and landlords rather than "the super-rich, who are harder to prosecute" (2013).

Where firms do not seek to evade taxes entirely, economic competitiveness leads them to seek out nations with more favorable tax rates in which to do business, and nation states impose differential taxation rates in line with this rational choice, lowering tax rates on businesses in order to be competitive. Genschel explains that modern multinational corporations have moved from a "confederative structure" towards "integrated transnational production," which allows them to essentially legally pick-and-choose where profits will be taxed as the production of a single good takes place across a variety of geographic locations (2005: 7–8).

Corporations including Apple, Google, Starbucks, Amazon and Vodafone Group have recently been taken to task for the minimal amount of tax they have paid to countries of the EU in which they have been doing business. Reuters has reported a number of ways these companies have exploited loopholes in laws (e.g. Apple in Ireland), abused tax residency requirements (e.g. Google in the United Kingdom), and/or booked their profits in other jurisdictions (e.g. Starbucks' British, German and French units) (Reuters, 2013b). Banks also exploit existing loopholes. For example, the UK "fair value on own credit rule" allows banks to post phantom losses based on increasing values of IOU bonds that they already own, a strategy that has netted them billions of pounds in tax cuts (Kennedy, 2013). The EU Parliament has recently insisted that banks disclose tax and profits in each country of operation rather than an overall figure by 2015, whereas other potential tax avoiding businesses will not have to undertake such disclosure (Coates, 2013). Tax fraud is a widespread and seemingly intractable problem. Nearly half of Greek businesses are said to avoid taxes in that already economically strapped country (*Los Angeles Times*, 2013).

With regard to taxation responses, Genschel finds that increasing European economic integration has concurrently increased interdependencies between internal national tax regimes in order to coordinate tax rates and attempt to abolish tax havens, although any concept of a "Euro-tax"—moving taxation to the supra-state—has to date been a "non-starter" (2005: 5–6, 16). According to Eurostat, as of 2012, however, the EU still lost an estimated €1 trillion a year to tax evasion and avoidance. In June of 2012, the European Commission presented an "Action Plan to strengthen the fight against tax fraud and avoidance." Common EU measures promoted include instituting common EU taxpayer ID numbers (TINS) and an EU-wide European tax code (European Commission, 2014). Even where there is a common system of taxation for EU member states, such as with the Value Added Tax (VAT), abuse and fraud still occurs. An AIV Report elaborates that this is partly due to the fact that the timely exchange of information encounters difficulties. The loss of VAT to member states is approximately €100 billion for the EU as a whole (AIV, 2013: 99–101).

The impetus, then, for real improvements in closing down loopholes and tax havens under their control remains upon individual member states, who to date have not been able to stem the flow of tax money away from the public treasury.

Journalist Eric Reguly has put forth the truism that "The rich have endlessly clever ways to shelter income ... The poor pay little or no tax because they use all their income to survive. That leaves the middle class" (2013). Cato Institute senior fellow Daniel J. Mitchell agrees that the European nations must collect a lot more from the middle class since "rich taxpayers usually have more control over the timing, level, and composition of their income" (2012).

While the above has focused on tax evasion and avoidance rather than tax levels, there are other potential side effects to a business model that uses the tax code to its advantage. Because corporate elites often live where they do business, not only are corporate taxes often kept low for the sake of competition, but other tax rates trend in favor of the more wealthy segments of the population. Bruce Scott points out that, at its extreme, such as under conditions of oligarchy:

> Great inequalities in wealth and power can become the basis for low (i.e. insufficient) taxes and the under-provision of public goods, creating a situation comparable to an incomplete state, where the rich can take care of themselves while ignoring the needs of the middle and lower classes.
>
> (2011: 135)

This in turn, then has the potential to lead to human suffering at the lower ends of the economic continuum and, with the demise of a significant group in the middle economic strata, any hope for social mobility for those not already at the top. In London, there is already some evidence of trends in this direction. It has been said that the square mile of the City of London earns 19 percent of Britain's GDP or nearly one-fifth of the nation's net wealth (Parker, 2013). London's Poverty Profile 2011 shows how London is becoming less representative of the country at large. Some key findings relevant here include: (a) the poverty rate in London is 28 percent compared to 22 percent in the rest of England and the gap has grown in the last decade; (b) housing is becoming increasingly unaffordable for lower income families, even renters; and (c) the poorest 50 percent have less than 5 percent of financial or property wealth, while the richest have 65 percent and 45 percent, respectively (MacInnes *et al.*, 2011).

An article from Reuters offers three factors responsible for the shifts creating this marked increase in inequality in London—the fact that finance is the most important economic sector; the role of the lack of taxation on "non-domiciled" short- or long-term residents with ties to other countries; and the popularity of London real estate as an investment for wealthy elite (Vellacott, 2012). The Office of National Statistics reported in 2013 that to July of that year property prices in London had risen by almost 10 percent (Brignall and Osborne, 2013). Of the top ten purchasers of £1 million-plus properties in London in 2010, nine were non-nationals, and total non-national property purchases in that price range amounted to over £200m more those of UK nationals (*Telegraph*, 2011). It has been further noted that the head of the Qatari Investment Authority has also undertaken significant investment in major development projects in the capital (Moore, 2013). Chrystia Freeland has observed:

> In some ways the British experience of global plutocracy is much more extreme. America is mostly run by its own plutocrats but to have outsiders come in and exert influence on your country is much more of a cultural challenge.
>
> (*London Evening Standard*, 2012)

Globalization's effect on the workings of the IPE—including the concentration and flow of global capital—is our second factor in state indebtedness. Michel-Rolph Trouillot commented in 2001 that, while capitalism was always a transnational process, what was new was the "spatialization of the world economy" (p. 128). He explains this had originally resulted in the movement of financial capital primarily amongst the triad of the United States, Japan and Europe, the rise of "oligopolies" in which the market is controlled by only a few firms, and the positioning of individuals—even within the same industrialized countries— on opposite sides of an economic gap (ibid.: 129). Globalization in this scenario has not meant a move toward the homogenization of social condition on a global scale but rather the inverse. The concentration of capital, moreover, is beginning to change venues, with a shift to emerging economic centers in the BRIC countries (Brazil, Russia, India and China). As jobs have withdrawn from earlier economic centers and moved to new ones (or have been eliminated entirely), debt was accumulated to fill the gap in living standards. Richard Wolff explains that the effect of the bursting of the credit bubble upon which this rested, caused western Europe and other centers to "face the full force of a withdrawing capitalism without the debt cushion" and—with reduced government services—the sharply deepened inequalities were a "a new experience for the capitalist system" (2013). Chrystia Freeland points out that surging income inequality is thus taking place across such diverse nations as the United States, United Kingdom, China, India and even "cozy social democracies like Sweden, Finland, and Germany" (*TED Blog*, 2013).

The move by the nations of Europe toward increased economic regionalization was meant to provide them with a strong basis from which to weather the negative winds of a globalized economy through regulatory harmony and market efficiency. Caroline Warner has examined the EU and found, even in the core nations of Western Europe, that instead:

> Phenomena not integral to the Single Market project but that accompanied it, such as privitisation, decentralization, and campaign finance regulation, come with opportunities and incentives for corruption, and the EU, as a supranational institution, has a low capacity to moderate those opportunities.
>
> (2007: 2)

She goes on to note that the situation in the EU illustrates "parallel worlds in the universe of markets and politics" wherein these "violate geometry" and intersect in political cartels, funded by those seeking political decisions in their economic favor (2007: 43–44).

It is easy to see the potential here for global capital to undermine national democracy in the pursuit of its economic self-interest in any number of ways. A classic case in point, although later dismissed, was the scandal involving illegal donations to the French UMP for Nicolas Sarkozy's 2007 presidential campaign by Lillian Bettencourt, France's richest woman worth over €20 billion. Bettencourt, heiress to the L'Oreal fortune, herself was said to have been participating in illegal tax evasion through offshore accounts, in the face of which the government was said to have looked the other way (Paine, 2010; *BBC News*, 2013b). A second example can be found in a long-term bribery scandal between the German-based electronics corporation Siemens and officials in Greece's two main parties, PASOK and New Democracy, averaging €15 million annually. In return, Siemans received lucrative telecommunications and security contracts during the 1997–2004 period, including the 2004 Olympic Games in Athens (Mavrava and Papatheodorou, 2012). The tip of a much larger iceberg of allegations of corruption, these monies helped Greece fund its infamously bloated public sector.

The Bettencourt and Siemens incidents, and so many more like them, portray the ability large donors—whether individuals or corporations—have in influencing politicians and the political parties that back them in order to secure their election in what has increasingly become in the European states and EU Parliament elections a market driven contest with victory going to the better funded campaigns. Warner sees this as evidence that "diminished state sovereignty within the EU has not reduced politicians' desire for obtaining and holding onto national office" (2007: 135). For these politicians, this process has opened up the doors to co-option by plutocratic interests. Corruption is always a byproduct of low and nonexistent state capacity to moderate it because the proper governmental checks and balances do not exist. An even worse situation is the one now found in those states that institutionalize such corruption in a self-reinforcing process.

The concern of course, as expressed by Noam Chomsky, is that "Concentration of wealth yields concentration of political power. And concentration of political power gives rise to legislation that increases and accelerates the cycle" (2012). Incumbent officials establish mutually beneficial relationships with their donors who each "profit" from their long-term association. The official is able to continue to win reelection and remain in office and the donor, who now has very real political leverage, is granted special privileges and dispensations—typically of an economic nature. Large campaign donations under such instances can be considered shrewd investments open only to the very rich that allow them to reap special dividends and gains. Contrary to predictions by noted economist Joseph Schumpeter, it has been pointed out that in today's world, "Prime ministers and finance ministers flock to Davos not to lay down the law to businesspeople but to court their favors" (*The Economist*, 2013c). Beyond any legal and moral unacceptability of these undertakings, the financial gains gleaned by politicians seldom trickle down to the public at large. Further, it is clear that the transactions would not be undertaken in the first place if the financial gains for business didn't outweigh the costs of doing business with politicians.

Beyond its contribution to the net loss of state economic resources, national government representative involvement in "crony capitalism" has combined with governmental imposition of terms of austerity on its citizens during the economic crisis in response to EU official dictates, and ultimately led to the sense of an overall loss of sovereignty by national governments. Basically, the perception by ordinary citizens is that, at any particular time, either the global plutocrats or the supranational European Union are the ones actually steering the ship of state. Whereas the relationship between national governments and business interests are more blatantly in conflict with the democratic process, the relationship between those governments and the EU are more opaque in terms of its effects on sovereignty and national interest.

For the most part, citizens regarded the relationship of their member state with the European Union as a positive development prior to the 2008 economic crash and subsequent Eurozone crisis.[7] It was the effects of the imposition of terms of austerity on the citizens of member states in response to the economic crisis that put the EU in the spotlight with regard to perceived widespread negative effects of regionalization. The negative effects of austerity, in terms of record high unemployment, rising costs of basic necessities, and sharp cuts in welfare benefits and social services at a time when people needed them most, fell primarily on the middle and working classes. In particular, it has led to vilification of the representatives of what has become known as the troika—the European Commission, European Central Bank and International Monetary Fund. For countries not in the Eurozone, austerity has sometimes combined with pressure for IMF contributions, amounting in some cases to billions of euros, towards assistance with Eurozone loans (Warner, 2012a). For countries in the Eurozone, the crisis highlighted a lack of control of their own currency and the ability to manipulate inflation rates rather than being forced down an immediate path of spending cuts and increased taxation, as was the case in Spain (Hill, 2013).

Austerity packages for different nations consisted of varying combinations of tax increases and spending cuts, including reduced subsidies, decreased spending on public services, and a lowering of employment levels, pensions and salaries. Some were imposed by the EU and the IMF on states seeking external funding or "bailouts," while other packages were self-imposed by those nations needing to comply with SGP rules or Maastricht criteria for admittance to the EU, and were often less severe and/or with longer timelines (Theodoropoulou and Wyatt, 2011: 11–13). The later "Fiscal Compact" enacted in 2012, meant to extend SGP rules and give them teeth by setting a "debt brake" with fiscal penalties for noncompliance by Eurozone members, was signed by all but two of the then EU members—the United Kingdom and the Czech Republic—although Sweden also agreed its terms were unreasonable for non-Eurozone members

(Mason, 2011; *BBC News*, 2012a). The fiscal compact required a vote under Ireland's constitution and, in the ensuing debate, its terms were seen by some as giving the EU "intrusive rights to police the budgets of debtor states" and were renounced by Sinn Fein as "feudal bondage" (Evans-Pritchard, 2012). It is perhaps not unrelated that Ireland's pending exit from the terms of its EU-IMF bailout were linked by prime minister Enda Kenny to his being the leader who vowed to retrieve the country's "sovereignty and independence" (AFP, 2013).

A place where plutocratic self-interest, "crony" capitalism, and the demands of European Union austerity have come together is in the privatization of public assets. Joseph Zacune of the Transnational Institute argues that privatization in Europe, coupled with deregulation and austerity, has amounted to a "fire sale" in which private companies have been able to "scoop up public assets in a crisis at low prices." State owned public services subject to privatization have included the following sectors: energy, water, transport, postal services, arms manufacturing, media, and health insurance and services (2013: 3, 8–14). Similarly, health reform of the NHS in the United Kingdom has been likened to effective privatization in which competition (in line with EU competition laws) under the Health and Social Care Act opens it to being effectively run by large health firms—who are said collectively to have donated £750,000 to the Conservative Party (Huitson, 2011). Privatization as an austerity measure has generally not proven to realize a fraction of the total value those assets were predicted to bring in (Zacune, 2013: annex).

It is widely agreed that all around austerity fell short of expectations in terms of results. The International Labour Organization—a UN agency promoting human and labor rights—has reported that "austerity has not produced more economic growth" and instead had "devastating consequences" by fueling unemployment (McKenna, 2012). A 68-page report by the International Red Cross looked at the effects of the economic crisis and found that across the region the social impact had been immense and worsened during the period of austerity (Traynor, 2013; IFRC, 2013). The EU has recently set about quantifying austerity's social costs in the form of a "scoreboard" of its ill-effects (including effects on unemployment, education, poverty, the wealth gap, and disposable income)—the completion date unspecified—but has also failed to specify what measures it will take in response (Deutsche Welle, 2013; Holman, 2013). UK Labour MEP Stephen Hughes has been quoted as responding that such indicators are "useless if not binding" to a solution given that "Drastic austerity policies in Europe and the lack of effective social governance have caused mass unemployment, falling wages, cuts in social protection, and growing poverty and social exclusion, and a whole generation of people in despair" (Holman, 2013). Further contributing to the sense that the EU is making demands counter to the interests of the citizens of member states, even the IMF—infamous for its imposition of fiscal discipline—has begun pushing the EU to move away from austerity towards stimulating growth, while Angela Merkel continues to advocate staying the course (Chu, 2011a).

Compounding the ill effects of the economic crisis and the imposition of austerity is the role of the cross border labor mobility put into place with membership in the EU, particularly in countries of the Schengen region. EU commissioner Laszlo Andor has reiterated the EU contention that only a truly European labor market with the free movement of labor can help mitigate the issue of EU unemployment over the long term (European Commission, 2013). Under the current economic conditions and high levels of unemployment across the European Union, especially among younger segments of the population, this contention does not seem self-evident to the general population, leading to feelings of resentment towards migrants from other countries of the EU and a sense that their sovereign borders are being "overrun." A survey in the United Kingdom undertaken by Conservative Party chairman Lord Ashcroft, revealed that an overwhelming majority of 77 percent of individuals believed a major reduction in immigration would alleviate pressure on public services and make it easier to find jobs (*London Evening Standard*, 2013b). Reciprocal arrangements allow European nationals actively looking for work in the United Kingdom to claim unemployment benefits although some EU nations must be on a registration scheme for 12 months prior (Winnett, 2012a). Decision-making with regard to border issues is thus seen as largely out of the hands of national government. In 2012, French president Nicolas Sarkozy caused controversy by saying there were "too many foreigners" in France and supporting the deportation of Roma gypsies (*BBC News*, 2012b). A study by Maribel Casas and colleagues have made the point, pertinent here, that:

> The EU border is not only at the edge of those member states forming the outer limit of the union. The EU border is multiplying both within and without the territories of the EU ... Here, the border is no longer the "edge" and limit of political sovereignty.
>
> (2010: 74)

The latest of the treaties guiding the EU is the Lisbon Treaty. The Lisbon Treaty, which became law on December 1, 2009, has alternately been described as "an attempt to streamline institutions" to allow an enlarged European Union to function more effectively and as "part of a federalist agenda that threatens national sovereignty" (*BBC News*, 2011). It was enacted as a result of the non-passage of the proposed EU constitution that was rejected in French and Dutch state referenda. Many believe it accomplished most of the same things (see Caughlan, 2007). Emilie Ciclet makes the case that: "The Member States of the European Union (EU), which derive their power from their citizens, have renounced much of this power in favor of the EU" (2013: 246).

It is through the Lisbon Treaty, she holds, that definitional weaknesses in the delineation of limits to EU regulatory functions have allowed for the "stretching" of the limits to EU competences which, once established, have pre-emptory powers over member states (Ciclet, 2013: 247). By citing "common European interest," moreover, the European Commission implies it knows better what is in the interest of the member states and their citizens than they do themselves (Ciclet, 2013: 255). Citizen's direct input into policy at the EU level is severely constrained; in order for EU citizens to directly call upon the European Commission to bring forward new policy proposals, at least one million citizens must sign a petition supporting it (Europa, n.d.-a). Even their representatives—in the form of national government leaders seated on the European Parliament—are not in a position to broach new policy measures (Europa, n.d.-b). Others have voiced concerns over potential EU usurpation of national sovereignty in terms of the rule of law within a country and the jurisdiction of the European Court of Human Rights (ECHR). Beyond questions of whether the states within the EU actually have a common heritage with regard to universal rule of law, Charles Moore argues that while British laws can ultimately be reformed through its Parliament, the same cannot be said for laws imposed on British citizens under the ECHR (Winnett, 2012b).

Further, resentment of the imposition of technocratic oversight of member state governments (in the case of Italy) and the electoral demise of leaders of those governments due to their perceived connection to the negative effects of austerity measures (for example, Ireland, Portugal, Greece, Italy, Slovakia and France) reflects the perception that national leaders have "sold out" their sovereignty to the EU (Chu, 2011b; Lee, 2011. Finally, with regard to European Union policies, having a single country, Germany, de facto at the helm in the person of Angela Merkel—due to its position as the region's strongest economy—has not been overlooked. Resentment in EU southern states, which have been most subject to outside intervention, particularly Greece, has resulted in a re-dredging up of tensions dating back to World War II (Chu, 2011b, 2012: A3; *Daily Mail*, 2012).

Perhaps the ultimate crisis of sovereignty is taking place in those states where fragmentation—in the form of a move toward subnational regionhood—threatens not only its social cohesion but also its territorial integrity.

These states are being subject simultaneously to the stresses of a move toward supranationalism and EU citizenship from above along with the strain of internal devolution and differentiated "citizenship" from below. With regard to the current era of globalization, Samir Amin has been quoted as saying that:

> The present epoch is surely characterized by an awakening, or reawakening, marked by collective social identifications which are starkly different from those defined by membership of a nation-state or a social class. Regionalism, linguistic and cultural assertion, tribal or ethnic loyalties, devotion to a religious group, attachment to a local community are some of the multiple forms this reawakening has taken.
>
> (Perez, 2012: 98–99)

If building a supra-sense of European-ness among members of the EU has been difficult due to the existence of pre-existing nationalism, Schmidt has observed that, "Complicating this even further is that in some nation-states, subnational regionhood constitutes a local territorial identity which outweighs the national" (2006: 19). Those making recent arguments for increased self-determination, if not outright statehood, have included such diverse regions (and reasons) as Scotland, Catalonia, Corsica, Flanders, the Basque Country, Northern Ireland, Padania and Wales. Both Scotland and Catalonia have already set dates for referenda to decide what their continued role in their respective nation states should be.

Scotland, a country of approximately 5.3 million people and currently part of the United Kingdom, which also includes England, Wales and Northern Ireland, has set the date of a referendum on Scottish independence for September 18, 2014. British prime minister David Cameron has given approval for the Scottish Parliament to hold the referendum, which will potentially allow the Scottish government to negotiate independence, but it will not state exactly what the terms of that independence will be, with questions of debt assignment and ownership of offshore oil resources still undecided (Warner, 2012b). Charles King stresses that the Scottish government is not basing the move toward independence on cultural or linguistic heritage, but on the fact that "the people of Scotland embrace political and social values that set them apart from the inhabitants of England, Wales, and Northern Ireland" (2012: 114). King voices the concern that a decision for independence based on a claim of "a simple desire to do things their own way" will "reverberate throughout Europe, setting a precedent for dealing with fundamental questions of governance and sovereignty" (ibid.: 114). David Cameron continues to hold that the two nations are "better off together" and has offered Scotland more powers if independence is rejected (Jowitt, 2012a, 2012b). The latest polls seem to remain in favor of preserving the union (ibid.).

In Catalonia, contrastingly, the situation is one in which the region in northeastern Spain, with a population of 7.5 million, wants to hold a referendum on its independence on November 9, 2014 in conflict with the Spanish government, which plans to block it as unconstitutional (Frayer, 2014). Spain, which until tentative settlement in 2011 had been in violent conflict with Basque separatists, banned a similar vote by the Basque country—another culturally distinct region on the Spanish–French border—in 2008. (Roberts, 2012). Tensions across Spain find their basis in racial, religious and cultural diversity, and are heightened by the tensions of a country severely impacted by the economic crisis, austerity and allegations of corruption (Beith, 2013: 2). The economy of Catalonia, a wealthy industrial region, represents one-fifth of Spain's total GDP and is said to resent paying taxes that then go to fund other poorer Spanish regions (Frayer, 2014). A pro-independence march in September 2012 brought out an estimated 1.5 million demonstrators and 80 percent of Catalans are said to want the referendum (Abend, 2012: 3).

The planned referenda reflect, in microcosm and in sharp relief, a number of the larger questions regarding sovereignty discussed above. Issues revolving around decision-making, taxation, debt, economic inequality between regions and the flow of wealth between them all come into play. Ultimately, however, the Scots and Catalans "no longer regard political institutions headquartered in London and Madrid as meeting their needs" (Barber, 2014). The most pressing issue, then, is the ability of the state to both provide for the welfare of its people and serve as its legitimate representative.

The crisis of legitimacy

The crisis of legitimacy in Europe has its basis in the movement toward a polarized society with a vanishing middle class, a public perception of decreased representation by decision-makers and a lack of a shared feeling of national identity.

Robert Reich, Secretary of Labor under the Clinton Administration, predicted today's crisis decades earlier with his observation that:

> Each nation's primary political task will be to cope with the centrifugal forces of the global economy which tear at the ties binding citizens together—bestowing ever greater wealth on the most skilled and insightful while consigning the less skilled to a declining standard of living.
>
> (Perez, 2012: 98)

Today, however, even the educated and "skilled" members of the middle class are suffering the same decline as the working class—perhaps more, having fallen farther—while the wealth of the top earners grows exponentially higher. The legitimacy of the Westphalian state as representative of its people and serving in their interest is being sorely tested. While the existence of a strong middle class post-dates the Westphalian state, it has come to be representative of that state as one of its greatest achievements along with the promotion of democratic ideals and freedoms, universal suffrage and religious tolerance. An economic polarization of the state's citizenry would mean a move backward in the welfare of its people, who in turn would look elsewhere in the fulfillment of that function.

In the aftermath of a banking crisis that sparked the recession in Europe, the number of bankers based in the EU who earn at least €1 million per year were said to have gone up 11 percent in 2012 (Slater, 2013). That same year, the headline in the UK *Sunday Times* read: "Wealth of the richest grows to record levels" (Sawer, 2012). Conversely, hourly wages across the EU have on average fallen by 0.7 percent between 2010 and 2013 (*London Evening Standard*, 2013a). As statistics like these have become public, the concept of a "wealth gap" in society has increasingly become a part of the political discourse across the nations of the European Union, and researchers have sought to measure the extent of the problem. A study published in 2012 by Kaja Bonesmo Fredriksen of the OECD Economics Department looked at income inequality across the European Union. Her findings, using OECD data, reveal a trend where the top tenth of the population of European countries have been capturing an increasing part of the income generated by the economy, while the poorest 10 percent are losing ground. Further, using an aggregate measure of EU-wide equality, the study found inequality in Europe to be high and having increased over the past 25 years (Fredriksen, 2012: 8–9).

The most recent Eurostat data on inequality and income distribution date to 2012. The "inequality of income distribution" figures measure the ratio of total income received by the top 20 percent of the population with the highest income to that of the 20 percent of the population with the lowest income, weighted by population. The findings across the EU (including all 28 member states) were that the top 20 percent received 5.1 times as much income as the bottom 20 percent, the same as for 2011. This figure, however, varies widely by country. Countries of Southern Europe (Greece, Italy, Spain and Portugal) tended to have higher levels of inequality, averaging 6.3 times, than those of Northern Continental Europe and Scandinavia, averaging 4.2 and 3.8 times respectively, with the United Kingdom falling in the middle, at 5.4 times higher inequality between these groups (Eurostat, 2014a).

Perhaps an even more alarming set of statistics is in the area of unemployment. A Eurostat news release showed that the unemployment rate for the Eurozone and EU-28 were 12.2 percent and 11.0 percent, respectively, in September 2013—both up from one year prior. The unemployment rate was said to have risen in 16 of 28 states. Further, youth unemployment rates are 24.1 percent and 23.5 percent in the Eurozone and EU-28, respectively. Greece continues to have both the highest overall unemployment (27.6 percent) and youth unemployment (57.3 percent) rates in the EU (Eurostat, 2013a). With regard to inequality and unemployment variations within the region, it is illustrative to look at the situations of Spain, the United Kingdom and Germany.

Spain, a Eurozone nation, has been called "the most unequal society in Europe" by the Catholic charity Caritas, with three million Spaniards in "extreme poverty," while a study by Credit Suisse found the number of millionaires rose 13 percent in 2011. Caritas' general secretary for Spain, Sebastian Mora warned of a divided society with a disappearing middle class (Hamilos, 2013). Spain's unemployment rate in September 2013 stood at 26.6 percent, with its youth unemployment rate a discouraging 56.6 percent (Eurostat, 2013a).

The United Kingdom does not belong to the Eurozone. An OECD study indicates income inequality in Britain increased more in the first three years of the crisis (2008–2010) than in the previous 12 years and it had the seventh largest gap between its richest and poorest out of all 34 OECD countries (Dugan, 2013). HM Revenue and Customs' figures show 18,000 people earned at least £1 million, almost a doubling of its 2010–2011 figures (Boffey, 2013). Unemployment rates for the United Kingdom in September 2013 were 7.6 percent, with the last available data for youth unemployment in July of 2013 at 20.9 percent (Eurostat, 2013a). London is also the most unequal region in the United Kingdom with the top 10 percent of households in London accounting for 40 percent of all income, and the bottom 50 percent accounting for only 15 percent (MacInnes *et al.*, 2011). London unemployment rates for this same period were 8.7 percent (Greater London Authority, 2014) with youth unemployment at 25.5 percent in April 2013 (Institute for Public Policy Research, 2013).

Germany, long said to be the success story of both the EU and the Eurozone, has not been immune to the growing "wealth gap." German unemployment rates have been nearly the lowest in the EU at 5.2 percent, with youth unemployment at 7.7 percent (Eurostat, 2013a). Beyond unemployment, however, there is widespread systemic underemployment, with individuals reliant on part-time, underpaid mini-jobs, masking the true extent of the problem. A European Central

Bank survey showed 25 percent of all German workers earn less than €9.54/ hour—the upper limit of the low wage sector (Connolly and Osborne, 2013). The German Institute for Economic Research reports that wages fell in real terms for all but the top 10 percent of earners in Germany between 2005 and 2010 (Ferguson, 2012). According to Germany's non-profit Bertelsmann Foundation, approximately 5.5 million Germans have lost their middle class status over the last ten years, while half a million others became high income earners (Traynor, 2013).

In Germany, the United Kingdom, Spain, and so many more EU countries, citizens who were in the middle and working classes as few as five years ago have now become today's "new poor" (Sanchez-Vallejo, 2012). In 2011, Eurostat analyzed recent statistics on monetary poverty and income inequalities in the European Union. They found that 16.9 percent of the EU-28 population was assessed to be at-risk-of-poverty (after social transfers), with that rate stable between 2009 and 2010, before increasing between 2010 and 2011 (although eight of the 28 countries did report a decrease during that time). The Eurostat study also found that the unemployed were a particularly vulnerable group with almost half of unemployed persons at-risk-of-poverty in 2011 (Eurostat, 2013b). Aid workers with Klimaka, a Greek psychosocial assistance organization, report that "the middle class is increasingly becoming our target group" as former professionals have become unemployed and eventually homeless (Korge and Batzoglou, 2012). *International Business Times* UK reporter Lianna Brinded writes of individuals "one cheque away from a crisis," noting that:

> While it is important to stress that in the economic climate that the poor are getting poorer, the number of middle-class individuals and families that used to earn average or above-average wages, living in enviable family homes and flats and working in white-collar jobs, are now falling below the breadline and are turning to foodbanks for help.
>
> (2012)

The "squeezing of the middle class," as it has become known, is due to a number of factors. It was mentioned in the prior section that the middle class is often turned to for taxation when money is needed basically because the poor can't pay and the rich won't. Nowhere is this clearer than with regard to Europe nations dealing with economic crisis. In order to keep up with the revenue necessary to service debts and fund services in the face of austerity, states have sought to cut wages and services and raise taxes. This has fallen squarely on the shoulder of the middle class. Greece, for example, passed new 2012 tax measures designed to raise a needed €2.2 billion by limiting family tax benefits and increasing the amount of income tax paid by those earning €19,000 or more, with the rate increasing from 40 percent to 42 percent for those making more than €41,000—said to be the higher end of the middle class average (Reuters, 2013). In France, a population long tolerant of high taxes has become concerned about continued increases as tax deductions have been narrowed and tax ban thresholds frozen while public services have suffered (*The Economist*, 2013d). In the United Kingdom, Labour leader Ed Miliband criticized the government for helping "the poor and the wealthy" while hurting "the living standards of those in the middle." He cites cutting child benefits, raising tuition fees, and the fact that the number of taxpayers in the middle forced to pay a 40 percent rate of income tax has risen to 1 in 6, as the wage requirements for this bracket have been continually cut (*Telegraph*, 2014; Collinson, 2013). Rising taxes, lowered benefits, an increased cost of living, and stagnant wages are leading to widespread disillusionment.

A related trend is the pressure on local governments, which provide those welfare and municipal services that many citizens utilize on a daily basis, from libraries and bin collection to senior citizen and youth services and jobs programs. A 2011 Council of Europe Report found that "local budget revenue contracted in real terms in most Council of Europe member states surveyed over the period 2008 to 2010," while "expenditures on social welfare and support have increased as a result of economic pressures on households" (2011: 43). An additional issue is that the impact of the financial crisis and the potential for extension of EU influence create added uncertainty (ibid.: 44). More recently, many local governments have been undergoing cuts that, if continued, are said to threaten not only "local government as we know it" but the solvency of cities themselves (Taylor *et al.*, 2013; Parker, 2013). This contrasts sharply with the reality that many of the elite in the top percentiles of income rarely utilize public services and therefore have no stake in their survival. As one financier was quoted as saying, "The only time that I use the state is when my driver drives on public roads" (Oborne, 2012).

Across the continent, a realization is setting in for the masses that dreams of sustaining, or ever achieving, a middle class lifestyle for themselves and their children is quickly fading away:

> The European dream is under assault, as the wave of inflation sweeping the globe mixes with this continent's long-stagnant wages. Families that once enjoyed Europe's vaunted quality of life are pinching pennies to buy necessities, and cutting back on extras like movies and vacations abroad.
>
> Potentially more disturbing—especially to the political and social order—are the millions across the continent grappling with the realization that they may have lives worse, not better, than their parents.
>
> (Dougherty and Bennhold, 2008)

An October 2013 Red Cross societies report, viewed as a damning critique of the response to EU debt crisis, highlights "unemployment, the widening poverty gap, and growing risk of social unrest" (Traynor, 2013). The Resolution Foundation, dedicated to improving living standards for the United Kingdom's low and middle income population, argues that this squeeze is not just due to the current austerity but "a much longer-term and deeper-seated trend" (Wintour, 2013). This reflects the impact of technology and globalization on employment in

Europe, leading to the loss of middle class jobs over the long term. In 2012, respected international finance expert Sony Kapoor was quoted as asking, "With catastrophic unemployment levels in Spain, Portugal, and Greece that are still rising, the real question is, how long before the social fabric gives way?" (Stewart, 2012). A year and a half later, that question was still being asked. In 2013, Jack Ewing, European Economics correspondent for the *New York Times*, acknowledged that the European unemployment rate is a critical indicator in that, the longer record levels persist, the harder it will be for leaders to push the necessary changes for economic growth while at the same time "contain discontent" (Ewing, 2013). As unemployment rates in many countries continue to go up, especially for young adults, the social contract is seemingly being stretched to its limit. Such concerns over agitation and social unrest have not been lost on many other commentators over the last few years, for example:

> Juan Somavia, director-general of the International Labour Organization, a United Nations agency, has warned that social unrest could worsen if stimulus packages are not seen to benefit ordinary people, saying "There's a sense that it's billions for bankers but pennies for the people."
>
> (Thornhill, 2009)

> For the members of today's mainly young middle class, all avenues for advancement have been blocked by billionaires, old men, or people whom they assume should belong in one of these two categories. This is an explosive situation.
>
> (Krol, 2013)

> As a result, Europe under the leadership of old-fashion politicians, a business elite, which through monopolies and cartels does not permit new innovative forces to get into the creation process, and under the strong influence of trade unions, is running at full speed toward the catastrophe ... The end is coming with the cross depletion of the middle class, which started with the PIGS and is now expanding to the north.
>
> (Koronakis, 2013)

Over the course of the economic crisis, discontent has indeed on occasion overrun its containment, and frustration by citizens has seemingly "exploded" onto the streets. Across the southern member states of the EU—Greece, Italy, Spain and Portugal—the protests have often turned violent, clashing with police. A report from 2010, relatively early in the crisis, showed demonstrators displaying the slogan "plutocracy should pay for the crisis" but, by the beginning of 2012, Greek protestors directed their hostility more squarely on the EU leadership, burning German flags (Wherlock, 2010; *Daily Mail*, 2012). In November 2012, hundreds of thousands of people took to the streets in their respective nation's capitals in coordinated protest organized by the European Trade Union Confederation (*BBC News*, 2012d). In Portugal, demonstrators carried banners denouncing the Troika (*BBC News*, 2012d). Spanish union leader Ignacio Fern-andez Toxo called it "a political strike against the policies of a suicidal and anti-social government," which implemented "impositions from Brussels" (Kington *et al.*, 2012). In Italy, it was students who were on the front lines while, in the northern member states suffering less from austerity, the protests were more restrained but held in solidarity (ibid.: 2012). The 15-M network sparked the "Occupy" movement that staged sit-ins around the world—most famously at St. Paul's Cathedral in London—and, by 2013, had morphed into "Blockupy," which hoped to cut off access to a number of European financial institutions in a critique of global capitalism and globalization (*BBC News*, 2012c; *Aljazeera*, 2012). After three years of protests, however, demonstrators still see no clear redirection of policy.

As a result, any national sense that "we are all in it together" is decreasing and the essence of the social contract between state and citizen—in which citizens submit to the state in exchange for a guarantee of their welfare—has been violated. Amitai Etzioni explains the process—which becomes cyclical—thus:

> As governments fail to deliver the public and private goods they are expected to provide, they are considered less legitimate by the public, and the fact that they lose legitimacy is one factor that diminishes their ability to govern, i.e. their competence.
>
> (2012)

He ascribes this to the fact that technological and economic developments occur much more rapidly than "political and ideational institutions" can adapt to them (ibid.). In that sense, the European Union seems to be an appropriate example.

Jurgen Habermas sees the EU as the adaptation by which the peoples of Europe seek to recover "political room for manoeuver" in the face of globaliza-tion, but laments that the "long shadow cast by nationalism continues to obscure the present" (2012: 28, 47). Citizens still want to believe that the Westphalian state can fulfill its role but it is continually coming up lacking.

Increasingly, citizens not only feel that they have an unequal economic share from those at the top percentiles of society but also that their vote does not matter.

Economic columnist Philip Coggan aptly assesses the problem as having mul-tiple parts. The first part of the problem lies in the fact that individuals "have become complacent about our democracies and deeply cynical about the politi-cians that run our governments." The second part, he says, is that the representa-tive model of democracy—where voters choose those who represent them—has given way to a third model in which those representatives "delegate decisions to experts"—such as central banks, international courts, and technocrats—who act in a way that suggests that the economy is rigged in favor of the rich (2013). The cynicism with politicians is no doubt partly linked with a number of the sover-eignty and legitimacy issues aforementioned, but the trend toward reduction in voter turnout and political party membership seems also linked to a more general disconnect between democratic institutions and citizenry. A number of individuals have commented on these trends in participation to this end.

Ferdinand Mount has explained how in the 1960s total UK political party membership was around ten million or one-fifth of the population but by the end of 2007 it had fallen to not much more than half a million or 1 percent—largely due to the decline of a role and opportunity for active membership and the rise of the role of media and professional advice (2012: 131–143). Adding these trends to a dramatic drop in voter turnout, Mount concludes, "something had gone badly wrong with British politics" (2012: 145–146). It is happening, however, not only in British politics but also across Europe. In Germany, for example, party membership numbers have fallen and the average age of members risen, while voter turnout has dropped from 80 to 70 percent in a decade (Seiffert, 2013). In discussing the trend across Europe, Professor Ingrid van Biezen notes on average only 4.7 percent of national electorates are members of a political party today and the absolute number of members has almost halved since 1980. She further notes that the parties themselves are less representative of a wider constituency but seem rather to constitute "the outer ring of an extended political class" (2013).

The latter is perhaps key and ties in with Coggan's second part of the diagnosis of the problem. Increasingly, people perceive they are being governed by an out-of-touch elite operating in the interests of plutocrats. Elected leaders themselves are in some cases seen as a part of an economic elite themselves, having been "well-born" and privately educated in exclusive schools (West and Nelson, 2013: 1). It is the role of the unelected in governance, however, that ultimately fuels disenchantment and a great deal of "unelected governance" is thought to come by and through the EU. Most directly, the installations of technocratic oversight into national governments struggling with noncompliance with EU debt and deficit rules has spurred the ire of a public already antagonized by the effects of austerity. Whether or not the technocratic governance was indeed better that what had gone before is not the question—it is that in a democracy the people do not perceive as legitimate governance in which they so blatantly did not have a say. *Telegraph* business correspondent Louise Armistead wrote that "As if in wartime, democracy has been sidelined and public opinion ignored under the assumption that the state—or superstate—has a higher cause" (2012). UK deputy prime minister Nick Clegg said at the time that "It would be a very bad precedent indeed if it was felt that somehow democratically-elected governments can't sort out the things for which they have been elected" (Churcher and Woodcock, 2011).

An even bigger concern may be the legitimacy issues posed by the European Union project itself. The EU's founding principles clearly state a commitment to three primary tenets: democratic equality, representative democracy and participatory democracy (Europa, n.d.-c). It has long been held, however, that the workings of the EU entail a "democratic deficit" in that they lack transparency and citizen participation and ultimately a lack of democratic recourse. The EU itself recognizes and has set about addressing this issue, proposing for example that the European parliamentary elections could also include a partisan race for president of the European Commission based on the former's electoral outcome—an idea seen as likely making the problem worse not better (Grabbe, 2013). In fact, this type of proposal is symptomatic of the ad hoc way in which the EU has been progressing. Jurgen Habermas has critiqued both the incrementalism of EU integration and any regime of central steering that transfers "the imperatives of the market to national budgets," stating: "In this way, the heads of government would invert the European project into its opposite. The first transnational democracy would be transformed into an arrangement for exercising a kind of post-democratic, bureaucratic rule" (2011: 52). Ultimately, there is general agreement that the European Union is an unfinished project—necessary to deal with the transnational issues of today but which will require further economic and political union to succeed. This will be a difficult task at a time when EU leadership approval has earned some of its lowest ratings and when the national political moods seems to be more for continuing to muddle through as is than to upset the political extremes (Manchin, 2014).

Vivien Schmidt maintains that not only has EU "governance *by* and *of* the people" been much weaker than "governance *for* the people" but that they could not help but be since the "EU has no collective identity, which is a *sine qua non* to constitute a demos, or to express a collective will" (2006: 21–2). Neil Fligstein has looked at length at the idea of a European collective identity and would agree with Schmidt, finding that only 12.7 percent of people living in Western Europe primarily think of themselves as European, while 44 percent still have only a national identity and the remaining 43.3 percent put their membership of a nation state first. While he ultimately concedes that it just might be too early to see the emergence of a European identity, Fligstein maintains that, as of 2008: "Europe so far has been a class project ... Ironically, those with a European identification clearly represent one set of social groups to the exclusion of others" (2008: 156). If it can be asserted that the EU has not yet fostered such an identity, the question that needs to be asked is whether the Westphalian nation state of today indeed itself has such a collective identity, and what that encompasses, or whether there are multiple identities within the state fractured along differential lines of identification both within and across borders. Michel-Rolph Trouillot recognized two decades ago that increasingly "new social movements" and trans-national organizations were creating identities that bypassed the state, suggesting that "globalization renders the state irrelevant not only as an economic actor but also as a social and cultural container" (2001: 125). Perhaps it is more apt to say that the state is not yet irrelevant but that new economic realities have made it appear to its citizens as alternately both an essential and insufficient container for protecting their interests, depending on where threats to those interests are seen as arising from. If, for example, EU policy is seen as benefitting other states to the detriment of one's own then an emphasis on state-as-container in terms of reflexive nationalism is a likely result. In this case, inequality is often seen as a zero-sum equation in which one state's middle and working classes are in competition with those of other states.

Brian Burgoon has studied inequality and the anti-globalization backlash by political parties and finds that: "income inequalities, left unchecked by social protections, do indeed tend to dampen support of global engagement and spur backlash against it in party position-taking, including trade protectionism, anti-internationalism and anti-EU backlash" (2012: 431). While on one hand, this can take the form in mainstream parties of a reversion to concerns centering on "national interest," it can on the other also foment the development and expansion of fringe parties who embrace "extreme" platforms, which play on the current economic climate to seemingly normalize their views. With regard to the current economic climate, Saskia Sassen points out that: "This is also then fertile ground for disadvantaged citizens and the expanded number of middle class citizens who are losing economic and social ground to turn their fears against immigrants" (2010: 24). Ian Traynor states that "two big contemporary issues— the euro crisis and Muslim immigration—have fueled the rise of illiberal populism" nearly everywhere in Europe (2012). Aditya Chakrabortty argues that the power of populists lies less in their message than that they represent a "vast and growing dissatisfaction with the professional political class" (2013). While these groups by their nature are "nationalist," their common concerns regarding the EU have started to forge cross-national alliances.

The rise of "extreme" political parties, primarily on the far right, has garnered enough attention to cause concern, and national governments have begun to respond to the social currency of some of these issues as recent debates over burqas and minarets will attest.[8] Peter Sutherland, former special representative to the UN under Kofi Annan, states that this resurgence of national identity is due to the "pressures of globalization and the threat of international terrorism" but that the issues surrounding multiculturalism are not really about the revival of "national identity" but rather are against behavior that offends democratic and civil norms that almost all Western nations have in common (2008: 74, 76). He sees the consequences of globalization and multiculturalism as having united people globally, but divided them locally in a "tribalization" of society (ibid.: 83). The end result is a ghetto-ization of economically deprived segments of the population who might also be ethnic minorities. When riots take place in these communities, as has happened across Europe in the past few years, they raise complicated questions of whether it is cultural bias, youth unemployment, or policies that fail to foster social inclusion that are to blame. There is also a sense that at least in some sectors a semblance of "economic identity" over "national identity" may also be taking hold. Hintjens sees "unofficial and semi-legalized hierarchies" as an emerging response among EU citizens to both the state's "besieged legitimacy" and increased securitization of governance (2007: 410). She has noted that Europe has "no new notions of citizenship to offer" and that, as state's legitimacy declines, efforts are instead increasingly made to "police the growing insecurity of people's lives" (2007: 409). A second order effect to the process, then, is that when social and economic ghetto-ization is combined with a reactionary response to security issues on the part of the government, the result becomes a trend towards the police-like state others have described as developing in the United States (see Corbin and Hendrix, 2014).

In the final accounting, without a secure sense of identity linked either to the nation state or the EU on the part of its citizens, both entities are surely in jeopardy.

Conclusion

This chapter sought to make the case that the overarching trend across the Westphalian nation states of the European Union is one in which they are experiencing a decline of both sovereignty and legitimacy. This has been a result of forces acting from both within and without that are serving to deconstruct its functioning as a modern welfare state. Ultimately, the deconstruction of that state—and the protections it provides to its citizens—is correspondingly leading to the demise of that productive social strata, protected by labor laws and earning beyond a living wage, that developed into what we call the middle class. Consequently, its members no longer reliably enjoy their "comfortable" existence of the past nor can they count on having years of secure retirement.

As was shown, its sovereignty has been targeted in multiple ways. The 2008 financial collapse set off by the housing bubble triggered a crisis that made plain that national debt levels had become unsustainable, compounded by tax evasion and avoidance, the movement of global financial capital to new economic sectors, and the contingencies of economic regionalization. In such a scenario, those in positions of political power are subject to manipulation by those wielding large sums of money both at the personal and organizational levels. As these funds fail to trickle down to those citizens below and as the lack of control of its currency and the imperatives of austerity measures dismantle social services, the state is forced to violate its social contract. Pre-existing subnational fractures are also exacerbated, leading to a direct threat of fragmentation of a state's national territory—prime examples being the near-term planned referenda on independence by Scotland and Catalonia.

The threat to Westphalian state legitimacy thus follows in that it is increasingly perceived as no longer representative of those which it governs. A polarization of the citizenry economically and a horizontal fracturing culturally have caused a decline in a sense of national identity. Extreme unemployment (and underemployment) and the demise of vital social services at the local level have intensified a feeling that the government works to the advantage of the rich, disillusioning the general populace. Increasingly, the onus is on the middle class to make up financial shortfalls and the realization has set in for many that the next generation is unlikely to achieve what their parents have. The decline in the middle class is profound and the implications broad. Mario Pezzini, director of the OECD Development Center, makes plain this group's importance:

> middle classes are not only a motor of consumption and domestic demand, their social role remains equally important. Middle classes are believed to support democracy and progressive but moderate political platforms. Strong middle classes can influence economic development through more active participation in the political process, expressing support for

political programmes and electoral platforms, in particular those that promote inclusive growth.

(2012)

The result of the pressures squeezing the middle class has been explosive public protest on one hand and a withdrawal from mainstream political life completely on the other—with frustrations obvious in the cross-European growth of "extremist" political parties, particularly on the far right and the tribalization of society as it turns inward in fulfillment of its needs.

It has been suggested that these tribulations are the birthing pains as society moves from one state form to another. The continued expansion of the European Union and its umbrella of regionalism, both in terms of members and mission, have been pointed to by some as the way of things to come. Certainly, it is clear that many of our most important issues cross borders at the very least at regional levels. Still, given the evidence that this chapter offers, the EU as currently conceptualized is clearly not fulfilling its role as heir to the Westphalian state, exacerbating existing problems as it somehow falls short of providing the region's citizens with either a new identity or a social contract that fulfills their needs. It remains to be seen whether the Westphalian states of Europe will deem to reassert their authority, will acquiesce to the European Union as a sovereign entity in its own right—perhaps allowing it to grow into itself, or whether something new lies on the horizon. None of these forms, however, can ultimately reassure us of the fate of the European middle class.

Notes

1 See Perez, 2012, for discussion of the origins of the nation state concept and debate over whether borders of the state and nation actually coincide.
2 For the sake of brevity, this chapter has compressed 350+ years of development of the capitalist system in Europe into a paragraph. For a more comprehensive examination, see Scott, *Capitalism*, 2011.
3 A more detailed history of the development of the European Union is online, available at: http://europa.eu/about-eu/eu-history/index_en.htm.
4 See, for example, Etzioni's 2012 look at the questioning of the competency and legitimacy of the nation state on a global basis.
5 In addition, while much of the data for the EU includes all EU member states, the focus of this chapter is upon the Western European states as they are the more established representations of the Westphalian state.
6 In this chapter, we focus on the effects of the sovereign-free economy but this is not to deny the importance of the illicit economy in challenging state sovereignty. For more details on the significance of this side of the equation, see Schneider and Williams, *The Shadow Economy*, 2013, and Europol's "2013 Serious and Organised Crime Threat Assessment."
7 The EU has not been without its own issues of corruption. See, for example, the case regarding Eurostat, in Warner, 2007, p. 172.
8 For example, Koukouzelis' 2008 article elaborates arguments regarding the extent to which visible religious symbols such as Muslim headscarves are differentially interpreted under both France's principle of "laicite" and the European Convention of Human Rights.

References

Abend, L. (2012) "Catalonia's Call for Succession." *Time Magazine*, 24 September: 3.

AFP (2013) "Ireland set to Exit EU-IMF Bailout on December 15." October 14. Online, available at: http://uk.finance.yahoo.com/news/ireland-set-exit-eu-imf-204959733.html.

AIV (2013) *Crime Corruption and Instability: an Exploratory Report*. No. 85, May. The Hague: Advisory Council on International Affairs (AIV).

Alessi, C., Wolverson, R. and Sergie, M. (2013) "The Credit Rating Controversy." Council on Foreign Relations. October 22. Online, available at: www.cfr.org/financial-crises/credit-rating-controversy/p22328.

Aljazeera (2012) "Anti-austerity Protests held across Europe." June 1. Online, available at: www.aljazeera.com/news/europe/2013/06/2013619152349261.hml.

Armistead, L. (2012) "Could Democracy Derail the Euro?" *Telegraph*. April 28. Online, available at: www.telegraph.co.uk/finance/financialcrisis/9233886/Could-democracy-derail-the-euro.html.

Baker, L. (2013) "S&P Cuts EU's AAA Rating, European Officials Dismiss Move." Reuters. December 20. Online, available at: www.reuters.com/article/2013/12/20/us-europe-creditrating-sp-idusbre9bj0fi20131220.

Barber, T. (2014) "To Revive Trust in Europe, Rebuild Faith in Democracy." *Financial Times*. January 2. Online, available at: www.ft.com/intl/cms/s/0/d06b0f6c-696d-11e3-89ce-00144feabdc0.html#axzz2pqtXUCb5.

BBC News (2011) "Q&A: the Lisbon Treaty." January 17. Online, available at: http://news.bbc.co.uk/2/hi/europe/6901353.stm.

BBC News (2012a) "EU Summit: All but Two Leaders Sign Fiscal Compact." March 2. Online, available at: www.bbc.co.uk/news/world-europe-17230760.

BBC News (2012b) "Nicolas Sarkozy says France has too many Foreigners." March 6. Online, available at: www.bbc.co.uk/news/world-europe-1728064.

BBC News (2012c) "Spain's Indignados Protest here to Stay." May 15. Online, available at: www.bbc.co.uk/news/world-europe-18070246.

BBC News (2012d) "Violent Clashes as Austerity Protests Grip EU Cities." November 15. Online, available at: www.bbc.co.uk/news/world-europe-20320993.

BBC News (2013a) "Fitch Downgrades UK Credit Rating to AA+." April 19. Online, available at: http://bbc.co.uk/news/business-22219382.

BBC News (2013b) "Bettencourt Scandal: Key Players." October 7. Online, available at: www.bbc.co.uk/news/10539846.

Beith, M. (2013) "Between Crime, Separatism, and Racial Tensions, can Spain Pull Through?" *Atlantic*. July. Online, available at: www.theatlantic.com/international/print/2013/07/between-crime-separatism-and-racial-tensions-can-spain-pull-through/278074/.

Boffey, D. (2013) "Super-rich on Rise as Number of £1m-plus Earners Doubles." *Guardian*. June 1. Online, available at: www.theguardian.com/politics/2013/jun/01/top-earners-millionaires-inequality-city-finance.

Bonesmo Fredriksen, K. (2012) *Income Equality in the European Union*. OECD Economics Department Working Papers No. 952. Paris: OECD Publishing.

Brignall, M. and Osborne, H. (2013) "London Property Boom Leaves Super Rich Scrambling around for a New Pad." *Guardian*, September 20. Online, available at: www.the-guardian.com/business/2013/sep/20/london-property-beem-super-prime-market.

Brinded, L. (2012) "Britain on the Breadline: Middle Class, Hungry, and Homeless." *International Business Times*. April 30. Online, available at: www.ibtimes.co.uk/

articles/334864/20120430/society-big-human-interest-foodbank-recession-budget. htm#.

Burgoon, B. (2012) "Inequality and Anti-globalization Backlash by Political Parties." *European Union Politics*. Vol. 14. No. 3: 408–435.

Businessweek (2013) "European Debt Balloons: What each Country Carries, Per Capita." Special Issue. September 16–22: 74.

Casas, M., Cobarrubias, S. and Pickles, J. (2010) "Stretching Borders Beyond Sovereign Territories? Mapping EU and Spain's Border Externalization Policies." *Geopolitica(s)*. Vol. 2. No. 1: 71–90.

Caughlan, A. (2007) "These Boots Are Gonna Walk All Over You." *Brussels Journal*. December 13. Online, available at: www.brusselsjournal.com/node/2773.

Chakrabortty, A. (2013) "The Age of the Political Idiot." *Businessweek*. July 3: 8–10.

Chomsky, N. (2012) "Plutonomy and the Precariat." *Nation*. May 8. Online, available at: www.thenation.com/article/167763/plutonomy-and-precariat#axzz2XRPmdEvY.

Chu, H. (2011a) "Growth Vital for Europe." *Los Angeles Times*. October 28: A1, A6.

Chu, H. (2011b) "Europe's New Rules, Written in German." *Los Angeles Times*. December 3: A1, A6.

Chu, H. (2012) "Eurozone Ministers Hold off on Approving Second Bailout for Greece." *Los Angeles Times*. February 16: A3.

Chu, H. (2013) "Debts Catch Up with the Dutch." *Los Angeles Times*. June 9: A9.

Churcher, J. and Woodcock, A. (2011) "'Difficult Times Ahead' for Economy, says David Cameron." *Independent*. November 11. Online, available at: www.independent. co.uk/news/uk/politics/politics/difficult-times-ahead-for-economy-says-david-cameron-6260786.html?printService=print.

Ciclet, E. (2013) "Does the Lisbon Treaty Effectively Limit the Power of the European Union?" *Economic Affairs*. Vol. 33. No. 2: 246–256.

Coates, S. (2013) "Banks Fear Storm of Protest over how Little Tax they Pay." *London Times*. March 1: 6–7.

Coggan, P. (2013) "The Threats to Western Democracy." *Policy Network*. September 5. Online, available at: www.policy-network.net/pno_detail.aspx?ID=4452&title=The-threats-to western-democracy.

Cohen, D. (2009) *Three Lectures on Post-Industrial Society*. McCuaig, W., trans. Cambridge: MIT Press.

Collinson, P. (2013) "Budget 2013: Extra 400,000 People to be Caught in 40% Higher Tax Band." March 20. Online, available at: www.theguardian.com/uk/2013/mar/20/budget-2013–40pc-higher-tax-bracket.

Connolly, K. and Osborne, L. (2013) "Low-paid Germans Mind Rich–Poor Gap as Elections Approach." *Guardian*. August 30. Online, available at: www.theguardian.com/world/2013/aug/30/low-paid-germans-mini-jobs.

Corbin, T. and Hendrix, N. (2014) "The Demise of the American Middle Class and the Rise of the Police State." Bunker, R. and Bunker, P. eds. *Global Criminal and Sovereign Free Economies and the Demise of the Western Democracies: Dark Renaissance*. London: Routledge.

Daily Mail (2012) "Greeks Brand German 'Nazis' for Driving through Painful Cuts and 'Taking Control of their Economy.'" February 15. Online, available at: www.daily-mail.co.uk/news/article-2101614/Greece-debt-crisis-Greeks-brand-Germans-Nazis-taking-control-economy.html.

Deutsche Welle (2013) "EU 'Scoreboard' to Tally Austerity's Social Costs." October 3. Online, available at: www.dw.de/eu-scoreboard-to-tally-social-costs/a-17133131.

Dougherty, C. and Bennhold, K. (2013) "For Europe's Middle-Class, Stagnant Wages Stunt Lifestyle." *New York Times.* May 1. Online, available at: www.nytimes.com/2008/05/01/business/worldbusiness/01middle.html?pagewanted=all&_r=0.

Dugan, E. (2013) "Poor Hit Hardest by Financial Crisis and Welfare Cuts will make it Worse." *Independent.* May 15. Online, available at: www.independent.co.uk/news/uk/politics/poor-hit-hardest-by-financial-crisis-and-welfare-cuts-will-make-it-worse-8616344.html.

Elliott, L. and Inman, P. (2012) "Eurozone in New Crisis as Credit Agency Downgrades Nine Countries." *Guardian.* January 13. Online, available at: www.guardian.co.uk/business/2012/jan/13/eurozone-crisis-france-credit-rating-aaa.

Etzioni, A. (2012) "The Domestic Sources of Global Adhocracy. *Social Change Review.* December, Vol. 10. No. 2: 99–124.

Europa (n.d.-a) "Treaty of Lisbon: The Treaty at a Glance." Online, available at: http://europa.eu/lisbon_treaty/glance/index_en.htm.

Europa (n.d.-b) "EU Institutions and Bodies." Online, available at: http://europa.eu/about-eu/institutions-bodies/index_en.htm.

Europa (n.d.-c) "The Union's Founding Principles." Online, available at: http://europe.eu/scadplus/constitution/democracy_en.htm.

European Commission (2013) "Labour Mobility: Europe's Chance to Battle the Crisis." August 5. Online, available at: http://ec.europa.eu/commission_2010-2014/andor/head-lines/articles/2013/05/20130508_en.htm.

European Commission (2014) "Fight against Tax Fraud and Tax Evasion." Taxation and Customs Union webpage. February 12. Online, available at: http://ec.europa.eu/taxation_customs/taxation/tax_fraud_evasion/further_reading/index_en.htm.

Europol (2013) "EU Serious and Organized Crime Threat Assessment (SOCTA 2013)." The Hague. Online, available at: www.europol.europa.eu/sites/default/files/publications/socta2013.pdf.

Eurostat (2013a) "Euro Area Unemployment Rate at 12.2%." October 31. Online, available at:http://epp.eurostat.ec.europa.eu/cache/ITY_PUBLIC/3–31052013-BP/EN/3–31052013-BP-EN.PDF.

Eurostat (2013b) "Income Distribution Statistics." December 18. Online, available at: http://epp.eurostat.ec.europa.eu/statistics_explained/index.php/Income_distribution_statistics.

Eurostat (2014a) "Inequality of Income Distribution." January 17. Online, available at: http://epp.eurostat.ec.europa.eu/tgm/printTable.do?tab=table&plugin=1&language=en&pcode=tsdsc260&printPreview=true.

Eurostat (2014b) "Government Debt in % of GDP-Quarterly Data." January 22. Online, available at: http://epp.eurostat.ec.europa.eu/tgm/table.do?tab=table&init=1&plugin=1&language=en&pcode=tipsgo20.

Eurostat (2014c) "Private Debt in % of GDP-Consolidated-Annual Data." January 22. Online, available at: http://epp.eurostat.ec.europa.eu/tgm/table.do?tab=table&init=1&plugin=0&language=en&pcode=tipspd20.

Evans, M. (2013) "Middle Classes Targeted as Tax Evasion Prosecutions Double." August 5. Online, available at: www.telegraph.co.uk/finance/personalfinance/consumertips/tax/10221452/Middle-classes-targeted-as-tax-evasion-prosecutions-double.html.

Evans-Pritchard, A. (2012) "Irish EU Treaty Vote Threatens Chaos." *Telegraph.* February 28. Online, available at: www.telegraph.co.uk/finance/financialcrisis/9112155/Irish-EU-treaty-vote-threatens-chaos.html.

Ewing, J. (2013) "Jobless Rate in Euro Zone Stays at Record." *New York Times.* October

31. Online, available at: www.nytimes.com/2013/11/01/business/international/jobless-rate-in-europe-stays-at-record-12-2.html?_r=0.

Fairless, T. (2013) "EU Threatens Action Against Big Three Ratings Firms." *Wall Street Journal*. December 2. Online, available at: http://online.wsj.com/news/articles/SB1000 14240527023043551045792336238411378120.

Ferguson, K. (2012) "All Work and Low Pay: Getting By Without Minimum Wage in Germany." *Spiegel Online*. May 14. Online, available at: www.spiegel.de/international/germany/low-paid-workers-struggle-despite-germany-s-booming-economy-a-832724.html.

Fligstein, N. (2008) *Euro-Clash: The EU, European Identity, and the Future of Europe*. New York: Oxford University Press.

Frayer, L. (2014) "Catalonia Seeks Succession Vote." *Los Angeles Times*. January 17: A4.

Garton Ash, T. (2012) "The Crisis of Europe: How the Union Came Together and Why It's Falling Apart." *Foreign Affairs*. Vol. 91. No. 5: 2–15.

Genschel, P. (2005) *Globalisation and the Transformation of the Tax State*. TranState Working Papers 10. Bremen: Collaborative Research Center, University of Bremen.

Gilman, N., Goldhammer, J. and Weber, S. (2011) *Deviant Globalization: Black Market Economy in the 21st Century*. New York: Continuum.

Grabbe, H. (2013) "How Not to Fix the European Union's Democratic Deficit." *Financial Times*. November 4. Online, available at: www.ft.com/intl/cms/s/0/663ab 6b6-3da2-11e3-9928-00144feab7de.html#axzz2pqtXUCb5.

Greater London Authority (2014) "Unemployment Rate, Region." January. Online, available at: http://data.london.gov.uk/datastore/package/unemployment-rate-region.

Habermas, J. (2012) *The Crisis of the European Union*. Cronin, C., trans. Cambridge: Polity Press.

Hamilos, P. (2013) "Spanish Wealth Gap Biggest in Europe, says Charity." *Guardian*. October 10. Online, available at: www.theguardian.com/world/2013/oct/10/spanish-wealth-gap-inequality-charity.

Hill, S. (2013) "To Hell and Back: Spain's Grotesque Recession and Its Surprising New Economy." *Atlantic*. October 18. Online, available at: www.theatlantic.com/business/archive/2013/10/to-hell-and-back-spains-grotesque-recession-and-its-surprising-new-economy/280678/.

Hintjens, H. (2007) Citizenship under Siege in the Brave New Europe. *European Journal of Cultural Studies*. Vol. 10. No. 3: 409–414.

Holman, K. (2013) "Europe Counts the Cost and Faces Up to the Huge Social Damage Caused by Austerity." *Tribune Magazine*. October 19. Online, available at: www.tribunemagazine.org/2013/10/europe-counts-the-cost-and-faces-up-to-the-huge-social-damage-caused-by-austerity/.

Huitson, O. (2011) "Is Britain a Plutocracy? According to the NHS Reforms…" *Opendemocracy*. February 5. Online, available at: www.opendemocracy.net/ourkingdom/oliver-huitson/is-britain-plutocracy-according-to-nhs-reforms.

Institute for Public Policy Research (2013) "Youth Unemployment set to Top 1 Million Again." April 16. Online, available at: www.ippr.org/press-releases/111/10638/youth-unemployment-set-to-top-1-million-again.

International Federation of Red Cross and Red Crescent Societies (IFRC) (2013) "Humanitarian Impacts of the Economic Crisis in Europe." Geneva: IFRC. Online, available at: www.ifrc.org/PageFiles/134339/1260300-Economic%20crisis%20Report_EN_LR.pdf.

Jowitt, J. (2012a) "David Cameron Flags up Flaws of Independence for Scotland." *Guardian*. February 15. Online, available at: www.guardian.co.uk/politics/2012/feb/16/david-cameron-scottish-independence-flaws.

Jowitt, J. (2012b) "Cameron Offers Scotland More Powers if it Votes No to Independence." *Guardian*. February 16. Online, available at: www.guardian.co.uk/politics/2012/feb/16/freedoms-scotland-no-independence-cameron.

Kennedy, D. (2013) "Phantom Losses that Wipe Out Tax Bills." *London Times*. March 1: 7.

King, C. (2012) "The Scottish Play: Edinburgh's Quest for Independence and the Future of Separatism." *Foreign Affairs*. Vol. 91. No. 5: 113–124.

Kington, T., Roberts, M., Connolly, K., Willsher, K. and Smith, H. (2012) "European Strikes: Who is Protesting and Why?" *Guardian*. November 14. Online, available at: www.gurdian.co.uk/business/2012/nov/14/european-strikes-who-protesting-why/print.

Korge, J. and Batzoglou, F. (2012) "'New Poor' Grows from Greek Middle Class." February 14. Online, available at: www.spiegel.de/international/europe/0,1518,druck-814571,00.html.

Koronakis, V. (2013) "Depleting Europe's Middle Class is Europe's End." New Europe. January 29. Online, available at: www.neweurope.eu/kn/article/ongoing-depletion-middle-class-will-bring-end-europe.

Koukouzelis, K. (2008) "Neutrality, Religious Symbols and the Question of a European Public Sphere." *Politics in Central Europe*. December, Vol. 4. No. 2: 41–60.

Krol, M. (2013) "The Day the Middle Class will Rise Up." *Presseurop*. April 10. Online, available at: www.presseurop.eu/en/content/article/3656741-day-middle-class-will-rise.

Lee, D. (2011) "In Europe's Pecking Order, it's 'Merkozy,' then Everyone Else." *Los Angeles Times*. November 11: A1, A6–7.

Lilico, A. (2010) "Household Indebtedness in the EU. European Parliament Directorate General for Internal Policies, Special Committee on the Financial, Economic and Social Crisis." Briefing Paper. April 2010. Online, available at: www.europarl.europa.eu/activities/committees/studies.do?language=EN.

London Evening Standard (2012) "If a Man is not an Oligarch, there's Something Wrong with Him: Welcome to the New Breed of Plutocrat Running London." December 10. Online, available at: www.standard.co.uk/news/london/if-a-man-is-not-an-oligarch-theres-something-wrong-with-him-welcome-to-the-new-breed-of-plutocrat-running-london-8398932.html.

London Evening Standard (2013a) "Sharp Fall in UK Wages puts us in Bottom Four EU Countries in Terms of Decline." August 11. Online, available at: www.standard.co.uk/news/uk/sharp-fall-in-uk-wages-put-us-in-bottom-four-eu-countries-in-terms-of-decline-8756245.html.

London Evening Standard (2013b) "60% say Immigration is Hurting UK." September 1. Online, available at: www.standard.co.uk/panewsfeeds/60-say-immigration-is-hurting-uk-8793161.html.

Los Angeles Times (2013) "Tax Fraud Found to be Widespread." August 10: AA2.

MacInnes, T., Parekh, A. and Kenway, P. (2011) *London's Poverty Profile 2011*. Trust for London and New Policy Institute. Online, available at: www.londonpovertyprofile.org.uk/downloads/povertyreport2011-web.pdf.

McKenna, B. (2012) "Europe's Austerity Measures Worsen Jobs Crisis, ILO Report says." *Globe and Mail*. April 30. Online, available at: www.theglobeandmail.com/report-on-business/international-business/european-business/europes-austerity-measures-worsen-jobs-crisis-ilo-report-says/article4104013/.

McKinsey Global Institute (2012) *Debt and Deleveraging: Uneven Progress on the Path to Growth*. January. Online, available at: www.mckinsey.com/insights/global_capital_markets/uneven_progress_on_the_path_to_growth.

Manchin, A. (2014) "EU Leadership Approval at Record Low in Spain, Greece." Gallup. January 8. Online, available at: www.gallup.com/poll/166757/leadership-approval-record-low-spain-greece.aspx.

Mason, R. (2011) "Sweden Sides with Britain over 'Unreasonable' Europe Treaty." *Telegraph*. December 9. Online, available at: www.telegraph.co.uk/finance/financialcrisis/8947324/Sweden-sides-with-Britain-over-unreasonable-Europe-treaty.html.

Matlack, C. (2013) "Greece's Financial Woes Are Far From Over." *Businessweek*. September 26: 23.

Mavrava, L. and Papatheodorou, V. (2012) "Forgiving Siemens: Unraveling a Tangled Tale of German Corruption in Greece." *Corpwatch*. June 11. Online, available at: www.corpwatch.org/article.php?id=15740.

Mitchell, D. (2012) "The European Evidence shows Why the Left's Real Goal is Higher Taxes on the Middle Class." *Commentator*. April 16. Online, available at: www.thecommentator.com/article/1100/the_european_evidence_shows_why_the_left_s_real_goal_is_higher_taxes_on_the_middle_class.

Moody's (2013) "Rating Action: Moody's Downgrades UK's Government Bond Rating to Aa1 from Aaa Outlook is Now Stable." Moody's Investors Service. February 22. Online, available at: www.moodys.com/research/Moodys-downgrades-UKs-government-bond-rating-to-Aa1-from-Aaa–PR_266844.

Moore, J. (2013) "Sheikh Hamad bin Jassim bin Jaber al-Thani: Meet the Man who bought London." *Independent*. June 21. Online, available at: www.independent.co.uk/news/world/middle-east/sheikh-hamad-bin-jassim-bin-jaber-althani-meet-the-man-who-bought-london-8669134.html.

Moore, T.L. (2014) "The Contemporary Clash *in* Civilization." Bunker, R. and Bunker, P. eds. *Global Criminal and Sovereign Free Economies and the Demise of the Western Democracies: Dark Renaissance*. London: Routledge.

Mount, F. (2012) *The New Few or a Very British Oligarchy: Power and Inequality in Britain Now*. London: Simon & Schuster.

Neate, R. and Ball, J. (2013) "100 of UK's Richest People Concealing Billions in Offshore Tax Havens." *Guardian*. May 9. Online, available at: www.guardian.co.uk/politics/2013/may/09/100-richest-uk-billions-offshore-tax-havens.

Oborne, P. (2012) "The Rise of the Overclass." *Telegraph*. January 20. Online, available at: www.telegraph.co.uk/finance/financialcrisis/9027846/The-rise-of-the-overclass.html.

Oxfam (2013a) "Tax on the 'Private' Billions now Stashed Away in Havens Enough to End Extreme World Poverty Twice Over." Press Release. May 21. Online, available at: www.oxfam.org/en/eu/pressroom/pressrelease/2013-05-22/tax-havens-private-billions-could-end-extreme-poverty-twice-over.

Oxfam (2013b) "Lost Tax Haven Cash Enough to End Extreme Poverty—Twice Over." Press Release. May 22. Online, available at: www.oxfam.org.uk/media-centre/press-releases/2013/05/tax-haven-cash-enough-to-end-extreme-poverty.

Paine, H. (2010) "France's Plutocracy—the Bettencourt Scandal Shakes the Republic." *Global Policy Forum Blog*. Global Policy in Brief. September 14. Online, available at: http://globalpolicyinbrief.blogspot.com/2010/09/frances-plutocracy-bettencourt-scandal.html.

Parker, S. (2013) "A Greek Tragedy on the London Stage: the City, the Eurozone Crisis and an Urban Dark Age to Come." *Opendemocracy*. July 20. Online, available at: www.opendemocracy.net/print/74184.

Perez, A. (2012) "Ch. 4 the Sustainability of the Nation-State Model in a Globalizing World." Rodriguez, M. and Martinot, S., trans. Durand, C. and Martinot, S. eds. *Recreating Democracy in a Globalized State*. Atlanta: Clarity Press.

Pezzini, M. (2012) "An Emerging Middle Class." *OECD Observer*. Online, available at: www.oecdobserver.org/news/fullstory.php/aid/aid/3681/An_emerging_middle_class.html.

Reguly, E. (2013) "As Europe's Middle Class Goes, so Goes the Euro." *Globe and Mail*. September 20. Online, available at: www.theglobeandmail.com/report-on-business/international-business/european-business/as-europes-middle-class-goes-so-goes-the-euro/article14448319/.

Reuters (2013a) "Middle-class Greeks to Fork Out over 40% of Annual Salary in Tax." *Reuters*. January 12. Online, available at: http://rt.com/news/greece-income-tax-increase-846/.

Reuters (2013b) "Factbox: Apple, Amazon, Google and Tax Avoidance Schemes." *Reuters*. May 22. Online, available at: www.reuters.com/article/2013/05/22/us-eu-tax-avoidance-idUSBRE94L0GW20130522.

Roberts, M. (2012) "Catalans Start Voting in Election that could Lead to Independence." *Guardian*. November 25. Online, available at: www.guardian.co.uk/world/2012/nov/25/catalans-voting-election-lead-independence.

Sanchez-Vallejo, M. (2012) "Poverty Trap for Middle Classes of Europe." *Presseurop*. January 29. Online, available at: www.presseurop.eu/en/content/article/1469391-poverty-trap-middle-classes-europe.

Sassen, S. (2010) "Ch. 2 Membership and Its Politics." Hsu, R., ed. *Ethnic Europe: Mobility, Identity, and Conflict in a Globalized World*. Stanford: Stanford University Press.

Sawer, P. (2012) "Sunday Times Rich List 2012: Wealth of Richest Grows to Record Levels." *Telegraph*. April 28. Online, available at: www.telegraph.co.uk/finance/9233605/Sunday-Times-Rich-List-2012-Wealth-of-richest-grows-to-record-levels.html.

Schmidt, V. (2006) *Democracy in Europe: The EU and National Politics*. New York: Oxford University Press.

Schneider, F. and Williams, C. (2013) *The Shadow Economy*. London: The Institute of Economic Affairs.

Scott, B. (2011) *Capitalism: Its Origins and Evolution as a System of Governance*. New York: Springer.

Seiffert, J. (2013) "Why Germans are Losing their Interest in Politics." *Deutsche Welle*. September 22. Online, available at: www.dw.de/why-germans-are-losing-interest-in-politics/a-17102465.

Slater, S. (2013) "London Leads 11 Percent Jump in Bankers Earning 1 Million Euros." *Reuters*. November 29. Online, available at: http://uk.news.yhoo.com/london-spearheads-11-percent-jump-bankers-earling-1-093628813-sector.html#.

Stewart, H. (2012) "Eurozone Unemployment Adds to Gloom Ahead of Polls." *Guardian*. May 2. Online, available at: www.theguardian.com/business/2012/may/02/eurozone-unemployment-elections.

Sutherland, P. (2008) "A Golden Mean between Multiculturalism and Assimilation." *Studies: An Irish Quarterly Review*. Spring, Vol. 97. No. 385: 73–86.

Taylor, M., Burn-Murdoch, J. and Butler, P. (2013) "Council Cuts will Bring Local government 'to its knees.'" *Guardian*. March 25. Online, available at: www.guardian.co.uk/society/2013/mar/25/council-cuts-local-government-knees/.

TED Blog (2013) "The Age of Global Plutocracy: Chrystia Freeland at TEDGlobal 2013." June 12. Online, available at: http://blog.ted.com/2013/06/12/the-age-of-global-plutocracy-chrystia-freeland-at-tedglobal-2013/.

Telegraph (2011) "Russians Snap Up Luxury London Homes." October 28. Online, available at: www.telegraph.co.uk/property/8855270/Russians-snap-up-luxury-London-homes.html.

Telegraph (2012) "'Mafiosi' Stand to Gain Most from EU Bail-out of Cyprus." November 4. Online, available at: www.telegraph.co.uk/finance/financialcrisis/9654709/Mafiosi-stand-to-gain-most-from-EU-bail-out-of-Cyprus.html.

Telegraph (2014) "The Squeezed Middle Deserves Far Better." January 14. Online, available at: www.telegraph.co.uk/comment/telegraph-view/10571637/The-squeezed-middle-deserves-far-better.html.

Tett, G. (2013) "Markets Insight: Europe and US Lines Cross on Household Debt Ratio." *Financial Times*. May 9. Online, available at: www.ft.com/intl/cms/s/0/fca4054c-b8b6-11e2-869f-00144feabdc0.html#axzz2tyYbPb1P.

The Economist (2013a) "Household Debt." June 1. Online, available at: www.economist.com/news/economic-and-financial-indicators/21578669-household-debt.

The Economist (2013b) "On a Wing and a Credit Card." July 6: 52–3.

The Economist (2013c) "Schumpeter: Cronies and Capitols." August 10: 59.

The Economist (2013d) "Why do the French Tolerate such High Taxes?" September 24. Online, available at: www.economist.com/node/21586765.

Theodoropoulou, S. and Wyatt, A. (2011) *Withdrawal Symptoms: an Assessment of the Austerity Packages in Europe*. Working Paper 2011.02. Belgium: European Trade Union Institute.

Thornhill, J. (2009) "Agitation as Middle-class Europe Struggles to Cope." *Financial Times*. March 11. Online, available at: www.ft.com/intl/cms/s/0/3a090842-0e84-11de-b099-0000779fd2ac.html#axzz2rk0l02Fm.

Traynor, I. (2012) "Europe's Elites Feel the Backlash." *Guardian*. April 23. Online, available at: www.theguardian.com/world/2012/apr/23/europe-elite-democratic-backlash.

Traynor, I. (2013) "Austerity Pushing Europe into Social and Economic Decline, says Red Cross." *Guardian*. October 9. Online, available at: www.theguardian.com/world/2013/oct/10/austerity-europe-debt-red-cross.

Trouillot, M. (2001) "The Anthropology of the State in Globalization." *Current Anthropology*. February. Vol. 42. No. 1: 125–138.

Van Biezen, I. (2013) "The Decline in Party Membership across Europe means that Political Parties need to Reconsider how they Engage with the Electorate." Blog, EUROPP, London School of Economics and Political Science. Online, available at: http://blogs.lse.ac.uk/europpblog/2013/05/06/decline-in-party-membership-europe-ingrid-van-biezen/.

Vellacott, C. (2012) "London Impoverished by Rise of the Plutocrats." Reuters. March 20. Online, available at: http://uk.reuters.com/article/2012/03/20/uk-london-incomedisparity-idUKLNE82J02420120320.

Walter, M., Bryan-Low, C. and Forelle, C. (2013) "UK Stripped of Triple-A Rating." *Wall Street Journal*. February 22. Online, available at: http://online.wsj.com/news/articles/SB10001424127887323549204578320613007137362.

Warner, C. (2007) *The Best System Money Can Buy: Corruption in the European Union*. Ithaca: Cornell University Press.

Warner, J. (2012a) "Britain Falls for Lagarde's Charms and Coughs Up another £10bn." *Telegraph*. April 20. Online, available at: http://blogs.telegraph.co.uk/finance/jeremy-warner/100016478/britain-falls-for-lagardes-charms-and-coughs-up-another-10bn/.

Warner, J. (2012b) "Why Would Scotland Turn Itself into Greece?' *Telegraph*. October 11. Online, available at: www.telegraph.co.uk/news/uknews/scotland/9602126/Why-would Scotland-turn-itself-into-Greece.html.

West, E. and Nelson, F. (2013) "The Strange Death of the British Middle Class." *Spectator*. August 24. Online, available at: www.spectator.co.uk/features/9000951/the-missing-middle/.

Wherlock, C. (2010) "Greek Demonstrators say 'Plutocracy Should Pay for the Crisis.'" *Les Observateurs*. February 24. Online, available at: http://observers.france24.com/print/226422?print=now.

Winnett, R. (2012a) "370,000 Migrants on the Dole." *Telegraph*. January 19. Online, available at: www.telegraph.co.uk/news/politics/9026401/370000-migrants-on-the-dole.html.

Winnett, R. (2012b) "Taxpayer Stumps Up another £10bn to Save Euro." *Telegraph*. April 20. Online, available at: www.telegraph.co.uk/finance/financialcrisis/9217926/Taxpayer-stumps-up-another-10bn-to-save-euro.html.

Wintour, P. (2013) "Squeezed Middle must wait another Decade for Rise in Living Standards." *Guardian*. February 12. Online, available at: www.guardian.co.uk/business/2013/feb/13/resolution-foundation-report-squeezed-middle/.

Wolff, R. (2013) "US Political Dysfunction and Capitalism's Withdrawal." *E-International Relations*. October 27. Online, available at: www.e-ir.info/2013/10/27/us-political-dysfunction-and-capitalisms-withdrawal.

Zacune, J. (2013) *Privitising Europe: Using the Crisis to Entrench Neoliberalism*. A Transnational Institute Working Paper. Amsterdam: The Transnational Institute.

9 Afterword

The twenty-first-century international political economy—Westphalian state and middle class futures

Robert J. Bunker, Pamela Ligouri Bunker and John P. Sullivan

This short afterword to *Global Criminal and Sovereign Free Economies and the Demise of the Western Democracies* provides some commentary and thoughts on the major trends identified and findings reached in this special volume. Specifically, it addresses the impacts new IPEs have on the Westphalian state and the middle class and their related futures. Further, a few of the emergent and near distant trends taking place—not organic to the chapters of this work—will be brought to bear. At the outset, however, we have identified six important themes from the book project regarding the twenty-first-century IPE.

The first theme is that at least three IPEs can be said to exist: the formal (legitimate) economy, the criminal (illicit) economy, and the sovereign free (plutocratic) economy. A fourth—the semi-formal economy—is a transitional one that exists somewhat in the gray area between the formal and the criminal ones—removed from the sovereign free economy though multinational corporations will readily attempt to draw profit from it. This also raises the possibility that another transitional economy exists between the formal and the sovereign free economies; that is, the off the books economy.[1] These economies are ordered from the supra-national through the national and to the sub-national in Table 9.1.

The second theme is that significant profit is no longer in the formal economy. This is due to lack of margins, diminished buying power of the middle class (i.e. they have less disposable income) and increased state taxation. True profit margins are to be found in the illicit and the sovereign free economies where regulation is either non-existent or very lax and sales are either not taxed or taxed at very marginal rates since payoffs must be factored into the cost of doing business. These two economies, respectively, provide an economic foundation to sub-state actors (criminals) and supra-national actors (corporations) alike and, as a result, allow them to increasingly challenge Westphalian states tied to an eroding formal economy foundation. The semi-formal and the off the books economies—as transitional ones—would be expected to offer more profit opportunities than the formal economy but not as much those existing at the economic extremes. For example, MNC profit-maximizing schemes focused on avoiding formal economy taxation are ongoing and prevalent:

Table 9.1 Twenty-first-century international political economies

Economies	Characteristics	Benefactors
Sovereign free (plutocratic)	Supra-national, networked, (informational), high profit margins, no/low taxation, (payoffs).	Winners of globalization—multinational corporations, plutocrats (1.0–0.1 percent).
Off-the-books	Transitional/gray area, increasing profit margins.	Increasingly plutocrats.
Formal (legitimate)	National, hierarchical (industrial), low profit margins, state taxation	Westphalian states, middle class, lower class (via social mobility).
Semi-formal	Transitional/gray area, increasing profit margins.	Increasingly criminals.
Criminal (illicit)	Sub-national, networked (informational), high profit margins, no/low taxation (payoffs).	Winners of deviant globalization—criminals and gangs, organized crime, terrorists/ insurgents, cartels, warlords.

On 4 February 2014, the Tax Administration Service's (SAT) General Administrator of Large Taxpayers, Óscar Molina Chie, stated in an interview that 270 multinational companies operating in the country were using aggressive accounting methods in order to avoid paying Mexican taxes, despite generating profit locally. According to Molina Chie, the SAT will use data from chain stores, auto dealers and shopping centers to prove the liability of these multinationals, 269 of which are headquartered outside of Mexico, and end the tax evasion.

(Southern Pulse Correspondents, 2014)

The third theme is that variants of capitalism are in conflict—if not outright war—as are the differing social classes of the capitalists themselves. In retrospect, globalized capital does indeed appear to represent the rise of a new gilded age based upon predatory business tenets. These capitalists have been early adaptors to globalization, effectively moving beyond the sovereign confines of the state. They can be considered the supra-bourgeoisie—a true global elite comprising 1 percent or likely less of the world's population. The multinational corporations owned by this supra-bourgeoisie are now extracting profits out of Western democracies at an alarming rate because state moderated capitalist systems and the petty bourgeoisie that operate within them are simply outmatched by this more advanced and sophisticated capitalist form.

The fourth theme is that this globalized conflict is not a conventional struggle as normally fought between states but is, rather, asymmetric in nature. No other way exists for one civilizational epoch to supersede another than via an indirect approach that attacks the foundations of a state form from the extremes—that is, from the top down and bottom up. The new insurgency constructs of "criminal insurgency" and "plutocratic insurgency" derived from Steve Metz's original 1993 commercial insurgency projections have developed to the point that they can now be said to reasonably well articulate this process taking place.

The fifth theme is that Westphalian states and sub-national and supra-national organizations are organized very differently. States still follow hierarchical patterns while sub- and supra-national entities are heavily networked, giving them an information processing edge that translates into quicker environmental adaption and exploitation. As aforementioned, they also each have their own unique relationship with the various IPEs that now exist. Further, ever shifting associations and factions have developed in order to facilitate mutual economic gain—primarily plutocrats in alliance with criminals—and blending as has taken place in Russia and other states. As a result, our increasingly post-Westphalian world is gaining a pre-modern flavor. Territorial states are in competition with cities, regional areas, sub-national groups, and supra-national state groups and entities such as multinational corporations, very reminiscent of the renaissance period with its multitude of fiefs and royal lands, city leagues, dynastic states, mercenary corporations and the Holy Roman Empire all competing for political power. The current amalgam of competing social and political forms and the changing nature of states has been commented on by quite a few scholars including Martin van Creveld (1991, 1999), Philip Bobbitt (2002), and Phil Williams (2008).

The sixth theme is that the IPE discussed and analyzed in this special volume is not the same IPE as is being taught in universities and colleges in the Western world. The latter promotes the façade that globalized capitalism and the supra-bourgeoisie are in alignment and exist in a functional relationship with state moderated capitalism and the petty-bourgeoisie. Nothing could be further from the truth. As a result, the dark and deviant globalization underpinnings of this work are very much in variance with that traditionalist school of thought. The traditionalist school is constrained by a modernist perceptual lens that provides a backward, rather than forward vision of the new world unfolding around us. This work is also estranged from both the international relations theories of realism and democratic liberalism. As stated in a February 2014 US Army War College Op-Ed related to this subject matter:

> we must move beyond the blinders of both realist (state focused) and liberal (free markets are infallible) school tenets in our perspectives on international relations and accede that: a) nonstate entities now have the power to challenge states; and, b) globalized capitalism is increasingly in variance with Western state moderated capitalism which seeks to mitigate large inequalities in our social class structures.
>
> (Bunker, 2014)

Many of us involved in this research project thus see the unfolding twenty-first century very differently—we have essentially "paradigm shifted"—with a new perspective on capitalism, political economy, social class structures, MNCs, plutocracy, criminality and insurgency very alien to even late twentieth-century thinkers.

Criminal and plutocratic insurgencies are two challengers to the current West-phalian state construct. They both seek to extract wealth and power from the existing state forms. Indeed, they are likely emerging due to the changing nature of states themselves. That is these state challengers emerge as a consequence of the rise of networks and the shifting power dynamics that result (Castells, 2009).

Power is the key factor in this relationship between states and wealth-making potentials. Violence (the absence of power), disciplinary discourses, the institu-tionalization of power relationships, values and legitimacy are all interactive ele-ments in the formation and transmission of power relationships, social structures and organizational forms. As networks become central in the social construction of power relationships and organizations, violence, money and trust become pivotal indicators of emerging social foundations.

Networks (both social and technological) benefit from new modes of commu-nication, such as Internet communication technology and new (social media). Proximity in a spatial and temporal sense is no longer necessary to exert or project power. States are inherently territorial—that is they are bound to the "space of place." The "space of flows" (that is global markets: formal, sovereign free, or criminal) on the other hand, is not solely bound to physical turf. Thus the actors dominating the space of flows can choose where (and when) to act. This flexibility allows them to challenge static political and economic structures.

The new political actors—plutocrats and criminal insurgents—act on a global stage, avoiding national power or shaping national power through corruption, co-option and direct confrontation when necessary to gain political advantage. The frame of reference for contests between power and counterpower thus becomes network nodes at global, national and subnational levels. These interac-tions can confer great advantage to agile, adaptive actors or can cripple those unable or unwilling to change. Both criminal insurgents and plutocratic pretend-ers have leveraged an ability to exploit gaps in state and increasingly global security capacity to remove themselves from regulation. The result is a combina-tion of virtual and physical free-state zones (temporary autonomous zones or enclaves) where they can maximize profit and plunder and avoid sanction from regulation.

In this transition to the network (Castells) or market (Bobbitt) state the crimi-nal insurgents (cartels and gangs) and plutocrats are in effect waging a counter-power struggle against the state. Both are squeezing the state: the transnational gangsters from below and the sovereign free raiders from above. These two strands of state competition are not necessarily mutually exclusive. Certainly both sets of actors seek to avoid regulation by states and both have used corrup-tion and violence to further their ends. In one sense, they are both actors in the process of "deviant globalization." Profits—whatever the source—become the desired end to maximize wealth generation and resource extraction. Both crimi-nal insurgents and plutocrats therefore can and likely regularly collude to maxi-mize their respective wealth and power (as seen in money laundering and securities crimes). Indeed, both criminal and plutocratic insurgent networks challenge state solvency (capacity and legitimacy) and hence sovereignty (Sullivan, 2013).

Certainly the conflict between state challengers creates a struggle for power. Indeed, a second power–counterpower struggle can emerge (as is seen in the Occupy and *Indignadas* movements in response to plutocratic exploitation and *autodefensas* in response to criminal cartels). The counterpower challengers to institutionalized criminal and plutocratic insurgents also are organized as networks exploiting new media and the space of flows (Castells, 2012).

The networked social protest movements that emerged in the wake of plutocratic exploitation and the resulting assault on the middle class presents a potential counter to the rise of plutocratic and criminal insurgent power grabs. Here the Internet (space of flows) and public square (space of places) interact to become the venue for political communication and organization—that is they become new assemblages of power (actual or potential). It is these assemblages (e.g. Tahrir Square, Zuccotti Park, Spain's *acampadas*) where the virtual on-line discourse realized physical reality. These forays into political action and rebellion may form the beginning of a social movement to counter (or temper) the rise of plutocratic and criminal enclaves and the assault on the global middle class.

With these themes in mind, we will now look at Westphalian state and then middle class futures.

Westphalian state futures

Three of the chapters in this special volume, those by Luis Jorge Garay Salamanca and Eduardo Salcedo-Albarán on Colombia, Guatemala and Mexico, Tanya Buhler Corbin and Nicole Hendrix on the United States, and Pamela Ligouri Bunker on the states of the European Union present case studies. Major themes from these chapters, along with supporting themes presented in other chapters as they pertain to those states, are summarized in Table 9.2. They are listed in relationship to the underlying theoretical foundations of this work articulated by T. Lindsay Moore in his chapter concerning the present clash *in* Western civilization—that is epochal change from the modern to post-modern era. This is further supported by the criminal and plutocratic insurgency constructs developed by John Sullivan and Robert Bunker, respectively, along with the collaborative deviant globalization inputs of Nils Gilman.

The Colombia, Guatemala and Mexico case study provides insights into the effects of criminal insurgency on those states. Such states threatened by subnational groups present very real bottom up threat concerns as expressed by this project. While some plutocratic insurgent elements are evident—like privatized city potentials in Honduras and the multinational corporate profiting across the board—they are presently a second tier concern to the loss of state territories, violence and corruption. The rise of the illicit economy that has helped to make up for a lack of state revenues and the rich/poor divide characterizing their

Table 9.2 State(s) and epochal change

State(s)	Colombia, Guatemala, Mexico	United States	States in the European Union
Primary threat	Criminal insurgency (sub-national).	Plutocratic insurgency (supra-national).	Plutocratic insurgency (supra-national).
Secondary threat	Plutocratic insurgency (supra-national).	Fear of sub-national violence and criminality; not criminal insurgency.	Organized crime; not criminal insurgency.
Processes	Lack of revenues/illicit economy profiting, loss of state territories (via coercion), rich and poor divide.	Lack of revenues/public debt, loss of state assets (via privatization), loss of middle class.	Lack of revenues/public debt, loss of state assets (via privatization), loss of middle class.
State impacts	Criminalized-state; impunity and corruption, state deconstruction; reconfiguration (criminal futures).	Becoming police state-like; homeland security, follow on to prison building, state over-centralization (sovereign status quo); and plutocratic influences.	Economic authoritarianism; elite dictates, state deconstruction; EU reconfiguration (plutocratic futures).

societies has created conflict environments fertile for violent non-state actor emergence and growth. State impacts have been a steady progression toward criminal futures via state deconstruction and reconfiguration. We have already witnessed in all of these states the emergence of areas of impunity—criminal pseudo-state or statelet enclaves—where local mafia chieftains, narco warlords and associated criminal leaders hold de facto political authority. They have access to a lot of money and gunmen and, while presently lacking in proper titles and legitimacy, they are the true wielders of power within the areas they operate.

The above can be contrasted to the US case study that primarily looks at the threat of the plutocratic insurgency to the middle class and a concomitant decline in the perception of government legitimacy followed closely by an overreaction by the state to the fear of sub-national violence, not insurgency, being directed against it in the post 9/11 security environment. Terrorism fears have built on earlier ones, focusing on the fear of rampant criminality and drug use from the 1980s onward. While the initial fears resulted in massive prison building programs, the new fear has resulted in the establishment of overarching security mechanisms that can threaten civil liberties. In these instances, the state solution to countering the threats of criminality and terrorism—which are intractably linked to the illicit economy—are in many ways as bad, if not worse, to society than the initial threats themselves. For many multinational corporations, however, the focus on US domestic security with its numerous privatized prisons and security guards and DHS contracts has been a boon to their balance sheets. Compounding the present impacts are lack of revenues for federal, state and municipal governments, with a concurrent rise in massive debts and the loss of state assets via incremental rounds of privatization over the preceding decades. Thus, the sovereign free economy is also limiting much-needed corporate revenue streams into the public coffers in addition to hollowing out the American middle class. These stressors placed on the United States are resulting in state over-centralization, bureaucratic inertia and a lack of congressional consensus—a true crisis of governance. As a result, the United States has become increasingly status quo seeking and is now manifesting police state-like behaviors. Further, it has been argued that it has been co-opted to varying degrees by plutocratic entities whose interests are in variance with that of the American public.

The states of the European Union provide yet another interesting case study. These states are being influenced by the rise of a supra-national entity while at the same time being economically challenged by a plutocratic insurgency threatening their middle classes and the solvency of their governments. Additionally, a number of these states—including the United Kingdom (with regard to Scotland) and Spain (with regard to Catalonia)—are also being threatened by potential succession of their indigenous territories. The political gestalt is resulting in both a "crisis of sovereignty" stemming from mounting public debt, loss of economic resources, and loss of control over decision-making and a "crisis of legitimacy" with the polarization of society and a vanishing middle class, the public perception of decreased representation by decision-makers, and a decreased shared feeling of national identity. Organized crime, increasing levels of tax evasion, and corruption are also threatening the revenue streams and integrity of many of these states. The overriding concern is that of states becoming deconstructed into new forms that fail to provide for the social welfare of their citizens while, at the same time, the new supra-national form that has arisen in the form of the EU also fails to fulfill that role. The end result is a form of "economic authoritarianism" devoid of democratic principles both at the state level and potentially taking hold within the corridors of power in Brussels. More than one scholar has commented on the growing social unrest that is taking place amongst the middle, and formerly middle, class of many EU states.

The above case studies very much complement theoretical perspectives on Westphalian state futures. These states can be said to have only a certain number of future trajectories. They can attempt to stay as they are—remain in a "steady state" condition—as the United States is attempting to do by aggressively fighting change. They can lose internal control, fail, and ultimately fragment, losing parts of their territories to sub-nationals as Colombia, Guatemala and Mexico are struggling against. The United Kingdom and Spain with their potential succession issues are among others that risk fragmenting via a different mechanism— regional referenda at the ballot box. Finally, Westphalian states can attempt to evolve into something else—a different and more evolved form of social and political organization. This trajectory of course is represented by those Westphalian states having joined the European Union, though the tradeoff may be the loss of democratic representation, at least during the near term, and an unknown future for the middle class.

This special volume has also highlighted the fact that competitors to the Westphalian state have arisen. Euphemistic terms for armed sub-national and supra-national entities include cartels, transnational organized crime, illicit non-governmental organizations and multinational private security corporations. More pessimistic terms for them are emerging "war making entities" and "nation state killers." The contest between the Westphalian state and its competitors will be that of a war over social and political organization—it will determine what the post-modern state form will look like, how people will live, and how they will organize themselves. The victor will be determined by what entity—in essence, which population vessel (territorially contiguous or not; either place or more likely space dominant; most assuredly networked)—will be able to efficiently fulfill the needs of its citizens in the areas of force (military), bribery (economics), and fraud (ideology) (Moore, 2003). Another requirement of this entity is that it must be able to function as a "post-modern street fighter"—one that is competent in engaging in twenty-first-century conflict—a skill that is presently lacking in most Westphalian states as they are unable to function in blurred crime and war operational environments. As T.X. Hammes has highlighted in his chapter, converging technologies (e.g. information, robotics, nanotechnology and additive manufacturing) will be a major component of such conflicts. In order to economically sustain itself in these conflicts, it is imperative that this entity be able to secure resources from the IPE and, since the real profits have moved to the margins of this economy (e.g. the illicit and supra-national levels), it may very well be required to gain such a non-formal extractive capacity. How the gaining of such an extractive capacity will be reconciled with modernist notions of national sovereignty, or if it will result in the rise of new state prerogatives, is presently unknown.

Middle class futures

The relationship of the middle class to the Westphalian state since the time of mid-to-late nineteenth-century industrialization has, at least until the last few decades, been a symbiotic one. This rising socio-economic class was critical to the economic and war making power of great states with their mass assembly lines and industrial armies and fleets. Operating under the paradigm of state moderated capitalism, this represented our traditional perspectives on IPE—the old IPE. With the current discontinuity stemming from the rise of globalization and information age advances, this symbiotic relationship has been broken. Operating under the paradigm of globalized capitalism, an emerging form of IPE—a new and dark form as highlighted in this volume—has developed. This form of IPE is heralding near future changes to the middle class in the Western democracies and can be considered an early phase component of the epochal transition from the modern to the post-modern eras. What must not be forgotten is that a later phase transition is expected as the epochal shift and the new IPE matures.

Near future

The near future of the middle class in the Western states suggest that an hour-glass phenomenon is fully emerging. At the apex of the social structure is a small plutocratic elite supported by a highly skilled and competent meritocracy. Both of these sets of individuals may be nationals of the host state but not necessarily so—in fact, non-domicile residents (foreign nationals) enjoy many tax advantages in London, New York and other global cities where the super-rich congregate (Florida, 2013). While a middle class most certainly still exists in these states, it is increasingly being culled out with only a minority of individuals and their families able to join the meritocracy as knowledge workers, upper level governmental bureaucrats and other highly skilled professionals. For the rest, a retrograde process is in effect, with their social class status and incomes both impacted as they increasingly join what has become a servant economy (Faux, 2012). In the United States this has led to more Americans now identifying themselves as members of the lower rather than the middle class (Florsheim, 2014).

Social mobility is correspondingly being negatively impacted and the societal mythos—derived from the "Horatio Alger" construct—bonding the socio-economic classes together in a "continuum of prosperity" is also being deconstructed (Gardels, 2012; Cox, 2014). Further, a "debt free" vs. "indentured servitude/debt" (economic based) and "citizen" vs. "criminal" (legality based) dynamic appears to be developing in American society. The debt free articulation does not mean free of debt—as investment debt can be functional—but rather that on balance these individuals have amassed positive wealth. This dynamic can further be further divided into high wealth and moderate wealth individuals. Given this schema, American socio-economic class stratification appears to be forming along these lines (from highest status levels to lowest):

Debt free—high wealth citizens: The highest status socio-economic class is the plutocratic one where individuals have accumulated high levels of wealth. Ranging from the 0.1 to 1 percent of citizens, it operates primarily in the sovereign free economy at the upper levels and in the off the books economy at the lower levels.

Debt free—moderate wealth citizens: This socio-economic class is formal economy-based and has been able to accumulate moderate levels of wealth. It represents the remnants of the old middle class and increasingly is comprised of the meritocracy, knowledge workers and still successful petite bourgeoisie—small business owners. This class is being increasingly taxed by the state because the plutocratic class has learned how to avoid taxation and the lower and criminal classes have little to no income to tax.

Indentured servitude citizens: Representative of the lower classes with no criminal records, this socio-economic grouping is indicative of the working poor and the new servant economy that has emerged. These individuals hold negative wealth and in a sense have fallen into "indentured servitude" for the rest of their working lives. Given new bankruptcy legislation—which benefit plutocratic investments—personal debt increasingly follows an individual like an economic anchor dragging them down. Economic mistakes made early in one's life—just like legal transgressions—increasingly shadow them for years to come.

Indentured servitude criminals: Increasingly the label of criminality sticks to individuals and at some point no social redemption exists—a person becomes digitally branded in state databases for life and is viewed as less than a citizen of the state. This stigmatized socio-economic class is preyed upon by predatory capitalism in the sense that prison has become an industry and criminals have become a resource to be exploited. Still, at least these individuals are able to obtain credit, which means they have some sort of menial jobs skills linked to the formal economy. While owning some assets, this socio-economic class has on balance negative wealth.

> *No wealth criminals:* This stigmatized socio-economic class is even lower in status than the one immediately above it because the individuals comprising it have no assets and are not even able to obtain credit. These individuals are fully removed from the formal economy—other than gaining possible governmental subsistence handouts—and can only operate in the semi-formal and illicit economies. Like the social class above them they are also preyed upon by for-profit prison and probation industries and are saddled with court fines.
>
> (Gambino, 2014)

Of course, an even higher-level socio-economic class is that of *debt free—high wealth foreign nationals* who do not have any of the burdens of local US citizenship and, being extra-sovereigns, can effectively side-step domestic taxation if they can create legal and corporate shielding that ensures that they are not directly linked to any trade or business activity taking place in the United States (IRS, 2014). Similarly foreign nationals—whose high wealth is drawn from the illicit economy—can also effectively be considered to enjoy high societal status and privilege up until the point that they have been arrested for their criminal transgressions by the American authorities. Of note is that foreign nationals can also be integrated into the lower level socio-economic classes of *indentured servitude citizens* and below—though in those instances their status is usually lower than that of citizens.

Various states within and associated with the EU, such as Britain, also appear to be following the US socio-economic class trajectory, however, they presently are much further behind in having police-state like mentalities (Hintjens, 2007). Instead they are facing their own economic crises while at the same time grappling with multi-level issues of authority being brought to bear with the continued expansion and integration of the European Union and issues of mobilized populations that are not being effectively integrated into the dominant cultures of the various European states and which often face marginalization on an economic and ethnic basis, further feeding dissent.

Far future

In the coming decades, human civilization will continue to globalize and change. We will increasingly see migration between states and an increasing presence in cyberspace itself. Our world will witness at times both a wealth of resources due to the implementation of advanced technologies such as the geo-thermal cracking of oil deposits, additive 3D manufacturing (e.g. replicators) and new forms of bio-technology, and a scarcity of resources due to too many humans populating our planet along with adverse effects on the environment, such as global changes in climate, and weather patterns will change with productive areas becoming unproductive and vice versa, ocean levels obliterating coastal regions, and hot regions becoming cold and cold regions becoming hot.

How the Western democracies, or what is left of them by the time the far future is reached, will respond to such a challenging world is unknown. What is known is that, on our current trajectory, the new IPE presents us with a crisis of capitalism with very few winners worth billions and literally billions of losers worth nothing. This is not a sustainable global politico-economic system and will lead to seething unrest for most of the world's population. It will also be negatively affected by two projected major events impacting human civilization. The first event is that of the eventual full-scale introduction of robots into the labor force.[2] Great powers will no longer require large human populations because robots will be able not only to engage in economic production but will also be deployable on the battlefield. Further, states and other political entities will thus view an overabundance of population as a liability. The second event is the projected transition from desktops and laptops to wearable computing and ultimately their implantation in humans. In retrospect, pioneering experiments such as Google Glass will be seen as primitive artifacts of what is yet to come. This bio-technical evolutionary process will result in humans increasingly interacting in both physical space and cyberspace simultaneously via artifacts such as smart optical interfaces. Of concern is whether robots will become the labor force and enforcers of a computer augmented globalized elite—the techno-warlords and kleptocrats of the future (Galeotti, 2014)—or if these technologies will be applied in a more democratic and egalitarian manner befitting the social welfare principals of late Westphalian states. Further, which politico-economic ideology wins out in the far future will determine how states will address the welfare, or lack thereof, of excess non-productive human populations living in slum cities throughout the globe.

Conclusion

The subtitle *Dark Renaissance* was chosen for this special volume with due consideration of its implications. The level of change taking place in the international community is equivalent to that of the shift from the classical to the medieval epoch and the medieval to the modern epoch. Elements of both epochal shifts are evident in this one—hence the fusion of the terms dark ages and renaissance. From the lens of the IPE, the current shift from formal based capitalism to something else is equivalent to the earlier transitions from classical slavery to medieval feudalism and from medieval feudalism to modern capitalism. Concerns over that "something else" formed the basis of this book's genesis because the trends to date clearly indicate that both Western democratic state and middle class futures appear somewhat dim. However, such a fate should be expected as epochal change shatters one civilization in order to give rise to a new and more advanced one.

Notes

1 See the chapter by Yelena A. Tuzova, "The Illicit and Sovereign Free International Political Economies" in this work for more on these economies. It should be noted that she does not make a distinction between the off the books and sovereign free economies. Our proposed twenty-first-century IPE typology with its gray economy areas should of course be open to discussion and debate concerning its accuracy.
2 Per the T. Lindsay Moore chapter in this work such robots will require the fielding of a new energy source—some sort of fuel cells that generate electrical power to energize these systems presently appear to be the most likely candidate technology.

References

Bobbitt, P. (2002) *The Shield of Achilles: War, Peace, and the Course of History*. New York: Anchor Books.

Bunker, R. (2014) "Op-Ed: Not Your Grandfather's Insurgency—Criminal, Spiritual, and Plutocratic." Strategic Studies Institute, US Army War College. February 20. Online, available at: www.strategicstudiesinstitute.army.mil/index.cfm/articles/Not-Your-Grandfathers-Insurgency-Criminal-Spiritual-and-Plutocratic/2014/02/20.

Castells, M. (2009) *Communication Power*. New York: Oxford University Press.

Castells, M. (2012) *Networks of Outrage and Hope: Social Movements in the Internet Age*. Cambridge: Polity Press.

Cox, A. (2014) "If the 1% wants Class Warfare, Maybe it's Time to Start Fighting Back." *Guardian*. February 18. Online, available at: www.theguardian.com/commentis-free/2014/feb/18/tom-perkins-1-percent-class-warfare.

Creveld, M. van (1991) *The Transformation of War*. New York: Free Press.

Creveld, M. van (1999) *The Rise and Decline of the State*. Cambridge: Cambridge University Press.

Faux, J. (2012) *The Servant Economy: Where America's Elite is Sending the Middle Class*. New York: Wiley.

Florida, R. (2013) "Global Cities of the Super-Rich." *Atlantic*. March 21. Online, available at: www.theatlanticcities.com/jobs-and-economy/2013/03/global-cities-super-rich/4951/.

Florsheim, L. (2014) "Americans Have Stopped Thinking of Themselves as Middle Class." *New Republic*. January 30. Online, available at: www.newrepublic.com/article/116413/expanding-ranks-lower-class.

Galeotti, M. (2014) "Introduction: Kleptocracies, Warlords and Mafias in Uniform." Bunker, R. and Bunker, P. eds. *Global Criminal and Sovereign Free Economies and the Demise of the Western Democracies: Dark Renaissance*. London: Routledge.

Gambino, L. (2014) "Thrown in Jail for being Poor: The Booming for-Profit Probation Industry." *Guardian*. March 2. Online, available at: www.theguardian.com/money/2014/mar/02/poor-.

Gardels, N. (2012) "The 'Land of Opportunity' is Becoming Hollywood Fiction: Rising Plutocracy Threatens American Democracy." *New Perspective Quarterly*. December 5. Online, available at: www.digitalnpq.org/articles/global/620/12-05-2012/nathan_gardels.

Hintjens, H. (2007) "Citizenship under Siege in the Brave New Europe." *European Journal of Cultural Studies*. Vol. 10. No. 3: 409–414.

International Revenue Service (IRS) (2014) "Taxation of Nonresident Aliens." January 17. Online, available at: www.irs.gov/Individuals/International-Taxpayers/Taxation-of-Nonresident-Aliens.

Metz, S. (1993) *The Future of Insurgency*. Carlisle: Strategic Studies Institute, US Army War College. December 10. Online, available at: www.strategicstudiesinstitute.army.mil/pubs/display.cfm?pubID=344.

Moore, T.L. (2003) "Early Fourth Epoch War Research." Bunker, R., ed., *Non-State Threats and Future Wars*. London: Frank Cass: 159–170.

Southern Pulse Correspondents (2014) "Mexico—SAT Claims Hundreds of Multinationals Evade Taxes." February 11. Online, available at: www.info@spcorrespondents.com.

Sullivan, J. (2013) "Chapter 10: How Illicit Networks Challenge Sovereignty." Miklaucic, M. and Brewer, J. eds. *Convergence: Illicit Networks and National Security in the Age of Globalization*. Washington, DC: National Defense University; 171–187.

Williams, P. (2008) *From the New Middle Ages to a New Dark Age: The Decline of the State*. Carlisle: Strategic Studies Institute, US Army War College.

Index

Page numbers in *italics* denote tables, those in **bold** denote figures.

Printed by PGSTL